The Center for Western Studies is a cultural museum and a study and research agency of Augustana College, Sioux Falls, South Dakota, concerned principally with South Dakota and the adjoining states, the Prairie Plains, and the Trans-Mississippi West.

The Center serves as a resource for teachers, research scholars, students and the general public, through which studies, research projects and related activities are initiated and conducted, and by which assistance can be provided to interested individuals and groups. Its goal is to provide awareness of the multi-faceted culture of this area, with special emphasis on Dakota (Sioux) Indian Culture.

The Center was founded in the conviction that this region possesses a unique and important heritage which should not be lost or forgotten. Consequently, the Center for Western 4tudies seeks to provide services to assist researchers in their study of the region, to promote a public consciousness of the importance of preserving cultural and historical resources, to collect published and unpublished materials, art and artifacts, important to the understanding of the region, and to undertake and sponsor projects, to sponsor conferences and provide permanent displays and shows which reflect the art and culture of the West, particularly the Sioux.

The Center maintains an archive and possesses one of the finest collections available of books relating to all aspects of the American West. The Center continally seeks to expand its collections in order to provide maximum assistance to interested scholars, students at all levels, and the general public. The collections include excellent representative Sioux Indian art, bead and quill work, western art consisting of original oils, water colors, bronzes, photographs, and steel engravings.

DAKOTA VISIONS

A County Approach

David J. Holden

1982

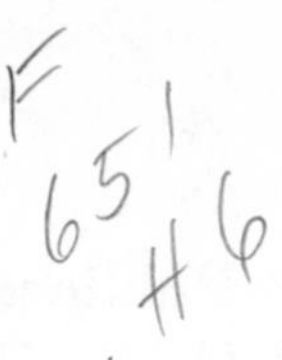

Dedication

This book is dedicated to Arthur J. Holden, whose inspiration for the future is grounded in our ability to provide a connection with the past. We work toward this objective so that he will be able to find his biological roots in the natural heritage of our country.

Published by
THE CENTER FOR WESTERN STUDIES
AN HISTORICAL
RESEARCH AND ARCHIVAL AGENCY
of
Augustana College
Sioux Falls,
South Dakota

ISBN Number 0-931170-21-4
Library of Congress Number 82-072870

First Edition
Printed by Crescent Publishing, Inc., Hills, Minnesota
Manufactured in the United States of America

COVER PHOTO

(Courtesy Eros Data Center and U.S. Geological Survey)

An image mosaic of the state of South Dakota, created at the Earth Resources Observation Systems (EROS) Data Center, is in effect a "color photo" from 570 miles in space.

The mosaic has the characteristics of color infrared photography. Green, growing vegetation is red with variations in the red tones indicating different plant species, stages of growth, and the health of the vegetation. Deep, clear water is black; water that carries silt or sediment is light blue or white. Cities appear light blue and are bright spots on the image because of the reflective qualities of combined different quantities of asphalt, concrete, rooftops, trees, and grass.

Predominant features on the South Dakota mosaic are the heavily forested Black Hills, the stark bright Badlands, the Missouri River with its series of huge dams, and the multitude of lakes in the eastern part of the state.

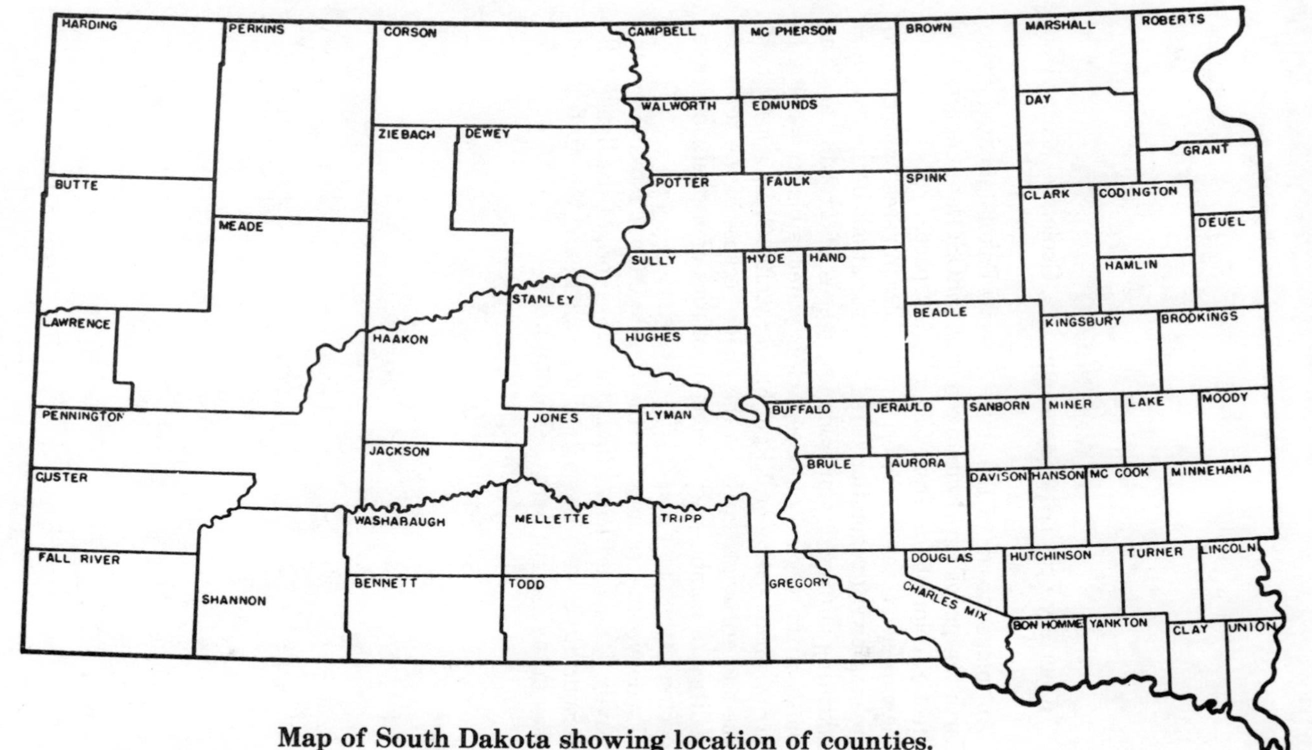

Map of South Dakota showing location of counties.

Table of Contents

LIST OF PHOTOGRAPHS

Acknowledgements

The progress that is listed here is to be credited to hundreds of people who have provided bits of information, verbally or by letter. To attempt a complete listing of individuals would be to forget some. So suffice it to render gracious thanks to all those who have helped and to hope they will continue to be willing to gather and provide information.

Special thanks must be given to Professor Ruth Laird, who had the patience and provided the encouragement to guide me through my first attempts at writing. To the National Park Service that provided grant money to start the project. To Bill Dean and Francis Ugolini of National Park Service, who provided information. To Ron Howard, H.L. Hutcheson and Ron Shave, who helped work on the initial survey of natural areas. To The Nature Conservancy, which helped with the preservation of some of the natural areas. To Jim Chamie and Dave Ode, who read the initial drafts. To Ode, who with Dilwyn Rogers and Larry Zimmerman, contributed to the book. To the South Dakota Agricultural Station, Ray Moore, Director, for the opportunity to work on related projects. To Dr. L.A. Deitrick and nephew Tim Jackson, whose help in northwest South Dakota was invaluable. To the Extension Home Makers, who allowed me to use information from their publication "South Dakota, a Land to Behold." To the South Dakota State University cartography class under the direction of Orville Gab and Lee Opheim. During the final stages of the book to Marvin Riley, who provided population data and to the staff from the Center for Western Studies, especially Dr. Sven Froiland and Dr. William Geyer who provided editorial help. And to all others whose courtesy, coffee, and collaboration made this effort worthwhile, I give my wholehearted thanks.

Finally to my wife Nelda, whose understanding and typing made this effort reach a successful conclusion, I give a special thank you.

David J. Holden

Introduction

For those of us who take pleasure in observing the wonders of the world there is no doubt that God created a system, not just man. Moreover, it is a system into which man was born, nurtured, and fitted with a consciousness that enables him to reflect on both his own humanity and his relationship to the rest of creation.

Here in South Dakota one finds many familiar systems all functioning to channel diffuse unusable energy into concentrated forms called living organisms. It is man who is dependent upon these living systems, but for 3½ billion years the systems operated without the presence of man.

Present conditions leave little doubt that man is becoming a burden in many of these systems. To be convinced, one has only to witness the deterioration by soil erosion, ecological simplification, mineral depletion, water and air pollution, overpopulation, urban blight, fossil fuel removal, and extinction of species at 1000 times the natural rate. It makes one wonder if God should issue an ultimatum: save the system if you're to save yourselves.

Here in this book, in a small way, I look at parts of these functioning systems in South Dakota. I examine the interconnected biological, geological, ecological, historical, and sociological relationships sometimes carried along by human interest stories to heighten the readability.

The book gathers the author's experiences and observations that have for years accumulated in a box in the closet only to be hauled out and assembled during a year's sabbatical from South Dakota State University. For convenience, material has been organized into the 67 counties in the state and divided into seven sections, each section carrying a main theme and several subthemes.

I have started the book with geological and biological themes of the state, followed with contemporary issues in energy and conservation, and then have considered human interest themes relating to pioneers and settlers. The last sections deal with our Indian heritage and finally "Dakota Images," those impressions of the past that have led to our images of today. Perhaps such an examination today will lead to positive images for our future generations.

The reader, however, may choose as time or desire prompts to skip around and read the book as he would a collection of short stories. Each county is an independent story.

In addition, the reader is directed to search for other themes that run through the book, to experience the rich ornithological heritage of the state, to find the human interest elements, the humor, and perhaps, if one has a religious bent, to understand the experience of seeing God through the splendor of nature. Where else can one witness the presence of God with so little effort?

For those who have previously taken little note or interest in the living system, it is hoped that in some small way the book might turn their thoughts in that direction and that it could in some way illiminate the misconception, in this battle for survival, that always God and the natural systems are the ultimate victors. Instead, the need is clear for man to temper his present attitude if he is to be successful in the living system. This also is a concern of the book.

The stories about the people of various counties are simply vehicles for the author to express an idea or concept. By localizing a concept, I hope to create more interest. Obviously, flattery would have been easiest, but we all know that flattery is cowardly. So those counties where flattery has been replaced by constructive criticism have really fared the best. At any rate, read on and view the book in its broader purposes.

Whether these recollections, observations, and feelings should have been better left in the closet, I leave up to the reader. Of course, I hope the reader too will have found some repayment for his efforts that matches mine in having written the book.

BIOLOGICAL REFLECTIONS

Biological Reflections

County	Title
Bennett	Endangered But Not Forgotten
Brookings	An Eye on Migration
Day	Plenty of Prairie Pot Holes
Edmund	The Year the Antelope Vanished
Gregory	The Eagle Makes a Comeback
Hamlin	Care and Feeding of a Marsh
Hughes	A Gathering of Birds
Kingsbury	I Thought I Saw a . . . an Egret?
Lake	Lake Herman is Dying
Lawrence	The Plant Lovers
Lincoln	The Hog Peanut — Seen Any Lately?
Moody	Living Antiques of the Coteau des Prairie
Sanborn	The Year of the Pheasant

First, come with me for a sampling of some of the biological systems that South Dakota has to offer. Come and get a feel of the systems as the forces of life pulse through its creatures, large and small, turning our state from a wasteland into a verdant cover of life. Experience some of the birds, animals, and plants that make the exploration of little known places a memorable experience. You don't have to be rich to see miracles. Just have patience, good eyesight, and a willingness to seek out those creatures that make the system operate.

Once upon a time, long, long, ago, there was in a far-off unknown country a stretch of land, a small part of a great whole, which lay for ages swept by beating winds and seared by heat and drought in the summer suns, or covered by a blanket of snow, frozen and silent through long winters. Here were strange prehistorical animals, a distinctly different vegetation, and an aboriginal people of whom we have but slight traces . . . While centuries rolled away this wild region lay waiting . . . Then grew the sage brush, blue grass, buffalo and bunch grass, and the delicate prairie flowers of our present day, covered by an infinite brooding silence.

—Nina Farley Wishik
Along the Trail of Yesterday

To be a bird is to be alive more intensely than any other living creature . . . Birds live in a world that is always in the present, mostly full of joy . . . with little memory of the past and no real anticipation of what is yet to come—intensely conscious of sight and sound, strongly swayed by joy and anger, and sometimes petrified by ecstasy or fear.

—N.J. Berrill

I give my pledge as a world citizen to respect all of life as I respect my own kind, to cherish nature's creations and riches which I shall neither use thoughtlessly nor abuse willfully, since man and nature are of one earth and of one spirit.

—Michael W. Fox

Bennett County

Area, 1,173 square miles
Population, 1925 - 3,186; 1945 - 3,298; 1980 - 3,236
County Seat, Martin. Population 1,018

After the Indian allotments were made in 1911, the government opened the remaining land for homesteading. The drawing took place on October 24, 1911, at Gregory, and again there was a host of people flooding the county to place their fate in 160 acres. Martin was awarded the county seat at an election in which only Indian and white men with Indian wives were allowed to vote. During the first few years county offices were filled with educated men of Indian and white extraction, but in recent years Indians have lost control of the voting.

Bennett County, surrounded on three sides by Indian Reservations, is a colorful place because of its composition of Indians, farmers and ranchers. Its population once reached over 4,500 in 1935, but for the most part has remained stable.

Interesting sites reflect the black pipestone found in nearby Mellette County. The county has, or has had, a blackpipe bank, saloon, store, and school.

Other sites are the Nelson Rock Collection, the Rice Fossil display, and over by Swett, that town that is almost not there, is the site where the prehistoric camel bones were discovered.

Endangered But Not Forgotten

Bennett County

Mary Ann slammed the lid of her suitcase with a finality that startled her. She knew she would never come back, except for brief visits. She knew she was cutting the umbilical cord to her home and the countryside she enjoyed. She was torn with anger, sadness, and frustration. Why, she wondered, were her friends so cheerful about leaving the "old dump" and getting out into an exciting world? None ever came back, except possibly on Christmas, when she rarely ever saw them. Mary Ann felt that finishing high school was almost the end of the world—her world— with some invisible force driving young girls out of the community.

With sudden determination she picked up her worn jeans jacket and headed for the spot on the marsh near the Lacreek Wildlife Refuge.

She edged her way out on a spit of land, where hunters had built a duck blind, and settled down to watch. She had come to say goodbye to "her" birds. She hated to leave, for she had come to feel a kinship with them, as she did with all wild things. She had watched their coming in 1963 when she was a small girl. She had watched the first pair build a nest on an old muskrat pile. She had watched them raise their first cygnet. Now the family group consisted of twelve fully grown trumpeter swans.

She settled down to await their arrival. She was to experience one of those rare surprises that so often greet one who has the pa-

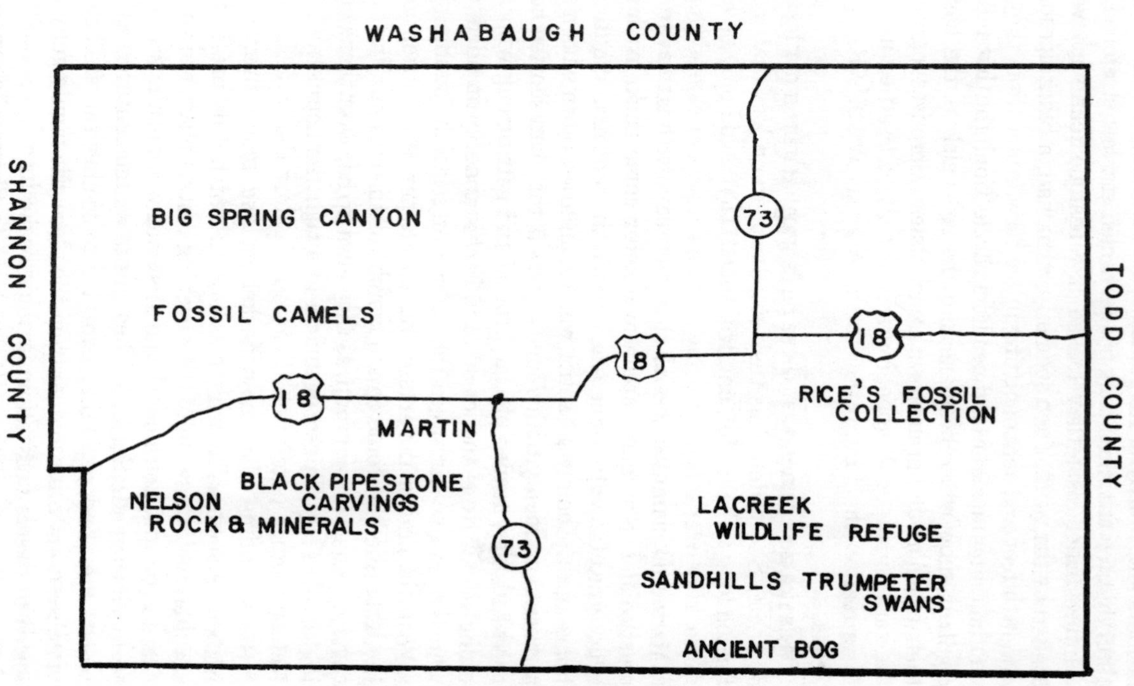
BENNETT COUNTY
WASHABAUGH COUNTY
SHANNON COUNTY
TODD COUNTY
STATE OF NEBRASKA
BIG SPRING CANYON
FOSSIL CAMELS
73
18
18
18
73
MARTIN
BLACK PIPESTONE CARVINGS
NELSON ROCK & MINERALS
RICE'S FOSSIL COLLECTION
LACREEK WILDLIFE REFUGE
SANDHILLS TRUMPETER SWANS
ANCIENT BOG

tience and perseverance to observe the diversity and complexity of the marsh. Distant calls drew her attention to a black-dotted V, stamped out against the flaming red fingers of the evening sunset. The sounds resonated through the wild marsh and tied her into the totality of the place. Closer they came to Mary Ann's observation point, their long beaks, necks, and feet stretched out. As they sailed past they looked like flying sticks with wings shaken by the wind. Then suddenly, with wings acting as rudders and with feet and necks shifting into a forward position, they settled on a hummock of land near the shore. The light that fell full on their snow-white plumage and the red mask at the base of their beaks made her gasp with excitement. Here was a group of the rare endangered whooping cranes that had settled near her for a rest on their migration to the Aransas Wildlife Refuge in Texas.

Was it a good omen that these birds greeted her on her last day at home? She watched as they stood around on legs that looked far too long to be useful, and with necks that could only be made for looking over fences, peering around corners, or eavesdropping at parties. Of what use was all that overextended anatomy to wild creatures? The human watcher was being entertained by clowns, oddly graceful with their exaggerated movements, standing as tall as men. Their wild spirit was exemplified by their constant alertness. Suddenly with a loud cry, as if they had spotted her in the blind, they leaped off the ground and with strong wing beat caught the drift of the jet stream. Feet and neck extended, they split the air like arrows as they disappeared to the south.

With the cranes' departure, Mary Ann turned her attention to the birds she had come to the marsh to bid farewell. The swans came in as a graceful group, as they always did, to settle down for the night. They flipped in unison in a tight semicircle and with feet and wings outstretched came in against the wind in an effortless landing. The now darkening sky made their snowy whiteness seem even whiter as it reflected the dimness of the evening. As they swam to their evening resting place, they passed near the blind. Their black beaks glistened wetly as the water rolled in globules off the tips. They hesitated momentarily as they passed the blind, as if they expected to see her there. They had often seen her come and go from the place. Then gracefully bowing their heads and plunging their beaks into the water, they decorated the air with jewel-like droplets of crystal clear water.

What force was pushing her away from these beautiful birds?

And why did she have to leave home in search of her destiny? She sank deeper into the blind while night pulled its dark curtain over the land.

As a young girl she had studied about endangered species in school. She remembered the slogan "Extinction is forever," and she hoped that people would care enough to help the trumpeter swan and the whooping crane back from the brink. In 1934 there were only 14 whooping cranes left; now they were on the increase. Trumpeter swans had survived in small numbers only near Yellowstone, but now they too were on the increase. She hoped when she came back home there would still be beautiful birds to see.

Next Mary Ann remembered a trip with her father to White River, where they had stopped at a prairie dog town and spotted a black-masked, weasel-like animal peering out of a prairie dog's burrow. Her father told her the strange looking bandit-like weasel was a black-footed ferret, which preyed on prairie dogs. The town was one of the few places in the United States where a remaining speciment might be seen. She was happy to have been able to see the ferret and marveled at the intense vitality of its eyes. Was it now extinct? There had been no sightings for the last two years. Was this unique species, the product of millions of years of evolution, wiped out without so much as a ripple in the stream of public consciousness? Such a finely tuned, living machine, adapted by years of adjustment to a specific niche in the environment, gone. Surely some penalty must be exacted for such genocide. Who would be convicted? Who would levy the fine? Those intensely vital eyes staring at her years ago . . . had their spark of life been rubbed out? She remembered lines by Blake about the wildness of a predator.

In what distant deeps or skies
Burnt the fire of thine eyes?
On what wings dare he aspire?
What the hand, dare seize the fire?

The evening grew colder and darker. Her body felt cramped in the small blind. It was time to leave. She arose, walked slowly home, listening to the sounds of the night.

In the morning, as she finished the last packing details and walked to the car, she listened. They would be spiraling up to fly out to their favorite feeding grounds. In the east, the eerie morning light laced ribbons of color into the clouds. She hesitated. Then muffled sounds, like French horns in a Wagnerian symphony, drifted faintly back to her to be locked forever in memory. It was the early morning call of the swans. The sounds lifted her spirit, and she hoped the sounds of the swan, and those of the crane, would never be locked in the silence of the past.

* * * * * *

Now Mary Ann was back. College over, family growing up, teaching career launched. She had looked forward to a summer's vacation with her family in the old home town. And at first opportunity she took them to the spot where she had watched the swans. Now instead of 12 there were some 138 swans in the group. When they winged in, as from some distant swan Valhalla, they circled the group. Their muted French horn trumpeting sent a wave of nostalgia through her. Was there a hint of recognition? Then, as if in an aerial ballet, they settled upon the water.

The young 12-year-old, an image of her mother, glowed with wonderment. "They're beautiful, Mother," she gasped.

Mary Ann turned, tears of joy mixed with the salt of sadness, and said softly, "Thank God, there are still things wild, free, and beautiful." She closed her eyes for a moment and imagined again the clarion call of the whooping cranes bidding her back into communion with wild, free spirits. Then she opened her eyes, looked at her family enjoying the white swans swimming with elegant grace over the placid water, and said, "It's good to be back."

The endangered black-footed ferret is so rare that only a few people have ever seen it. It preys on prairie dogs and is endangered because of the poisoning of the prairie dogs.
Photo — SDSU Cooperative Wildlife Unit

Brookings County

Area, 801 square miles
Population, 1925 - 17,320; 1945 - 15,022; 1980 - 24,332
County Seat, Brookings. Population 14,951

They settled there along the eastern edge of the wooded Sioux River (1857) where the ford of the Noble Trail crossed to the west. There were thirteen happy Norwegians and one half-Swede. They were either very happy or just tired, because it would have taken some such state to account for their staking out a town with Indians camped across the river. They called the new settlement Medary. The next year the Indians led by Smutty Bear burned the settlement and drove out the pioneers. Undaunted, in 1869, they rebuilt bigger and better and dreamed the dream of a shopping center with connections in Chicago.

However, fortune never travels along rivers and the railroad track missed their town by seven miles. Medary evaporated into stillness with only a sign on the highway and the longest avenue in Brookings to commemorate its existence. Now on the prairie a lone gnarled boxelder, the site of the village well, stands vigil over a few bumps where scattered broken bits of china marked W.H. Grindley, Lancaster, England, reflect the sunlight. Now and then a bottle labeled McLean Volcanic Liniment is the prize of one who can beat the neighbor out to scrounge after a heavy rain.

Also in Brookings County is Fountain, that town which disappeared and left a graveyard of young children covered with European cemetery spurge. Its tattered fence and crumbling gravestones now are memories of pioneer pain. The spurge, a symbol of European influence, lives to compete with its other weedy relatives.

Throughout the country are the lakes — Oakwood, Hendricks, Sinai, Campbell, Goldsmith, and Oak Lake. There are the woody ribbon of trees along the Sioux River and Gilleys, Hushers, and Hidewood groves. The latter is a site of aspen and pond lilies. There is Paul Errington Marsh near Bruce. Near Aurora are a giant glacial erratic and the flower-spangled Aurora Prairie. The latter is a preserve of the Nature Conservancy and is a living museum dedicated to reflect the conditions when prairie covered the entire county.

An Eye On Migration

Brookings County

It's little appreciated that one can live in Brookings County and observe the ceaseless ebb and flow of the planet's life. We do not have to travel halfway around the world to observe the miracle of creative living.

The miracle comes to us. It comes in the form of geese, flipping and flapping out of the sky to settle on a cattail marsh after a summer stay near the Arctic. Some pass overhead in military fashion, wedging their way along and honking a cry of confidence understood only by other geese. The miracle comes in the form of colorful warblers that have dressed for the occasion before leaving their southern estates and are now flitting in search of food along the tops of trees in the back yard. It comes with the upland sandpiper (upland plover), which has just made a 4,000-mile trip from Argentina and stops to whistle his claim to a spot on the

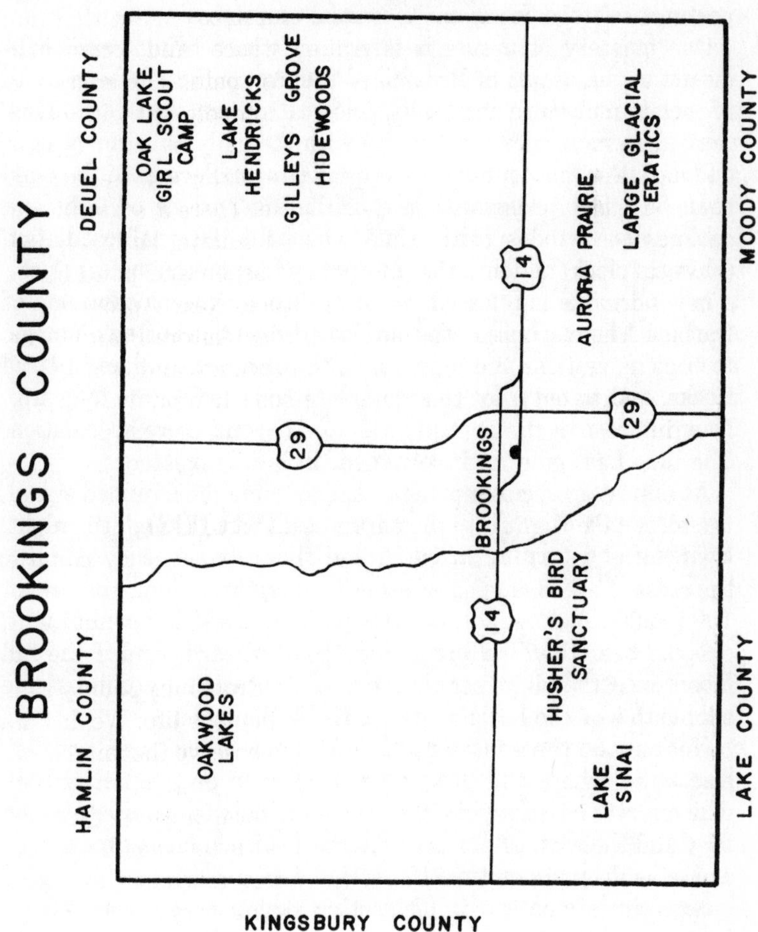
BROOKINGS COUNTY
MINNESOTA
DEUEL COUNTY
OAK LAKE GIRL SCOUT CAMP
LAKE HENDRICKS
GILLEYS GROVE
HIDEWOODS
AURORA PRAIRIE
LARGE GLACIAL ERATICS
MOODY COUNTY
14
29
29
BROOKINGS
14
HUSHER'S BIRD SANCTUARY
HAMLIN COUNTY
OAKWOOD LAKES
LAKE SINAI
LAKE COUNTY
KINGSBURY COUNTY

rolling prairie from atop a fence post. This is the flow of seasons and the patterns of life.

Through all the seasons, many creatures pass across one's view. They form a woven pattern of interrelated complexity. But if the senses are not attuned, if mind is not conditioned, this pattern is not recorded on the tapes of memories that roll endlessly through the mind. It's unfortunate that so many people relegate such opportunities to be observant to cranial emptiness.

One mystery of nature is migration which brings wonderful events to the people of Brookings. It starts out as the sensitivity of certain molecules of a bird's biological system. At a certain instant these molecules synchronize with the daily patterns of light and darkness (photoperiod). The oscillating molecules of the birds come in exact phase with the oscillating periods of light and darkness. At the specific time when the external oscillation (physical clock) matches the internal oscillation (biological clock), a new hormone is released. It flows through the bloodstream of the bird. The response in the bird is to dress up in spring plumage, to become restless and aggressive, to form with others in large flocks, and to eat a lot to accumulate body fat for its long trip. Now interest in the opposite sex goes beyond mere speculation. The time has come for involvement in family matters.

At almost a precise moment, as if by some prearranged signal, the birds take flight into the darkness and fly through the night. Swirling and turning in one grand flying ballet, they climb to the crest of an advancing weather front and fly along at a rate of 100 to 200 miles a night. If one is patient on a still moonlit night, one can hear them calling as they go overheard. And if the full moon is in the right position, one can occasionally glimpse the silhouettes of the birds as they pass by the moon.

Not only do these master migrators know when to go, but they also know where and how to go. Locked in on a celestial body which serves as a compass, they fly unerringly to the site to which they and their ancestors have returned since ancient times. They arrive as if by appointment.

Sometimes men set up distracting structures such as tall TV towers. The light on the top can misguide birds on cloudy nights. Their navigation fix, instead of a distant star, is now a local light. It causes them to fly in a tightening spiral, eventually to crash into the guy wires or the tower. Such a place lies across the Brookings County line near Flandreau. On some mornings hundreds of dead birds lie stewn around the base of the tower. These carnages have not been corrected by a new type of light, and the slaughter goes on at all the towers.

Back to migration. A bird arriving at its destination quickly gets to the business of staking out a territory and raising a family. When the oscillation of its internal molecules (its clock) has measured the proper day length (photoperiod), it repeats the performance in a southerly direction.

Some large shorebirds, such as the golden plover, fly from South America to the Arctic Circle and back, a trip of over 6,000 miles. Even the tiny hummingbird, no larger than a teaspoon, flies nonstop over the Gulf of Mexico to make a 3,000-mile trip.

The question arises as to why these birds undertake such long hazardous journeys. Maybe they are, like Jonathan Seagull, incurable fliers. Maybe their original habitat was the northland, and they were forced south by the glacier and continued this pattern after the glacier retreated. But most probably the space, the solitude, and the abundant food produced by the almost nightless days in the north account for the odyssey. Most of this food would go to waste if it were not for the annual migration of the birds.

Every bird watcher has his favorite stories. For example, there is the saga of Wilbur, an abandoned baby barn swallow left in a paper sack by campers. Wilbur, a contraction of the phrase, "Well, bird, what do we do with you now?" was addicted to insects. He started life with hardly any feathers, a bad disposition, and uncivilized bathroom habits. Yet in spite of it all, he grew up to be a sleek model barn swallow. He learned to distinguish between grasshoppers, flies, hamburger, and earthworms. He detested earthworms. Once, after swallowing one, he spit it up and never again would he try another. He did not require flying lessons and learned to swoop with ease, but he still did not get the idea that it was not respectable for a swallow to perch on the ground. He maintained stubbornly that the most important thing in life was to sit on a ledge with his mouth open for food.

Wilbur was one of a late season hatch and had little time to adjust to the swallow's world before time for migration. He spent his time in preparation for migration by swooping around his human friends. At a distance, the local swallow population swooped too, as if trying to entice him away. If Wilbur noticed his wild friends, he paid little heed. Finally came the day of departure. The local swallows had been congregating for days. The molecules of their bodies were finally in tune with the proper day length. The migratory urge had reached a climax. Wilbur's biological clock was working too. He came to the window near dusk, fluttering and looking in at us for almost a minute, as if to say good-bye before he departed. Maybe he felt we should prepare to migrate with him.

Next day no swallows were to be seen. Wilbur, ill prepared and ill equipped, had followed the primeval urge to migrate. Perhaps he found a mate or friend on that long journey to teach him the ways of a swallow.

To this add the story of Waxy, the cedar waxwing which learned to fly again after recovering from a damaged wing. Waxy, already an adult when injured, never did quite trust his human friends and remained aloof and wary. His only concession was to take the food, water, and shelter offered. When released to the wild, he quickly rejoined a resident flock of cedar waxwings.

And don't forget Robby, a fledgling robin whose mother had been lost. His greatest delight when growing up was to sit in a tree, fly high in the air, and land on the unsuspecting shoulder of a student on the way to school. After riding for a block, he would return to his perch and repeat the performance.

Memories of Wilbur, Waxy, and Robby have made the candle of life burn a bit brighter. They join memories of all the other birds that have turned a dull day into an occasion upon their arrival after a year-long trip. They are friends returning for a meal of cracked corn and sunflower seeds.

By having a bird feeding station and banding a few passing migrants that stop for a meal or two, you can add interesting facts to bird literature. Some 15,000 individuals of 125 species have been banded at the Brookings station. Many have returned year after year. Their migration pathway from Brookings is primarily into Texas and Mexico. The farthest recovery is that of a little flycatcher which made it all the way to Guatemala. The oldest known hairy woodpecker ever recorded, 16 years old, ate his suet at the Brookings station. In addition, such rare birds for eastern South Dakota as the whippoorwill, barn owl, shrike, and hooded warbler have been banded. One winter 600 redpolls and a host of evening grosbeaks were banded before they returned to their northland.

A bird feeding station is an island in the stream of life that flows continuously through the Brookings area — an island of stories.

Day County

Area, 1,061 square miles
Population, 1925 - 15,175; 1945 - 12,883; 1980 - 8,133
County Seat, Webster. Population 2,417

Its many lakes, marshes, hills, and plains make this a diversified wildlife county. There are mink and muskrat, ducks and geese, pheasant and partridge, pike and pan fish, and altogether they reflect the productivity of the land.

Located on the Prairie Coteau, Day County boasts some of the better natural lakes in the state. These lakes — unpolluted, sometimes uninhabited, and always unparalleled in their natural beauty — are a haven from the urban sprawl. Enemy Swim, Pickerel, Waubay, Blue Dog, and Bitter Lake are a few of the more popular lakes in the area.

The county is rich in Indian tradition and Enemy Swim Lake has a large Indian population. On the eastern border of the county are the Poles, to the north and west are the Norwegians, and on the south the Germans and scattered in between are the Swedes.

Early history of the area dates back to the French fur traders. In 1830 Joseph Brown, followed by Francoise Rondell and Albert Barse, established trading posts. And today Rondell, who was said to have had five wives, still is a common name in the area.

The many small towns in the county no longer portray their pioneer vigor. Only Webster, Waubay and Bristol seem to grow. Pierpont, Roslyn, Grenville, Andover, Butler, Crandall, Lily, and Holmquest are but reflections of better years. Most towns have been stripped of schools, railroads, grain elevators, and banks so that finally all that remain are the saloons, churches, and post offices. They too eventually disappear. The most painful loss is the post office for with it goes a name, a place on the map, as if a death has occurred on the once thriving prairie. All that remains is history.

Finally, there is remembrance of the prairie chicken that was once so abundant in the county. It was last seen in the grasslands in the northwest part of the county in 1930. Its disappearance was attributed to the onrush of population. Today, 50 years later, the prairie chicken has again found a home in the county.

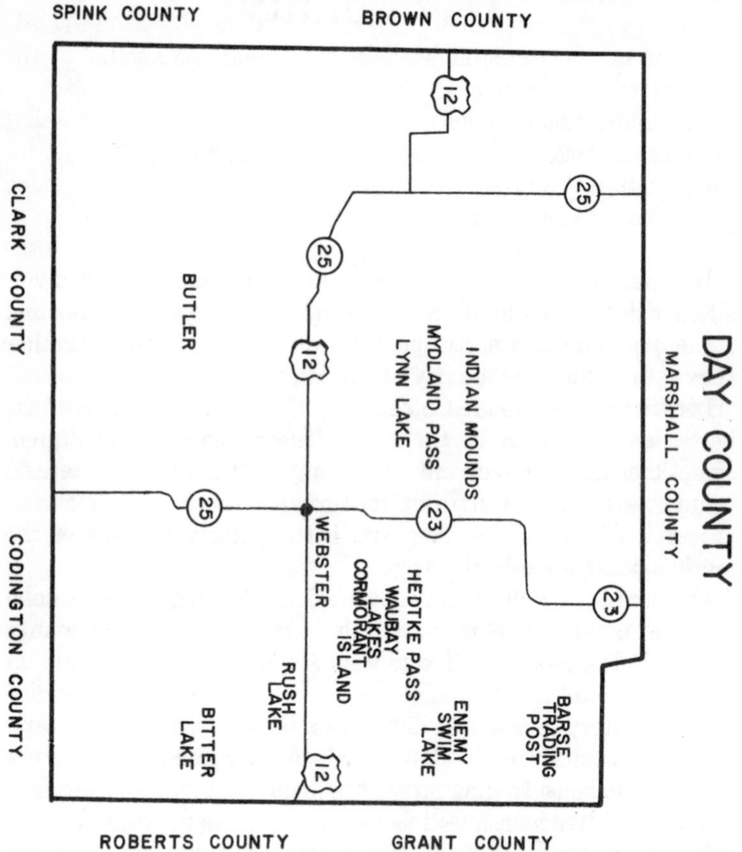

Plenty of Prairie Potholes

Day County

The glacier that came down from the north some 8,000 years ago deposited a legacy in Day County. Huge stagnant sheets of ice left terminal moraines, ice block lakes and sloughs, blocked drainage ways, and rocks — all reminders that there are forces on earth over which man has no control. The ever present rocks, called glacial erratics, especially remind us of the glacier. They break the plow, strain the back, and try the patience to a point where it is no longer the rocks that are erratic. But the obsession to clear the land never ceases, and a neat stone pile is a symbol of the diligent work of man.

Day County and the surrounding area served for many years, after the retreat of the glacier, as summer hunting grounds for the Indian. It is a mosaic of the prairie, woods, and ponds needed for abundant game and fish production.

On a high point at the end of a terminal moraine that rises some 500 feet above the surrounding lakes and prairies was an Indian holy site, a point from which the Indian could view the wide sweep of the surrounding area for buffalo, prairie fires, and enemies. Below the moraine, the Indian hunted amongst the numerous lakes for the deer, muskrat, ducks, buffalo, and other game that populated the area. He found, on the prairie, Tipsin (Indian turnip) and various plants with healing powers — alum roots to treat wounds and cattail fluff for bandages. For toothache there was purple coneflower and for headaches, willow bark. There was sage for the quest for ceremonial vision and sweet grass to bring in good spirits. The marsh yielded cattails and giant reeds for food and shelter. The woodland provided berries, acorns, and building material. The sloughy, woody prairie was indeed a beneficient hunting ground for the Indian.

The post-glacial lake shore lines are rimmed with boulders that show the lake level for a long period after the retreat of the glacier. The lakes of that early time were 15 to 20 feet deep and connected in a chain-like complex covering several miles. Each lake was given a name. Today these "lakes" are called sloughs. Only four to five feet deep, they are dry at least half of the time; if not drained, they are filled with sedges and rushes. During wet years, however, they are the sites of abundant waterfowl.

In the early 1900s the lakes were sites of the slaughter of wild fowl. Market hunters, supplied with cases of shells, traveled by horse and buggy to the lakes, below skies darkened by ducks. After an all-day shoot, they would ship their ducks and geese to Minneapolis and Chicago for one dollar apiece. Duck passes were sprinkled with red, green, yellow, blue, and black shell cases. The local newspaper contained pictures of the slaughter. A favorite pose was to string the kill on a line, ends held by bearded hunters grasping their favorite shotguns. Mercifully, the Migratory Bird Law of 1913 put a stop to this unregulated hunting.

In 1880 Day County, which the Indians had found appealing,

began to attract the early settler. It was beautiful country, and many farms had their own private lakes. The mosaic of prairie, woods, and lakes was ideally suited for the diversified farming of pioneer days. There was wood for fuel and building and abundant animal life for hunting, fishing, and trapping. Rich prairie grass provided grazing and suitable sites for breaking and planting. The early settlers had no way of knowing that what appeared to them a blessing clothed in beauty would eventually turn to dusty disaster, filled with pain and poverty.

The emigrating hordes continued until 1920, coming by wagon and oxen, horse and buggy, and finally the Model T. Norwegians, Swedes, Germans, Poles, and a few others sectioned off the county into distinct communities. Every quarter section, except sections 16 and 36, which were school sections, is claimed by either homesteading or by planting ten acres of trees, as allowed by the Timber Culture Act of 1878. The settlers built large homes and raised almost anything that would grow, including children. A visitor during the day would usually be greeted in the front yard by two or three curious children and four or five anxious chickens. Grass in the lawn meant the childbearing age was over. The pigpen and the garden were at opposite ends of the farmstead, and to get from one to the other meant passing by the kitchen window. On a typical summer morning, Mother would go to the stove, young boys for water and wood, daughters to the laundry, older boys to the field, and while the younger children were screaming in the yard, the father would go off to town. The activity was robust and hectic and lasted from sunup to sundown. But when the kerosene lamp was blown out at the end of the day, the land again listened to the sounds of the wild. A coyote howled from the hills, ducks and frogs clattered in the ponds, and darkness settled over the area as if no human being had ever existed on the land. For 16 hours man controlled the environment, but he had yet to conquer the night.

Typically on a 160-acre homestead stood a house, barn, granary, chicken house, and hog house. The livestock were cattle, sheep, hogs, horses, turkeys, chickens, geese, and ducks. The crops, in addition to the garden, were wheat, oats, barley, corn, flax, and alfalfa. Fences and roads radiated out from the farmstead. The land was full. It was to stay that way for only a generation.

A typical township of 36 square miles, Lynn Township, exemplifies a trend that was to take a century to complete. Situated in the north central part of the county, Lynn was the second township to be settled and is the site of Lynn, which was one of the first towns founded in northeastern South Dakota.

The town was situated at the base of the terminal moraine where the Indian ceremonial site was located. An outpost or scout camp for old Fort Sisseton, Lynn, on the shores of what was then called Lynn Lake, was the site of the last big buffalo hunt (1850) in the area, when 50 buffalo were slain. Along the trails and ruts that cut across the prairie in crooked fashion may still be seen dugouts of some of the old sod houses.

During those early decades of the twentieth century, it was as if some giant cornucopia was spilling forth golden promises of a glorious future for the people of Lynn. By 1925 the population of the township swelled to nearly 500, about 14 persons per square mile.

Then came the double whammy of Bust and Dust. In 1929 the stock market collapse resulted in losses and low prices. In the 30s the land, which should never have been turned over, caught the wind and rode the jet stream to the eastern seaboard. Dust, drought, wind, grasshoppers, and low prices turned the happy gleam in the eye of the pioneer to a glint of pain. He hurt all over, and neither tunes nor tonics brought relief.

The town, whose name was inspired by the Swedish opera star, Jenny Lind — the first map makers spelled it Lynn — had died without a song. Only a few twisted, rusty iron pipes from the creamery remained.

The population continued its decline. Only a few more than 100 people now live in the township. Except for three or four large families, the township is made up of the elderly . . . and emptiness.

Four-fifths of the early residents of Lynn, their aspirations worn away upon the grindstone of reality, shut out the twin blights of drought and disaster by moving on. They left memories and the graves of loved ones. The county today is more of a wilderness than it was in the early 1900s.

But there is a difference. The Indian grass, big blue stem, and little blue stem mixed with the wild prairie flowers are gone. All that remains is evidence of the disruption to the land caused by man. Today's children, and children for all time, may never experience the wonders of the tall grass prairie in the Lynn area. It is a concern that will be reflected in man's interaction with nature over the next century.

Under normal conditions, plant succession will take over to

turn abandoned land into tall grass prairie. But succession is a hollow sounding term when there is no seed source. Succession is especially hard when the area is populated with brome, Kentucky blue, and quack grass. An area in the Waubay Wildlife Refuge from which livestock has been excluded has remained about the same over a period of 30 years. It is still mostly brome and blue grass. If we want native prairie to be saved, we must be prepared to help it.

The rest of Day County has followed a pattern similar to that in Lynn Township. Only the larger cities have held or gained in population. The entire county has lost half its population since 1925, with the largest losses in rural townships.

Other small towns, such as Butler, have also tasted the bitter pill of decline. Butler has crumbled from a town of over 300, with five grain elevators, to almost nothing. It started later and continued longer than Lynn, but it's now only a memory. Its most enduring memorial is its graveyards. Once a town of five churches, Butler has contributed in no small way to its granite-punctuated cemeteries. It's ironic that even there, decay is taking a toll. After 100 years, tombstones are disintegrating under the triple threat of water, wind, and rain.

Counties on the Coteau des Prairie that are neighbors of Day County have experience similar events. The elements of topography, soils, and climate interact to reflect the prosperity of the country. The people are trapped into learning to live in balance with themselves and their environment.

Day County, tied by the strings of a changing environment, can be molded into a beautiful place to live. But, first, man must learn that he is not master of all his surroundings and must adjust harmoniously to the change.

A typical South Dakota marsh surrounded by prairie and woodland. Photo — D. Holden

Rocks outline the old hanging shore line of an ice block lake that has turned into a marsh. This shore illustrates the extremely high level mark of the lake just after the retreat of the glacier. Today the marsh to the left is nine feet lower and frequently dries out.

Photo — D. Holden

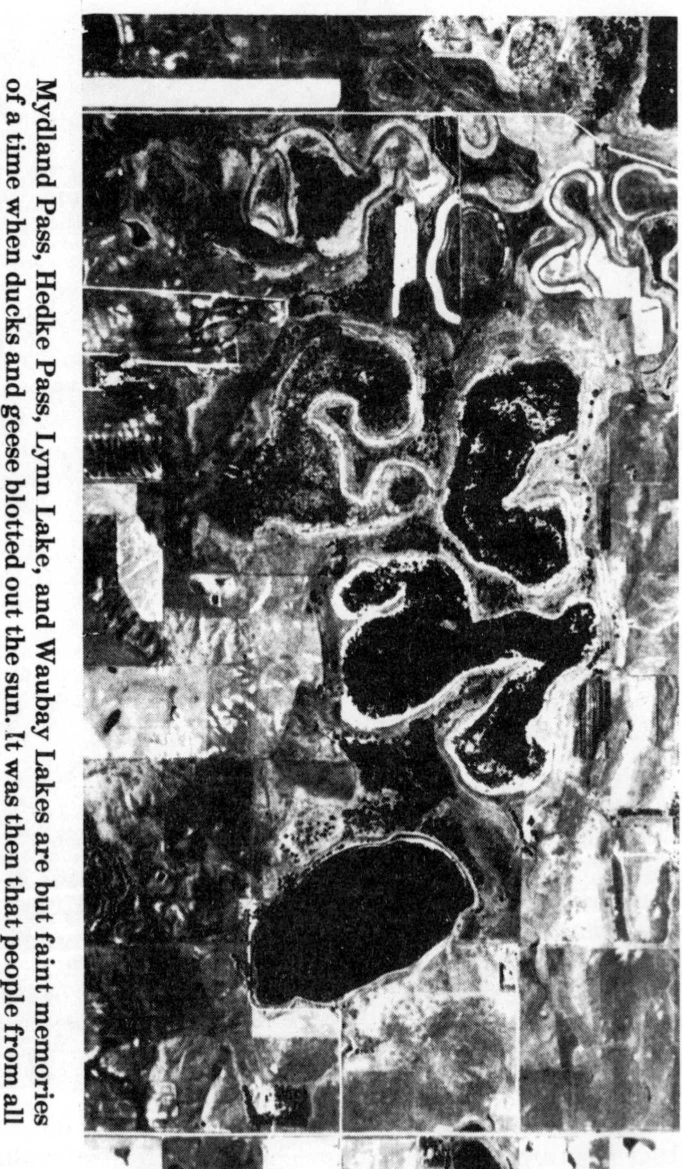

Mydland Pass, Hedke Pass, Lynn Lake, and Waubay Lakes are but faint memories of a time when ducks and geese blotted out the sun. It was then that people from all parts of the country and all walks of life came to the area to hunt. This picture shows the Mydland Pass area. Photo — SDSU Remote Sensing Institute

Edmunds County

Area, 1,158 square miles
Population, 1925 - 8,743; 1945 - 7,247; 1980 - 5,156
County Seat, Ipswich. Population 1,153

Edmunds County was not always trucks and tractors playing out a game of production economics on subdued grasslands. Back in the ancient days it was a giant inland sea, marine fossils, and in the county to the north, a 27-foot aquatic monosaur (lizard) reveals this past. The retreat of the sea brought land dinosauers like tyrannosaurs that ate triceratops for dinner.

The legacy of this sea is 200 to 2,000 feet of Pierre Shale that was later made fertile by the glaciers of the Pleistocene which left a 50- to 1000-foot veneer of glacial till over the Pierre Shale. During the retreat of the glacier the east edge of the county was the spruce studded shoreline of glacial Lake Dakota. Near the lake in a bog south of present-day Mina, an Imperial Mammoth perished. Its massive head now occupies a place of prominence at the School of Mines. This species of elephant was one of five that occupied the area during post and preglacial times.

Sometime after the retreat of the glacier came the Paleo Indians. They were followed in succession by Mound Building, Woodland, and Agricultural Indians.

During the time of Lewis and Clark (1805), Four Bears of the Mandan, trading parties of the Arikara, Waneta of the Cuthead Sioux, and other tribes of the great Sioux Nation were known to journey through Edmunds to Armadale Island for the annual James River Rendezvous. Then on to what seemed to the Indians the center of the nation, Council Rock, for it was here that the god of the Indians lived. So great was its power that the assemblage of skulls, rocks and poles were brought to the Chicago World's Fair and advertised as the Indian's Cathedral of the Plains. It was lost, and with it went a great focal point for Indians on the Great Plains.

Later came the sod-house frontier and the land of the straddle bug that turned back the Indians and buffalo. Next the Yellowstone Trail cut through the county and the east was connected to the west. By now wheat had become the king of commerce.

What else can one associate with Edmund County? First there is Ipswich, once the nation's greatest shipping point for buffalo bones and a railroad boom town. Within two weeks after the town was founded there were three newspapers, two banks, the county seat, and a host of other businesses. It competed with Eureka as the largest primary wheat shipping center in the nation. It also became an important sheep and wool shipping point. But as Ipswich grew three other boom towns died. They, too, sought a railroad line but finding none Edmunds, Freeport, and Georgetown joined the company of Beebe, Craven, Gretna, Loyalton, Powell, and Vermont City in achieving ghost status.

But Ipswich, home of the Yellowstone Trail Association, commemorated the completion of U.S. Highway 12 from Plymouth Rock to Puget Sound by building a Memorial Arch over the highway. After several moves the Arch is now in the city park.

Along the Yellowstone Trail are also Bowdle and Roscoe, rivals of Ipswich for the county seat. Both were boom towns that grew rapidly after the railroad arrived but have lost people in the last years.

Indian campsites are scattered in the hills in the west part of the county. Near the library in Ipswich is an Indian prayer rock.

The Year the Antelope Vanished

Edmund County

They stood, white rump patches flashing a signal of alarm, bright, dark eyes like large marbles, sparkling with alertness. In unison they whirled, their white rumps bouncing in a powder puff ballet away from the danger. They left with speeds at times approaching 60 miles per hour and disappeared behind a hill, only to reappear upon the next distant hill. These were the antelope that in the early 1800s made the Missouri Coteau their home. Their number was almost as great as that of the buffalo that once roamed the plains.

Called goats by Lewis and Clark, who first sighted them in 1804 near Niobrara, they were not named, classified, and described by science until 1815. They were reported to increase in numbers as Lewis and Clark proceeded up the Missouri. Today, after the disappearance of the buffalo, the pronghorn antelope

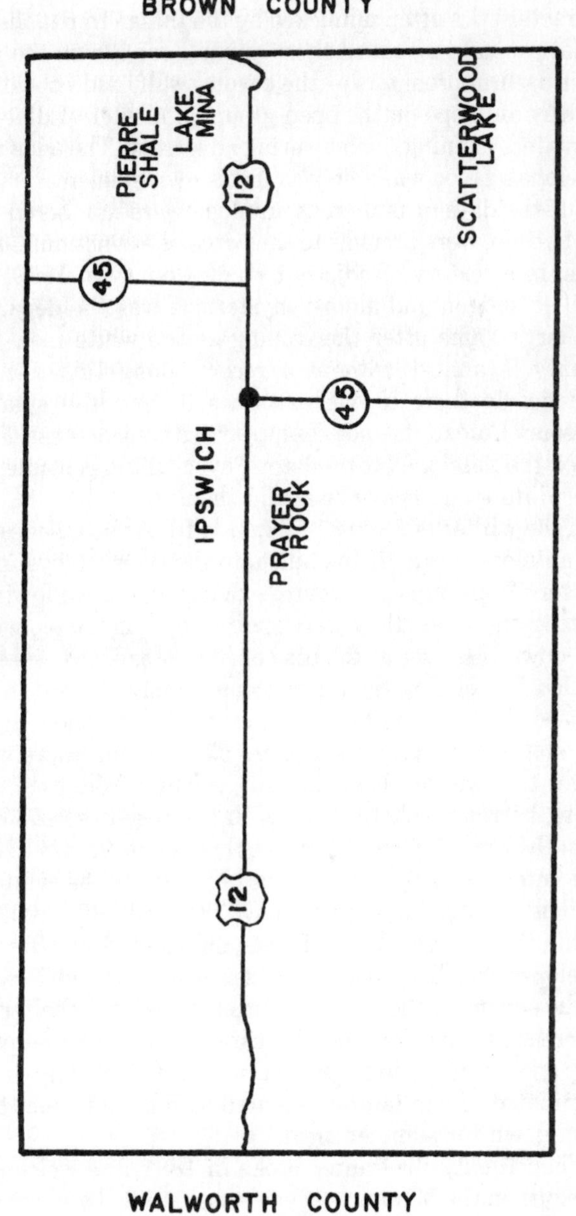
EDMUNDS COUNTY
McPHERSON COUNTY
BROWN COUNTY
WALWORTH COUNTY
FAULK COUNTY
POTTER COUNTY
PIERRE SHALE
LAKE MINA
SCATTERWOOD LAKE
IPSWICH
PRAYER ROCK
12
45
45
12

buck is the most characteristic symbol of the Western Plains. Its alert stance guarding a harem of females, its alarm signal flashing like a shiny pan in the sun, and its fleetness of foot are characteristics often mimicked by the Indian in ritualistic dances.

Nature had fine-tuned these animals for life on the plains, and their natural predators — the coyote, wolf, and bobcat — found a healthy antelope on the open ground a master of defense and an animated, cunning, maneuvering adversary. The odds were in the antelope's favor while he was in his own element.

But the days of numerous antelope were numbered. They, like the buffalo, were brought to the verge of extinction. Captain C.H. Ellis, in a history of adjacent Faulk County in 1909, wrote, "In fact, so sudden and almost mysterious was the departure of all the large game after the coming of the white man that Faulk County is almost without a record along this line." But the evidence is there if one examines it, and the symbol of the Missouri Coteau did not disappear without a cause. Fences corralled the antelope for predators, over-killing continued for food, and winters and heavy snow did them in.

In the winter of 1880-81, blizzards filled the gulches and drove the antelope down off the hills into the river valleys for food and shelter. There in large groups, exhausted and wallowing in snow up to their necks, they were spotted by hungry pioneers. All up and down the river at the base of the Coteau, the pioneers thanked God for sending them a welcome supply of meat in their time of need. The settlers had been surrounded by snow drifts, trains had stopped running, roads were blocked, and there was no way to get to town. So there they sat, isolated from each other, on a white, barren blanket of cold with few resources and blocked off from the rest of the world with only their ingenuity to save them. The antelope meat was a chance to survive the winter. A local resident wrote: "The deep snow that cut off outside brought within the reach of the settlers an unexpected source of food. The antelopes that had been so numerous on the prairie were driven by the storms to the river bottoms for food and shelter. These little creatures, so swift on the bare ground were helpless in the deep snow, and falling easy victims to settlers' guns were soon exterminated. Some families secured so many of them they salted them down for summer meat."

When finally the winter broke in 1881, the welcome sight of antelope on the Missouri Coteau was missing. Only rarely was one sighted, and these stragglers were wiped out by the big blizzard of

1888. This, coupled with continued hunting pressure, finished off the last of the antelope. A pioneer living near the area described the blizzard: "On the 12th of January, 1888, all nature smiled to usher in a most delightful day. It was a most beautiful winter morning, warm and gracious, with soft, variable breezes. One moment, bright, warm, glorious; the next moment, without the slightest warning, the terror fell with unexpected fury. An indescribable terror that pen cannot picture, swept over the great northwest. For fifteen hours it continued, blinding, impenetrable and intensely cold, the atmosphere filled with needles of ice driven by a furious wind with a terrific roar, producing an intense darkness and shutting out objects only a few feet away. In a moment it was gone and the sun came out as beautiful as a morning in May. Its work of death was ended." After the blizzard, the temperature dropped to 30° below, and 112 people in the state had perished. Of the livestock not protected 90 per cent were lost, and wildlife deaths went uncounted. The antelope definitely were extinct in Edmunds County, and in all of South Dakota once numerous antelope were on the verge of disappearance.

Too long had hungry bellies been filled with antelope meat, but the slaughter was about to stop. By 1911 it was made illegal to kill an antelope. So began for the pronghorn the long journey back from near extinction. By 1924 the pronghorn had increased to 680 in the state. Continued careful management speeded up recovery, and by 1941 the total had reached 11,000 head. A hunting season was allowed in 1942. Today the average number of pronghorn fluctuates between 17,000 and 43,000 with a management level of 30,000 considered optimum.

So the most beautiful and fleetest symbol of the Western Plains now occasionally can be seen again on the hills of the Missouri Coteau. To see the alert pronghorn antelope buck, standing as a sentinel on a distant hill, is a warming assurance that man is willing to share this planet with this beautiful animal.

Gregory County

Area, 1,023 square miles.
Population, 1925 - 13,091; 1945 - 8,690; 1980 - 6,015
County Seat, Burke. Population 859

The battle of Bonesteel wasn't such a big battle after all. Just 35,176 land grabbers trying for about 800 claims. When it was all over there were only one dead gambler, two severely wounded, and some 200 gamblers and unwanted characters shipped out of town on the next train. It could have been much worse with the town burned down as Dallas was in 1927. At any rate, such was the rather robust start of most of Gregory County and its towns. The county still has a bit of that distinct flavor, mixing western habits with eastern customs. It is an Indian, ranching, and farming community whose mix of traditions and life style provide colorful surroundings.

Though the early growth of Bonesteel and Dallas was nothing short of phenomenal, the flush of life known as boom lasted only a few years. Today the nostalgia remains but most of the people have gone. Gregory has lost 55 per cent of its people in the last 55 years. But lingering always are the memories of Sully Flats, Sully Grove, and Jack Sully, a successful local outlaw sometimes called the Robin Hood of Gregory County. Also there is Soper's Sod Museum, which recalls those days when construction was carried out with the always available prairie bricks. In the summer there are the annual pow-wows at Milk Camp and Bull Creek.

In addition the county has several woodland ravines near Bonesteel. These are the relicts of earlier days of cooler and wetter climate. On the Missouri River is Fort Randall Dam. On the banks of the Missouri, where the tall cottonwoods grow, is the Karl E. Mundt National Bald Eagle Refuge. Here some 300 eagles are known to winter.

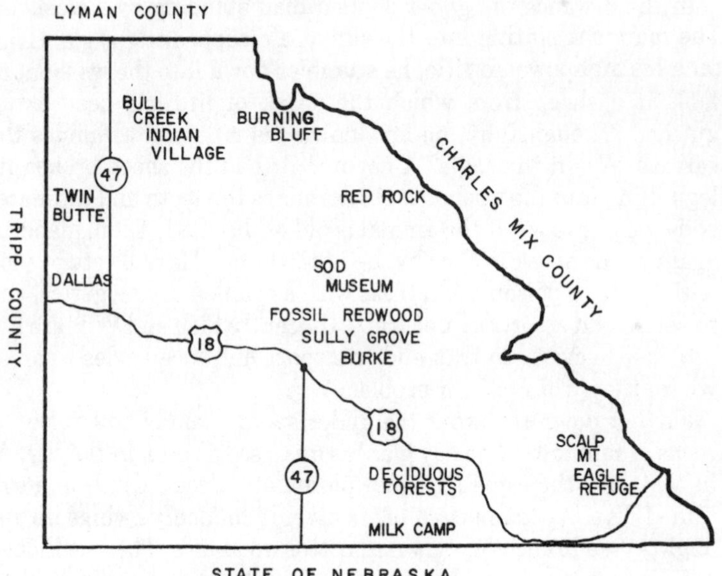

The Eagle Makes a Comeback

Gregory County

The eagle wears two hats. To some it is good; to others, bad. To some it is a killer of sheep; to others, a majestic symbol of bravery and freedom and the emblem of our country.

It is easy to find such contrasting sentiments out west in the land of grass and sky where a black eagle soars high on an updraft of air. The column of air carries the eagle higher and higher into the void. It is hard to tell at a distance if it is a golden eagle or an immature bald. Both are dark, since the young bald eagle does not develop its white head and tail until it is four to five years old. Soon the eagle is a speck in the sky.

It is also here in this country where the hang glider sometimes slips his wings into a tall column of air capped by a cumulus cloud. Then both the eagle and glider soar freely, filling the eye with sky, while below them roll the wonders of the earth in a panorama of colored patterns.

In the distance the glider spots a man standing by a washout. The man is squinting into the sun at a disappearing eagle. Gripping his highpowered rifle, he stumbles down into the washout to look at a sheep from which the spark of life has been extinguished. Thoughtfully, he lays down his rifle and examines the carcass. Was it the eagle? A coyote? Or had the sheep broken its leg falling into the washout? He examines the teeth and estimates body weight to see if the animal is old or diseased. Then, glancing again at the speck in the sky, he heads home. He will return soon with 1080, to poison the carcass with a cyanide coyote getter, and to set an odd assortment of traps. (Recently Fish and Wildlife has provided services to trap and transport nuisance eagles to areas where they will not be a problem.)

Farther down the creek the glider spots a young boy throwing rocks at minnows. The boy glances up to see a speck in the sky. As he watches, the eagle flips and plummets toward earth in a sustained dive. At the bottom of its dive, it suddenly swings up and alights on a branch in a gnarled cottonwood tree. There, silhouetted against the deep blue sky, its white head and tail reflecting the rays of the sun, it arouses in the boy a kinship with the wilderness. For a moment the boy is projected into the eagle's world and absorbs the power and freedom needed to lift his own spirits.

The eagle perching in the cottonwood seems to be a signal for other eagles in the area, and as the boy watches, the dark black eagle, which had hovered over the sheep ranch, appears. Inside of a half hour 17 eagles settle into the big cottonwood, eight black-headed and nine white-headed. It is a bit fanciful perhaps to describe their meeting as a showdown between good guys and bad guys, the white-headed American symbols of freedom and bravery and the black-headed, wicked sheep killers. To some people, stereotyping eagles is easy — they are all bad. Fortunately for the eagle, and the American public, fewer and fewer people dislike eagles so consequently more eagles survive. An added inducement is the $5,000 fine imposed on anyone who destroys eagles or eagle eggs. In spite of this, eight to ten eagles are wounded or killed by man each year in South Dakota. The wounded eagles are picked up and sent to the Eagle Rehabilitation Center at Laurel, Maryland.

Where did all the Gregory County eagles come from? Most moved in during the last 20 years because of the building of large mainstem dams on the Missouri River. Below these dams the water stays open all winter for a distance of one to two miles. This serves to concentrate the fish, overwintering waterfowl, and numerous predators, including both the bald and golden eagles. It is not unusual to find 400 to 500 eagles overwintering between Pierre and Yankton. Their presence created a need for a refuge, and the result was the Karl Mundt National Wildlife Refuge. The 1,135-acre refuge, created by the demand of the people, was paid for with a gift from the 7-Eleven Food Stores. It is run by our National Government.

It is here, among some of the largest cottonwoods along the Missouri, that eagles now make their winter home. It is here people have frequently reported seeing 15 to 30 eagles perched in a single tree — a sight almost unimaginable — attracting people from across the country, who gaze in awe at a spectacle that leaves them with a deep appreciation of the majestic bird. It stirs a response that, it is hoped, will awaken in the observer the responsibility to create a healthful environment that will support both eagle and man.

The endangered eagle has not always had it so good in South Dakota. A look backward at eagle populations of the past is revealing. In the 1700s to 1800s, eagles were reported to be nesting along some parts of the Missouri River and in most of the continental United States. As man encroached, the eagle population decreased.

When our nation was founded, a great debate ensued as to which bird should be our national emblem. Jefferson favored the eagle, Ben Franklin the turkey. Fortunately, Jefferson's vision of a symbol had more appeal than the mundane, gastronomic droolery of Franklin. The domestic turkey is a stupid bird that will sometimes drown itself in a rainstorm. This, plus its sometimes clumsy appearance, has led to a slang term which equates the turkey with stupidity. It would do little good for our country to be known as the "turkey" in the arms race or as one to turn "cold turkey" when the chips are down.

In contrast, the eagle has developed a positive image, and there is hardly a place or event that has not at one time or another projected the image of the eagle as symbol of America.

The fact that the eagle was made our national symbol did not at first give it any protection. Instead, it made the eagle a much sought after trophy. In the 1880s the <u>Times</u> in Okobojo — now a a ghost town — frequently reported the killing of eagles, and trophy hunters placed a high value on mature bald eagles.

In addition to being trophies, the eagles suffered from the fact that all birds of prey were regarded as chicken hawks and shot on sight. It was not until 1962 that legal protection was given to all eagles and to most birds of prey.

The eagle has recently been threatened by the increased use of persistent pesticides. These pesticides are concentrated in many food chains. The eagles are at the end of a food chain which includes algae, microfauna, minnows, and large game fish. Since the poison magnifies at each step, the result is a big dose of pesticide for the eagle, which causes it to fail to reproduce.

All these environmental factors have added up to the almost complete elimination of the bald eagle from the United States mainland. No more are the two-ton nests found in trees along the Missouri River. Only occasionally is a bald eagle reported to be nesting in the United States. In Alaska, eagles are still abundant.

A desire to save our national symbol from extinction has revived interest in the eagle. It is again coming back, and today Gregory County has the largest wintering population of bald eagles in the continental United States. There the eagles have found a home that provides them with a suitable habitat. There, and elsewhere, they are protected by laws that levy heavy fines on offenders who destroy an eagle. There is a feeling of public disapproval for shooting or killing eagles, and, in general, a healthy attitude toward the preservation of the eagle. With all these good things going for the eagle, perhaps it will again nest in South Dakota. It made a weak attempt near Gregory in 1975 but abandoned its nest before completion.

An even more basic concern with the eagle is that it has become an indicator of a livable environment: as goes the eagle, so goes our environment. So as a nation, if we face up to the issue and properly provide for a healthy, viable environment for eagles, we ourselves benefit.

We have finally come to the point where we can recognize eagles as the good guys with the white hats. If all goes well, we will soon be able to remove the eagle from the endangered species list. When this happens, man can breathe a sigh of relief for having saved a species. It will be a reversal of the patterns of events that lead to extinction — events that have been credited to the heavy hand of man. It will be a sign that if man can save a species, there is hope that he can contribute to his own survival. And it is indeed more inspiring to have a living symbol than to reflect over a picture of a dead emblem.

This bald eagle typifies the large number that now occupy the Karl E. Mundt National Wildlife Refuge. Between 300 and 400 eagles occupy the cottonwoods along the Missouri in the winter, and as many as 40 birds have been sighted in one tree. Photo — Willis Hall

Hamlin County

Area, 520 square miles
Population, 1925 - 8,232; 1945 - 6,600; 1980 - 5,261
County Seat, Hayti. Population 371

Hamlin County is a small county with small towns and large lakes. Its county seat — Hayti, named after the habit of the pioneers for tying hay for fuel — proved that being in the center of the county was an assist in gaining the county seat. However, it took 30 years to prove it.

The first county seat was the Spaulding Ranch, but as is often true in county seat matters the records were appropriated without the consent of the keeper and Castlewood was able to claim the status of county seat for several years. By being persistent, Hayti after several tries, finally legally won the right to be the county seat in 1914.

The lakes that make Hamlin County a resort center are Marsh, Dry, Albert, Twin, John, Mary, Goose, Norden, Clear, Johnson, and Poinsett. The latter — the largest lake in South Dakota, 8,205 acres — was visited by John C. Fremont and for a time it was called Fremont. People still are able to find Indian artifacts scattered along the south shore of the lake.

Hayden Carruth describes the life in the county when the railroad first entered Estelline in his book Track's End.

Care and Feeding of a Marsh

Hamlin County

In the center of Hamlin County is 2,500-acre Marsh Lake. On the lake's shore is Hayti. The town was first named Haytie, in a tribute to the ability of a marsh to produce the hay which was tied into knots to provide winter fuel for the pioneers, who stuffed the hay into a hay burner. A hay burner was usually one-half of an iron barrel, packed full of hay and placed upside down on a cook stove with one lid removed. The hay would burn slowly and drop down into the stove as it burned. While one barrel was burning on the stove, the men outside were tying hay and packing the next

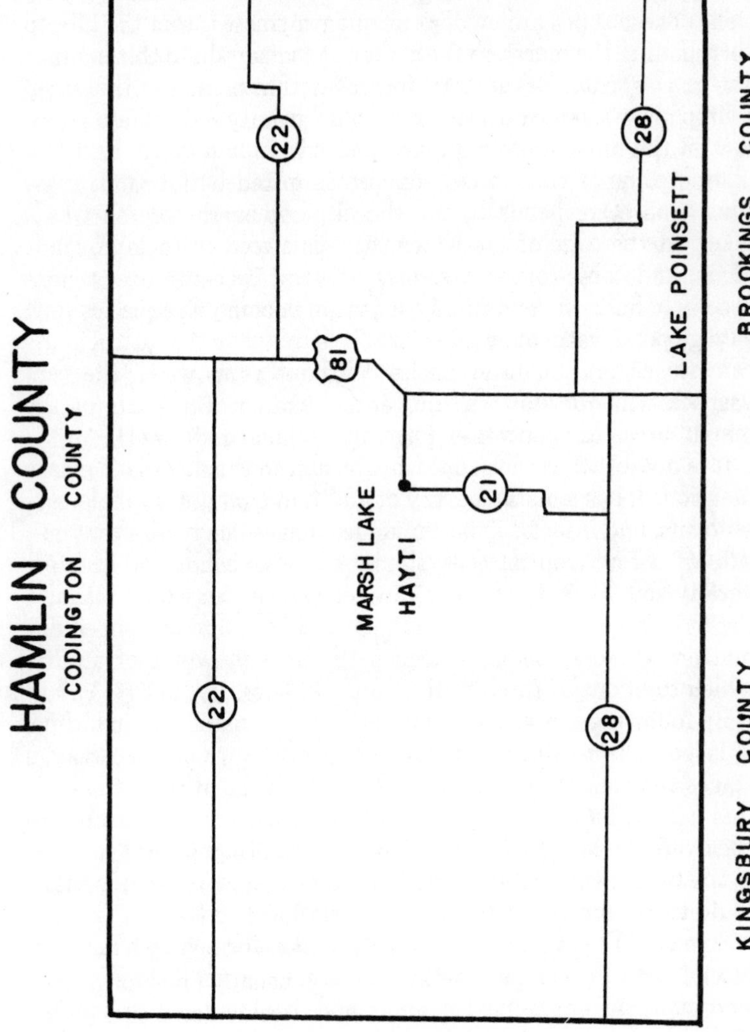
HAMLIN COUNTY
DEUEL COUNTY
CODINGTON COUNTY
BROOKINGS COUNTY
LAKE POINSETT
KINGSBURY COUNTY
CLARK COUNTY
MARSH LAKE
HAYTI
22
22
28
28
81
21

barrel. In this manner the marsh served the pioneer with fuel until the winter winds turned and headed back north.

Ecologically the marsh is a pond that contains one to two meters of water and goes through cycles of wet and dry years as it progresses in a successional manner to a tall grass prairie. Before the advent of men, this process took thousands of years to complete, and a marsh could be expected to have several distinct zonations. These zones are evident as one progresses from the hilltop surrounding the marsh to the center of the marsh. In this manner one moves from dryness to increasing wetness. On the steep hilltop grow western wheat grass, blue grama, and buffalo grass; low on the hillside are big blue stem and Indian grass; next is a distinct zone of cord grass, sometimes mixed with switch grass (this zone corresponds to the shoreline when the marsh was a lake). At the edge of the water there is a zone of cattails, giant reeds, and three-cornered sedges. Beyond the edge are various species of bullrush, and finally, a zone of submerged aquatics such as sago pond weed and wild celery. It is this zone that attracts the canvasback and redhead ducks. Without pond weed, the canvasback will not stay. In the center, and in deep parts of the marsh, areas of open water form an irregular patchwork.

It is notable that each zone, in addition to the dominant plants mentioned, has a distinct array of additional plants, animals, amphibians, and insects. This abundance makes one realize that outside of a few tropical ecosystems, the marsh has the greatest variety and diversity of life of any terrestrial ecosystem. It is also the most productive, with an annual yield of 15 to 20 tons of dry matter per acre. Compare this with three mowings of alfalfa, which total out to three to five tons per acre.

By following the successional pattern of a marsh through time, it is possible to select several marshes at various successional stages and thus study the time sequences in the life of a marsh. If this cannot be done, take a middle-aged marsh and extrapolate backward to the time it was a young marsh, then project forward to the time it will become a big blue stem prairie. Since it is easier to do the latter, one can explore Marsh Lake in Hamlin County.

Some 8,000 years ago it was truly a lake, formed by a large ice block from a glacier that melted in place. On several sides one can find hanging shorelines of sand and boulders which marked earlier high levels of the lake. Using these old shorelines, we can estimate that the early lake was 12 to 14 feet deep. By a bit of digging, successive shorelines can be traced to the present shoreline.

One now finds the present shoreline is a shore of cordgrass. It is now no longer a lake, and its name should be changed to Marsh Marsh or (since this is repetitive) to Once Lake Marsh. Today the lake has filled in so that only one meter or less of water is present. It was dry for a period in 1894 and again in 1934. The last few years it has been more dry than wet, with the dry periods increasing in length.

After the 1934 drought, all the seeds of the emergent plants, such as the bullrush, sedge, cattail, and associates, were able to germinate. (Most aquatic seeds need dryness to break their dormancy.) As the wet years continued, it again became a wonderful productive marsh. It is again in the middle of a cycle that keeps repeating itself until, after many years, it will become first a moist meadow then a tall grass prairie. However, no one will ever experience this remarkable process of nature because long before it can be completed the former marsh will have turned into productive cropland.

People have tried to place an economic value on marshes, but it is hard to compute benefits on something you cannot add on a calculator. However, everyone knows the Black Hills are valuable and unique, and we would feel a decided loss if they were to disappear. The unique physiographical unit of northeast South Dakota is the prairie pothole, but, unlike the Black Hills, the pothole is considered by many neither unique nor valuable. Nationwide, however, these marshes are known as the greatest duck and wildlife production areas on the continent. This wonderfully productive ecosystem is not studied. Neglected, it is on the verge of being lost before we have learned to understand its use and potential for providing necessary resources for the future.

Just what is a marsh good for anyway? It is a nutrient trap, a water trap, and a soil trap. It holds water in the area so that ground water is recharged. It prevents rapid runoff and erosion. It produces a harvest of ducks and geese. A good marsh can produce 400 to 500 muskrats at $6.50 apiece, and with the mink, fox and raccoon, it can provide the cash necessary to put a teenager through college.

The value of many plants in the marsh has not been assessed. Wild rice at $11.35 per pound can be made to grow in marshes. The more common cattail may be used as a vegetable in salads or boiled and eaten like cob corn. Cattails also provide flour, and their roots may be ground for their starch content. The ripe head produces fluff for pillows, mattresses, jackets, diapers, and wound dressings. The cattail has served as a livestock feed, and in Minnesota it is being pelleted and used for heating fuel. At 20 tons per acre, it certainly outdoes corn in the total amount of energy produced. It is so versatile that it sounds like something Jolly Sam the Medicine Man would peddle.

Since land in Asia is at a premium, farmers there purposely construct artificial marshes to purify water, remove nutrients, produce nitrogen, and raise rice. Marshes are their most productive land. Some day, when we get over the urge to destroy, we can accept marshes as an asset for the future.

When the non-Indian settled amid the marshes, he abused them. Nitrogen, phosphorus, and soil washed into the marsh at a rapid rate, causing premature filling. When the marsh was dry, the farmer burned, pastured, plowed, and raised good crops on it. It was, in fact, the marsh that saved many a farmer from bankruptcy during the Dust Bowl years. It was only in the marshes, which retained a trickle of moisture, that green plants grew. There the farmer raised a small crop and grew enough hay for his livestock. His regular fields were blowing away — all the way to Minneapolis, Chicago, and points east. It was also at this time, when marshes were dry, that marsh draining got started. Drainage progressed at a rate directly proportional to the land value. The higher the land price, the more rapidly the marsh was tiled and drained. In Iowa over 90 per cent of the marshes have been turned into fields. In South Dakota nearly half the marshes are gone, and the prospects for the rest are not good unless a reversal of the present trend takes place.

Today these marshes, once the feeding ground of thousands of redheads and canvasbacks, now harbor next to none. Only seven to ten areas in the state are known to have canvasbacks. The canvasback is listed as a threatened species. A similar, but not as drastic, decline has occurred with other ducks, shore birds, and all the inhabitants of the marsh. It may be but a short time before the people of South Dakota are crop long and duck short. We could be choking on economic abundance while starving from an inspirational deficiency caused by a shortage of what is wild and free, a deficiency not cured by plastic flowers and artificial turf.

There just could be a new resurgence at Hayti to haytie. They know that the Arab oil won't run forever but that those awful South Dakota blizzards will be back again to howl another day. And the people may be relieved to know that one acre of marsh yielding 20 tons of hay can supply one house with the necessary energy for three winter months.

Hughes County

Area, 759 square miles
Population, 1925 - 6,860; 1945 - 6,171; 1980 - 14,220
County Seat, Pierre. Population 11,973

Once a bear always a bear is not true about Pierre, county seat and state capitol of South Dakota. First named Mahto, Indian name for bear, it was eventually changed because it was opposite Ft. Pierre and called "Pierre on the east side of the river." Since then it has grown to a city of nearly 12,000. This leaves only about 2,000 people for the rest of the county.

The first settlers in the county were Frenchmen who married Indian women. The Rosseau brothers started a trading post at Medicine Creek in 1830. This was the first permanent fur trading post in South Dakota.

The Indian history of Hughes County dates back to 1492 when the area was occupied by the Arikara. Before that it was the Mandans; earlier it was the woodland Indians and mound builders. The last to arrive were the Sioux, who with the help of the small pox drove out the Arikara.

There are several Indian ceremonial sites in the county. On Snake Butte there is a line of boulders that ends with an outline of a turtle. It symbolizes the courage of a wounded Ree brave who warned his people of the Sioux before he died. Each rock was laid where a drop of blood had fallen. The Sioux so impressed by his bravery built this rock symbol for their enemy.

On Medicine Knoll, near Blunt, is a gigantic serpent outlined in rocks. The Sioux were said to come here to gather medicinal plants and perform rituals around the serpent.

About four miles north of Pierre is the Center Monument which marks the geographic center of South Dakota.

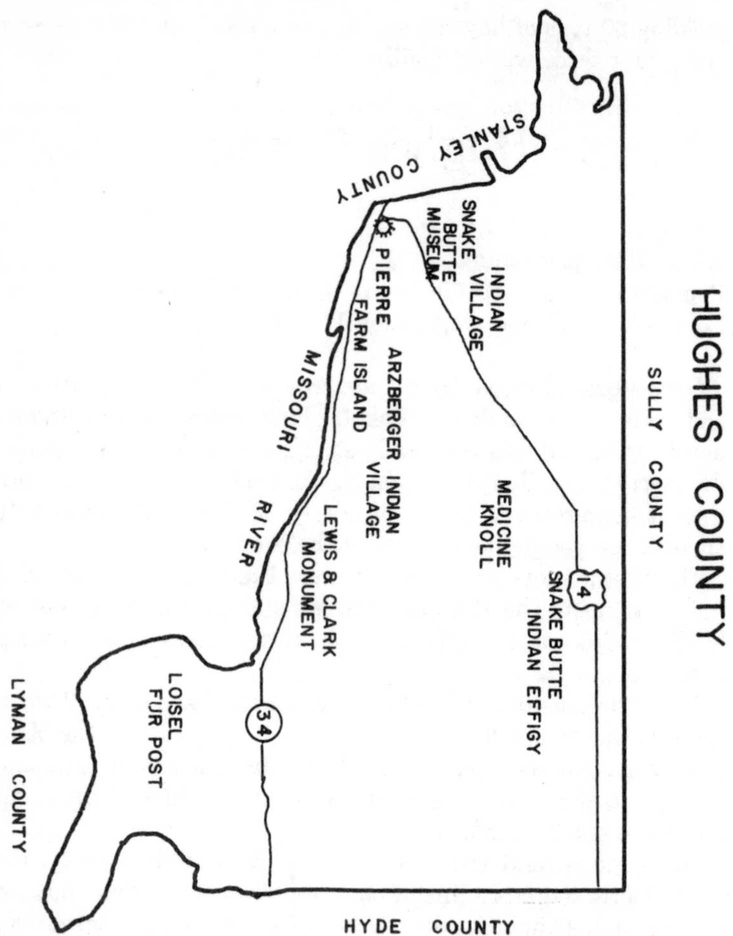

A Gathering of Birds

Hughes County

The intricate process of making new species is happening along the Missouri River. There, on the twisted, winding, braided river that has been a treelined avenue on the prairie for thousands of years, the birds are gathering. There the birds from the east, west, north, and south are able to congregate and have a ball. And have a ball they do, if one is to judge by the great number of hybrids produced — hybrid flickers, buntings, tanagers, grosbeaks, orioles, and towhees.

Since the retreat of the last glacier, this treeless plain has served as a wide isolating barrier, separating western woodland birds from eastern birds and, to a lesser extent, birds of the north and south. Because of this isolating factor, there developed in the west a population of Lazuli buntings, western tanagers, black-headed grosbeaks, red-shafted flickers, Bullock's orioles, and spotted towhees. Their eastern counterparts were the indigo buntings, scarlet tanagers, rose-breasted grosbeaks, yellow-shafted flickers, Baltimore orioles, and red-eyed towhees. They were all once distinct species, no longer freely interbreeding. But still remaining for interspecific fraternization is the long ribbon of trees on the Missouri; to a lesser extent, some of the smaller streams also provide a reserve population.

These strange hybrids were observed for many years along the Missouri and smaller rivers. Lewis and Clark, 1804, and John James Audubon, 1843, collected birds along the river. That these birds and their hybrids are easily recognized can be shown by explaining some of the obvious features in flickers. The western red-shafted flicker is red under the wings and tail, and the male has a red mustache running back from the beak. It has a gray head with a brown cap. The eastern yellow-shafted flicker has yellow under the tail and wings and has a black mustache. Its head is brown, with a gray cap, and it has a bright red band on the back of its neck. The hybrid is a mixed up blend of the two. The color under the tail and wings is orange. The mustache shows the most variation. It may be half red and half black, or speckled with red and black feathers. In a few cases the mustache on one side of the head is black, on the other side, red. The head colors, including the red band on the yellow-shafted, may also be modified.

These mixed birds are a sight to see as they sing their garbled songs from atop their lofty perches. And these flickers, and hybrids of other species, are the subject of intense interest by bird watchers.

To know a bird watcher is to watch a bird watcher. Even at dinner time he is apt to be watching intently through his binoculars as he plunges headlong into the bush. Picking himself up, he yells at his hungrier friends, "It's a hybrid!" Dinner is no longer of concern. It chars on the campfire. It may be hours before the birders get back, because they have a tendency not to know exactly where they are. But when they do return, they will have documented the presence of several hybrids. Back at camp they discuss, at length, whether it's a male, female, or immature. They chew contentedly on dry bread and beef while occasionally glancing at the black mess left over from dinner.

The next morning — or is it still night? — birders awaken to a cacophony of melodious merriment. All those birds, concentrated in one place, are singing a symphony of songs in a disconcerting concert. Why are the birds concentrated in one place? Because man has built dams that drown out ribbons of trees and the thousands of small islands that once dotted the braided Missouri. Only a few of the larger islands, such as Farm Island, remain, and it is there the birds have gathered to continue their experiments with life.

It is at Farm Island, a state park a few miles southeast of Pierre, that many people have experienced a high in bird watching. Many people have also used the island for bird banding and have banded, at times, 80 species in one day.

It is a place where, besides bird watching, people can reflect on bird populations and the changes man has imposed, knowingly or unknowingly, on these populations. One can reflect also on the changes that have taken place in the landscape over the many years.

Imagine, some 8 to 6 million years ago, that there was a continuous population of woodland birds, running from east to west. This population was then slowly divided by an advancing band of prairie that moved in from the south. Only the river valleys remained wooded and allowed for some mixing of populations. Fire and drought maintained the treeless plain, as the bird population was being split into eastern and western races. The different races soon began to develop different characteristics in song and plumage and became species. They were all given species names when first discovered.

Then along came man, who planted trees, erected posts and poles, and put in dugouts and dugins. He provided water holes along the way. He stopped the prairie fires and provided several types of bird habitat. The isolating barrier of the vast treeless prairie was broken by shelterbelts and farmstead trees. The birds from the east and west used this additional habitat, and again the two populations mingled. The gene pool from those birds in the wooded river bottoms, which, over the years, retained characteristics of both species now acts as a bridge to allow for smooth assimilation of the two previously diverging populations. Today the species are again blending into one.

This was officially recognized in 1974 when new names were given to yellow and red-shafted flickers. The two species were combined and called the common flicker, regardless of the mustache color. The two oriole species were called the northern oriole, and the two towhees became the rufous-sided towhee. Other species have not been renamed. They may have diverged too far and remain true species, or they may continue to hybridize and finally merge into one species with a new name in the future.

Continued observation of the activities of man reveal that the vast ribbon of green, the Missouri River trees, has been drowned out with dam water as the flood control reservoirs fill up. There is again developing an isolating barrier. Tree populations are being decreased and destroyed. The bird populations which have depended on this avenue of trees have most disappeared. Only time will tell what will happen as a result of these changes.

In the meantime, the diversity, excitement, and beauty of the birds at Farm Island can be enjoyed by everyone. A visit is especially interesting during the spring migration, when nearly 200 birds species can be seen. It is at this time that the birds, pulsating with increased hormone flow and charged with energy accumulated during the winter, are at their best. Decked out in gay spring plumage and singing gloriously, they epitomize a vibrant quality of life that seems to wrap the earth in goodness.

It is there that, on a short hike, you can see many birds from the woodland, water, and prairie. It is there, if you look closely, that you may find a few hybrids and reflect on the dynamics of creating new species.

If you are inclined to look at yourself as a biological organism, you might recognize a parallelism between bird and human populations. At one time the human population was separated into three distinct races due to such strong isolating factors as lack of communication, commerce, and transportation. The races were well on the way to new species. But today, because of the rapid increase in mobility, the human population is again a melting pot. There is no reason why we could not have different species of people, just as there are different species of birds. In fact, anthropologists tell us early man was a composite of several species living together.

Wouldn't it be interesting to have a human species evolve that is dedicated to altruism and love? The Big News at 6 would then have to spend a half hour proving that love too can be engrossing. But enough of this speculation.

On Farm Island the study of birds and other species will not only prove interesting but will also help prove the old adage, "Know them and you shall know thyself." Ralph Waldo Emerson stated, "Nature is a mutable cloud and is always and never the same." It is this that makes life interesting. Farm Island, its birds, and the few islands left in the Missouri River are parts of that "mutable cloud" of nature.

Farm Island, with the Pierre Shale Badlands in the background. This island of trees, surrounded by a sea of prairie, attracts birds from all directions during spring migration.
Photo — D. Holden

Kingsbury County

Area, 814 square miles
Population, 1925 - 13,068; 1945 - 9,673; 1980 - 6,679
County Seat, DeSmet. Population 1,237

Kingsbury is again one of those rural north central counties that has shown a decreasing population. It has had a gradual loss over the last 55 years that amounted to about 50 per cent of its population. Only its two larger cities, Arlington and DeSmet, are maintaining a steady population.

The county is typical of the central coteau and it is prairie, plains, lakes, and marshes. It reflects the Laura Ingalls Wilder and Harvey Dunn traditions. But gone are Silver Lake, the old homestead, and most of the shoulder high prairie grasses.

The outstanding prairie lakes are Albert, Preston, Thompson, Spirit, and Whitewood. Thompson is a National Natural Landmark and is the largest lake in South Dakota. However, it is mostly dry, filled with sedges, rushes, and reeds. Thompson is the site of some of the largest grass fires in South Dakota. Lake Preston is also a lake that has suffered the fate of most prairie lakes; it is mostly dry. To the south of Preston is Whitewood, and during spring migration it harbors a spectacular concentration of ducks and geese. It is a sight that thrills even the most stoical into esthetic rapture at the wonder of nature.

Other heritage sites are buffalo wallows, Indian mounds, Swett's Grove, and the Laura Ingalls Wilder and Harvey Dunn homesites.

I Thought I Saw a . . . an Egret?

Kingsbury County

He drove along the country road after selling a load of wheat to the elevator. His mind was occupied with whether he was going to use the money to pay the first half of the taxes, to buy his wife a 25th anniversary gift, or to get teeth braces for his teenaged daughter. Suddenly he stopped, slammed on the brakes, and stared out the window.

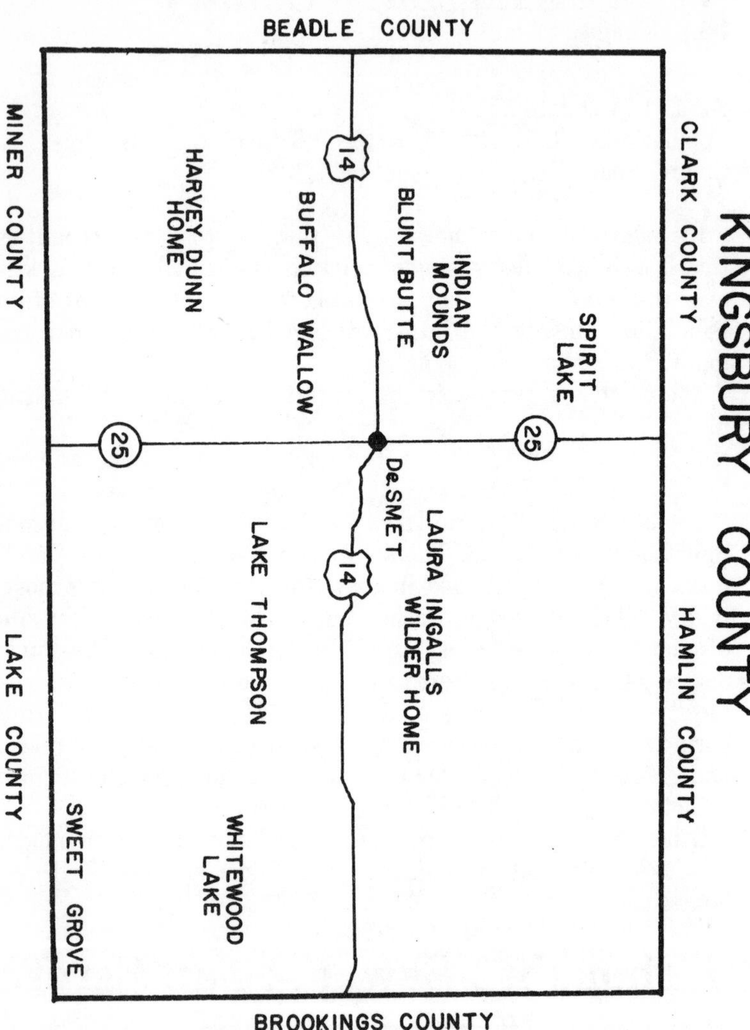

What were those long legged leghorns doing, walking around with his cattle? Were they some sort of storks? Had that last bottle of beer blurred his vision? Were the neighbors playing tricks on him? He forgot about taxes, the anniversary, the braces, and confronted the present with a burst of acceleration that sent him home in a cloud of dust. His wife looked at him suspiciously through the kitchen window. His daughter, hanging the wash on the line, was wondering about her braces.

He tried to act natural when he got out of the car, just another routine trip to town. But he felt he was being watched. Suddenly it occurred to him that, if he hadn't been seeing things, this was a good time to get his females' minds off the check in his pocket. Maybe he could stall long enough so that he could put a little money down on the new plow he was expecting to buy. So, bolstering his courage and hoping the birds would still be there, he strode into the kitchen and said. "There are some big white long-legged birds riding on the backs of the cattle in our pasture!" His wife forgot the anniversary, his daughter the braces, and he got his new plow. At least so goes the story of one Kingsbury farmer, who sighted the cattle egret on his way home from town.

The egrets came at a time that seemed to signal the end of a pioneer period. This pioneer period was a time when geese filled the sky, flying in V-shaped military formation as they split the blue with precision. The land resounded with the cacophony of a million honks as the big birds slid past the vestiges of a brilliant sunset to settle on Lake Whitewood. There, their honks, mixed with quacks and squawks of large northern ducks, produced a lot of night music. Some of the largest concentrations of waterfowl in the nation were found in Kingsbury County. It was there also that Harvey Dunn painted his pictures of the hardy pioneers and, on the shore of Silver Lake, that Laura Ingalls Wilder drew inspiration for the Little House on the Prairie series.

Kingsbury County residents will draw from the works of Dunn and Wilder for memories of their pioneer heritage. But the evidence of Kingsbury's physical heritage grows dimmer with each passing year. The great lakes that once produced for Kingsbury County one of the best hunting spots in the nation have dwindled to mere puddles. Silver Lake is gone, Spirit lake is mostly fields, Preston and Thompson are but large wet prairies, and Whitewood, Albert, and Henry are lakes on their way to marshes. The honk of the wild goose will not even be a memory if this trend continues.

Soon there was to arrive some newcomers to Kingsbury County. The cattle egret came about 1961, and today a population of between 40 to 60 is seen frequently in the county. The cattle egret is a beautiful white bird with long yellow beak and legs. It finds its niche living with cattle and feeding on insects around the feet of cattle. Often it can be seen standing on the backs of the cattle. Sometimes, standing on one leg on a back, it hints of a kinship with the daring bull rider. But most of the time it is on the ground, matching, step by step, the cattle in an unrehearsed pasture ballet. At times it strides underneath the cow and synchronizes its movements with the regular movements of the grazing cow. Only the darting movement of its head, as it snatches insects stirred up by the cow's feet, is out of synchronization. The cattle egret is indeed well named.

The cattle egret is the only Old World bird that has made it to North America without the help of man. First sighted in Florida in 1952, it began a northward spread. A bird of the field and open prairie, it has found a place among the cattle, and today its numbers exceed those of all the native egret species. If the present trend continues, there are big times ahead in the bird world for the cattle egret.

It moved from its Old World home in Spain, France, and Italy, where it never was numerous, into South America, Central America, and British Guiana. It is believed to have flown into Florida from one of these places. It then spread rapidly up the east coast as far as Canada and populated the southern coastal states toward Texas. It has now begun to increase rapidly in the inland states.

It nests in rookeries with other egrets and in trees with herons. It has been reported nesting in Sand Lake National Wildlife Refuge and at Scatterwood Lakes in South Dakota. It will probably soon be found nesting in other places.

Along with the cattle egret have come the great (common) egret and the snowy egret. They are, however, not so numerous. At one time these species were on the verge of extinction because of plume hunters. When new game laws provided full protection to these birds, and when it became no longer fashionable for ladies to wear plumed hats, the egrets made a comeback. Today they are increasing in numbers and spreading inland and northward.

In Kingsbury County the cottonwood that Pa Ingalls planted no longer casts its shadow on the prairie garden of Harvey Dunn. At 92, the old tree shades a completely changed countryside. There people have witnessed the passing of the prairie and its associated biota. They have been party to the introduction of a complete new set of flora and fauna. Many of these new organisms have been a boon to the country, others a bane. No regrets are anticipated in the coming of the egrets. It is hoped they will fit into their proper biological niche and can be appreciated for their beauty.

Worried about the poor wife and daughter? You needn't be. The following week the farmer hauled <u>two</u> loads of wheat to town.

Added Note: In the fall of 1980 some 200 egrets were spotted. During the summer of 1981, Bruce Harris and Ken Husmann discovered a large population of cattle egrets, snowy egrets, white faced ibis, little blue heron, and one Louisiana heron on Lake Whitewood. Many of these birds were nesting.

The cattle egret, now becoming common in South Dakota, is often sighted around the Hetland area in the fall. First, in 1970, a few birds were sighted; in 1978 some 60 birds were counted; and in 1979, over 120 were counted and photographed. Photos — Vernon Kirk & J.W. Johnson

Lake County

Area, 562 square miles
Population, 1925 - 12,616; 1945 - 11,606; 1980 - 10,727
County Seat, Madison. Population 6,210

The Dakota Territorial Legislature created Lake County in 1873, and settlers moved in so rapidly that it was organized the same year. The Swiss settled around Lake Badus and the Norwegians around Nunda.

The numerous lakes in the county are the main attractions in the county. The two largest are Madison and Herman. The latter is a state park. Other lakes are Brant, Henry, and Badus. On shores of Lake Herman, Prairie Village has been started by a group of concerned citizens who wished to authentically preserve the past.

The village has over 40 1890-vintage buildings restored, over 100 gas tractors, 10 large steam tractors, and countless types of farm implements. They all are woven into the archaic lifestyle of the 1890s.

The village lies dormant over winter, but when spring blossoms it is fully operational and the seeding of crops begins. When people come to the village in the summer, they can attend theater in the opera house, go to church on Sunday, and shop in the old village store. For those bent on working, there is the annual fall steam threshing bee when all the crops are harvested and threshed.

Also, another place of interest in Lake County is Buffalo Slough. This slough is a National Natural Landmark and is known for its large concentrations of waterfowl.

Lake Herman is Dying

Lake County

The prairie lakes in Lake County are like jewels in a sea of grass. Fringed with trees and framed with grass, they represent spots of beauty where people find fun and relaxation. There, alternately bathing and boating, people find time to spring loose

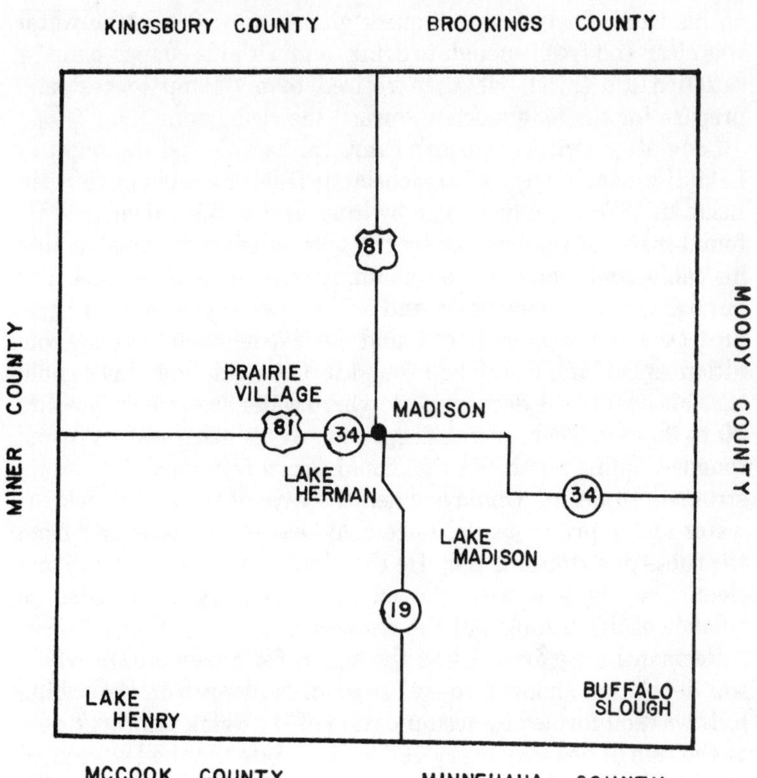

from the ponderous problems of the world and allow their minds to be lulled to rest by the constant splashing of the water on the sandy shores.

Drifting Goose once stopped on Lake Herman with his small band of Indians in the early 1800s, on his way to collect catlinite for his ceremonial pipe. He noted the deserted camps left by other Indians on their journey to the land of pipestone. All about him were spread signs of those earlier camps. Bleached white buffalo bones and ashes of old camp fires littered the area, reflecting the great number of Indians who had passed that way. Now and then the wind wafted the stench from a not-too-recent butchered buffalo.

Drifting Goose's careful eye surveyed the numerous bur oak that threw a complete canopy of shade over the spit of land that jutted out into the lake. He threw his moccasins on the clean sandy shore and waded out into the cool blue water, splashing water on his tired, dusty body. A quick glance showed him the water was clear and fresh enough to drink, and with his cupped hand he satisfied his thirst. He then retired to his camp to rest and prepare for the long journey toward the rising sun.

Long after Drifting Goose's campfire had pierced the night at Lake Herman, a new light reached out from the cabin of Herman Luce. In 1870 Luce had come by himself into the wilderness. He found many of the bur oak by the lake suitable for constructing his cabin, and many of the remaining ones he used for fuel. The bur oak canopy disappeared, and only a few oaks remained to give protection to his cabin. Luce found the lake in much the same condition as Drifting Goose had found it. On a quiet day Luce could take his boat to the deepest part, where water sometimes measure 20 to 30 feet. There in the deep, cool, oxygen-rich waters rested tongue-tingling northerns that could turn a frying pan into an instrument of desire. On days when the rays of the sun struck the water at the proper angle, Luce could see colors reflecting from the backs of swimming fish. He then knew the lake was fresh and clean and charged with the oxygen necessary to maintain a balance of life throughout the seasons.

Herman Luce's arrival was the signal for a new era, in which soil deposition changed to soil erosion. No longer on the rolling hills was soil formed by accumulation of the dying prairie grasses at the rate of one inch every 100 years, a rate that had stockpiled 18 to 20 inches of organic soils in the last 8,000 years. It was this rich soil that had made the settler prosperous and the prairie land the breadbasket of the world. But continued intensive use made the soil disappear at a rate of one inch every 10 years on sloping land and one inch every 100 years on flat or gently rolling land. Simple calculation reveals that there is only enough soil to last a bit over 1,000 years — less in areas of shallow soil. The grass that had held the soil together and acted as a sponge to slow the runoff has disappeared.

Where is all this soil going? Much has washed into drainage ways which eventually end in Lake Herman or similar reservoirs. The deposition in Lake Herman is at the rate of at least one inch every 10 years. Compare this with one inch every 400 years during the days of Drifting Goose. Today Lake Herman has 10 to 12 feet of silt and soil on its bottom. The last 10 feet were deposited in the last 100 years; it took nearly 8,000 years to add the first two feet. What was once a lake filled with 20 to 30 feet of water is now a lake four to eight feet deep. The depth of the lake depends upon the year. The predictable life of the lake is only 20 to 30 more years, under present conditions.

The changes that have taken place in the lake have been rapid. A gradual increase in minerals, especially nitrogen and phosphorous, has stimulated the growth of blue green algae, especially Microcystis, which float upon the upper layers of the lake in a velvety scum. These algae blooms are a disaster to the lake. Not only are they smelly when they die, but they also tie up all the oxygen as they decay and affect the entire lake. The lake loses its buffering capacity, and the alkalinity shoots up to a pH of 10. Toxins, diseases, and death are symptoms of a dying lake.

The sandy shores develop a dense stand of weeds, fertilized by the dying algae washed upon the shores. The small shallow bays fill up with cattails, bullrushes, and slough grass. All these things hasten the dying of the lake and its transformation into a marsh. Fish requiring high oxygen disappear in favor of the bottom feeders, bullhead and carp. Carp, a species introduced from Europe, winter kills in years when heavy snow prevent sunlight from stimulating the algae to manufacture oxygen. Anaerobic organisms and mud-dwelling worms take over the lake.

All these symptoms of a dying lake are present in Lake Herman. The aroused citizenry have started many projects to increase the life of the lake. Herman has become one of the 20 lakes selected for the Clean Lake Project by the U.S. Government, and efforts will be made to restore it. Unfortunately, the cure, rest, and rehabilitation of a sick lake are not a routine process. And Lake Herman is not a special case. It is typical of what is happening to all the lakes in the country. Some die faster than others, and man must learn that preventing sickness is the best cure for a lake if it is to enjoy a long life.

Today the great grandchildren of Drifting Goose still drift through the area. One, who retains some of the old traditions, came one day to the shore of Lake Herman with his ceremonial pipe. There he contemplated the tradition of the great circle of life that was such an integral part of the old Indian way, a life in which sun, soil, plants, animals, and man were joined in a never-ending circle. He lit his pipe and reflected on the old Indian idea that the earth, sun, moon, and stars were but a part of a massive substance put together by the Great Spirit. The deer, buffalo, eagle, spider, man, and all plants and animals were but animated parts of this massive substance. He viewed men as small gears in a massive group of gears meshed together to make a livable environment. As he drew on his pipe, he watched the white puffs of smoke drift upward to become one with the Great Spirit of the universe. A gust of wind wafted the odor of decaying carp from the winterkill, and his heart grew heavy and his mind weary as he contemplated the cost of progress.

As the fire in his symbolic pipe slowly died, the spirit connecting him with his universe seemed to be lost. He no longer had the feeling that all things and all beings were his relatives. To him the great circle of life had been broken. Will man ever learn, he wondered, to bring his actions back into harmony with the Great Spirit of the universe? He unfolded his legs and arose from his sitting position on the shore. Pouring the ashes of his pipe into his hand, he knelt and dissolved them into the waters of the lake. Then, as darkness deepened over the shallow bays, he said a final Goodbye to Lake Herman.

*Lake Herman is a state park two miles southwest of Madison. In addition to soil and bank erosion, the lake suffers from wind-deposited sediments and various effluents entering from the many activities of man.

Lawrence County

Area, 800 square miles
Population, 1925 - 14,665; 1945 - 13,575; 1980 - 18,339
County Seat, Deadwood. Population 2,035

It isn't easy to be a progressive, forward-looking county when the past seems more glamorous than the future. First, there are all those ghost towns: Big Bottom, Brownsville, Dumont, Crook City, Carbonate, Gayville, Iron Hill, Terriville, Trojan, Squaw Creek, Tinton, Roubaix, Galena, Nemo, and Two Bit. The latter deflated by inflation is nothing, and the other places can be described as just a bit more. Then there are the Ghosts of Deadwood Gulch and Mt. Moriah Cemetery, where the dead seem more famous than the living. Also there is Deadwood, itself a gulch of dead wood, forest fires, gold craze, dancing girls, and saloon fights. So who wants to live for the future when the glow of the past still illuminates the present?

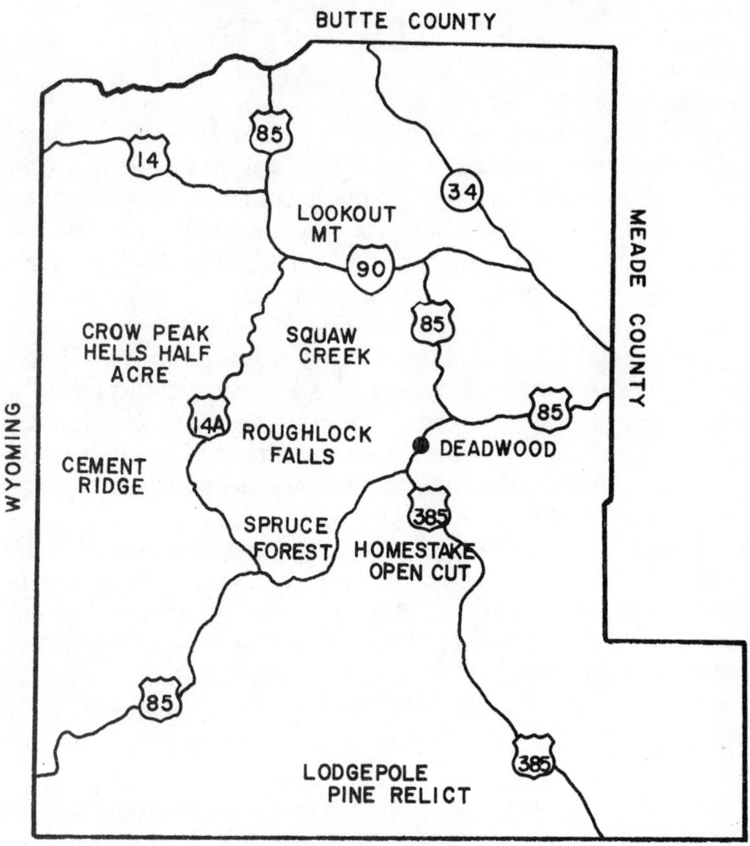

So Lawrence County, one of the smallest of the west river counties, is big on history, gold, and tourism. In addition to Deadwood, there are Lead and the Homestake Mine, Spearfish, Spearfish Canyon, and the Passion Play. Out on the plains there is the old French settlement of St. Onge.

The mountains to mention in the county are Terry, Crow, Lookout, Roosevelt, and Sunrise. The latter is where the ghost of Deadwood Dick still rides; and, it is said, if you listen when the wind is right, you can still hear the call of "gold" much like it rang across the hills in 1876. It was the call that depopulated Custer County overnight and turned Deadwood into a living legend.

Plant Lovers?
Lawrence County

Lawrence County residents have always been excited about their beautiful mountain setting. Now they're becoming excited about the infinite variety of plants found there — diversity that matches or surpasses any in the Midwest. Mountainous topography, jutting abruptly out of the prairie, combines elements of the west, east, north, and south. On a trip of a few miles, the traveler can experience climatic zones he would have to travel several hundred miles to experience on level land. He can start from a desert-like sagebrush environment, to prairie, to ponderosa pine zone, to a white spruce forest characteristic of the far north — all in 20 miles. This topographical diversity is the host for hundreds of plants, animals, and insects in each zone. It offers an invitation to study plants.

The study of plants these days has sometimes taken a weird twist. A recent best seller is titled The Secret Life of Plants. Articles bear such titles as "Sex and the Single Plant," "Sex and the Soybean," "The Power of Prayer on Plants," and "The Effect of Rock & Roll Music on Plants." This seems to imply, perhaps in some cases only by the title, an anthropomorphic purpose to plants. It is as if a plant has emotions and feelings and can react to pain and love.

Interest may have been stimulated by the recent connection of plants to very sensitive electronic instruments, such as polygraphs. Also, some fascinating discoveries have been made recently about plants. For example, muscle-like proteins have been discovered in some plants, and nerve-like impulses have been shown to exist in plants, although propagated at a much slower rate. Plants are able to control development in many insects by hormones, and in some cases bees actually copulate with orchids. These beautiful and fantastically shaped flowers have a special way of getting pollinated. In some cases the floral anatomy of the orchid appears similar to that of a receptive female insect so it can better copulate with its favorite bug. All this is enough to develop a nice anthropomorphic scenario to compare with what actually happens.

Imagine, if you wish, a buzzing male bumblebee flying around on a lazy Sunday afternoon. Suddenly he finds himself in the midst of a population of flowering orchids, all of which look like receptive females. His first instinct may be "Oh, my God!" The next instant he stumbles into one of the flowers, plays around a bit, stumbles out and onto the next, and next, and next, and so on until he falls exhausted on a nearby leaf. The stumbling bumbling bee has finished.

Meantime, back at the camp, the female bees are wondering what has happened to their "honey." When finally he does come back, he arrives frustrated, drunk with nectar, and having done his duty by pollinating a few hundred orchid flowers. What a life!

The tendency of man to attribute human instincts to the actions of birds, bees, and plants offers many behavior alternatives. Consider the revelation in a recent book that plants feel good about love and sex. "A chemist became so attuned to his house plants that they reacted excitedly when he made love to his girlfriend eighty miles away." The book reads like the Masters and Johnson of the plant world.

If plants do indeed have human emotions, we may one day have to learn to discriminate against phytosexuals. Do you want your child taught by a phytonymphomaniac? Or will you have to protect your plants from a phytosexual by having them watered only by a licensed waterer? All this, of course, is enough to make a biologist shudder. Is there a plant psychiatrist in the yellow pages? Or maybe it is the biologist who needs one.

The anthropomorphic trend dates back at least to some ancient religions, which attributed souls to flowers and drew plants with faces. Recently the idea that plants have emotions and are engulfed in an aura of mystic power has received much coverage in the popular press, usually with an accompanying explanation of what science believes happens.

Back in Lawrence County and surrounding area, some 16 species of orchids continue their weird means of getting pollinated. Each species is usually pollinated by a specific insect. The event is not one of pleasure. These species have coevolved, a process that allows both species to survive. The bee needs the nectar and pollen for survival, and the orchid needs to be pollinated. They benefit each other but are not in love. One cannot survive without the other.

In Lawrence County one is able to study and find the true relationship between plants and their biotic surroundings. These relationships are fascinating enough without having to make up strange behavior. Much of the mimicry and the mutual aid among plants and insects is an adaptation for survival. Lawrence County offers a host of these interactions in a wonderful range of plants set in mountainous scenery. This scenery — green with spruce and pine in spring and summer, laced with the yellow of aspens in fall, and dressed with sparkling frost in winter — is some of the best in the country.

Enjoy a mountain experience in Botany Canyon, where in places orchids are as frequent as dandelions. Mosses, ferns, and higher plants are a touch of the Far North. Enjoy the bogs of the Black Fox Camp Ground and their unique flora. Attune yourself to prairie islands in the forest, where the sun penetrates to the ground to create a whole new floral arrangement. Enjoy the sparkling water of Spearfish Canyon and Squaw Creek, where a strange bird, the dipper (water ousel), walks under water in the stream. Enjoy the forest openings, which team with birds from the various life zones. And when you have looked at them all and studied them all, you will find there are no weird plants, just people who write weird things about them. In Lawrence County so many interesting things await the eye of the trained observer that there is no need to develop mysticism and fantasy.

The beautiful yellow lady slipper is still a delight to find along streams, but it is becoming rarer and needs protection. The small white lady slipper is found with the yellow in the eastern part of the state, but the showy pink lady slipper has never been reported. Photo — N. Holden

One of the scenic little mountain streams and pools near where attractive orchids grow. Photo D. Holden

Lincoln County

Area, 574 square miles
Population, 1925 - 14,218; 1945 - 12,621; 1980 - 13,942
County Seat, Canton. Population 2,886

Lincoln County is a highly tillable county with little land that has not been turned into corn, soybeans, alfalfa. It is so productive that the community of Hudson boasts that farmers here have never had a crop failure.

The city of Canton, named because it is diametrically opposite Canton, China, is the center of this progressive farming community. This ability to always produce has led to high land prices and a stability in population in the county.

Tea, settled in 1894, had a bit of a time deciding on its name — it first was called Byron, next considered "Beer," before finally deciding on a family beverage for a name. Near Tea is located Old Klondike, an historic old mill that is considered a landmark in the area.

The spot for recreation in the county is Newton Hills State Park. This native woodland along the upper bank of the Sioux River is filled with campers on Memorial Day, the Fourth of July, Labor Day, and weekends that are made for picnics. Here in the hills the beauty of the woodland engulfs the visitors in the natural flow of creation. It gives them an understanding of the gifts from the land.

The Hog Peanut— Seen Any Lately?

Lincoln County

The hog peanut? You've never even heard of it? It's a little hard to find, even if you know what you're looking for and have the time for an early summer's outing. As to why anybody would want to look for a hog peanut . . . well, it's a plant rarity that some people get a kick out of tracking down.

But first, let's look at our present state of plant recognition.

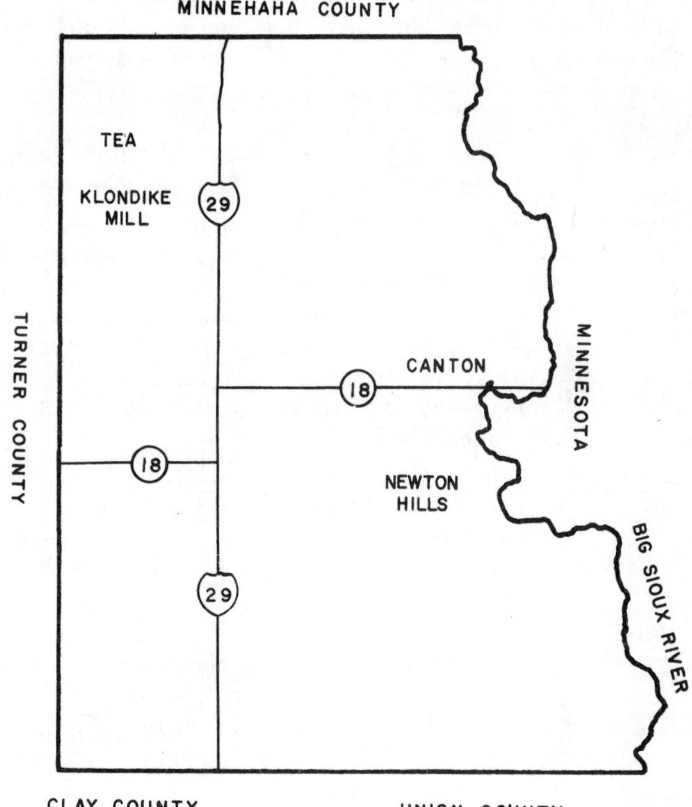

Most of us categorize plants as those which help us to live and which help beautify the earth; those which are unwanted weeds and "opportunists" that colonize disturbed ground; and those "forgotten" plants which have diminished in usefulness to man or which were never useful to him. A surprisingly large number of "forgotten" plants are maligned, abused, neglected, and, in general, ignored. It is in this category that we find our friend, the hog peanut.

Today's youngsters in search of new experiences can probably get along without the hog peanut. But imagine the delight of a youngster, or the pride of a parent, in discovering a secret known only to hogs. "So what?" you ask. But it just might be one step your youngster takes in man's constant struggle to prove his intelligence is greater than that of lower animals.

Before we look at the hog peanut itself, we've got to find where it grows. It's easier to describe the place than find it because hog peanuts grow in areas which have not been greatly disturbed. How many places — even a fraction of an acre — do you know which have not been disturbed by man in the past 25, 75, or even several hundred years?

One of these undisturbed places is Newton Hills State Park in Lincoln County. There in the hills and valleys are some 500 different plants, living together with bugs and animals in an undisturbed balance. We can now start looking for the hog peanut. On a shady, well drained forest floor we will find it.

In such places, three-leafed (trifoliate) hog peanut plants form a mosaic of green over the ground in an attempt to capture all the sunlight that filters through the trees. Under the trifoliate leaves, several long runners appear in late July. But unlike the strawberry, these runners bear a flower at their tips. The flower, instead of raising its petals to the world, buries its head in the ground. This plant is unique in that it flowers underground. The subsequent bullet-sized bean developed from the flower has been known for many years as the hog peanut. Why? Because among hogs it is considered a delicacy, and they are known to root up an entire patch in search of them.

Pigs were not the only animals that knew about the hog peanut. Birds, 13-striped ground squirrels, and small white-footed mice loved a batch for brunch. Mice, especially, in preparation for winter, gathered large caches of hog peanut and hid them in small cavities. The Indians, who had yet to learn about pork and beans, liked hog peanuts to go with their buffalo meat. They took to robbing the white mice, but the Indians, never ones to rob without leaving something in return, left corn so the mice would not starve to death over the winter. This was a smart move, since the mice could then gather more peanuts the next year and hide them in a place where the Indians would again return to harvest them.

The peanut became a prized food of Indians and brought a good exchange on the local market. Explorers Lewis and Clark wrote in their journals that a sack of the peanuts was one of the first items traded for with the Indians. Thus, with both Indians and early explorers, the hog peanut — although not called that at the time — was one of high value.

The hog peanut served man, mouse, and hog long and well, then faded rapidly to near obscurity. As the white man invaded the area, he brought with him his own new seeds and way of living, which were in many ways superior to those of the Indians. The hog peanut became virtually forgotten. So it remains today.

But should such plants as the hog peanut be entirely "forgotten" when they are replaced or unused? A lot of people say "No." To some people the matter becomes an ethical question: how can we so willingly relegate to oblivion a plant which has served so long and so well? To others, the hog peanut might serve as a novelty crop (it tastes a lot like a garden bean) or as a "buried treasure" to seek on outings.

Of great importance to all of us is what such plants represent. They have adjusted over eons to survive disease, pests, and the elements. They are potential sources of germ plasm, from which scientists might obtain certain desirable characteristics that have been lost or repressed in current varieties of some plants. Such materials might be of great value in "building" plants to meet specific requirements or needs.

Actually, undisturbed areas like Newton Hills Nature are performing a vast experiment which is useful to man. By a process of natural selection, playing upon the variation of biological organisms, a vast number of plants and animals are selected which are adapted to their environment. Man is thus able to go back and select those genes or gene combinations that he needs to provide food and fiber for a changing world. By the use of new techniques, many possibilities exist in transferring desirable traits into cultivated plants, thus tailoring them for new environments. We must therefore save the source of raw material upon which Nature acts to provide the "new" — actually, old — traits.

The hog peanut is one of some 500 plants in Newton Hills upon which Nature is performing this great experiment. It is a never ending process — unless man disturbs it by destroying the source of new plants.

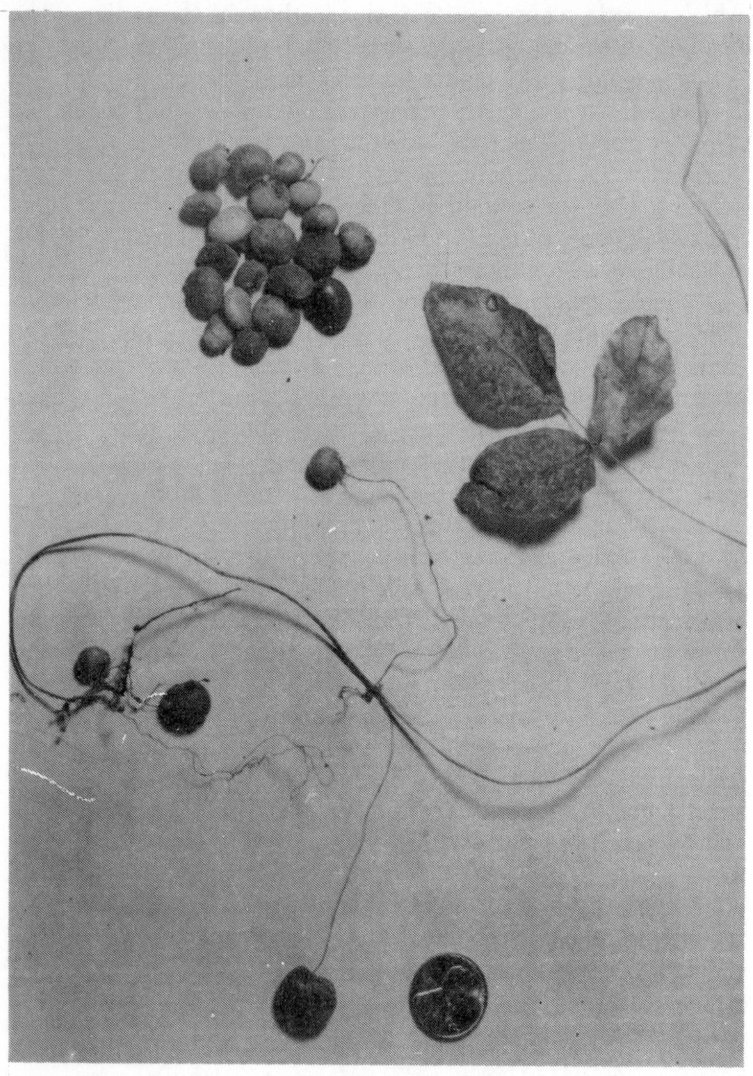

The hard-to-find hog peanut is not so hard to find if you look for it. It is abundant in the woodland, and it produces a small pod with diminutive bean above ground. Below ground are prized penny-sized beans that were sought by hogs, mice, Indians, and pioneers. Photo — SDSU Photo Lab

Moody County

Area, 515 square miles
Population, 1925 - 9,974; 1945 - 9,029; 1980 - 6,692
County seat, Flandreau. Population 2,114

The county as a whole has a smooth, uniform surface with few or no outstanding topographic features. The elevation is 1,550 to 1,700 feet above sea level. The most notable drop is along the Sioux River, where the drop ranges from 100 to 200 feet.

Flandreau, Medary, and Sioux Falls are the three places in Dakota settled in 1957. Here, as in the two latter places, the settlers were driven out by the Indians in 1858. In 1859 the Santee Sioux settled the area, and by 1871 a post office was opened by the Indians and called River Bend. Today the Santee Sioux Reservation is the smallest in the state.

Along with the reservation is the Flandreau Indian School reported to be one of the largest in the nation. It draws Indians from a large area and provides high school as well as vocational training. The July pow-wow is a great event held every year.

Lone tree is a historical marker in Moody County. The large cottonwood tree, recently cut down, was planted in a hole left by a claim stake. Its symbolism was so strong that it detoured a national highway. Today a marker stands in the crook in the road.

Blizzards also left their mark on Moody County. People remember 1880 and 1888. They tell of that afternoon on January 12, 1888, when the temperature dropped 39 degrees in one hour. It is here in Moody County that Ole Rolvaag turned the pioneer experience with blizzards into a lasting remembrance in his Giants in the Earth.

Located along old Highway 77 in the western part of the county is the Sioux Prairie, a relict of waving grasslands that covered the entire region.

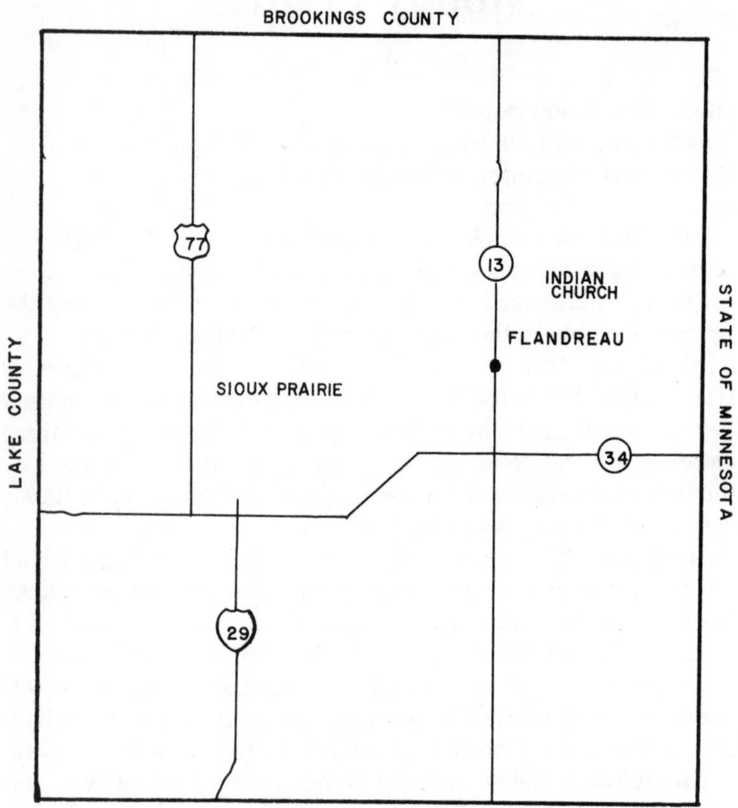

The Living Antiques of the Coteau des Prairie

Moody County

Stretching from the plains of Canada to northern Texas lies a band of tall grass prairie. The rich black soil of this prairie has nourished and produced the countless bushels of grain flowing to all corners of the world. Well-tended corn fields and the family farm are living monuments to the richness of this abundant, fertile resource.

Used and abused, the prairie has changed from a sea of waving grass, roaming buffalo, and raging fires to a patchwork quilt of green, black, and gold spreading as far as the eye can see through Iowa, Kansas, the Dakotas, and adjacent states. Nestled in this patchwork quilt are the rolling hills of the Coteau des Prairie in eastern South Dakota, which contain a few examples of prairie where living antiques remain and flourish. Here the remnant prairie ecosystem spreads over the landscape as a mosaic of changing patterns and colors. It is a living blanket in which the plants are woven together in a system that reflects the past and adjusts to the future. It continually produces the genetic variations that are selected by the environment. It is a system that assures, in spite of man, that a mantle of life will continue to clothe the earth.

The fabric of this blanket is 200 to 300 species of plants plus numerous species of animals and insects per section of land. These species represent a gene pool which is the present day answer to a long evolutionary history. It is a system whose stability is measured by its diversity and therefore designed for survival.

Let us examine a section of prairie on the Dakota Coteau in Moody County called the Sioux Prairie* and watch its panorama of color and activity through the seasons. Beginning in spring the prairie changes to a new coat of gaily-colored flowers every two weeks. In April, a relic of the last continental glacier, the pasque flower, senses the thawing spring breeze and bursts into quick blooms. Having failed to move north with the retreat of the glacier, the pasque flower finishes its seed production during the comparative arctic conditions of early spring. The flowers, produced long before the leaves of the plant, appear as lavender bouquets waving in the brown of last year's grasses. South Dakotans, seeing this flower bursting into bloom from the gravelly hillsides, hearken to the promise of a new growing season. They have designated it their state flower.

Following the pasque flower is a patchwork of yellow formed by the low growing Pedicularis (lousewort). A relative of the snapdragon, it furnishes the first nectar for the prairie bees. The prairie, now energized by the warm spring sun and flushed with

*A project of The Nature Conservancy, a national private land preservation organization.

the spring rains, moves into a more rapid procession of plants, with the dry, well-drained slopes favoring the more xeric plants and the low wet spots the more mesic flora. May and early June find the buffalo bean, Indian turnip, white camas, golden ragwort, buttercup, puccoon, and Canada anemone forming a mosaic of warm colors.

The American Indians followed this procession on the prairie with much interest. In fact, the "survival kit" of the Indian was the prairie, and he learned to recognize the various medicinal and food plants. Perhaps the most commonly used plants were the cattail, buffalo bean, and Indian turnip. They are still used today by many Indians, and older pioneers will also tell you that they found these important as survival foods. Today, however, they are as obsolete as the Model T Ford and as forgotten as last week's newspaper. Many prairie plants are indeed threatened species, especially the Indian turnip, which takes three to five years to form a turnip and which fails to set seed in eastern South Dakota because of a parasitism. The continued digging of this plant has all but eradicated it in some areas.

Moving into the last of June and first of July, the prairie seems to be flushed with radiance by a combination of pink prairie phlox, orange wood lily, and silver Psoralea sprinkled among the warm season grasses. It is indeed a delightful time to visit the prairie and marvel at the cosmic method of gardening.

Following the prairie garden into the middle of July, we are greeted by the purple coneflowers, yellow prairie coneflowers, and the brown-eyed Susans. Here again the Indian found a wealth of material for his medicine bag. The seed and root of the purple coneflower furnished toothache medicine, a sort of Indian novocain. The alum root gave him an astringent for his cuts and bruises, and willow bark (salicylic acid or aspirin) was used for his headache, puccoon root for birth control, and tannic acid from several species for upset stomach. In addition, medicinal tea from yarrow and sage and juices from the fruits and berries offered material for many types of beverages.

The first to the middle of August brings on the Liatris (gayfeather). The herbaceous plants that bloom now are taller than the ones in the spring. They have to be, in order to wave their enticing blossoms above the growing grasses at the pollinating insects.

Following the purplish blaze of the gayfeather, the warmth of the goldenrod and sunflower herald the coming of autumn.

Dispersed among the yellow and gold and extending well into autumn are the many hues of prairie aster. Finally, the end of the growing season is punctuated with the small blue prairie gentian. Blooming after the first frost in September, it is scattered among the changing colors of the prairie grasses. The golden red of the prairie grasses finally blends into the white blanket of winter, only to be greeted again in the spring by the welcoming appearance of the pasque flower.

Consider again what you have seen through the seasons as the basis for new varieties of plants to beautify the home, highway, and landscape. Here are found the genetic variations that the plant breeder is seeking. During the summer on one small prairie patch on the Dakota Coteau, we were greeted with white purple coneflowers; brown-eyed Susans with partially white ray flowers, others with partially maroon ray flowers, and one with a tendency to form all ray flowers (doubling); red, pink, blue, and white vari-shaped phlox; maroon and yellow prairie coneflowers; and pink yarrow. Finding these unusual creations provides an exciting sense of discovery for the keen observer.

Beneath all this obvious show of color and grandeur on the prairie is a strong and complex design. The very survival of the species depends upon it. The beautiful colors, the aromatic smells, and the elaborate and delicate structure of the flowers are mere devices to insure that the proper pollinating agent makes its appearance and the result is a continuing supply of seeds for dissemination. That this prairie beauty is aesthetically pleasing to man is merely a fortunate coincidence.

On the prairie it is always a source of wonder to note the interesting adaptations that have been made by the various organisms to avoid danger and win the battle of survival. Here are numerous examples of protective coloration, protective thorns, mimicry, and species that accumulate disagreeable chemicals. Plants, especially, have developed some unusual features, since they are unable to move away from danger or seek a more favorable site for growing. It may be noted that exotic chemicals and biocides are the results of many years of adjustment by the plants to the voracious herbivores' appetites and that biologically active compounds like nicotine, pyrethrium, and 1080 (a mammal poison) were first found in plants. Some insects also accumulate disagreeable chemicals when feeding on certain plants. The viceroy butterfly gets protection because it mimics the monarch's color pattern. The upland plover, mallard, meadowlark, and vesper sparrow nesting in the brown grass all find security by their protective coloration. While some plants are developing mechanisms to prevent them from being eaten, other plants are dependent upon at least being partly eaten. The buffalo bean, an important vegetable for the Indian, depends upon the action of the hydrochloric acid of the digestive tract of small mammals and birds to soften the hard seed coat before germination. These seeds are easy to find because they are lying by the thousands underneath the plant, and if they were all to germinate in place, there would be a population explosion. The small bird, however, after a good belly-filling meal with small caloric benefit, will probably spend the rest of the day proving it is a valuable part of the prairie ecosystem by planting buffalo beans over a wide area. Another prairie plant wins its battle for survival by tumbling along with the wind to scatter its seeds as it goes. The whole plant acts as a leaf and abscisses at the ground surface. This plant, the Indian turnip, was also a favorite Indian food and supplied starch to the Indian diet. The turnip mixed with bits of buffalo meat and seasoned with some wild onion makes a tasty stew for an Indian table.

The continual study of the prairie reveals many additional examples of the interaction of plants and animals with their environment. However, the most important aspect that comes through in the study of the prairie ecosystem is the fact that the successful species, surviving millions of years of change, obeyed three cardinal rules: they did not pollute, they did not over populate, and they recycled the elements of the environment. If a species broke one of these rules, it was on the way to extinction. Is man an exception to these rules? Perhaps we should reflect for a moment on an old Sioux Indian saying:

> "With all beings,
> and all things,
> We shall be as relatives."

We must realize that we, too, are a part of the prairie ecosystem and learn to better appreciate our prairie relatives.

Sanborn County

Area, 576 square miles
Population, 1920 - 7,877; 1945 - 4,972; 1980 - 3,213
County Seat, Woonsocket. Population 799

The land of watermelons and pheasants became Sanborn County in 1883, but before this it was first a part of gigantic Buffalo County (1864), then Hanson (1870), next a long narrow Bramble (1873), and then turned into a big Miner County (1879). It was the year (1883) when the railroad arrived with a host of new inhabitants that it was finally organized.

Before the railroad, the James River, which bisects Sanborn, was noted for its fords. The first white man's road authorized by Congress, the Noble's Trail, crossed the river in the northern part of the county; the Big Cheyenne wagon road crossed in the central part of the county, and the first bridge built over the James in 1883 was near Forestburg.

Forestburg, one of the main cities in the county, also had a hard time settling down. It was plotted out in 1875; it moved two miles north in anticipation of the railroad; it flooded out in 1881 and moved to higher ground where it is now located.

Not far from Forestburg was Rusken Park, a popular resort center that is now closed. It was the site of a former race track, ball diamond, golf course, dance hall, and picnic ground. It, like the entire county, felt the bite of population loss. In all Sanborn has lost 59 per cent of its population since 1920.

In addition to the watermelons, the sandy soil produces pumpkins, squash, muskmelons, and morel mushrooms. During the fall this produce is sold all over the state.

Natural sites in the county are the Pony Hills in the western part, a former sod church, and numerous artesian wells. Some wells are used to create lakes, some for heating and farm water systems, and some just run. One well in Woonsocket was known as the most powerful artesian well in the world. It shot a stream of water 96 feet in the air.

In the center of the county is John Brown's Mound, a huge sand dune left over from the post glacial days when the James River was a massive river that drained Lake Dakota. It was a period that also produced the sandy soil that now produces the melons.

The sand blowing off old Lake Dakota turned the Forestburg country into a massive dune area — now stabilized — and has today made Forestburg the Watermelon Capital of Dakota.

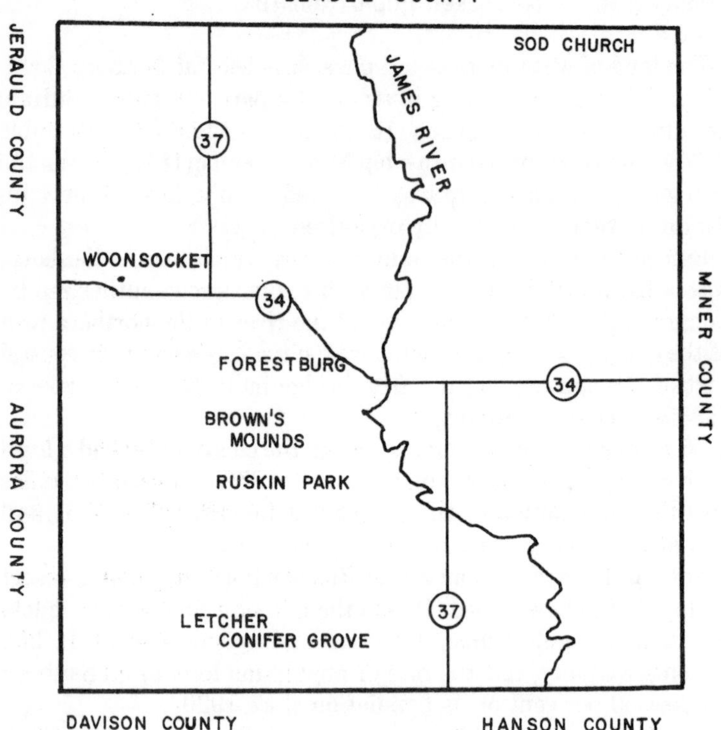

The Year of the Pheasant

Sanborn County

Bird introduction was the big thing in the United States before the 1940s. Some 44 species of song birds and four game birds were introduced. One, the cattle egret, got in by accident. Of these species, the English sparrow, European starling, and rock dove (pigeon) have become so successful that they are common household names. They are better known than many of our native species.

The reason for their success is their compatibility with the messiness of man — so great a compatibility, in fact, that they are considered pests. All the rest of the song bird introductions failed. Game bird successes were the chukar partridge, gray partridge, and Chinese pheasant. The pheasant was so successful that South Dakota became known as the Pheasant State. We boast a Pheasant Capitol, Pheasant Queen, Pheasant City, Pheasant Festival, and, of course, the Redfield Pheasants teams, which do battle with Tigers, Bearcats, and Badgers.

The pheasant was first successfully introduced in 1908 by private individuals on their farms along the James River in Spink County. Additional introductions then occurred along the eastern edge of the James River in Sanborn, Beadle, and Spink Counties. The pheasant continued to spread north and south along the James and in an irregular pattern eastward toward the Minnesota border.

The pheasant belt extended from Aberdeen, south through Redfield, Huron, Forestburg, and Mitchell and southwest to Winner, with numerous bulges to the east. Sanborn County was about the center of the belt. The pheasant population increased rapidly, and the first hunting season of one day was in Spink County in 1919. The limit was two birds. The count continued to increase. By 1945 it was estimated at over 32 million birds. This calculated out to roughly two to three birds per square mile on the prime pheasant range. Concentrate these birds into their proper habitat and "pheasants as thick as chickens" becomes an appropriate comparison.

Indeed, pheasants did mix with the chickens. Many farmers in those days of diversification raised leghorns — wild, white, skinny leghorns — and it was easy to spot leghorns and pheasants eating together, running in the same field, and roosting in the same tree. There were times when a hunter's bag would contain a white bird, which he would try to pass off as an albino pheasant to his gullible friends.

Since pheasants do not migrate but establish definite territories, they stay pretty much in one area as long as the food holds out. Thus pheasants almost became part of the livestock on the farm, especially in winter. They drank with livestock, they ate with livestock, and they knew exactly when a farmer would pull out into the pasture with a load of hay and grain. If they were not satisfied with the menu at one farm, they walked over in a group to inspect the fare at a neighboring farm.

In the spring they scratched up the seeded grain, especially the corn, and kicked the kernels out of the rows so that corn rows were seldom straight. Fortunately, the corn was not treated with mercuric fungicide in the early days.

Why was there such a population explosion that peaked in 1945? Food and habitat were at an optimum. Farming methods of the time led to an abundant production of annual weeds. Right after the dust bowl days, the farmer was still recovering from its effects. He had failed to produce much crop, but weeds still grew and left a large supply of dormant weed seeds, which germinated in the following wet years. He farmed with horse power and left low wet spots in the fields, stone piles, sidehills, and odd corners to grow up into weeds. He drilled in corn, using open pollinated seed corn, and frequently the field got too dry to cultivate. The corn rows become pocked with dust bowls, where pheasants took dust baths to suffocate the bird lice. The birds scratched for weed seeds all through the rows.

The flax which farmers planted was often too late and turned out to be 40 per cent weed and 60 per cent flax at harvest time. During the harvest of flax and other crops, the weedier spots in the fields were often left uncut because green weeds were hard for the binder to handle. These conditions added up to plenty of annual weed seeds. The farm was a pheasant paradise.

Almost everybody hunted. Businesses stopped during hunting season, and the population swarmed over the country — everybody on work release to the Promised Land. Not only the local people hunted. They came from all over the country, by plane, train, car, and bus. Lone road hunters drove with one hand while pointing a gun out of the car window. They shot at almost anything that jumped out of the ditch (an illegal practice now). Celebrities came, sometimes with retinues of 25 or more, to help with a drive through a cornfield. The celebrity circuses were followed by the not-so-famous, who wanted a look at the famous. They would all drive over the farmer's fields, tracks crisscrossing in all directions. Occasionally they would get out and walk to drive the pheasant. At the end of the drive, they would scare up flocks that numbered in the hundreds. The shooting started at one minute past noon the first day. It was the Fourth of July, Chinese New Year, and World War I, rolled into one. The limit of seven birds (five cocks and two hens) and a possession of 28 birds were enough to make the out-of-state hunter smile all the way back home. The in-state hunter ate pheasant until New Year's Day. It was an image of South Dakota that has vaporized into a pipe dream.

Then came the bust of what was for a short time South Dakota's second major industry. After the collapse, seeing a pheasant was almost an event. The bust started in 1946, and by 1976 the state's pheasant population had dropped to a mere 1.4 million birds, much less than the annual kill in the 40s.

Why such a reversal? The farmers quit raising weeds. In 1940 and during World War II, farm power changed from horse to tractor. The farmer, farming more intensively, began to make more money and to recover from the dust bowl. Farm fields stretched from road to road. There were no fence rows, no margins, no wet spots, no untilled hillsides. Fields stretched, black and bare, over an entire 40 acres. Herbicides were used in increasing amounts, and no longer did a field turn yellow with mustard and sunflower in July. Better seeds were used, and corn was planted in hills so it could be cultivated both ways. The farmer was now a clean farmer, and he went to the bank twice a year with his profits.

In addition to the loss of habitat and food supply, cold winters on the northern edge of the pheasant range seem to have affected the population. In the Webster-Sisseton area, where pheasants were once abundant, there still is much wasteland and cover but hardly any pheasants. It is there, where winters have become so harsh, that weather is a factor in limiting the bird. Cold winters are more numerous, according to weather statistics reported in Science.

If pheasants as thick as chickens are wanted, habitat that provides plenty of food is needed, such as Artemisia, Polygonum, Chenopodium, Ambrosia, Helianthus, Amaranthus, Rumex, Setaria — a listing that makes weeds sound important. Lacking sufficient weeds or habitat, we may have to add pheasants to the list of declining species that were once numerous in South Dakota.

When this decline happens, we can then treat pheasants as we treat the other species in our state that have diminished in numbers over the years. They will become completely dependent on man, and we can restock when the supply runs out. Pheasants will then be treated as the buffalo, elk, big horn sheep, antelope, quail, turkey, prairie chicken, swan, crane, and recently the canvasback. All are having a hard time making it by themselves and are now candidates for tender loving care. Will the pheasant be the next entry on the endangered list? In the most recent publication of the Blue List (threatened species list), serious consideration was given to listing pheasants in some areas of its range! If this happens, we will have a case of population boom and bust in only 60 years.

Or if we wish to increase the pheasants, we might try the soil bank system as was done in the 50s. Set aside acres were areas for pheasants, and their numbers increased during the soil bank years. It was weed seeds, nesting cover, and habitat all over again. If people want pheasants, they must provide habitat.

GEOLOGICAL REFLECTIONS

Geological Reflections

County	Title
Custer	Little Devils Tower
Fall River	Elephants, Elephants, Elephants
Grant	A Rock for All Ages
Harding	Castle in the Sky
Jones & Jackson	A Sea Called Createaceous
Marshall	Windy Mound—A Glimpse to the North
Minnehaha	People Pastures
Perkins	Living by the Sea

Next, open your eyes to the systems of the past, the geological time machine that stretches back some 4.5 billion years in the state. Watch it unwind, at what seems a frightening pace, as man in his frantic efforts tries to pack an understanding of the eons of history into a brief span of a lifetime. Search out for yourself the records in the rocks and imagine the strange life forms that once occupied the earth. Stretch your mind to an inland sea, a tropical rain forest, desert, giant redwoods, and to a slow-moving glacier plowing through the edge of an extensive spruce forest. This, my friend, is South Dakota of the past — imagine, if you will, what the future may offer.

> This wonderful anomaly in nature, which is several hundred miles in length, and varying from fifty to a hundred in width, is undoubtedly the noblest mound of its kind in the world: it gradually and gracefully rises on each side, by swell after swell, without tree, or bush, or rocks, and is everywhere covered with green grass, affording the traveller, from its highest elevations, the most unbounded and sublime views of -nothing at all, - save the blue and boundless ocean of prairies that lie beneath and all around him, vanishing into azure in the distance, without a speck or spot to break their softness.
>
> —George Catlin on the Coteau des Prairie 1840

> Time, geological time, looks at us from the rocks as from no other object in the landscape. Geologic time! How the striking of the great clock, whose hours are millions of years, reverberates out of the abyss of the past!
>
> —John Burroughs

Custer County

Area, 1,573 square miles
Population, 1925 - 4,354; 1945 - 4,196; 1980 - 6,000
County Seat, Custer. Population 1,830

They couldn't make a soils map of Custer County because they couldn't find enough level land to start. For it is here in the southern hills, where a dome shaped mountain has worn down to its granite core. It is a county that has become a monument to rocks and ponderosa pine. These granite rocks, filled with mica, feldspar, quartz, and a spattering of other minerals, are on display at the Cathedral Spires, Needles, the Pinnacles, Sylvan Lake, Little Devil's Tower — everywhere. There are colorful rose quartz, tourmaline, garnet, spodumene, and graphic granite — all often masked by a blanket of pine.

Custer is associated with the discovery of gold in 1874. Horatio N. Ross, the discoverer, died a pauper. Within a few months Custer was a boom town with thousands looking for ways to dig into solid rock. In the spring of 1876 the gold fever turned to Deadwood, and within a week Custer City was reinfected and deserted.

Here in Custer County is also Jewel Cave with the largest unexplored sections of cave in the world. The county also sports such places as Buffalo Gap, Calico Canyon, Custer State Park, Norbeck Wildlife Refuge, and Wind Cave. The latter is the home of buffalo, elk, antelope, mule deer, and prairie dog towns. These dog towns attract the hawk, owl, weasel, coyote, fox, and ferret — all predators looking for dogs for dinner. The burrowing owls, looking like they are standing on stilts, use the abandoned burrows for home as do the rattlesnakes.

For the rock hound in Custer County, there are the rock shops, perhaps the largest single collection in the nation, all displaying the minerals of the hills and Fairburn, Teepee Canyon, prairie and moss agates, not to mention the petrified wood and the Black Hills gold jewelry.

Yes, Custer County, too, must be classified as a vacationland.

Little Devils Tower

Custer County

Ryan was in the Hills for the first time. He looked around and wondered why they were called the Black Hills. As his eyes stopped on distant Harney Peak, jutting 7,242 feet to the sky, he saw the shadow of a cloud pass over the top of the mountain, turning it from green, to mottled shades of light and darkness, to almost total blackness. Under the low light intensity of shadows, ponderosa pine absorbed all the incident light, and the Hills looked dark and mysterious.

Ryan glanced at his mother making dinner on the camp stove. His feet were itching to explore the Hills, but he knew the family would be reluctant to take the nine-mile Harney Peak trail. He hit on a solution. "Mom," he said, "why don't I explore the Hills a bit and discover the best places for the family to hike?" His mother, up to her ears in cooking and crying — No. 3 was sitting in a puddle again — said, "Go ahead, Son." So off on the trail he went, armed with maps and a description of the Hills. A half-hour hike on the back leg of the Harney Peak trail took him to some monolithic, columnar granite pillars.

He looked at his map and found he had just passed through the Needles and was entering the Cathedral Spires. The book said he was gazing at the roots of an ancient mountain. Looking up from his map, he noticed to the west a massive monolith, called Little Devils Tower, that jutted above all the smaller pillars. It was there he must go to get a panoramic feel of what it was like to be surrounded by the things that make mountains. But first he would go back and get the rest of the family.

Back at camp he studied the origin of the Hills so that he could explain to his parents the strange and interesting formations he had found. Some 30 to 60 million years ago, forces within the earth's mantle, in western South Dakota and eastern Wyoming,

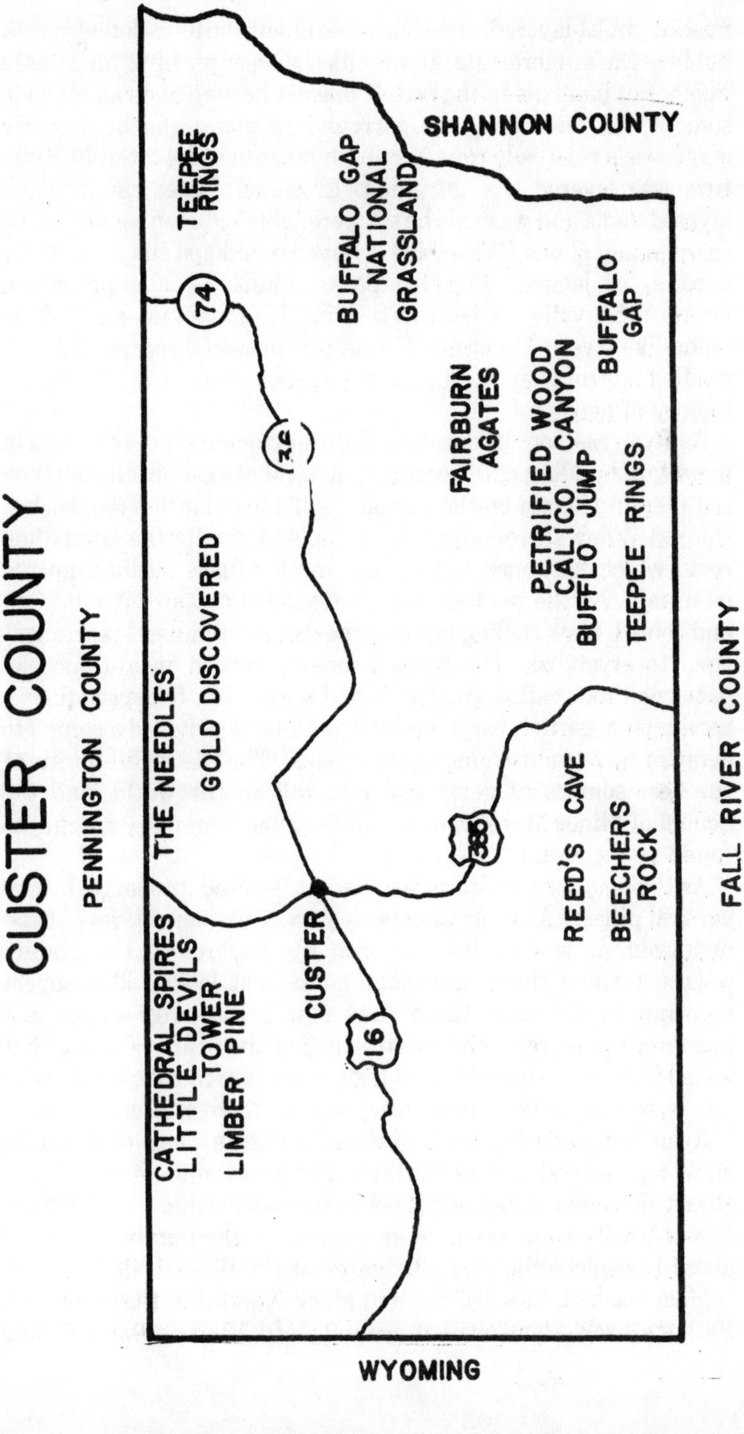

CUSTER COUNTY
PENNINGTON COUNTY
SHANNON COUNTY
FALL RIVER COUNTY
WYOMING
CATHEDRAL SPIRES
LITTLE DEVIL TOWER
LIMBER PINE
THE NEEDLES
GOLD DISCOVERED
CUSTER
16
385
36
74
TEEPEE RINGS
BUFFALO GAP NATIONAL GRASSLAND
FAIRBURN AGATES
PETRIFIED WOOD
CALICO CANYON
BUFFLO JUMP
TEEPEE RINGS
BUFFALO GAP
REED'S CAVE
BEECHERS ROCK

pushed multi-layered, overlying sediments into a dome-shaped bubble. On a microscale, it was like a knee pushing up a large number of blankets in the bed. It pushed its way up to an altitude some 4,000 feet above the surrounding plain, and in its early stage was a relatively round, smooth mountain. Its internal structure was layered like an onion. Erosional forces cut into the layered dome and washed the soft, erodable sediment out onto the surrounding plains. The bubble lost its dome shape and turned into a series of jagged, dissected peaks, pinnacles, and projecting points. The valley sides exposed in the mountain showed its onion-like layers. Underneath it all was primeval rock, which had swelled up from below. This rock and strata reflect the geological history of ages past.

As Ryan read on, he discovered the entire sequence of events in mountain building and wearing down. He read about the uptilted sedimentary strata on the periphery of the mountain (hogbacks), the red valley surrounding the Hills, and finally the crystalline rock, which had once been a hot, molten mass pushing up the mountain. As the molten magma expanded upward, it solidified and cooled. Slow cooling allowed the different minerals sufficient time to crystalize. The molten magma turned into a speckle-patterned rock called granite. Mixed with mica, feldspar, quartz, spodumene, garnet, beryl, and tourmaline, it provided a complete array of rare quality minerals and gems. (The Black Hills is one of the best sources of gems and minerals in the world, and the School of Mines Museum of Rapid City has exemplary specimens found in the area.)

As the massive granite core cooled, it fissured into large, blocky vertical pillars. After erosion peeled away the outer layers of the mountain, it worked its way into the fissures of the granite pillars, turning them into monuments that looked like fingers pointing to the sky. There they stand, scattered among the ponderosa pine, reflecting what is left of the primeval force that gave birth to a mountain. It is a story written in rocks that takes one back one to two billion years into the core of a mountain.

Ryan put aside his book, finished eating a plate of delicious stew, complained a bit about the slightly sour milk, and annoyed Hilary, his older sister, about being so poky getting ready. Before it was finally time to go, he announced to the family they were about to explore the crystalline area of the Black Hills.

Mom washed, bundled up, and stuck No. 3 into the carrier on Father's back. Ryan waited around until Hilary unwound hair curlers, then gave her the lunch to carry. He was in charge of the water. It was easy to go off by himself, but to move the family was like moving boulders.

They started out walking beside a rapidly running stream. The blue of the lupine and the larkspur, spattered with an occasional wood lily, brightened the trip. They hiked around an area that John Raek named Rocktower Mountains, then began their ascent on Little Devils Tower. All the while No. 3 had been gurgling and bubbling in her carrier, but now her tune had changed to a wail that glanced and echoed off the rock pillars like billiard balls. A shift of the carrier to Mother's back solved the situation, and No. 3 was soon asleep.

Now the problem was how to get Mom up the mountains. Unfortunately, all that was left were a rather vertical 100-foot cliff to scale, a 50-foot rickety ladder to climb, and a narrow path to the summit. Yes, Mother would need a bit of encouragement. She faced the situation squarely by sitting down on an uprooted tree and called for a miracle. Ryan felt disgust for being stymied. Hilary started to read a book, and Father, being his usual resourceful self, looked pleadingly at his beloved spouse and said, "Are you getting tired, dear?" With a look that seemed to pull forth years of ingenuity, Mom gritted her teeth, got up, followed the trail around to the other side of the monolith, and there walked by an easier trail to the top. Ryan breathed a sigh of relief as they reached the top. The family could at last enjoy the panorama of beauty that spread before them.

It was truly a wonderful sight, with the Cathedral Spires, the Needles and the Pinnacles, like grotesque granite toothpicks sticking up through the green ponderosa pine. To the west they saw Harney Peak, with its lookout station, collecting clouds. All around protruded the peaks and precipices of the green hills, dissolving into a patchwork of green and brown as they disappeared into the distant plains. Haze ringed the plains, where plain met cumulus clouds. The family had the eerie sensation that they stood at the center and could reach out, like the spokes on a wheel, to all parts of the world.

Hilary, looking over the view, remembered the poem she had read about majestic mountain grandeur. She felt like writing her own poem to place in the box John Raek had left for that purpose. John encouraged poets to share their thoughts and had left his words of inspiration:

A soul-restoring mountain ark
In South Dakota's Custer Park,
Where time and life are reconciled,
And man-of-years is like a child.

Dad felt the power and the enormousness of the mountain which dominated the landscape. He wondered if God had reserved this spot as a place to observe His handiwork.

Ryan, proud that he had discovered the place, kept asking everyone if they liked it. He felt the exhilaration of discovery and was anxious to go on to greater heights. But poor Mom, she sat there, spread out to the four directions, in a state of exhaustion. She hoped No. 3 would be ready for lunch. She knew if she could get some food into her, she would be quiet, and big Daddy could carry her again. The thought seemed to revive her. She began to look around and enjoy the beauty of the place. It lifted her spirit, infused her with new strength. She was glad she had made the effort to reach the summit. Even No. 3, after being fed, seemed to enjoy the sight as she pointed off into the distance and gurgled.

Mother went over to the side, where she could see the limber pine, a relict pine, and sat down. She watched the shadows of the clouds, playing patterns of color over the green of the mountains.

Ryan and Hilary finished their poems and put them into the metal container. The sun was beginning to set, its red rays stretched out to send streaks of color through the green pine. The clouds above the trees, edged in rose, turned deeper and deeper red until finally, as the sun set, they were a dark purple. Ryan had heard that when the sun arose out of the Big Badland to the east, it looked as if it came out of eternal fire.

It was soon time to go. Mother was the first on her feet, for she wanted to make sure Dad would be given every opportunity to carry No. 3 on the way down. As Mother firmly attached the child on her father's back, No. 3 realized she was given special attention. She gazed out as if to take one last look at the beauty. Then with a burst of gurgling, she pointed out to the hills and uttered her first words, "La, la, la — wanda, wanda." From that time on, No. 3 had a name, La Wanda.

The trip back to camp was hiked in silence, each occupied with his own thoughts and happy that there were mountains, trees, and streams to enjoy. Back at camp Hillary said, "That sure was a groovy place."

Ryan, content with his effort, said, "It sure was."

A view of Cathedral Spires framed by limber pine on the right and ponderosa pine on the left.

Photo — D.J. Holden

A view showing the vertical fractures that occurred as the hot molten magma cooled. Subsequent erosion removed the sedimentary material, and now the granite columns stand like fingers pointed at the sky.

Photo — D.J. Holden

Fall River County

Area, 1,756 square miles
Population, 1925 - 6,903; 1945 - 6,119; 1980 - 8,437
County Seat, Hot Springs. Population 4,742

Any place with a name like Sowbelly Canyon must have something going for it. That something was gold seekers who didn't find gold but discovered that the place had hot, naturally medicated water in natural rock bathtubs. These bathtubs, long used by the Indians, turned Fall River County into a health resort. The temperature of the river remains approximately 90° F. summer and winter.

In 1881 Dr. Jennings put a shed over one of the Indian baths and opened the first health spa at Hot Springs. It was said to cure inflammatory rheumatism, profanity amplified by aches and pains, and, in general, to improve the disposition of those who were classified as sore heads or cranks.

In addition to the numerous springs, baths, and plunges, Fall River County spreads out into the range country and the following are noteable: Smithwick and Claude Barr gardens; Buffalo Gap with Calico Canyon, a natural bridge, and petrified wood; Ardmore with Ardmore agate fields; and Igloo. The latter is an abandoned U.S. Army Ammunition depot. In this same area is the Buffalo Gap National Grasslands.

The part of the county that stretches into the Black Hills has Flint Hills, a quarry where the Indians obtained material for arrows; several Indian pictograph sites, such as in Craven Canyon; and also a place where fossil cycads were found. The latter was once a National Monument, but because of all the illegal picking of specimens it has been closed.

Fall River County has the highest average annual temperature of any county in South Dakota. Its southwest corner is also one of the driest parts of the state.

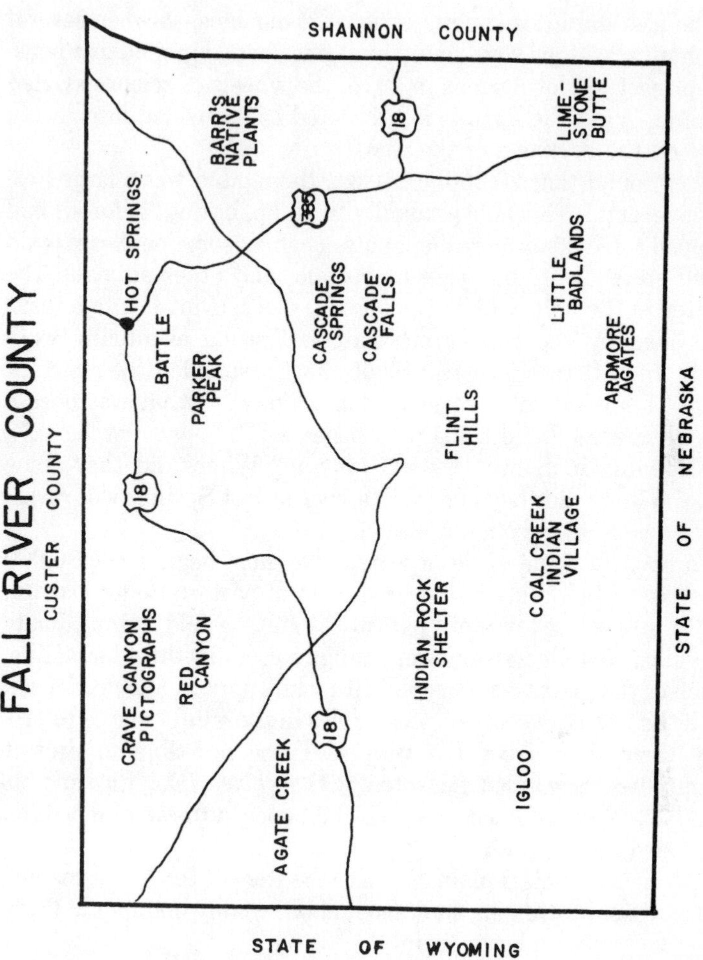

Elephants, Elephants, Elephants

Fall River County

There in Hot Springs in soil red as rust,
While digging a basement they uncovered a tusk.
Elephants, Elephants, Elephants, 35 all in a hole
A solution to the puzzle must be our goal.

The past dumps many mysteries into our laps, so when several elephant skeletons were found in a cone-shaped mound in a housing project in Hot Springs in 1976, the wheels of science started turning. What the scientists discovered has provided fascinating light on the darkness of the past.

They found that 20,000 years ago, the mound was a large hole in the ground. This hole gradually filled up, but not before it had trapped some 35 or more elephants, a camel, some peccaries (wild pigs), ancestors to our present buffalo, and other animals. The matter in the hole, which was porous, was cemented into a resistant plug by the percolating waters. Erosion eventually wore away the soft red Spearfish Shale that surrounded the resistant plug. This resulted in reversed topography — what was once a hole is now a mound filled with bones.

Elephants in South Dakota, you say? Where did they come from? Where did they go? Well, a visit to Hot Springs will reveal secrets you never believed existed.

To uncover some of these secrets, we must begin some 30,000 years ago when a glacier covered most of eastern South Dakota. In the unglaciated western part of the state, a cold, rainy climate prevailed. Swollen rivers were rapidly eroding the Black Hills. Much of the plains was covered with white spruce, and musk oxen with their shaggy coats formed circles in the winter snows to protect themselves from the wolves. Those not able to protect themselves were killed and eaten by the wolves. (Don Rice and his family have found musk ox skulls and bones in the stream beds on his ranch near Tuthill.)

Out on the treeless plain and near the edge of the forest roamed the caribou, ptarmigan, snowshoe rabbit, woolly mammoth, hairy rhinoceros, and a large buffalo.

During the summer, and as the yearly average temperature gradually rose, a group of animals moved into the region from the south. Camels roamed the area, and numerous camel skeletons have been found around one of South Dakota's younger villages, Swett. In addition to camels, there were tigers, sloths, mastodons, and a couple of ancestors of our modern-day horse. These and other strange megafauna gave the area an African appearance.

That everything is so similar to Africa is not surprising. In the distant past a land bridge across the Bering Strait connected Siberia to Alaska. Animals were free to roam back and forth at will, and they did, if they could manage the glacial conditions in their path. During this time there was a continual exchange of animals between the two continents. The horse, which originated in North America, migrated to Asia, and the elephant, which orginated in Afro-Asia, moved into North and South America.

Somewhere between 16,000 and 10,000 years ago, the land bridge disappeared. But just before it did, man and the modern-day bison moved into North America. The bison probably arrived first. Appearing on the northwest edge of the continent, mankind eventually spread, in about 1,000 years, throughout North and South America.

When they arrived in North America, they found a pristine wilderness from which the glacier had just retreated. But shortly after they arrived, this wonderful assemblage of megafauna disappeared. One theory is that the animals were unaccustomed to man and not fearful. The result was overkill by the primitive hunters. Other theories include failure to adapt to changing climate and competition from the recently invading bison. Probably a combination of all these factors caused extinction of the saber-toothed tiger, the elephant, and associated organisms. In the end, only scattered skeletons remain from which modern man may interpret the events of our past.

The state of Nebraska has contributed much to the elephant story. The loess and sand formed by the retreat of the last glacier covered over the skeletons. Today elephants have been uncovered in 84 of the 93 counties in Nebraska. Some excavations are the sites of elephant kills by the Indians. The University of Nebraska has a museum full of elephant skeletons, called "Elephant Hall," acknowledging the days when elephant reigned supreme.

But in no region has there been a concentration of elephant skeletons of such magnitude as in Hot Springs. There mammoths with tusks eleven feet long died as they slipped into a sink hole created by the dissolving away of underground limestone. Such holes are called karst sinkholes.

Unraveling the history of the skeletons in the sinkhole provides a vision of the past. Revealed is a panorama of red soil covered with a scattering of green plants. Roaming in the distance is a herd of camels. Nearby a hot spring, erupting from the Minnekahta Limestone, sends billowing clouds of fog rolling down the valley. At the edge of one pool stands a group of wild North American horses. Peccaries scoot off into the bush. Farther down, at the edge of a really large sinkhole, an elephant is trapped in the bottom muck. The trumpeting of the dying elephant is said to attract other elephants. Could this be the beginning of our modern-day find? How about a Hot Springs safari to find out about the interesting things that are happening at the Hot Springs Mammoth Dig — a place where history is unfolding before our eyes?

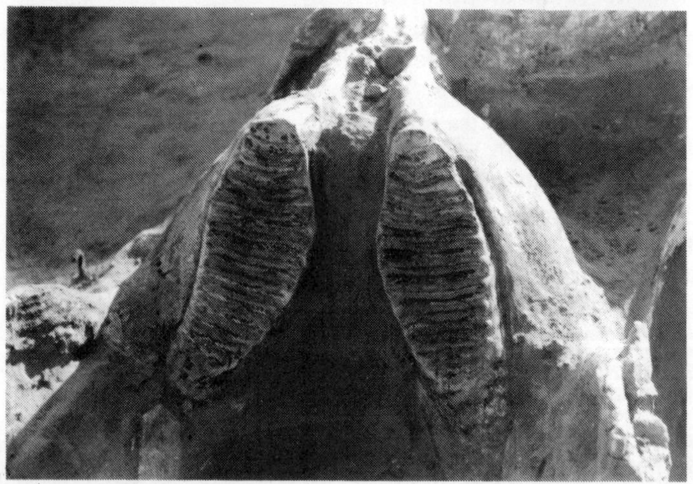

Workers removing the skeletons of the prehistoric mega fauna in the Hot Springs Mammoth Site. Below, the large grinding teeth of the Mammoth. So far 29 Mammoth skeletons have been removed and several more are estimated left. Also camels, peccaries, and numerous other kinds of plant and animal remains have been found.

Photo — Keith Morrill

Grant County

Area, 691 square miles
Population, 1925 - 11,114; 1945 - 9,872; 1980 - 9,013
County Seat, Milbank. Population 4,120

Grant County is a prosperous farming community with a range of hills in the western part reaching an altitude of 1,253 feet. These hills dip down eastward into the Minnesota River Valley which then spreads out into vast acreage of corn and soybeans. The lowest point in the valley reaches 962 feet above sea level. The location is on Big Stone Lake and is the lowest point in the state.

It was here on Big Stone Lake where the first settlers made a home. Moses Mireau and Solomon Robar started out in 1865 as fur traders but turned to farming in 1873 when the Indian left for the Reservation. Today Big Stone City is known as a resort city, for its cheese factory and in the last few years for its coal-burning power plant, which uses 80 train carloads of coal a day to generate electricity.

Milbank is also known for its historic mills that ground wheat flour with wind power in the pioneer days. Just east of Milbank are the granite quarries, supplying granite which has become a part of almost every cemetery in the nation. Royal Mahogany is not just a nice sounding name, but a grade of granite into which memorial messages are carved. So, "if you care enough to send the very best" send it carved in granite.

Producing these monuments and carving these messages are six large companies. The spoils of their efforts appear like pyramids on the plains. In one of the quarries shark teeth and vertebrae have been found.

Landmarks and historical sites in Grant County are Big Tom, an especially large isolated glacial hill; an old Indian church at Stockholm (founded in 1878); and Blue Cloud Abbey, a monastery that works with Sisseton Indians.

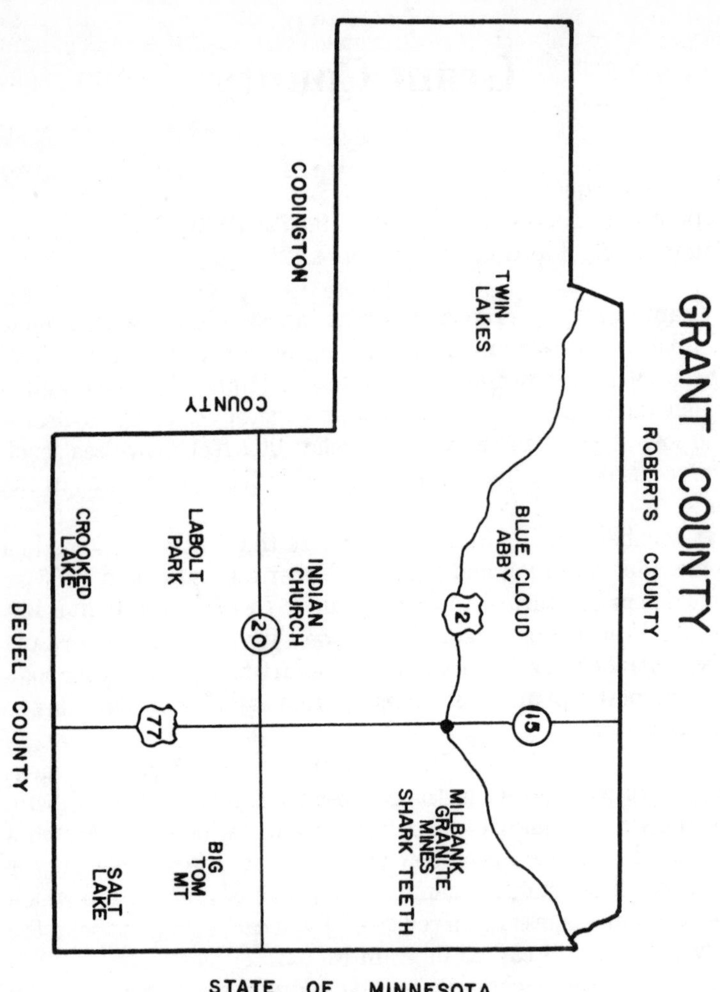

A Rock for All Ages

Grant County

One gets no feeling of ancient wonders as he looks around Milbank. The Chamber of Commerce has not erected signs on the highway proclaiming it to be situated on the oldest part of planet Earth. There are no visitor center, no parking area, no literature relating its history. Only large piles of rock that look like the pyramids of an ancient civilization, built against a prairie landscape. These giant rock piles turn reflective, curious minds toward an exploratory effort.

A superficial survey of the area seems to indicate there are only the usual corn, beans, and Norwegians. A closer view, however, shows numerous outcrops of massive, well eroded, rich red granite. The granite is part of a massive formation of granite that stretches from Big Stone, South Dakota, to Montevideo, Minnesota. It outcrops in various places in the Whetstone and Minnesota River valleys, largely exposed by the action of the Glacial River Warren.

Merely walking on the worn red rocks gives one no feeling of antiquity. But recent investigation shows them to be among the oldest known rocks on Earth. The seams in this formation have been dated at 4.2 billion years. The only place where older rocks have been found is on the moon.

Time boggles the mind. Looking so far back, the mind grows giddy as it tries to discern a lucid picture of events of the past. But recent scientific events have now opened a window. The past is glimpsed only faintly, but by using the principles advanced by the study of plate tectonics and the origin of our planet, we come up with the idea that we are standing on the roots of an ancient mountain. Starting some 4 billion years ago by the crashing together of two large granite plates, floating upon denser ferromagnesium minerals, a mountain was built and is today known as the Canadian Shield.

Time has erased visible evidence of the mountains. Some 200 to 100 million years ago, the area was covered by an inland sea. The sediment from the sea has since been eroded away by glaciers. But trapped in large cracks and fissures of the granite are the petrified teeth and bones of sharks. During the last million years, numerous continental glaciers ground over the area, and only 50 to 100 thousand years ago it was covered by a large inland lake called Glacial Lake Agassiz — a lake larger than all the Great Lakes combined. Little wonder that after all this time the mountains have disappeared, with only their roots wedged into the earth's core.

This beautiful granite is, indeed, a rock for all ages. It is the site of six nationally known producers of monuments and building materials, producers who are responsible for the pyramid-like piles of granite southeast of Milbank. Thousands and thousands of tons of the beautiful granite have been quarried from the earth and now rest in all parts of the nation. Royal Mahogany grave stones and markers with other equally pleasing trade names have sprung up at a rate of 12 per thousand population in local cemeteries. In a state with a population of 700,000, that means that 8,400 granite obelisks will mark man's passing in South Dakota over a year's time. These will be mixed with a few grey Vermont granite stones and even fewer marble headstones. All this comes to a total of 1,200 acres of granite grandeur, with carefully carved epitaphs, planted in South Dakota soil each year. If all the cemeteries in the state, after almost a century of statehood, were placed together, they would cover an area of 14 square miles. put them all in Clay County, our smallest county, and in another 100 years all of Clay would be a resting place for the dead.

Back to that vanished mountain range. This story may seem stranger than the legend of the Scotch city that vanished in a bog, only to reappear every 100 years. But here we find a vanished mountain reappearing as a symbol of the everlasting. Here we find an industry, built on dying, that makes money for the living. The past is mystic, but the present is real and earnest. So one picks up a piece of the ancient rock to see what makes it so attractive. To see what is happening, one must visit a site where some of the first Royal Mahogany granite grave markers were set to preserve a memory.

It is just a short distance to an abandoned Indian cemetery, tucked into the hills of the Coteau northwest of Milbank. Today the cemetery looks like a wildlife sanctuary, with trees, vines, and grass spreading over the monuments. Examination discloses some of the oldest grave markers in South Dakota. Many have fallen down and some are partly buried, but in one corner rests an old granite marker with the words "May His Rest Be Peaceful," which is slowly disintegrating in place.

The granite, no longer protected by Mother Earth, is exposed to the elements. It responds by exfoliation (or peeling) and will end as a shapeless stone. The first mineral of the granite to disintegrate, under the force of weathering, is orange potassium feldspar, called orthoclase. It will form clay and potassium fertilizer for the plants. On the ground are small flecks of black mica biotite (isinglass), the second mineral to disintegrate. It furnishes clay to the soil and mineral to the plants. The last mineral to break down is the translucent quartz. Virtually resistant to oxidation and weathering, it forms the sand of the soil. So the beautiful granite marker, set up as a Rock of Ages, has become a victim of time. In another 200 to 500 years it will turn into a forgotten, shapeless rock. Like the vanished mountain, it will pass from the memory of man.

Over a long time, the sands, clays and elements of the granite are eroded away and washed out to distant oceans. Here they sink into a rift or trench, where two tectonic plates are crashing together in a new period of mountain building. The old elements are reworked and become part of the granite of the new mountains. It is a cycle that is measured in billions of years.

Time and the restless earth go continually on. Only man tries to develop a chronology, in a futile effort to penetrate the depths of darkness. He projects time into the future and traces it back into the past, until both blur into almost nothing. According to modern-day science, time and the origin of the universe started some 10 billion years ago with a big bang. It will end, so it is postulated by some, when matter, again by gravity, condenses back into a giant black hole. Will this dense mass of matter again explode to form a new universe? Some believe so.

If all this is true and one can continue to follow time around, one finds that the end is just the beginning, and time, like everything else, appears to be cyclic. If ideas are the stuff dreams are made of, maybe we can all get together again in that next great new universe. Here on the Milbank granite, one can partly unwind the spool of time to reveal a part of the past and a glimpse of the future.

Molecules which don't wear out
May fall apart and wash away.
Then come together in strange new forms
And create another world some day.

So, for those on earth whose luck ran out
And life was filled with grief and curse—
For them, a hope of new beginnings
Out there in space, another universe.

So dust to dust and down and out
Is not so awfully hard to bear.
Instead of just goodbye, we'll say,
"I'll see you sometime, way out there."

Ancient red tombstone, made from billion-year old Milbank granite, disintegrating back into the soil in an abandoned cemetery. The atoms and molecules are released to begin their journey back to the sea as part of the age-old rock forming cycle. Photo — D.J. Holden

Harding County

Area, 2,682 square miles
Population, 1925 - 3,508; 1945 - 2,546; 1980 - 1,700
County Seat, Buffalo. Population 453

A tourist once remarked as he headed back to the interstate, "Hardly anyone gets to Harding." And so it is, the northwest county remains our most isolated and thinly populated county in

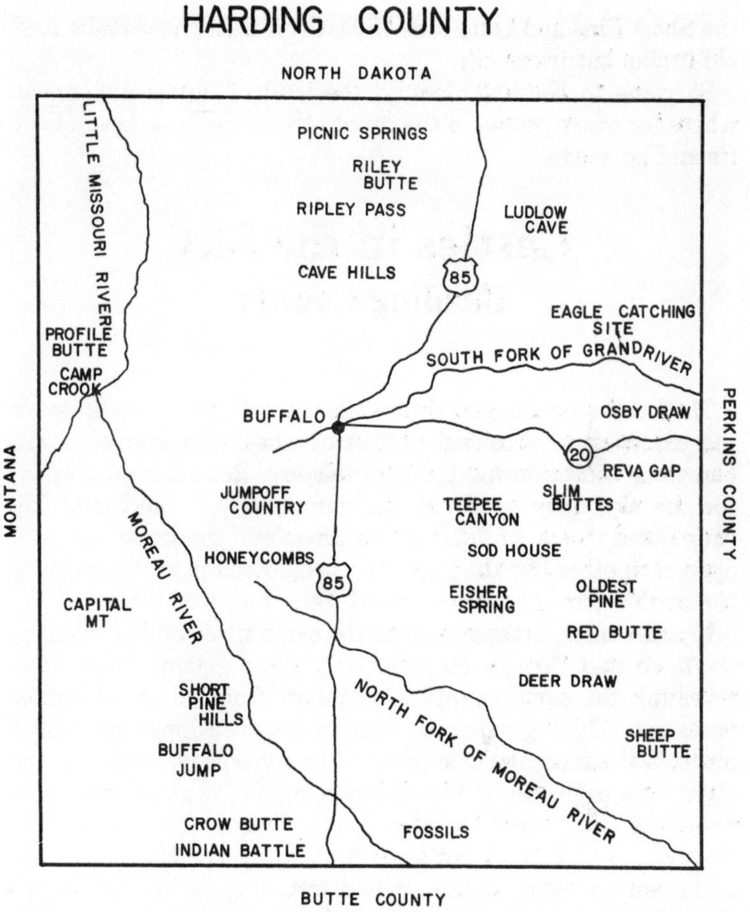

HARDING COUNTY

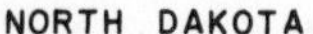

the state. It dropped from 0.9 persons per square mile in 1970 to 0.7 in 1980. It is again one of those counties that continues to lose population, having lost 52 per cent of its population the last 55 years. Its county seat, Buffalo, is small but busy.

Located in Harding County are some of the most scenic places in the state, places where one can be woven into the fabric of the living world without being caught up in the clutter of urban masses.

There in the southeast corner of the county are the Slim Buttes, Red Butte, Deer Draw, Sheep Butte, Reva Gap, and Paradise Valley. The latter is a place where one can't go wrong. In the northwest there are Table Mountain, Cave Hills, Ludlow Cave, Profile Butte, Government Knob, and Camp Crook. In between are the Short Pine and Long Pine Hills. Crow Butte near Redig is an old Indian battleground.

So come to Harding County, the land of buttes and draws, where for every person in the county there are three head of cattle and 28 sheep.

Castles in the Sky

Harding County

The Castles of the Slim Buttes are not a dream. They are striking examples of erosional patterns etched into sandstone and limestone strata during the Cenozoic era. Reaching grotesquely for the sky, they spell out the chronology of the earth. The varicolored strata, of different hardness and thickness, are piled upon each other like the pages of a book. Each page, by revealing the earth's geology, pictures the different ages of the earth.

In some cases, pressure within the earth tilted and buckled the strata so that they lie stretched out like a gigantic open book, revealing the earth's geological history from 40 to 90 million years ago. The top pages are usually resistant limestone, which protects the more delicate pages of easily eroded sandstone and clays. One page, nearly 60 million years old, is a coal seam that reveals a time when the area was an oxygen-poor bog. This, however, is a localized, not a continuous, layer. Situated near the coal seam are weird, hollow, cylindrical, or spherical concretions that, if broken open, make natural flower vases.

Located at about the 40-million-year level is a stratum that attracts local fossil hunters and geologists. Within this layer are the fossilized bones of small rodents and mammals. Usually only the jaw bones and teeth are found, but they are enough for paleontologists to date the layer. Some strata are heavy and dark red, with oxidized iron layers and concretions. Others are pure white, with fine grain limestone, but most layers are pastel bands of varying thickness.

Upon this varicolored strata of tinges, textures, and thickness play the changing patterns of light, turning the castles into different hues. Storm clouds filter the red rays and give the castles a cold blue hue. In the middle of the day, when the direct rays of the sun hit the buttes, the intensity is so great that all colors blend together into a light brown. It is at sunrise and sunset that the Slim Buttes are dressed in their most enchanting vestments. The red glow of the setting sun gives the buttes a warm color, laced with the dancing shadows of the pine trees. Cumulus thunderheads, spotting the bright blue sky, form marshmallowy caps. Some clouds reflect a rainbow of colors, as the sun sets. It is indeed a fairyland, as the panoramic play of colors recedes with darkness. If there's a full moon, the enchantment continues through the night.

Woven around and under the buttes is a blanket of vegetation. Contending with seasons that are dry and warm in summer and cold in winter, it reacts in a predictable way. In the spring, the greenness contrasts with the browns of the buttes. In summer, the grasses turn to brown and, from a distance, blend into the buttes in an overall pattern of brown punctuated by exclamation points of ponderosa pine. In the fall, there is a brief burst of color as the deciduous trees radiate their autumnal colors. On the ground the little blue stem and a few patches of big blue stem splash in with their patchwork of purplish-red. These blue stems, once common to the prairie, are now found only in isolated places. In winter, the area is a mottled mosaic of white, brown, and green.

Anyone in a reflective turn of mind, gazing on the buttes, might give thanks for the gift of being able to perceive this phenomenon, turn it into a cognitive response, and finally develop a concept that relates to our presence in the endless flow of time. We would surely be confused if we were required to make all our adjustments to life from observation of man-made phenomena. Animals, on the other hand, do not have the cognitive ability to interpret these phenomena. In some respects it appears that a great number of people, whose eyes have not adjusted to their surroundings, lack the ability also.

Whether the Indians found the panaroma of color and beauty attractive, or a place mainly to hide and hunt, is speculation. That they did use the area, however, is confirmed by the numerous signs left by them.

One of the more interesting signs is the evidence of scaffolds in the Indian burial trees located at the north edge of the buttes. On some of the taller buttes, eagle-catching pits have been located, and human skulls have been found peering out from under the protective ledges on some buttes. A few miles north of the buttes is a ledge of rock with numerous petroglyphs, and across from the ledge is Ludlow Cave, which shows signs of many years of Indian occupation. Between Ludlow Cave and the Slim Buttes are many teepee rings.

When the Indians left, so did some animals. Exodus of the Indians, driven out by General Crook in 1876, was followed by the rescue from extinction, by Fred Dupree, of some 200 buffalo. The animals were later transferred to the Scotty Philip ranch near Ft. Pierre. The last "free" buffalo seen in the area was in 1884. The grizzly bear had disappeared a few years earlier. The last prairie wolf was killed in 1945.

One of the most interesting areas to visit is a deep northwest-running canyon, about three miles north of the castles. There a large spring erupts from the side of a butte, feeds a three-acre stand of aspen, runs down the canyon a few hundred feet, then disappears into dry sand. In this dense aspen thicket — one of few in northwest South Dakota — are the remains of an old Indian teepee. It was discovered in 1878 by buffalo hunters who came north to obtain their winter's buffalo meat. The teepee symbolizes the time when the Indians occupied the area.

Through the respect and love of Ralph Waugh, the integrity of the teepee has withstood the elements. Ralph's father was one of the buffalo hunters who discovered the teepee in 1878. In 1909 Ralph filed a homestead in the area and in 1914 took his first picture of the teepee. From that time on he carefully replaced the rotting logs with new ones, and the teepee has stood tucked away in the woods, a symbol of the times when red men rode the ridges of the canyons.

It is interesting to speculate on the role of the lonely teepee. A possible explanation is that it served as protection for a wounded or sick warrior, left to die or recover as the tribe was forced on the reservation by General George C. Crook at the close of the 1876 Indian Wars. Whatever its role, it remains a relic of the free spirited Indian who no longer roams at will over the plains.

In the southern part of the buttes are Deer Draw and Sheep Mountain, with their legends of moonshiners, outlaws, and frontiersmen.

Just west of the southern edge of Slim Buttes and in several areas in Harding County along small streams where erosion is so rapid that vegetation cannot maintain a foothold, are many areas of small badlands. These bare slopes, which resemble a fault line, expose all the strata in detail. Locally these areas are known as the "Jump-Off." In one area of the Jump-Off, where a particular type of erosion is occurring, the resulting pattern is known locally as the "Honeycombs." If you ever wish to see a Honeycomb Jump-Off, go to Harding County. It is well worth the effort. There is no other in the world.

The most impressive feature about the Honeycombs is their unique erosional pattern. The geometrical configuration creates an artistic design that defies duplication. It is one of the most photogenic sites in nature. Even the novice may appear professional when photographing the area, for no matter from what angle you photograph, you still get the pleasing effect of soft angular shadows playing upon angular sandstone and forming repeated geometrical patterns.

If you are not awed by the various patterns of nature and art, the Honeycombs will leave you uninspired. But you can still appreciate their geological value. The Honeycombs lie directly on top of the Hell Creek Formation and consist of fine-grained micaceous sand. The sand grains from the Golden Valley Formation (originally called Slim Buttes Formation) are cemented together by clay. Weathering out of the sandstone formation are numerous sandstone concretions that resemble 50 calibre bullets. Occasionally you will find some twining of these sand crystals, but the interesting thing about them is that they all face to the northwest, indicating this once was the direction of flowing water. The sand particles are not bound together by lime, and the cementing agent is probably siliceous.

Of interest about the Honeycombs, really a descriptive name, is their unique erosional pattern, not duplicated in any other badlands formation. In addition, such abundant sand crystals are not commonly found in other areas. The main attraction of the area, however, is simply the pleasing patterns portrayed by the designing hand of nature.

Indeed, the Harding County badlands is not just a place to remember. It is a lesson in history and geology. It is a bending of the mind around the countless patterns etched into the rock by the enduring force of time. It is honeycombs and castles in the sky, imprinted on the imagination.

Cutting the sky like ships on the prairie stand the multicolored battleship rocks of the Slim Buttes (top). Below the tall buttes, the tilted eroded strata leaves a geological history that unfolds like the pages of a text (bottom).

Photos — D.J. Holden

**An old Indian teepee in the Slim Buttes, photographed in 1916. When it was discovered in 1889, sod lay along its sides, and it had a cattail floor mat and a painted buffalo skull for decoration. Ralph Waugh, local rancher, maintained this relict of the Indian by replacing each pole as the original rotted away.
Photo — courtesy Estelle Jarvi**

**With the death of Mr. Waugh in 1973, the entire teepee collapsed and today (1979) it is a shamble of decaying timber.
Photo — D.J. Holden**

(John C. Ewers in his book <u>Indian's Life on the Upper Missouri</u> describes the construction and use of a similar structure which he calls a war lodge.)

Near Reva is a sod house used by pioneers. Constructed in 1910 and still occupied, it is a reminder of the passing of the Indian and the coming of the settler.

Photo — courtesy Rapid City Journal

Near the Slim Buttes are geometrical designs of the honeycombs, a sculpture that dwarfs the talents of man.
Photo — Tim Jackson

Jackson County

Area, 816 square miles
Population, 1925 - 2,539; 1945 - 1,561; 1980 - 3,437
County Seat, Kadoka. Population 832

It's hard to become a real county when one keeps disappearing from the map, but Jackson County made it. It was finally organized in its present form in 1914, and in 1980 it engulfed Washabaugh. But such is the life of counties whose boundaries are always rearranged by legislators.

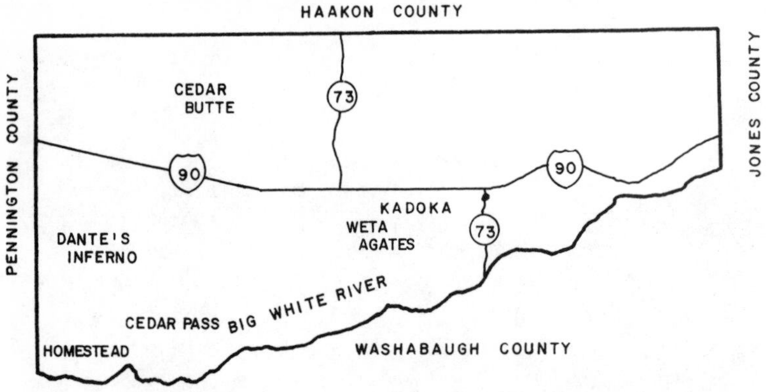

The county experienced an explosive growth period when the railroad reached Kadoka in 1906. During this period tar paper shacks, tents, or dugouts appeared on every quarter section south of Interstate 90 and east of Highway 73. But like so many of these starvation claims, they eventually ended up again in the hands of the cattlemen.

It is here at Kadoka that the tourists get their first look at the Badlands National Park. Kadoka, meaning hole in the wall, looks out at the vast panorama of erosional grotesqueness that only wind and water can arrange on an unstable landscape. This park with a visitors center at Cedar Pass attracts tourists from all over the world. They can view the changing pattern of light from sunup to sunset and be greeted by a world of fantasy. In the red glow of sunset, images of Dantes Inferno flit through the mind. In the cold blue of a thunderstorm, a similar mysterious darkness lurks within the purple pinnacles. During the sunshine of the day, cloud patterns make rippling, moving shadows that seem to animate the rugged landscape.

In the gorges and washes, the fossil bones of prehistoric animals are exposed to reveal the secrets of the past. It is here where the bones of the thunder horse of the Sioux (titanotheres) are found. This giant relative of the horse with a horn on his nose was a legend to the Sioux.

There are many other fossil sites, and the area is great for the rock hound. There are prairie agates, jasper, chalcedony, and fossils all over. But remember you can look but not collect in a national park.

Jones County

Area, 982 square miles
Population, 1925 - 3,995; 1945 - 2,045; 1980 - 1,463
County Seat, Murdo. Population 723

Jones County was not always prairie. It was once a part of a massive shallow inland sea that spread a deposit, the Pierre Shale, over the entire state at a depth of 100 to 2,000 feet. In the eastern part of the state a series of glacial events has spread a redeeming veneer over the land, but west of the river it is almost all Pierre Shale.

So massive is the formation that it has controlled the destiny of the land for 100 million years. Today it controls the destiny of the people.

It is out here in Jones County that people sit lulled into complacency by country music, cattle prices, machinery sales, and storm warnings, but with little awareness that six to twelve inches of soil are all that provide a thin line of survival between them and complete disaster. Prices, production, and a lack of rain, locked into the ever-present Pierre Shales, often turn the farmer/rancher to his God in hope of deliverance.

As the long-playing record of time turns its tune on the land, the ever-changing hills turn to knobs of slate and shale reflecting the power of erosion. As the erosion works its way into the hills with ever larger coalescing rings of destruction, the people of Jones County become fewer. For Jones County is a victim of the Pierre Shale Syndrome: infertility, drought, and barrenness.

But Jones County is more than Pierre Shale. It, together with the adjacent counties, also experienced the railroad syndrome, cattle barons, and honyockers. For awhile the county was a cattleman's utopia with unfenced range, ranches almost the size of counties, and women who came out from Chicago to entertain the cowboys. But this all evaporated with the railroad. Almost simultaneous with the influx of landseekers came an exodus of cattle to eastern markets, and as the railroad pushed westward towns sprang up. They were filled with gamblers, land sharks, petty thieves, ne'er-do-wells, and even some people who tried to make an honest living. Murdo was a busy place in its heyday, and that flavor of the western tradition still permeates the country.

First, the influx of people turned the county into a farming community, but as years passed the county again reverted to cattle raising. This shift has been reflected in the population of the county. Having lost 60 per cent of its population since the boom time, it is today the county with the smallest population and rivals Harding County for the lowest population density. Remove the urban complex of Murdo, Okaton, and Draper, and the rural scene dominates with less than 500 people making a living on 982 square miles. It is also the youngest county in the state, being organized in 1916 when it separated from Jackson County.

Scenic areas in Jones County are the old ghost towns of Capa, formerly a health spa, and Van Metre. Along the Bad and White Rivers are areas of scenic beauty to delight those who seek the unusual.

A Sea Called Cretaceous

Jackson & Jones County

There is something eerie about the crust of the earth. It seems to be stable and motionless but really isn't. It undulates, like giant waves on a petrified sea, so slowly that only after a thousand years can one really decide which direction it is going. This slow undulation accounts for one part of our continent going up and another part going down. Those parts going up form mountains, and those going down become inundated by the oceans. Such inundations become large inland seas and sometimes have covered over half of the continent. Records show three or four of these inundations once covered the Midwest. The last was between 100 and 200 million years ago, in what was called the Cretaceous period. It left a vast sediment, called the Pierre Shales, upon the land of the Dakota.

This great Cretaceous Sea extended from the Gulf of Mexico to the Arctic. It covered the entire Midwest from Ohio to the Rockies. What is now Jones County was near the center; if the God of the Sea, Poseidon, needed a home in the deepest depths, here was the place to go. Today the sea is gone, but it left an extensive deposit that covers all of Jones County, sometimes to a depth of 2,000 feet. This vast deposit is best seen in desolate bare banks along the Missouri River. It is probably the most extensive and abundant material covering the state, even more abundant than the ubiquitous glacial till found in the eastern part of the state. Remove the glacial till, and what do you have? Pierre Shale. It outcrops in the Sisseton Hills, the hills around Aberdeen, along the James River, and several other places. Well diggers often tap the Pierre Shales and wonder where the shale came from.

Picking up the dull, gray, platey material, the well driller reflects on the numerous times he has drilled into it and the numerous times he has seen it as he fished the Missouri River. Slowly the business of drilling wells fades, pushed out by the dark gray sediment that conjures up visions that here once rolled the waves of an ancient sea.

People living on the plains often glamorize the distant sea. They see in the watery depths the secrets of the past. The well driller wipes a speck of dust from his eye and wonders what it must be like to explore the bottom of a sea. Stories of a sea's wealth make him wonder if he too might find vast deposits of manganese, nickel, cobalt, copper, iron, zinc, silver, and, yes, gold. He's Jacques Cousteau on the bow of the Calypso, shouting to his men, "This must be it!" Only this Calypso has wheels because the sea has been drained dry. Still, he can explore the bottom of the sea with only his hiking boots and sunglasses. No pressurized suits, oxygen tanks, and other specialized equipment are needed. Anyone can explore.

On the vast sea bottom, now dissected by streams, one can explore for all those talked-about treasures. They're all there, especially the manganese nodules, the iron concretions, and the barite crystals. They are scattered here and there, but the problem of turning them into a valuable resource is that there is too much distance between here and there. They are too thinly scattered and too impure in composition to compete on today's market. They can be useful in the future if supplies grow scarce. People who speak of the treasures of the sea use "if" a good deal. This also holds true about products found in the Pierre Shales.

All one needs for exploration is the permission of the landowner, where the land is privately owned. Millions of acres of this sea bottom land, however, are managed by government agencies. So we, in fact, are the owners and are encouraged to explore this resource by such agencies as the Forest Service, Bureau of Land Management, Fish and Wildlife, and several other State and Federal agencies.

So one explores — to extend the mind, to seek a museum specimen, to discover an article of beauty. What does one find? Examples of an assemblage of ancient sea fossils known as the Pierre Shale Fossils. These are the scaphites, baculites, ammonites, chambered nautilis, belemnites, clams, turtles, shark teeth, and whale ear bones, to mention a few. Here one finds weird concretions and nodules, crystals of calcite, gypsum, and golden barite or desert roses. In some places agates, flints, cherts, jasper, and chalcedony are washed in with the gravel in the stream bed. But most of all, one finds solidified mud, shale, turned to gumbo, which sticks to the shoes like great balls of tar when wet.

Collect some of the Pierre Shale from different layers and places, and examine with a strong hand lens or microscope to see the multitudinous microscopic types and forms of organisms that lived, died, and settled out to form a part of the strata on the bottom of the sea.

Looking into the microscope and rubbing the gritty shale between the fingers, one wonders where it all came from. Mostly it is all gray shale, but here and there is a chalky layer of lime or of volcanic ash — now after a million of years of weathering, bentonite clay. These different particles have all settled to the bottom of the sea as part of the chemical and biological activity associated with the action of the sea.

The biggest supplier of material for the sea was the mountains. Erosion, the great leveler, moved the mountains into the sea, and as it did, it fertilized the waters. The waters then filled with teeming life. Diatoms and radiolarians, with their siliceous bodies, and foraminifera, with their carbonated lime bodies, mingled with the sharks and whales. They, together with the rest of the species of the sea, linked together to form a network of food chains. But in the end their remains settled like particles in a giant vegetable soup. They rained down onto the bottom like a continuous giant snow storm. The rate was rapid when temperatures were warm and slow when the temperatures were cold. This created layers of different sizes, which today look somewhat like the uneven pages of a massive book.

Today the story enclosed within these page-like layers is fascinating. It gives one an idea of the nature and extent of the great Cretaceous Sea. One can understand that the Pierre Shales are not only in the Jackson-Jones complex but almost everywhere in Dakota land. The fossils are especially abundant around Wasta and Eagle Butte. The scenic Badlands are particularly interesting along the Missouri in Lyman and Stanley Counties, but Jones is the only county whose surface deposit is completely Pierre Shale.

Visit a place where the Pierre Shales have been stripped of their vegetation. Wander through the barren hills. Sometimes, in the midst of the hills, one appears to be waking from a bad dream. All about are heaps and piles of ashlike materials, splotches of dark red iron concretions glowing like burning coals, producing a feeling of that awful place that twists and torments the spirit. But then, off on a little knoll, growing in utter desolation, stands a blooming yucca. Its spike of creamy white flowers tinged with pink pierces the sky. Like a flash of light, it washes away the mood of gloom spread by the somber shales.

All of this proves that people who ignore their surroundings do not benefit from observation and understanding. They become almost as dull as the shale. The well driller who speculated on a small piece of shale in his hand saw a whole sea before him. It opened his mind, illuminated his spirit, and filled him with a sense of understanding. He saw that the past was connected with the future.

The dark, somber, almost sinister Pierre Shales Badland seems to drift off into emptiness on the horizon. Deposited here by a vast Cretaceous Sea 100 million years ago, it is the most massive deposit in the state. Photo — D.J. Holden

Marshall County

Area, 889 square miles
Population, 1925 - 9,740; 1945 - 8,182; 1980 - 5,404
County Seat, Britton. Population 1,590

The first settler, Charles Bailey, in Marshall County in 1881 was an outlaw. He stole horses and engaged in shady deals. Accused of this undesirable behavior, he was killed trying to escape. From this somewhat less than inspiring beginning, Marshall County has developed into a prosperous country. Its soil, it is said, is as productive as any in the northwest. It is a county that abounds with 33 natural lakes, most of them in the southeast corner of the county atop the coteau. Here we find Clear and Stink Lakes, Red Iron and Alkali Lakes, and having run out of imagination, there are Two, Four, Six, and Nine Mile Lakes, named according to their distance from Sisseton. There are Hills, Buffalo, Owl, Kettle, Grey, Piyas, Cottonwood, and Little Cottonwood Lakes. And there, surrounded by most of these lakes, of all things, is a town called Lake City.

The most interesting part of Marshall County, however, is Sica (Sieche) Hollow State Park. Here in the tradition of the old Indian legends lurk the bad spirits of the world. After dark, ghostly glowing stumps, strange smells, and, out of the depth of the woods, moving and creaking sounds seem to come from the spirit world. There are sinking bogs and swamps that give off gas that burns. The place is loaded, the Indians say, with spirits.

To the botanist, bird enthusiast, and nature lovers, it is one of the best examples of the woodland ecosystem in South Dakota. It is sugar maples and aspens; it is woodland, spring flowers, and bog plants galore; it is indigo buntings, scarlet tanagers, and grosbeaks, mixed with birds of the upland prairies.

Leaving Sica Hollow one can next visit Windy Mound, Prayer Rock, Spirit Earth Gap, and Squaw Hill — the latter a site that relates to the legend of Enemy Swim Lake.

Probably the most famous site in the area is Fort Sisseton. This army post, turned social center, operated from 1864 to 1888. It took the Indian name Sisseton (dead fish) and turned it into a place of glamor and parties for sportsmen from Chicago and Minneapolis. It operated in the latter manner until 1910, when abandoned, it fell apart in the hands of vandals. It was reconstructed in the 1930s and today is a state park. The fort celebrates its frontier tradition every June with a gala three-day event.

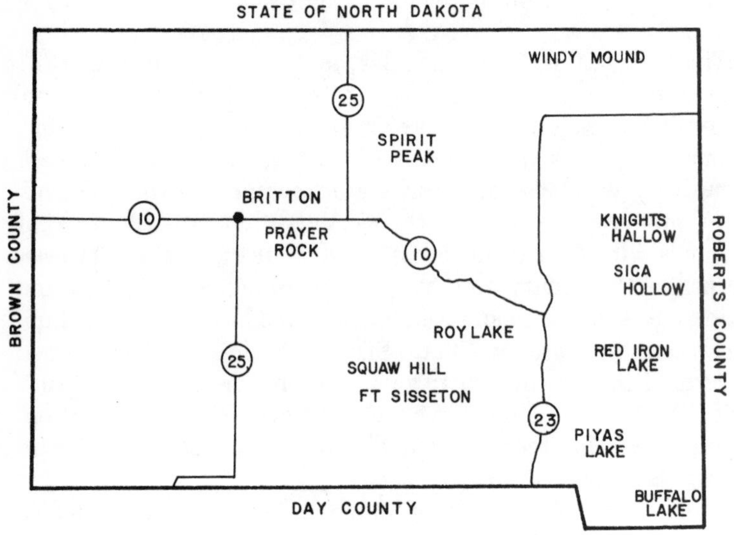

Windy Mound — A Glimpse to the North

Marshall County

A prominent feature of eastern South Dakota is a plateau of land that starts at Dell Rapids and gradually slopes upward until it comes to a point in Marshall County, near the North Dakota border. At its point is a large conical hill of stratified glacial outwash gravel known as Windy Mound. The base of Windy Mound has several tilted layers of stratified gravel, indicating it was once the bottom or edge of a rapidly moving stream. Dumped upon the glacial gravel is a mass of unsorted glacial till, which forms the top part of the mound. The entire plateau was named by French traders who settled among the Indians in the 1850s. They called it the Coteau des Prairie — the prairie tableland.

At its northern extreme, some of its higher points rise 500 feet above the surrounding lowlands. And on its northern extent the Coteau is flanked on the east by former glacial Lake Agassiz and glacial River Warren (now called the Minnesota River, which drains south, and Red River of the North, which drains north). On the west flank lie the glacial Lake Dakota and the James River, which drains south. The Coteau stands as a ridge on the edge of the Continental Divide.

As the adventurer walks to the top, he gets a feeling of why the hill is called Windy Mound. The wind becomes colder and stronger, and he mumbles about walking into a glacier. At his side, the little boy asks, "What's a glacier, Pop?" This sets the man's mind for the events to follow. When finally the summit is achieved, the father and son feel the wind as it sweeps down from the north, to be split apart by the wedge of the Coteau. They feel projected into space on the point of a piercing knife. All around, the land is below them. Off to the east and north lies the fertile valley of the Red River of the North. It blends into the farmland of Minnesota. To the north is North Dakota. They are standing at the junction of three states.

A massive cold front approaches from the north, its cold air clashing with the warm, humid air of the valley. Then condensing vapors billow forward, propelled by the wind. The fog deepens. Like the wind, it is split by the land wedge and rolls past in the valleys below. Finally, haze covers the top of the Coteau.

To the watchers, whose eyes squint and pupils dilate, the deep haze appears to be a huge wall, like a glacier. The valleys to right and left are shrouded in fog, blotting out the vestiges of civilization. The man and boy are projected back to the beginning of the Ice Age.

The ice flows forward at the rate of 100 to 200 feet a year. It crushes, grinds, smoothes, and piles everything in its path. It operates like a huge, slow-moving bulldozer, constantly hosed down by a fire hose. Much of the material in front is sorted by the running water; the rest is overrun by the glacier. As the glacier approaches the wedge point of the Coteau, it splits. One lobe moves down the Minnesota Valley toward Des Moines, the other into the James River Valley. Much material, in the form of lateral moraines, is plastered on the side of the Coteau by the valley glaciers as they move forward, building up the size of the Coteau.

In ravines and sheltered areas of the Coteau are vestiges of white spruce forests. Along the tree edge lumbers a giant wooly mammoth, its long curved ivory tusks almost as white as the frost on the bent boughs of the spruce. On the bare ground the giant bison paws at the frozen ground in search of forage. Camels, saber-toothed cats, and two species of elephants, along with the giant ground sloth and the horse, have been forced farther south. Giant beaver still work some of the streams pouring off the edge of the Coteau, and during the summer a variety of birds nest along the ponds just south of the glacier.

As the glacier proceeds southward, it thickens and covers the Coteau with a blanket of ice. For 60,000 years, the area is locked in a deep freeze. Only on the surface, where snow accumulates in the winter and partially melts in summer, is there much activity.

After centuries of moving steadily south, the glacier begins to retreat. It moves forward in winter, then retreats by melting in the summer. The net movement now, however, is north. The Coteau is the first land to appear as the thin ice sheet breaks into huge blocks. The larger blocks melt in place, forming the many Coteau ponds and lakes. The thicker ice pack in the valleys moves back more slowly and blocks the northern drainage ways. As a result of this ice dam, two large lakes form on flanks of the Coteau. The one occupying the James River Valley is called Lake Dakota, and the one on the east of the Coteau is Lake Agassiz. Remnants of these great lakes are known today as Lake Traverse and Lake Big Stone. The Continental Divide divides the two lakes. Traverse is the source of the Red River of the North and Big Stone, the Minnesota River.

The glacier retreats completely from the area, and rivers drain the glacial lakes. All that remains are large river channels, numerous terraces, and huge lake beds.

The glacier has left a vast legacy. It provided us a seed bed upon which our great agricultural enterprise can develop. It left us with lakes and streams and their associated wildlife and recreation. It shaped and renewed our landscape.

It was not until after the retreat of the glacier that man arrived. Browns Valley man dates back to 8,000 years. Along with man came the plains bison. Both trekked over a land bridge in the Bering Straits from Asia and the Old World.

On the Coteau itself, the spruce, which again invaded the area after the retreat of the glacier, gave way to deciduous trees in the ravines. The tall grass prairies invaded from the south at about the same time. The great megafaunal assemblage of elephants and associates disappeared. Recent evidence suggests overkill by the newly arrived Indian. However, a change in climate and competition from the population explosion of the newly arrived bison are possible other factors. The establishment of new food chains also entered the picture. Today skeletons of the camel, giant beaver, American horse, sloth, elephant, and other extinct mammals remind one of the pristine wilderness that must have greeted the first human being to set foot on our continent an estimated 12,000 years ago.

As the climate became drier, only a few relict areas of deciduous trees remained on the northeast facing slopes of the Coteau. Sica Hollow is a good example. The woodland Indian populated the area, and the rest is history.

The sun pierces the fog with a beam of light, and the father again reflects with the boy. Yes, my son, the glacier will be back. When is hard to predict, but it will be back to carry in a new supply of rocks, create new ponds and lakes, and remake and renew the streams and rivers. The entire surface of the land will be changed. It is a renewing cycle, as the Nile renews the land for Egyptians. Only it is a 100,000 year cycle, not an annual one. It creates lakes, so that they can start to fill up again. It creates farmland, so that man can destroy it again. The glacial cycle has repeated itself at least eight times in the last million years. Indications are that it is on its way again.

Yes, my son, man is a guardian of the land, not its owner. He is in charge for a fleeting geological moment, then must give up the land to a greater force. So learn to live with the force, and let your life be a creative understanding rather than a struggle in futility.

The land belongs to the future . . . .
That's the way it seems to me . . .
We come and go, but the land is always there.
And the people who love it and understand it
are the people who own it — for a little while.

—Willa Cather

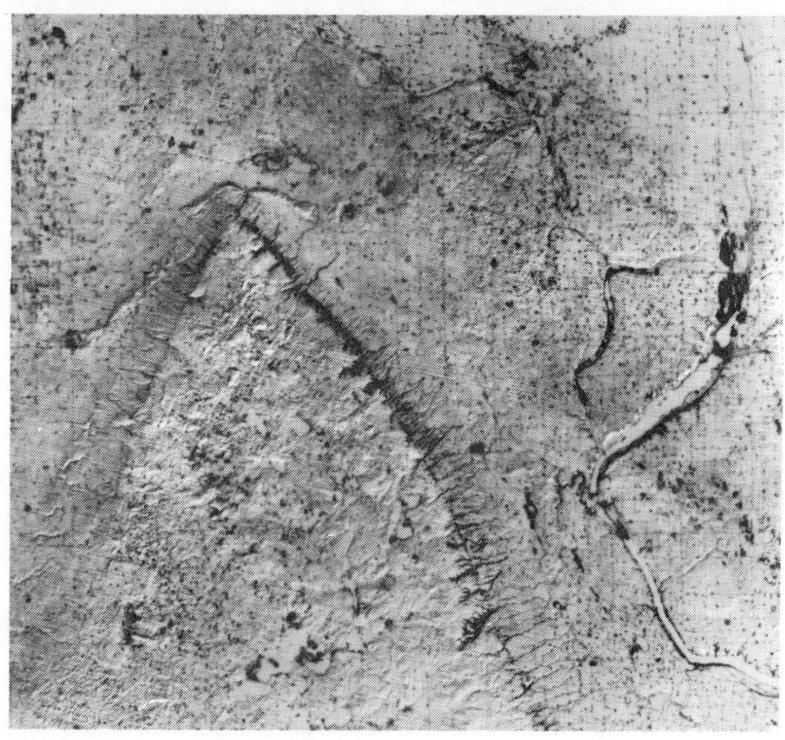

At the tip of the Coteau des Prairie juts the peak of Windy Mound. From it one can view the Red River Valley on the north, the Minnesota River Valley on the south, and the James River Valley on the west. To the right is the channel of the glacial River Warren. The lower part is Big Stone Lake and the Minnesota River. The upper, broad channel, is Lake Traverse, Club House Slough, and the Red River of the North. The Continental Divide is the point where the two lakes meet. The snakelike channel to the left of Traverse is a meander scar called Dry Run. Dry Run, Club House Slough, the glacial River Warren channel, and Sica Hollow on the coteau are National Natural Landmarks.

Photo — SDSU, Remote Sensing

Minnehaha County

Area, 815 square miles
Population, 1925 - 47,493; 1945 - 57,932; 1980 - 109,435
County Seat, Sioux Falls. Population 81,182

From the waterfall he named her Minnehaha, Laughing Water
—Longfellow

There on the Plains it flowed cutting through an endless grassland as a twisting ribbon of life, the Thick-Wooded River (Tchan-kasn-data) with its beautiful falls. So beautiful, enchanting, and compelling was the river that it attracted to its banks the Indians from all tribes on their way to the great red Pipestone Quarry. They camped on the wooded Seney Island by the Falls to bathe in the sacred pool that came from a spring in a hill facing east. They drank of crystal clear waters. They called it Minne Waukon, Sacred Water, and worshipped the Great Spirit of the land.

So powerful was the attraction of the Falls of the Big Sioux River that Joseph Nicollet wrote about it during his travels with John C. Fremont in 1836. His report, in the hands of an enterprising man from Iowa, Dr. George Staples, stimulated a different picture of the Falls. He saw in his mind an arena for commerce and planted the seed of a city in 1857, the Western Town Company.

From then on in rapid succession the area around the Falls grew: Fort Sod (1858), Fort Dakota (1865). These secured the area from the threat of the Indian by force and by treaty (1858). This early growth signaled the mighty transformation that was soon to take place.

There on the hill facing east, where the copious sacred water flowed, a bottling business turned the crystal clear water into colored flavors to quench the thirst of the white man. On the banks of the Falls there arose a power company, a flour mill, and the Dubuque House (1857), the first hotel. These stretched across the prairie skyline and punctuated the horizon as the symbol of a new world of progress.

MINNEHAHA COUNTY

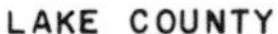

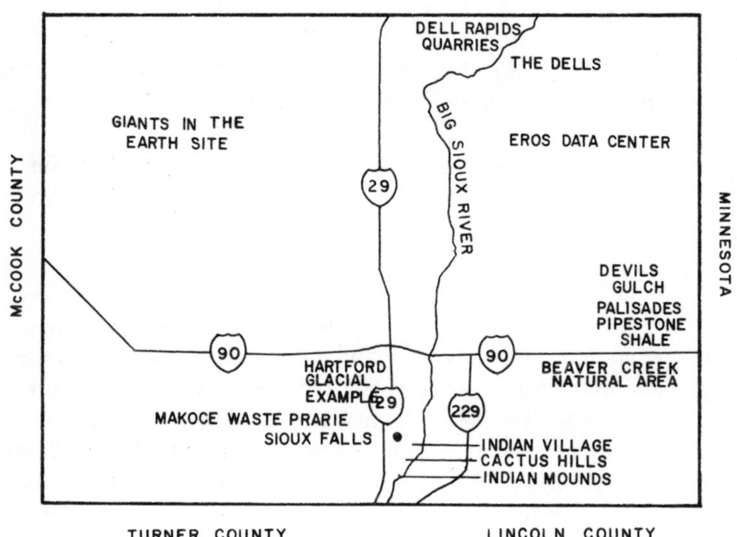

Later came the railroad tracks, stockyards, packing plant, biscuit company, and a host of other businesses. They sprang up as if the Falls and its waters were the source of a magic growth hormone. Their arrival spelled the end of enchantment for the Falls, the demise of Seney Island, turning the Historical Society, which tried to save the Falls, into arcadian dreamers. They spawned the nucleus that was to eventually become a city of over 80,000 souls.

Other attractions in Minnehaha are the Dells, the Palisades (a state park), Eros Data Center, Pettigrew Museum, Great Plains Zoo, Old City Hall Museum, Beaver Creek Nature Center, Cactus Hills, and numerous signs of old Indian villages.

It is a county that has 16 per cent of the population on about one per cent of the state's land, or a density of 133 people per square mile. It is the only county in the state that exceeds 100,000 in population.

Weekend People Pastures

Minnehaha County

Minnehaha County is our most populated county. Its 815 square miles would have some 150 people per square mile, if they were spread uniformly throughout the county. Contrast this with Harding County in northwestern South Dakota, where the population is 0.7 people per square mile, or rural Day County, where the population is rapidly declining.

On a weekend, the people of Sioux Falls buzz out from the city like bees to the honey field. Their goal — an outdoor experience. They depart in motorized metal shields of respectability for a weekend of roughing it, dragging their affluence behind them. Arriving at their lakeside destination (wilderness) with bus, boat, and bike, drivers relax with a beer, housepersons prepare lunch, and TV and terror reign among the youngsters.

They are seeking those aesthetic values of solitude, beauty, and diversity that they have spent a lifetime destroying. There is still embedded in their genes, however, the need for a wilderness experience, for a pristine wilderness where man and molecules may communicate in an endless process of creation. In this wilderness they are no longer glutted with economic constipation, and their vision is not clouded with pollution. Their minds are not troubled with dwindling resources, and social unrest does not threaten their lives. They no longer feel society slipping and collapsing into a chaotic cesspool. Their ancestral genes of greed and aggression, masked by the sheen of affluence, are subdued while they contemplate the rights and values of other things and other beings.

They come away from their experience in the wilderness recreated and refreshed, again ready to diminish the quality of life on the economic battlefield.

In coming and going they have, with no thought of its past or its present, passed through part of a wilderness that was once a tall grass prairie. They do not account for the time needed to form the endless waving grass and herbs that drift in playful resonance with the wind. They do not recognize individuality in the myriad forms and types of plants, animals, and insects living together in harmonious balance with their environment. They do not see the constant changes, as nature plays a game of fashion with a multicolored display to fit the seasons. The prairie doesn't awaken in them a feeling like the majesty of the mountains, the awesomeness of the oceans, the solitude of the forests, or the foreboding of the desert. It arouses no feeling, except in a few devoted souls who utter emotional proclamations into a sea of apathy. To most people, the prairie is shades of green turning to brown, covered in winter with a blanket of snow. It is a conglomerate of plants with vague names and even vaguer uses. To others it is a waste of space and land and calls for an economic solution. They regard the broad plains as "empty" land, in which the artful efforts of man are played out in crops of green and gold. The economic satisfaction thus gained sparks the objective that all native prairie must be subdued. What was once the tall grass prairie is the breadbasket of the world.

This western philosophy, that all things are created for man's use, is coupled with the technology that allows man to carry out this philosophy. Minnehaha County has become one big people pasture. There is little room for anything else. Now is the time for the people of Minnehaha to recognize that if there are to be natural areas and wildlife, the people must provide for them. They must develop a moral and ethical philosophy that in turn develops "rights" and laws that give protection to unique natural systems that have taken millions of years to build. To do otherwise is to be swallowed by the anthropocentric attitude that man is the only thing that matters on this planet.

Minnehaha still has a few small areas that reflect the biological heritage of the county, but some 100,000 people will need big pastures if their aesthetic spirit is to be nourished.

One big area or trail that the people of Minnehaha County could develop is the Sioux Quartzite Formation. A visit to the various outcrops that occur in the region would be a lesson in geology, biology, and history as well as a pleasant, scenic drive.

The Sioux Quartzite is a billion-year-old PreCambrian formation that lies just beneath the glacial till. Other geological formations either were never present or eroded away. The quartzite, a metamorphic sandstone, has been turned a pinkish color by highly oxidized iron. It is very hard and extends to depths of over a hundred feet in some areas. It is quarried and shipped to many parts of the country, where it is used extensively for construction. At certain places layers of clay in the quartzite have metamorphized to form catlinite (pipestone), which is scattered throughout the formation. Underneath the quartzite is the PreCambrian granite, like that exposed at Milbank.

A typical trip through quartzite land will eventually bring one to the Falls on the Sioux River (Sioux Falls), where pioneers founded one of the first settlements in Dakota. The Falls is also the site of Fort Sod and Fort Dakota, which were built for protection from the Indians. The beautiful Falls are now completely surrounded by the city of Sioux Falls, which maintains a small park at the riverside.

Continuing north on the trip, one arrives at Dell Rapids. This town also takes its name from a quartzite outcrop on the Sioux River. A series of dells in a deep gorge occurs just southwest of the city. Along the steep, dry cliffs, three species of cactus are found — an unusual occurrence. A lush growth of trees fills the gorge, and people look down to enjoy the warblers in the treetops during spring migration.

The city of Dell Rapids shows the influences of the massive pink rock. Almost all public buildings and roads are built with it. Pink roads radiate out from a pink city, to the delight of tourists. At the east edge of town is a massive quarry where great pink piles of crushed rock wait to be loaded on trucks and trains.

Athletic teams at Dell Rapids High School are known as the Quarriers, but the quartzite influence stops there. No one dares call the football team "the pink crush" or the basketball team "the pink machine." Nor is heard the cheer "Go, Big Pink." It should be pointed out to male students, however, that many a formidable foe has been conquered by the delicate mystique of desirable pinkness.

Split Rock Creek cuts through eastern Minnehaha and exposes several other outcrops of quartzite. The most notable of these is the Palisades State Park. Details about its history and use can be obtained from the Park Ranger.

Just a few miles north of the Palisades is the town of Garretson, site of a scenic spot known as Devil's Gulch. Outlaw Jesse James is said to have hidden in this area.

Just over the border in Minnesota is Blue Mounds State Park, where the quartzite has turned blue because of lichens growing upon it. There buffalo, grama grasses, native prairie, and a possible Indian calendar blend into an interesting story. Built into one of the park's quartzite cliffs is a visitors center, which among other services offers highlights in the life of Fredrick Manfred, prairie novelist.

The Pipestone National Monument is a must-see on the Sioux Quartzite Trail. Abundant information is available at the visitors center. It should, however, be noted that pipestone (catlinite) is found occasionally in layers in many places in the Sioux Quartzite, notably the quarry at Dell Rapids and scattered sites at the Palisades. Several sites are also near Jasper, Minnesota.

Jasper and Jeffers are pink cities in Minnesota. Near Jeffers is a site where the Indians carved numerous petroglyphs. Etched into the rock, along with glacial serrations and fossil ripple marks of an ancient sea, are hundreds of ceremonial figures. This quartzite outcrop is maintained as a state historical site and is a unique place to visit.

Gitchie Manitou is an outcrop of Sioux Quartzite just over the border in northwest Iowa. A picnic area and a beautiful patch of native prairie make it a prime spot to visit.

By connecting all these sites, the massiveness of the Sioux Quartzite formation becomes apparent. It extends from the James River, near Mitchell, well into Minnesota — over 150 miles. It is an education, an inspiration, and a scenic delight to study the history of this formation. It is a people pasture for the multitudes of Minnehaha County and the adventurous who want a unique outdoor experience. There is no other place like it in the world.

Jim Wilson used the term "People Pastures" and in remembrance we thank him for his enthusiasm for our natural heritage.

A couple of "people pastures" near Sioux Falls during the holidays display the newest in motorized comfort (the count in Newton Hills State Park on Labor Day 1979 was 7,800).
Photos — D.J. Holden (top), Jeanne Kilen (bottom)

Perkins County

Area, 2,914 square miles
Population, 1925 - 7,055; 1945 - 5,530; 1980 - 4,700
County Seat, Bison. Population 457

Perkins County, like the other counties in the northwest part of the state, was open for settlement in 1909. Its county seat, Bison, named for the buffalo of the plains, exceeds by four people its counterpart, Buffalo, in adjacent Harding County. These twin cities, connected by grassland, Prairie City, and Reva, are 60 miles apart. But given the optimism of a neighboring town, Chance, there could be big things happening out here.

Lemmon is the largest town in the area and has a large petrified wood park. Add to this the hamlets of Usta (Indian name of Ed Lemmon, local rancher), Meadow, Strool, Bixby, Zeona, Imogene, Ada, White Butte, Ellingson, Coal Springs, and Shadehill, and you have all of the combination post office, liquor, gas, gloves, and grocery stores in the county.

The highlights of Perkins County are the fossils, petrified wood, dinosaur tracks, Cedar Canyon, Moreau River badlands, and Shadehill Reservoir with its buffalo jump. Near the latter is the Hugh Glass Monument. It relates the tale of his fight with a grizzly bear and his long crawl to Fort Kiowa, the story told by Fredrick Manfred in his book, Lord Grizzly.

Perkins County is big, the second largest in the state, and together with Meade, Harding, and Butte constitutes about one eighth the area of the state. Most of this area is thinly populated and sometimes you can go for miles without meeting anyone, but when you do it's an occasion to remember.

Living by the Sea

Perkins County

People of Perkins County don't really live by the seashore. They live on the sediment of what was once the edges of a giant inland sea that covered the interior lowland of the nation. The sea, when it existed, formed a layer of thick sediment covering most of the

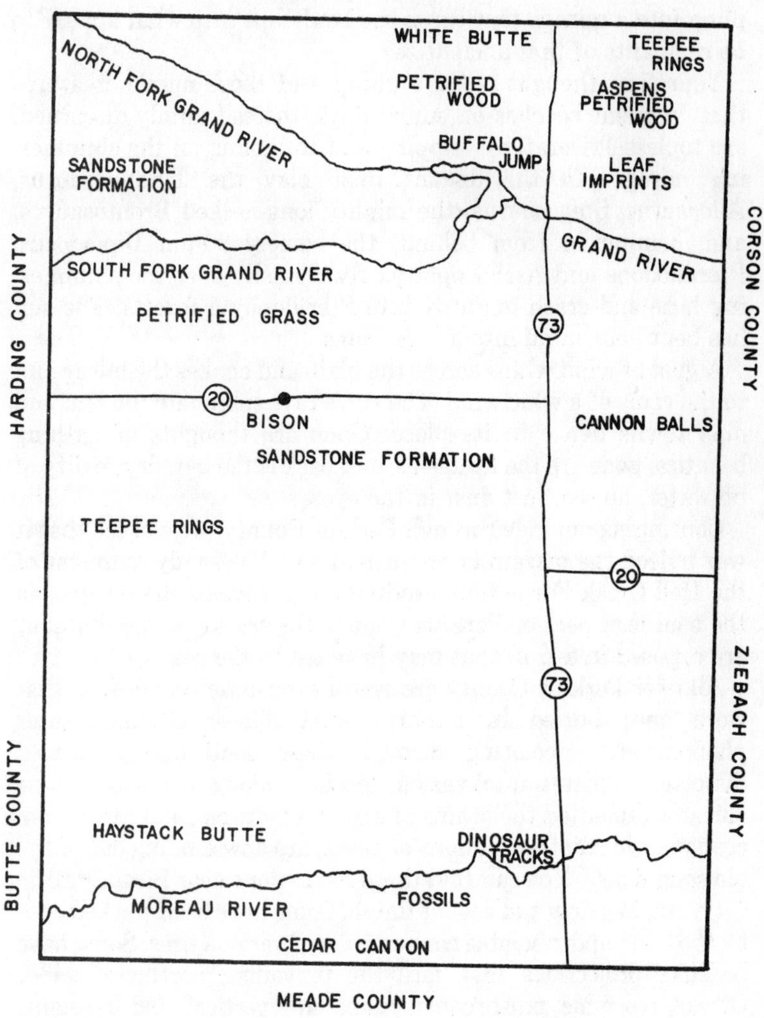
PERKINS COUNTY
NORTH DAKOTA
WHITE BUTTE
TEEPEE RINGS
NORTH FORK GRAND RIVER
PETRIFIED WOOD
ASPENS
PETRIFIED WOOD
BUFFALO JUMP
SANDSTONE FORMATION
LEAF IMPRINTS
GRAND RIVER
SOUTH FORK GRAND RIVER
PETRIFIED GRASS
73
HARDING COUNTY
CORSON COUNTY
20
BISON
CANNON BALLS
SANDSTONE FORMATION
TEEPEE RINGS
20
73
ZIEBACH COUNTY
BUTTE COUNTY
HAYSTACK BUTTE
DINOSAUR TRACKS
MOREAU RIVER
FOSSILS
CEDAR CANYON
MEADE COUNTY

state. The sediment is now known as the Pierre Shales. As the sea retreated, some 100 million years ago, it left sand dunes and sediment, called the Fox Hills and Hell Creek Formation, covering part of Perkins County.

So today, as you take off at a gallop across the plains of Perkins, you are frequently greeted with signs of what was once the shore of this sea. Stopping to rest and daydream on a sunny day, you can see heat waves radiating up from the hot soil surface and rippling into a mirage that turns the landscape into what appear to be remnants of that ancient sea.

Your first thought is for a glimpse of those nubile creatures that frequent beaches on sunny days. Instead, dimly discerned, are topless Triceratops, tripping and trembling on the shimmering mirage. In the distant mist play the Tyrannosaurus, Allosaurus, Stegosaurus, the mighty long-necked Brontosaurus, and, coming in from behind, the comely 30-ton Diplodocus. Pteranodons and Archaeopteryx fly clumsily over the shimmering haze and crash mightily into Pteridophyte forests. The sun has bent your mind into a time warp.

A gust of wind whips across the plain and chokes the mirage into the arms of a whirlwind. The sun's rays sublimate the sea, and dust devils dance in its place. Gone are thoughts of bathing beauties, gone are the fantasies, and back is the hot, dry reality of no water, no sea, just dust in the eyes.

Continuing our ride through Perkins County, we can see that it was indeed the margin of an ancient sea. The sandy sediment of the Hell Creek Formation, eroding away, reveals these signs. In the southern part of Perkins County the tracks of the dinosaur are exposed in a trail that may have led to the sea.

All over Perkins County are weird sandstone concretions that were once buried in massive sand dunes. Ground water phenomena, percolating through these sand dunes, carried dissolved silicates into various pockets along the way. These silicates cemented the grains of sand into strange and exotic concretions which, after millions of years, are now eroding out of the old sand dunes. You can find these formations near Bison, Prairie City, and Meadow and east of Ralph. Some have been worked over by the wind and resemble cannon balls of various sizes. Some have beaklike projections that face the prevailing northwest wind. Others resemble mushrooms. Some are vertical and resemble petrified lightning. Some, from a distance, resemble Grecian statues, with the horizontal ones lying back in repose. In some places where the sandstone is layered and can be split, beautiful leaf imprints can be found. When you find these, you know you are looking at the age when flowering plants came into existence — an age, some 80 million years ago, when the dinosaurs were disappearing, to be replaced by mammals.

These same percolating ground waters, carrying silica, have petrified organic matter buried in the sand. Trees and bones were replaced, atom by atom, until all the carbon atoms were exchanged for silica atoms. These petrified logs are found in most parts of Perkins County. In what was once a swamp, one finds layers of petrified ferns and grasslike plants. The Indians built teepee rings from the petrified slabs, and the pioneers built claim shanties.

In some areas a large sheet-like layer of a brown flinty material has formed, covering several acres to a depth of two to three feet. This layer is the remains of a large subsurface flow through the sandstone. In many places ancient forces broke it up, and people piled it along fence lines and roads. If you examine it closely, you will find it full of holes. Ranchers will use these rocks with holes to hold down fences that cross ravines. And they will curse its hardness when it breaks their machinery. It is this rock that contains the petrified wood. The holes mark where the wood has fallen out. Examine these rocks also for cavities which are sometimes filled with beautiful hexagonal quartz crystals . . . and sometimes with rattlesnakes.

One place where you can experience much of this geological grandeur is on the banks of the Moreau River. The lower strata of an eroded bank may reveal marine fossils; a bit higher one may find bivalves, which indicate shallow brackish water. Above the clam shells, petrified logs are found which have burn scars. These indicate that the brackish water pond filled up, a forest covered it, and later it was burned by fire. High on the bank and on the surface are the scattered bones of dinosaurs that once called this place home. Chalcedony is found washing out of the bank.

The atmosphere of the sea persists in Perkins County. The bank is a complete chronological lesson in geology and paleoenvironments. It is an outdoor classroom which should be left intact for future generations to study the history of the past. People of Perkins County must learn to preserve and protect this natural heritage.

Fossil dinosaur track left in sands of the retreating sea.
Photo — D.J. Holden

Cannonball concretions that were once part of the sand dunes left by the retreating Cretaceous Sea in Perkins County.
Photo — Tim Jackson

Petrified wood from trees that fell in a stagnant pool left by the retreating inland sea. Found in the area are lignite coal seams, petrified grass, and petrified lignite called Knife River Flint.
Photo — Tim Jackson

ENERGY

Energy

People, like molecules, bounce around at the expense of energy. Only people are usually going some place. They are going some place to use energy, buy energy, store energy, or make money to later spend on energy. Energy, a word that exploded into our everyday language when the gas stations closed, is now receiving new attention. It is important. I used up a bit putting this section together.

> Fortunately for us plants are very adaptable and exist in great diversity . . . they could thus continue indefinitely to supply us with renewable quantities of food, fiber, fuel, and chemicals.
>
> —D.C. Hall

> Up to this point in man's history, photosynthesis is the only source of food on earth and its capacity may ultimately determine the number of people who can live on this planet without starvation.
>
> —C.T. de Wit, Harvesting The Sun

> All life — human, animal, and plant — is ultimately dependent for its food-energy upon the photosynthetic process by which chlorophyll converts the sun's energy into food-energy usable by plants and by humans and other animals. Why do we not regard this as the most fantastic accomplishment ever, for all life in all its forms is derived from this?
>
> —Elizabeth Dodson Grey, Why the Green Nigger

Clay County

Area, 403 square miles
Population, 1925 - 10,569; 1945 - 9,382; 1980 - 13,135
County Seat, Vermillion. Population 9,582

Clay County, although small in size — the smallest in the state, is big in history. In its early days it was occupied by the Sioux, who gave the Vermillion River its name based upon the yellow limonite ore that turned vermilion upon heating.

In 1804 Lewis and Clark visited Spirit Mound, believed by the Indians to be inhabited by 18-inch devils with human forms. The expedition discovered artifacts and believed it to be an Indian burial ground. In 1822 Fort Vermillion was founded by a French fur trader named Francis Le Roi. He was followed into the area by John J. Audubon, the ornithologist, in 1843. In 1845 the Mormons made the area their winter camp. Settlement of the county began in 1859, and in 1861 Clay County was established.

Today Clay County is noted for the University of South Dakota, founded in 1862, and its prosperous farms. But not always did it have prosperous times. In 1873 a grasshopper scourge visited the area, lasting for six years. In 1881 the Missouri River flooded and destroyed Vermillion. The town relocated on higher ground, and today is still growing.

In the new University the first classes were held in 1883, and it established the W.H. Over Museum in 1913. The Geological Survey became part of the University in 1926, and today the University is the center of cultural activities for the entire area and the state.

About 70 per cent of the county's population is located in the city of Vermillion, 14 per cent live in 10 small villages, and 16 per cent are rural.

Understanding the Green Machine

Clay County

Clay County is the smallest county in South Dakota, with 403 square miles. It is the home of the University of South Dakota, the oldest university in the state. Over half of the population of

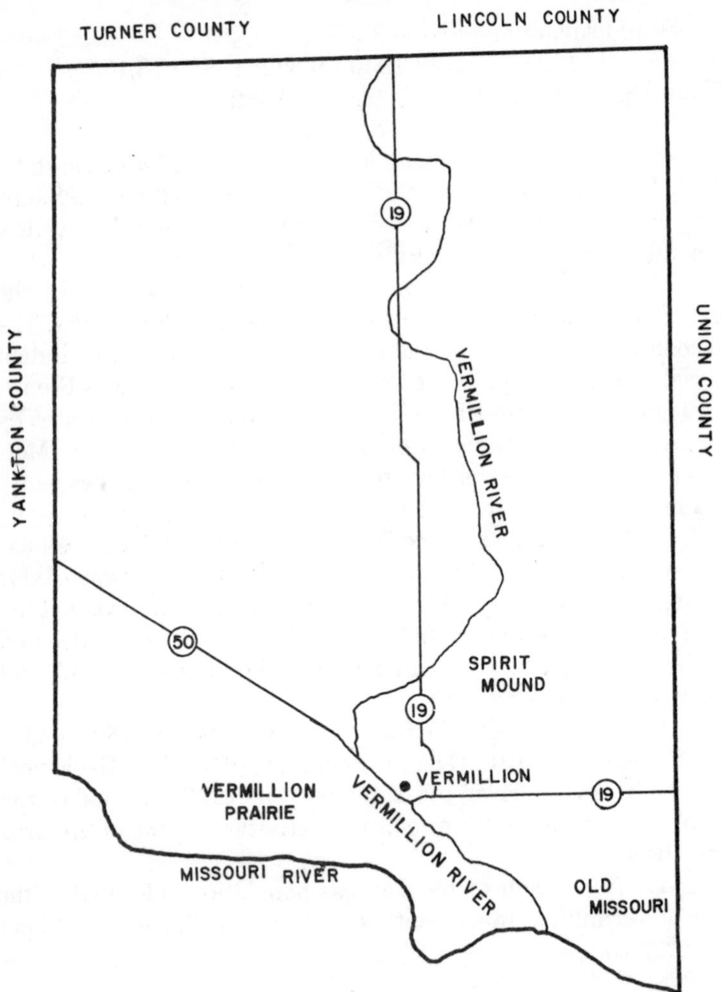

Clay County are students, staff, and people associated with the University. The county, therefore, is a center of intellectual activity. It is a place where one should learn to appreciate what goes on in the other counties of the state. It is a place where man is taught those humanistic values that enable him to understand and fulfill his life in a manner meaningful but not destructive to his environment.

Education teaches us about the aesthetic values of life as well as the necessity for surviving on a level that will enable us to enjoy these aesthetic values.

Today one of man's chief concerns is simply the energy supply needed to exist and still remain creative. It is not a simple problem. Our public educational institutions are the places where ideas are incubated, plans are hatched, and methods are tested and distributed to the people. They are where age-old problems associated with plants are studied. Plants, after all, are at least one-half of our living system.

In the study of plants and survival, some simple truths are hard to understand, ignored, or just plain forgotten. One is that man is, was, and probably forever shall be dependent on plants for his existence. As with all animals, man is parasitic on plants. He gains some momentary advantage by being able to use condensed, canned, or stored plant products, such as fossil fuels. But when the canned material is used up, he is back to direct dependency on the living plant.

There is no better system, and probably never will be, able to fix solar energy into a more usable form. The plant is the ultimate solar energy machine. We have been deceiving ourselves for years into believing that man can produce an abundant supply of cheap energy from innovative mechanical and chemical devices, including fission and fusion. To do so on a long-term practical basis would be a miracle.

To base our hopes on such a miracle is wishful thinking. We must continue to live within the confines of recycled and renewable biological resources. Our plant resources and diversity should not be continually destroyed, neglected or under utilized. We should not take for granted that plants constitute over one-half of the living systems in the world. We have assumed our supply of energy is inexhaustible. We are mistaken.

As man evolved over the past 2 million years, he knew how, where, and when to get the energy he needed to subsist. If he failed, he starved. It was not an easy way of life.

We have depended on industry, business, and government to supply us with all the energy we need, and we take for granted that they will continue to supply us. We are usually not aware, nor do we care, where the energy comes from. This is especially true of city dwellers, angered by even such small failures as lights going out for short periods.

Equally reprehensible is that large suppliers of energy appear not to be concerned with the laws of diminishing returns, going to greater and greater effort for less and less energy. The days of Jed Clampett's shooting holes in the ground for the bubbling crude are over. Only after spending much money and absorbing frequent abuse and disruption of the environment are new supplies of energy realized. This bull elephant-like behavior generates distrust in all citizens with closets full of china to protect. Contrast this social distrust with that of citizens living during earlier changes in energy supply. People welcomed with great anticipation the change from wood to coal, from coal to petroleum, and from petroleum to electricity. Why? Because the disruption was not widespread.

Our problems are becoming more numerous, our solutions fewer. An alternative is to look at a new approach — to couple our economy and energy supply to more stable renewable or cyclic resources. We need to tie ourselves (in reality we have always been tied) to a sun-plant-animal (man) cycle. We need tree farms for heating fuel, energy plants for motor fuels and rubber, and of course plenty of plants for food and shelter.

This then brings us to photosynthesis, the system that now furnishes us with approximately 80 percent of our usable energy. It is the world's biggest and most important biophysiochemical reaction. Six times more energy is produced by this system in a year than the total amount of energy, worldwide, used by man in the same period.

Why is photosynthesis important? If we understand the process, we can see why we are dependent on it and cannot replace it. Imagine, if you will, the fusion of two hydrogen atoms in the sun. This fusion is the source of the sun's energy, and it is what man is trying to bring about by the fusion reactor on earth. As hydrogen atoms fuse, particles of light (photons) are given off. They travel 93 million miles, at 186,300 miles per second, and arrive on earth in 8.3 minutes. If one could stand in the dark and watch only one photon, one would see a tiny flash of light go by and enter the leaf of a favorite plant. As the photon enters the leaf, its energy is collected by molecular antennae. Only the blue and red energy photons are used, with the rest radiated back into the air. The radiated light is mostly green, and that is why our plants look green. The light energy that is collected in the leaf accumulates in its energy-trapping antennae (chlorophyll) and is transferred into an electron that comes from water (H_2O). The electron is itself a condensed body of energy, and the energy photon from the sun fuses with it and gives it more energy. It is like a sugar molecule being absorbed by a jelly bean to give it more energy. This energized, excited electron is then forced, by the continual pressure of other sun-energized electrons produced behind it, through a chain of carriers. It flows through this chain like an electric current and furnishes electrons to an electron acceptor. This acceptor is carbon dioxide, which has been pulled in by the leaf. Each molecule accepts four electrons, and when 24 electrons have charged six carbon dioxide molecules, they are hooked together to form a molecule of glucose (sugar) via a series of chemical reactions. One hundred eighty grams of glucose have 689,000 energy calories of sun-activated electrons — enough to fill a cup and start a cake.

To summarize, the sun sends energy in packets, the leaf is attuned to catch them, and it converts the energy into sugar. This sugar can be stored as starch. But most important is the basic reaction. From it comes almost all of the world's energy, almost all of the organic material (plant and animal), and all of the fossil fuels of the world.

Is it not indeed a miracle to know that a nuclear fusion reaction on the sun provides the energy packets that form the energy bonds that hold us all together? Is it not indeed a miracle that our plants are able to absorb this energy from an atomic nuclear reaction on the sun and convert it to useful compounds and energy? Is it not indeed a miracle that these same plants, from these first simple compounds, form all of the other biological compounds necessary for life? Is it not indeed a miracle that the same building blocks that make up plants are, by simple transformation, put together again to form the animals, including man, of the world? Finally, when that supply of excited electrons being formed continually by the sun is no longer produced, all life falls back to the simple form of carbon dioxide (CO_2), water (H_2O), and nitrogen (N_2).

It is sheer arrogance to assume that man can design a better source or method of supplying the world with energy. The sun-activated system is a balanced, time-tested system. It does not pollute. It is not subject to sabotage. It does not produce life-destroying radioactive by-products; there is no problem with using materials to make illegal bombs. Obtaining raw material and storing the waste product are no problems.

Lewis Strauss, Atomic Energy Commissioner during the Eisenhower administration, said of the future of atomic energy: "We will soon be entering an era in which energy will be produced so cheaply that it will not pay to meter it." It is ironical to note that we have always had a free supply of energy, and Mr. Strauss did not realize that the best things in life are free. It is only after man handles energy a few dozen times that things become expensive.

We are being driven by force from the sun. Our educational institutions, including those in Clay County, should make it abundantly clear to our youth where their energy is coming from.

Like Walt Whitman, I "believe the leaf of grass is no less than the journey work of the stars." Or, as Longfellow put it, "Dust thou art, to dust returnest,/Was not spoken of the soul." All is held together for a fleeting geological moment by that ephemeral glue from the sun, energy.

Codington County

Area, 701 square miles
Population, 1925 - 17,760; 1945 - 16,750; 1980 - 20,885
County Seat, Watertown. Population 15,649

Codington County is in the north central part of the Coteau des Prairie. The county is divided just east of its center by the Big Sioux River, which begins north of Watertown. The county is relatively flat with an elevation of 1,700 to 2,000 feet above sea level. The main geological feature is the glacial drift which covers the county at a depth of 500 feet.

The lakes of the area are Medicine, Long, Grass, Nicholson, Pelican, Goose, Kampeska, and Punished Women. The latter is the site of an old Indian Church and an Indian legend. It seems that an old Indian chief desired a beautiful young Indian maiden, but she spurned him for her young lover. The chief killed the young man and tortured the girl to death. As the chief was preaching over the bodies of the two lovers, he was killed by a bolt of lightning.

Lake Kampeska has an equally interesting legend about a beautiful Indian maiden and her lover. This lake, called the Lake of the Shining Shells by the Indians, has a rock pile near Stony Point called "Maiden Isle," built there, according to the legend, by braves who threw rocks into the water to win the favor of the

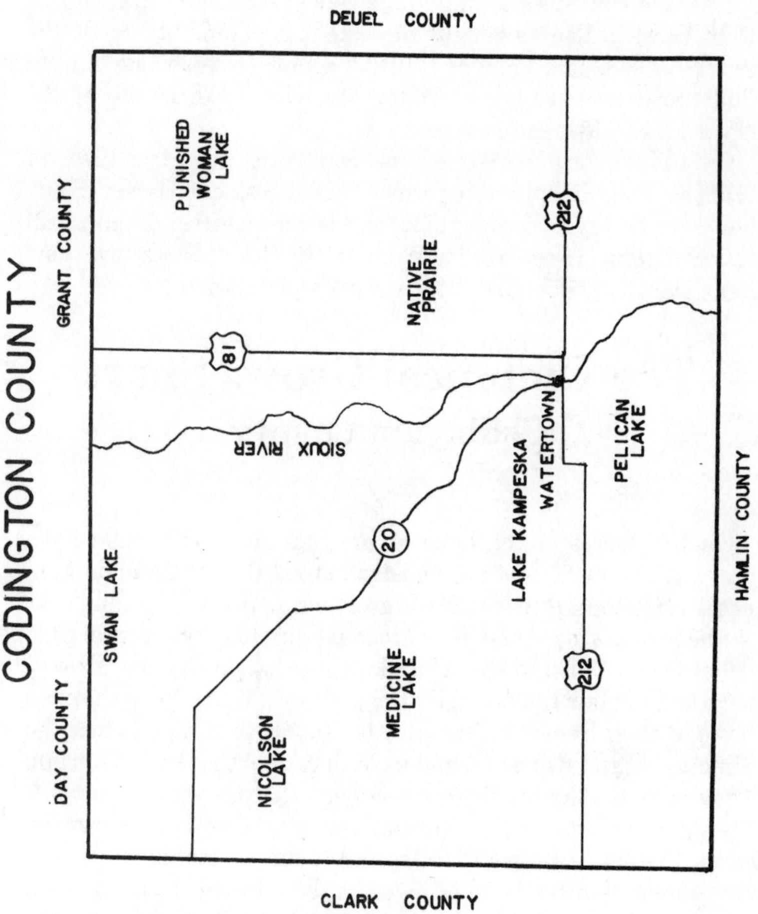

princess. Finally, angered by her coquettishness, they put her on the rock pile and threatened her with starvation. A pelican fed her fish until her lover returned to rescue her.

Other legends tell other stories about the rock pile: that it was the place where the Wauken Tanka stood when he counselled the tribe or that it was a place where Indians came to pray for peace.

Another interesting lake a few miles west of Kampeska is Medicine Lake. Noted for its salt content and medicinal properties, it had been an Indian source of purifying waters.

The lake having no outlet or inlet is fed by an underground

spring and continues to build up a concentration of minerals. In 1914 Howard Reeves bought the lake and planned to bottle the water for sale as a tonic or curative agent. However, he did not find too many customers. Today Medicine Lake is one of the newest State Recreation Areas.

On the western border of the county is the little town of Wallace, the birthplace of former Vice President Hubert Humphrey. It, however, because of its size never qualified for an urban renewal grant. In contrast to Wallace, the city of Watertown contains over three-fourths of the county's population.

The Umbilical Grows Short

Codington County

On the shores of the Lake of the Shining Shells walked the brave Wawenneta, and on the island stood the Indian maid Minnequa. He stopped to watch the great white pelican, circling over the head of his loved one. He watched it dip its wings, as if in final tribute, as it faded to a dim speck in the distant sky. To Wawenneta and his fair Indian maid, the pelican was the force that had brought their lives together. Slowly, they both turned to face the direction of the rising sun and gave thanks to the Great Waukan. They gave thanks for the nourishment that the earth provided. They gave thanks for their strong, healthy bodies, and with a look to the distant sky, they gave thanks to the glistening white bird that symbolized the bond of love that had drawn them together.

In the villages surrounding the Lake of the Shining Shells, the Indians lived in direct contact with the land. They were nourished by the abundance of its products. In many ways their mode of living contrasted with that of the present day.

Today we are still nourished, in one way or another, from the food, fiber, and fuel provided by the earth. But the distance these materials must travel and the number of times they are handled complicate our mode of living. The life line of nourishment, the umbilical cord of our existence, can be as long and complex as the energy we receive from Saudi Arabia or as simple and close as the nourishment we receive from our own garden.

In the land of the Lake of the Shining Shells, now known as Lake Kampeska, things are changing also. Families have found that the law of reciprocal supply and demand has oscillated to such an extent that pocketbooks are flat. People are looking for something more controllable. One answer is to shorten the life line, the umbilical cord that provides their nourishment.

One family has shortened the supply line in a unique manner.

> Our house is warmed by a wood burning stove this winter, and our bodies are warmed by the effort to supply it with wood. Our spirits are buoyed by having the strength and health to be able to get the wood.
>
> We have chosen this method to keep warm, rather than to have our supply of fuel shipped in from Saudi Arabia. We figured that it was cheaper for us to exert a bit of energy and burn up the elm wood available from the death of our trees from Dutch Elm disease than it was to have oil pumped out of ground, loaded and shipped 6,000 miles across the ocean; unloaded, refined, cracked, distilled, loaded and shipped overland 2,000 miles to Watertown; and unloaded, stored, loaded and delivered to our tank. So far we are warm, the Saudies are not mad, the local oil company has not figured out what happened and the family argues over who is to fill the wood box. It is almost like having an oil well in the back yard, when we can make all this free energy available.

The farm family is also manufacturing its own power sources and fueling them with energy from the hillsides. These self-reproducing machines come equipped with automatic refueling and a lifetime lubrication guarantee. Yes, on at least one farm located on the banks of the Sioux River, the cord has been shortened. The farm has become a self-sustaining unit by using horsepower. This, coupled with the other food producing capacities of the farm, makes it a unit that depends little on the outside world.

This was the style well into the 1930s and was responsible for the successful settling of America. In 1900, 80 per cent of the people were food producers; today 3.2 per cent produce the food. It is the marvel of modern agriculture that as food production goes up, the number of food producers goes down. This reciprocal relationship has required the weaving of a support system that is becoming entangled in its own complexities.

Farther down the river in a nearby county is an example of another family that has shortened its life support system. The visitor notices a modest looking structure that blends with its surroundings. In fact, he has to look twice to notice that it's a home, for it does not project a massive, imposing image against the sky that is the hallmark of the VIP's residence. Nor is its architectural style French, Colonial, Classical Greek, or English Traditional. It is Early American Honyocker, the dugout of the early American settler, constructed today with modern techniques and materials. It is an underground home that scarcely disrupts the environment, yet saves a good deal of energy. It takes advantage of the moderating effects of the earth — cool in summer and warm in winter, with an average temperature of 50° F below the frost level. It is landscaped with drought-tolerant and cold-resisting native species, and the lawn is a flowering panorama of native prairie. The backyard is a garden surrounded by fruit and fuel trees. Fast growing cottonwoods serve both as shade and fuel for the wood burning stove that heats the house. It is a home that recycles most of its wastes. It is a home where the umbilical cord has been shortened. The security thus generated is a paid-up insurance policy.

To be sure, such energy saving innovations are the vision of the future. They are still a long way from Walden Pond, where Thoreau spent 17 cents a day for living expenses. But they do point the way toward self sufficiency.

The idea of independence and self sufficiency has always been with us. In fact, it was a selective factor that helped man evolve to his present state of refinement. It was a sharpening stone that honed his brain into the keen-thinking organ that it is today. Its computer-like nature has allowed the brain to select the options that provide it with the best methods of survival. But somewhere along the line, after centuries of sharing, bartering, and trading, man invented money. With this new tool, it was no longer necessary to produce the commodities needed for life. Man could buy them.

Nature, however, does not select the fittest on the basis of wealth. Those are selected whose genetic capacity has allowed them to adapt and survive within the confines of their environment. Money cannot buy survival genes.

Finally, once again, around the shores where the shining shells are seen, people are beginning to realize what elements of life are really important. They are learning, as the prophet Isaiah said, that "all flesh is grass" and that their umbilical cord is really connected to the plants.

Davison County

Area, 532 square miles
Population, 1925 - 16,015; 1945 - 13,903; 1980 - 17,820
County Seat, Mitchell. Population 13,916

The first known residents of Davison County were the Arikara. There, dating back to 900 A.D., they lived along Firesteel Creek in mound-shaped mud houses until driven out by the Sioux.

In 1872 settlers came and settled in dugouts a short distance from the old Arikara village and gave the creek, Firesteel, its name. There at the junction of the creek and the James River pioneers experienced their first disappointment when the grasshoppers destroyed their crops. In 1880 the winter was long and severe and floods threatened the James River bottom.

In 1880 the railroad arrived two miles to the west, and this prompted Firesteel village to move to the newly created Mitchell.

In 1889 a prairie fire driven by a 60 mile-per-hour wind threatened the county. Mt. Vernon was almost completely destroyed.

Places to visit include the Corn Palace, the Middle Border Museum, and Big Medicine Butte — the latter a place where Indians built their ceremonial rock cairns.

The Power and the Plow

Davison County

Oops! We just slipped into an energy crisis. Something we said would never happen. But it did, for society no longer knows the basic elements of survival. The answer is there, but it's so simple and fundamental that we can't believe it's true. We keep grasping

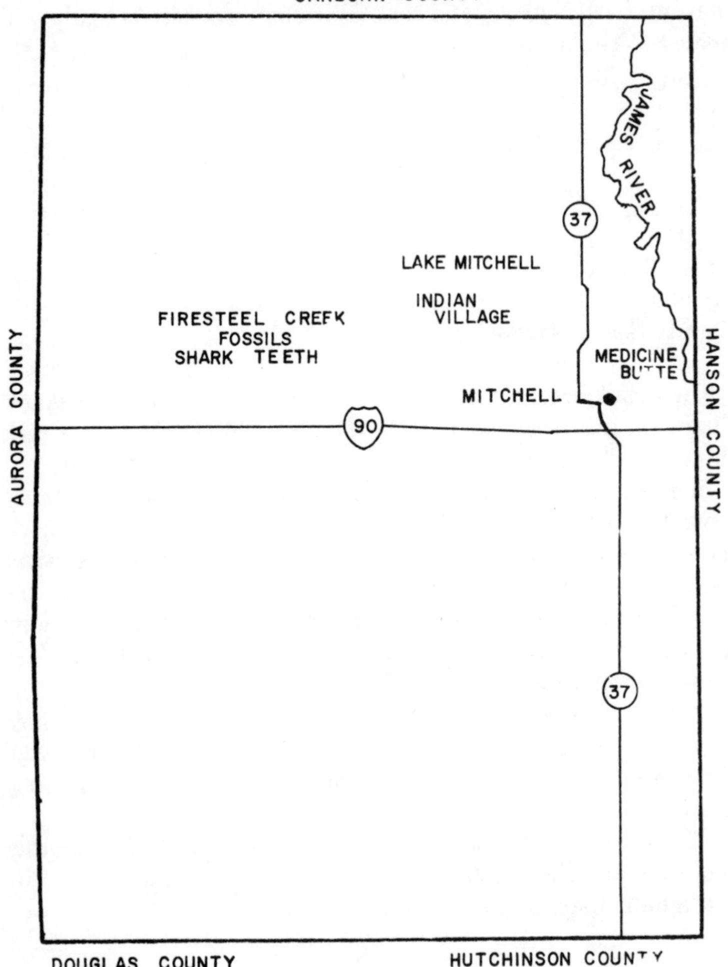

for a miracle cure, a technological solution. We walked on the moon and heard the boom of the atomic blast, but we never found the abundant source of energy that was promised. Instead, we slipped deeper and deeper into the tortuous depths of greater dependence on nonrenewable resources. It was a journey cold and dark.

Let's reflect on the dim, shadowy past and expose to the light the biological wonder called man. Man has carried for millions of years the germ of being able to transform the world. But he has never quite learned how to use that wonderful power.

We find the first sign of his existence, footprints made in the volcanic ash of Laeoti, Africa, almost 5 million years ago. Then he was a bit over four feet tall and looked with awe at the much more formidable and superior megafauna that surrounded him. In no way was he in control of nature. He was a product of it. He stood with stick and stone facing fearsome lions, tigers, and elephants and happy at the little things that came his way. Now all that remain are scattered skeletons.

Out of this 5-million-year experiment with life came several species of man before he arrived at his present refined, hairless, cloth encumbered state. All of these species were directly, or indirectly through animal foods, dependent on plants. This dependency has continued to the present, with nearly 75 per cent of the world's population, the so-called have-nots of the third and fourth worlds, still dependent on the plant.

Some 10,000 years ago agriculture and domestication refined the method of plant dependency. Starting with the digging stick and developing into primitive plows, large stable civilizations developed. Aztec, Inca, Sumerian, Egyptians, Greek, and Roman are examples of highly developed civilizations that flourished in direct connection with the plant (albeit human slaves helped them reach their zenith).

With the opening of the New World in 1492, settlers brought the seeds for more complete control of nature. They brought the idea of the iron plow, with its power to pull — first, by the cruel method of using the tail of the horse to pull the plow, and later by our present method of connecting power to the plow. This led to an abundant food supply.

It was about 1850 that settlers moved into Davison County, bringing with them the inventions of John Deere and James Oliver, chilled steel, moldboard plows. They used the newly invented plows to turn over the black prairie soil. At about this time their dependency on wood for energy changed to coal.

The chronology of events that changed the prairie are recorded in the Middle Border Museum at Mitchell. It is a story of the power of the plow — how the fertile soil of the plain became the breadbasket of the world. In Mitchell also stands the Corn Palace, symbol of agricultural greatness.

The period of coal dependency continued until after the dust bowl years, when the switch to petrochemicals was complete. For years power and the plow evolved to even greater accomplishments. The plow went from a single bottom, walk-behind breaking plow, to a riding sulky, to a stump jumper, to a 3-bottom gang plow, up to a 16-bottom tractor plow controlled by closed circuit television. Man now had a handle on nature, and nature became as useful as a fourth-string quarterback. Petrochemicals were a modern genie in the tractor tank. The farmer had at his disposal (if he was a large farmer operating three to four tractors) the equivalent of 5,000 energy slaves. Only the pharaohs in Egypt, during the building of the pyramids, could approach this in human equivalents. Man, what Power!

But by the 1940s, the great petrochemical age was overshadowed by the nuclear age. We were promised an unlimited supply of energy, so cheap we would not have to meter it.

But then it came — the energy crisis, beginning of the end of nonrenewable resources. The free energy promised by atomic energy is all but a forgotten dream, and the people in Davison County, and the rest of the world, are left with an unfulfilled promise because the energy slaves have run out.

Today, the people of Davison County can add lack of energy to their list of disasters that include drought, flood, hail, wind, rust, fire, insects, fungi, nematodes, and grasshappers.

After 5 million years of trying, 30 per cent of the human population was able, for some 40 to 80 years, to divorce themselves almost completely from the plant. Now that they have awakened from the dream, the people are slowly realizing that the affairs of our planet must be wrapped around the plant. It is entirely possible that great civilizations can, with population controls, be organized around the productivity of the plant. It is the ultimate living solar energy machine, a quality-controlled, time-tested machine, designed to provide the energy needed for making the world go around.

It is something for the people of the world, including residents of Davison County, to think about as mankind rides, flagellating his ego horse, off into the sunset.

Shades of the times when the farmer produced and cycled his own power and energy.

Photo — Brookings Register

Haakon County

Area, 1,819 square miles
Population, 1925 - 4,545; 1945 - 3,063; 1980 - 2,794
County Seat, Philip. Population 1,088

Haakon County remembers a roundup that covered 10,000 square miles. But that was before Haakon was a county. An area 100 miles long and 100 miles wide is big and it took a lot of cowboys working to get all those cattle into one bunch. The excitement, glamor, and hard work of these early roundups have left a chapter of history that stimulates the imagination of the new generation.

The abrupt end of those cowboy days came in 1907 when the settlers came west on one train and the cows were sent east on the next. But those days of the settler, too, were few because in 1911 a devastating drought hit the county and only the most hardy settler remained after a summer of blistering heat.

With the surge of settlers, the county was filled with embryonic towns that felt the pulse of life but later died with the loss of people. Today Powell, Willsburg, Hillard, Kirby, Carlin, Elbon, Lucerne, Moenville, and Cherry Creek are vacant spots where green grass grows.

Sites of interest in Haakon County include Grindstone Butte, Harding Grove — a natural woodland — and the Deadwood Trail of the goldrush days. This trail cuts across the southern edge of the county and its ruts, still visible in the prairie, are our link with the past. It leads our memories back to the days when all noses pointed west as if the smell of gold could carry to all with restless feet.

A Rip in the Mantle

Haakon County

Weak spots in the earth's mantle are places where geothermal energy may find its way to the surface, or where the energy may be tapped by deep wells. Such a place exists in Haakon County and northern Jones County. Sometimes the artesian water comes

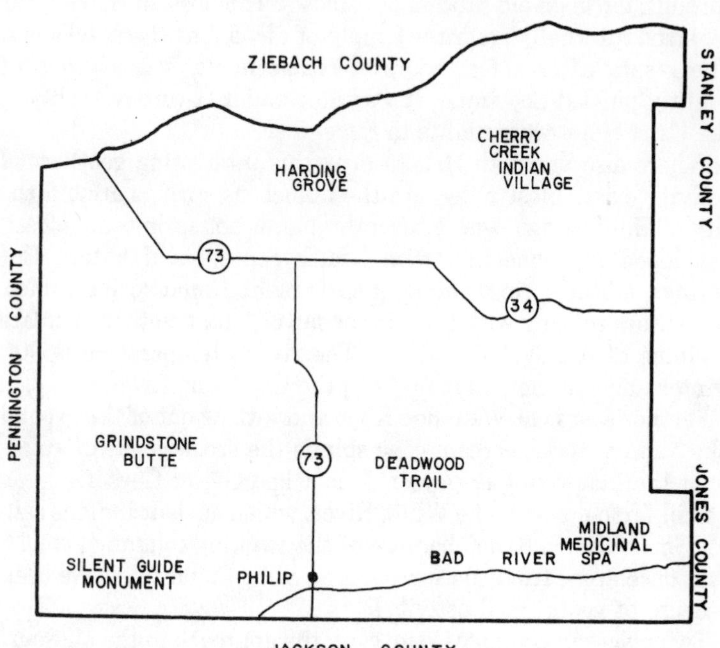

gushing to the surface with temperatures as high as 160° F, sometimes with geopressured natural gas, and always with salts. Salt concentrations of 24 grams per gallon (6 grams per liter) or greater have frequently been measured.

All the towns and people in Haakon County are beginning to think of using this geothermal energy, now that fuel prices have skyrocketed. The word "all" means Philip and Midland, the only towns surviving of the 10 or 12 that were started in the late 1880s.

Famous Capa, just over the border in Jones County, with its Capa Hotel and medicinal health spa, is but one ghost town in an ever lengthening list of forgotten places. It was in Capa that some of the old Scottish cattle barons, who were the first to settle the West, took their Saturday night baths. There they washed away the accumulation of range dust and soaked out the meanness, some would say, that accumulated from looking at cattle all week. After their baths, they felt like new men. They had lost the dust and dirt of the week, loosened up sore muscles, and improved their dispositions, all the while soaking in the hot mineral water.

But the soaking sucked out two or three pounds of body water through the good old process of osmosis. This loss, of course, was replaced internally from the supply of alcohol at the hotel's bar. The result, after a few hours of replacement, was a group of slightly pickled Scotsmen. It was no wonder Saturday nights at the Capa Hotel were nights to remember.

Where else in South Dakota does this interesting geothermal activity exist? Most noted are the numerous springs around the city of Hot Springs, where several mineral hot springs have been developed in connection with health centers and hotels. Hot springs, sulfur springs, mineral springs, and mud spring fumes, sometimes reeking with the odor of sulfur, mix together to create a plume of fog over Fall River. The river's temperature is 90°, winter and summer, as it flows to the Cheyenne River.

Farther east near Wounded Knee and jutting out of the ground like an inverted ice cream cone stands the eroded cone of an extinct thermal spring or geyser. It is called Gieser Geyser.

Still farther east is the White River, which ancient Indians called "Smoky Earth River" because of the twisting column of smoke that once arose from the surrounding hills. Could this have been because of geothermal activity?

Two places in Gregory County, on the approach to the Missouri River, suggest geothermal activity. Red Rock, a prominent formation, stands out in relief against the sky. It is a regional landmark. It is made up of Pierre Shale turned red by the oxidation of its iron. A few miles distant is Burning Bluff, from which smoke and odorous sulfur fumes spread across the river bottoms. Burning Bluff was drowned out by Lake Case. These two spots could be the result of past geothermal activity.

Back in Haakon County again, the promise of energy from the earth has resulted in intensified activity. Look at Philip, the county seat. It has a large industry heated with geothermal water. The spent water from the plant goes into the city swimming pool and from there back to the aquifer to be reheated again. It sounds like a good deal — no initial cost, no middle man, and no taxes, and one can't wear out water. But the water is briny, and the high concentration of salts can corrode copper pipe in 11 years. Swimming in the salty water, especially long dips, causes the skin to wrinkle. The water is, however, said to help rheumatism, arthritis, and muscle pain. It sucks out the poisons and, as mentioned, does a good job as a pickling brine.

The overflow from the swimming pool can be evaporated and

the salts harvested. There might be a market for some of the salts.

The people in Haakon County are heating up over geothermal energy. New and ingenious engineering techniques are being developed to make use of this natural resource. Schools, homes, ranches, hotels, businesses, and industries are beginning to use the energy supply.

It may even be that famous old Capa and its health spa will rise again. The hot artesian well is still there, awaiting some enterprising innovator. And while it will probably never again be able to pickle old Scottish cowboys, there are lots of Norwegians waiting around to try it.

McCook County

Area, 573 square miles
Population, 1925 - 10,392; 1945 - 8,596; 1980 - 6,444
County Seat, Salem. Population 1,486

The topography of McCook County is level to undulating with an average elevation of 1,400 feet above sea level. The most extensive flat area is in Pearl Township. The West Fork, East Fork, Little Vermillion, and Wolf Creek form the drainage patterns for the county.

The area between the East Fork and Little Vermillion is known as the Valley and is the more densely populated rural area. The settlers came mostly from the Scandinavian countries with a number of Irish settling around Salem.

The county was established in 1873, but it took awhile to establish a county seat. It seems that a game of whose got the county seat was played between Cameron, Bridgewater, and Salem. Cameron went out of existence, Salem, forgetting their Hebrew name of Peace, slipped in a window and stole the county records from Bridgewater. After a bit of unpleasantness, the county seat remained at Salem.

Canistota, Indian meaning "board on the water," has the Ortman Chiropractic Clinic and serves patients from a wide area.

Spencer is the site of a large Sioux quartzite quarry and furnishes crushed rock which is shipped to nearly every state in the union. A tile factory uses the sand by-product from the quarry.

Not far from the southern border of the county is Rumpus Ridge Store, perhaps started by some of those rowdies who swiped the courthouse records, or maybe they just wished to compete with Pumpkin Center, which is just across the line in Minnehaha County.

Centennials Are for Celebrating

McCook County

Salem, a city of peace (at least it was named for peace), celebrated its 100th anniversary in 1980. It followed the predictable pattern of all centennials. It concentrated on the noteworthy affairs and contributions of a few prominent old settlers, which are but a blink in the great eye of the region's history. There is something magical about being first. The first doctor, blacksmith, hotel, saloon, church, settler, baby, grave, etc., are apparently more important than millions of years of prehistory, 8,000 years of Indian settlement, and the natural heritage responsible for the fertile soil upon which men's livelihood depends. The natural, aesthetic beauty of the county is ignored. Salem residents live within a people-oriented culture, in which the car is more important than water quality, and more effort is spent on assuring human pleasure than alleviating human suffering.

So in 1980 they celebrated, as we all do, the settlement of the land and reflected on the hardships of the settlers. We bask in the accomplishments of 100 years of progress. We worship the growth, size, and culture that have been attained and look toward the next 100 years with a sense of greater prospects for growth, size, and accomplishment.

What will we celebrate on the bicentennial? Undoubtedly we will celebrate completion of the petroleum age and a switch back to coal. Domestic oil, Arab oil, and natural gas will be gone. We will have undergone a massive adjustment to coal-dependency as we begin our tricentennial years.

But what will we be celebrating at the end of those years — 200 years from now? All fossil fuels will be exhausted — oil gone, coal gone — and we will be back to living on the resources that man, with slow but continual success, lived on for some 3 million years. We might then look back, with satisfaction or despair, on 300

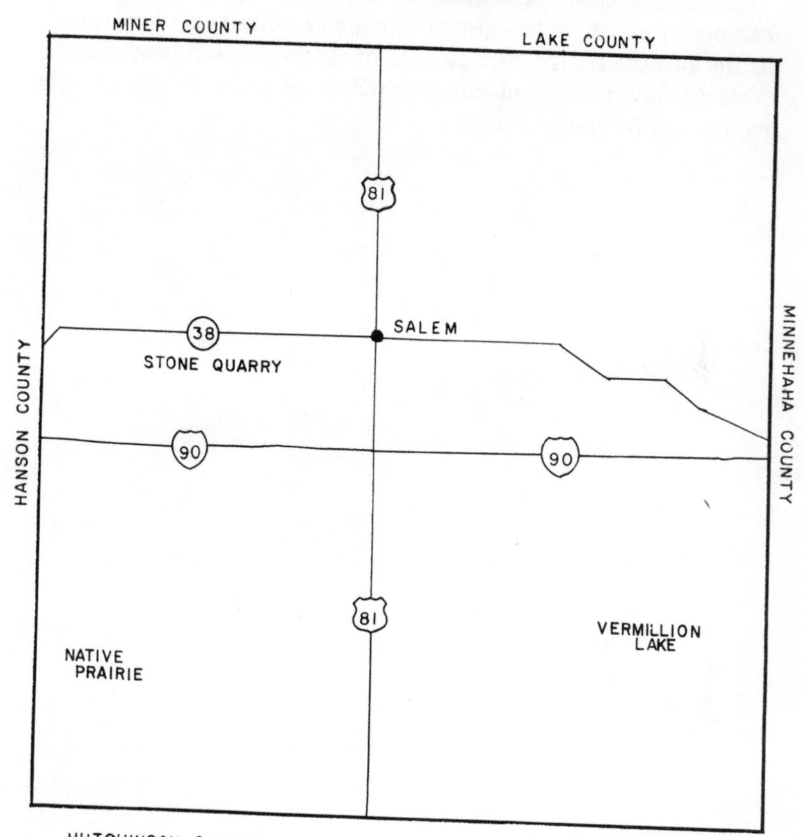

years of energy affluence. At this point a final adjustment must be made if humanity is to continue to celebrate centennials.

So it's a very narrow outlook — this tendency to view our land as if it is only 100 years old. We forget prehistory and assume the future to be more of the same grand and glorious past. If by some miracle a magnificant new source of energy becomes available, we can again live on a resource-filled planet. All we have to do is exploit it for our own benefit. Then the grass will be green, the birds will sing, and man will have dominion over all, to use as he sees fit.

To those who believe in this sort of science-fiction miracle, the future holds no problems, at least for a few years. But who believes in miracles these days?

Salem, the town that reached 100 years, has tested the turbulence of youth. It has grown into a city with its growth rooted in the future. The resourcefulness of its people and productivity of the countryside lead one to predict that the future of this region will be good.

ECOLOGY & CONSERVATION

Ecology & Conservation

County	**Title**
Lyman	A Gift from the Dust Bowl
Miner	Who Will Speak for the Flowers?
Pennington	The Wilderness Way
Potter	Prairie Fire
Turner	Gene Conservation
Union	The Urge for Life

It is fashionable today to play the ecology game with conservation becoming the password. Slogans became popular like: "Save energy, recycle," "Save our earth," "Give a hoot, don't pollute," "Pitch in," "Fish need water too," "Wildlife needs you," "Save our wetlands," and "Acid rain kills." These are all bumper stickers that warn about the impending disaster to our South Dakota systems. But whoever heard of "Don't drain the gene pools"? It could be we missed something. The following section deals with issues that should elicit more than just lip service from us all.

Human history becomes more and more a race between education and catastrophe.

—H.G. Wells
The Outline of History

For that which befalleth the sons of man befalleth the beast; . . . as the one dieth, so dieth the other; yea, they have all one breath; so that a man hath no preeminence above a beast; for all is vanity.

—Ecclesiastes 3:19

In Wilderness is the Preservation of the World.

—Henry David Thoreau

Nature bats last!

—Paul Ehrlich

The land belongs to the future . . .
That's the way it seems to me . . .
We come and go, but the land is always there
And the people who love it and understand it
are the people who own it — for a little while.

—Willa Cather
O Pioneers!

Lyman County

Area, 1,643 square miles
Population, 1925 - 7,432; 1945 - 4,275; 1980 - 3,864
County Seat, Kennebec. Population 334

The history of Lyman County parallels that of most of the west river counties. First there were only Indians (before 1810); then Indians, explorers, and fur traders (1810-1890); then removal of the Indians by action of Congress, which turned the land into an unfenced open range (1890-1905 — the era of the cattle baron); next the coming of the railroad, which deluged the county with land seekers (1905). The latter act resulted in an almost tenfold increase in population in a short time. These settlers first attempted to farm, failed, and finally shifted to a combination of farming and stock raising.

During the early times in Lyman County there were many forts: Fort Aux Cedars (Missouri Fur Company, 1802), Fort Lookout (French Fur Company, 1822), Fort Kiowa (1822), and Fort Defiance (1845). The last two were established by the American Fur Company. Also the military Fort Hale (1873) and an Indian trading post round out the early settlements.

This early colorful western history has been captured by Eudora Kohl in Land of the Burnt Thigh. It was a time when banks were operated day and night on two barrels and a plank. These were days when instant cash was obtained with a six-shooter instead of an instant cash card.

A Gift from the Dust Bowl
Lyman County

Those who do not know history are apt to repeat it.
—Santayana

On February 10, 1890, a gun sounded in Chamberlain, South Dakota, and 10,000 settlers rushed across the Missouri River into Lyman County. The land on the Great Sioux Reservation, between the White and Cheyenne Rivers, had just been opened for settlement. The settlers came in wagons, covered and uncovered. They came with oxen and horse, with and without families. Men, and a few women, were there to try their hand at homesteading. There was only one feeling — optimism. All doubts were submerged by enthusiasm as the newcomers sought out choice quarter sections, a search that culminated in pounding fresh-cut stakes in the corners of 160 acres to announce to the world that here stood the property of a new landowner.

One of the new landowners was a strong young man with a wife and small children. As he stood on the land, he fingered his hat in restless anticipation. A vision of the future shone in his eyes. He crumbled the dark, rich soil in his fingers. There, on the side of the largest hill, he selected a site for his home, and as he looked over and across the vast treeless prairie, he saw trees, vines, gardens, and wheat. The plain had become a vision of productivity.

When house and family were secure, and when signs of spring had awakened the land, the young farmer again stood on the hill surveying his newly won land. A breeze tugged playfully at his hat and cooled his brow. Then slowly the plow bit into the prairie sod, exposing the internal anatomy of the earth. It was the beginning of a giant wound, and the symbol of this wound was a tiny plume of dust that drifted off behind the plow. It was like a flag, warning those who could understand. All the plowman noticed was that the dust filled his eyes and choked his breath. But the Indian who watched from a distance shook his head and murmured, as he watched the turning of the sod, "Wrong side up."

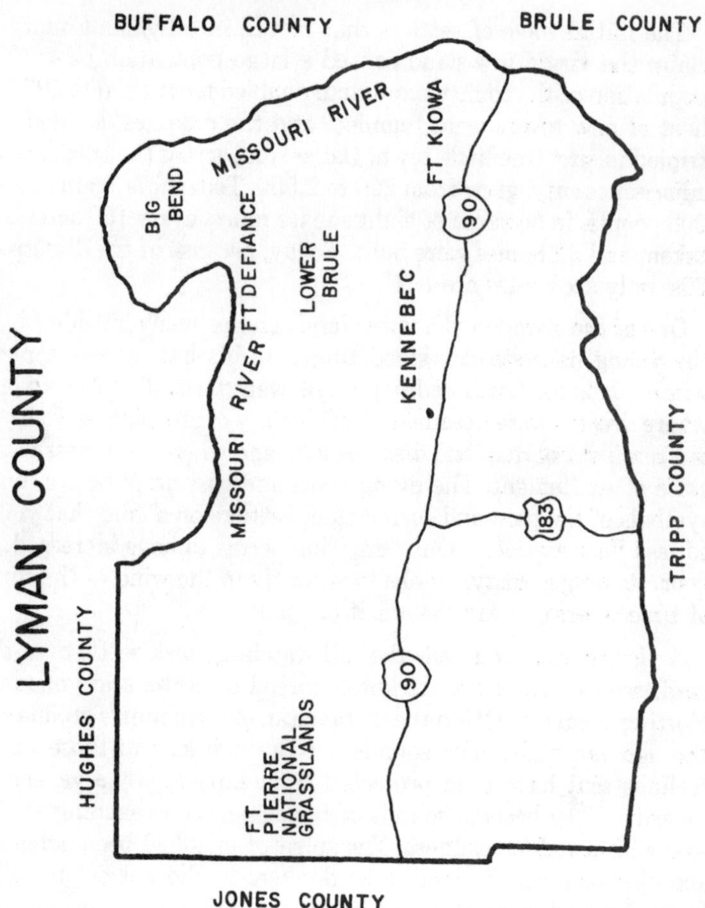

Years passed, and the youthful enthusiasm turned to drudgery. The calluses on the young man's hands grew harder, and the fertile soil grew thinner. The doubts that had been slumbering because of ambition were turning into reality. The small plume of dust that had arisen from the plow on that first day had grown to enormous size. Coalescing with the plumes on neighboring farms, it turned into a raging dust storm. The wind ripped the rich black soil from the dead and dying plant roots and piled it like snow on the fences. It blew dust over the entire eastern part of the nation, and the country recoiled under the impact of the Great Dust Bowl. The earth had reacted to a wound that had sheared the surface of its protective covering in a land where wind was king.

The initial wave of settlers that moved into Lyman County to claim the virgin grassland caused a large population boom. The population of the county more than doubled from 1890 to 1910. A host of new towns were founded, and the old ones doubled and tripled in size. One little town, Dallas, just across the border in an adjacent county, grew from 200 to 2,000. Today it is again around 200 people. In one area of eight square miles, every 160 acres was taken, and 32 homes were built. Today, because of the disastrous 30s, only six homes are left.

One of the abandoned homes stands on the lonely hillside where the young homesteader stood fingering his hat. It was a place where plans for home and happiness were formed. It was a place where dreams were dreamed of the bounty of abundance. Today it is a reminder of dust and disaster in a land where loneliness was a state of excitement. The dying trees and rusting plow are mute symbols of the pain and suffering of settlers on a land that yielded less than expected. Only the wind seems to have increased. A door, its hinges rusty, creaks incessantly in the wind — the force of time wearing away the spirit of man.

A visitor, standing near the hill watching dusk settle over the land, sees a blanket of darkness spread over the scars of man, blotting them out. Off in the distance an old windmill's groans cut through the night. The sounds cut through also to those inner feelings that have been protected from exposure by a veneer of security. They become sounds of hopelessness, wrenching at the soul with a sudden sadness. The spirit of man had been defeated and ejected from the land, a land where he did not belong. The lesson learned is painful and tragic. Only time and wisdom will heal the wounds.

At the height of the great exploitation by man, from 1890 to 1915, nearly half of Lyman County felt the bite of the plow. Inevitably the land was abandoned, and the adapted native grass again took over to heal the scar made by the disruption. This abuse of the land came to a climax during the Great Depression and Dust Bowl days of the 30s. Destitute people left, and the government bought up their properties to try to reclaim the land. So, born of poverty and baptized with dust, came two great gifts to the American people — 4 million acres designated National Grasslands, and the Soil Erosion Service (later, the Soil Conservation Service). One of the 19 National Grasslands, the Fort Pierre National Grassland is situated in northwest Lyman and adjacent counties. Today grasslands are models of how, with the proper use and management, land can maintain its productivity.

Two generations have gone by since the pinch of poverty was felt by the people of Lyman County. Now a new generation is again eyeing the vast grasslands. They see, not a dust bowl and poverty, but wheat fields and productive crops. Memories are a gift only to those who will dream. The lessons of history are more easily ignored than studied. So the plow bites into the ground to rip open the wound anew. The plume of dust enlarges and blinds the farmer. He does not see that the road leads to poverty.

The new generation does not remember that in the four or five years of the Dust Bowl, the land was lowered in some places three to four feet. They do not know that the power of the wind is relentless. In some places in southern Wyoming, the land has been lowered 150 feet over a long period. They only feel that if luck is on their side, the next few years will see big crops of wheat and money for machinery.

Again, Lyman County has reached a point where nearly 50 per cent of the land is under the plow. The frangible thin soil lies exposed to the wind and awaits the coming of drought. Five to 40 inches below this thin soil lies the barren, sterile Pierre Shales bedrock. A new erosion cycle will expose this unfertile substrate and enlarge the already present Pierre Shale badlands. When spreading and coalescing with the White River badlands, the Badland National Monument will have to be enlarged.

After a few hundred years, the newly exposed somber grey shale badland will have become oxidized, and the iron in the clayey shales will streak the landscape with bands of red, yellow, and brown. Then the government will announce to the world a gift to man — an enlarged new Badlands National Park.

A traveler approaching the park will be greeted with a sign at the entrance that proclaims: "Welcome. You are now entering your newest national park, recently expanded through the efforts of man. Watch for mud slides and washed out roads after heavy rains. Protect wildlife by observing the speed limit."

There will be no need for man to remember past abuses. This time the abuses will be etched forever in a scar across the breast of Mother Earth.

Areas of thin soils and poor management are often severely damaged by strong winds and heavy rains, to the extent they are no longer productive. **Photo — SCS**

Miner County

Area, 568
Population, 1920 - 8,560; 1945 - 6,057; 1980 - 3,739
County Seat, Howard. Population 1,169

Old timers state that "when Miner County was first created it was a treeless prairie covered with long thick grass and it had lots of wild game and the streams had good fishing. There were also many buffalo chips to use for fuel." Today there are larger farms with good livestock and all the newest methods of farming. The crops are corn, oats, wheat, alfalfa, beans, and once, it was reported, that 10 per cent of the county was brome grass.

It shares with Hanson County a town called Epiphany, a town built mostly on medicine. Father Kroeger, a priest-doctor, claimed to have a cure for cancer, and in 1900 as many as 400 people would be in town for treatment. He manufactured his own medicines. The clinic and much of the town disappeared after Father Kroeger's death in 1904.

In population Miner County has not fared well. From a high point of 8,560 in 1920, it has drifted downward at about 80 people a year to 3,739 — a loss of about 57 per cent of its people. Half the people in Miner County now live in Howard or small villages in the county.

Who Will Speak for the Flowers?

Miner County

"Where have all the flowers gone?" is not echoed through the plains of Miner County. It is an agricultural county with an agricultural bent. The farmers have learned to adjust to the soil and their surroundings and have found the land pliable to their efforts. Nothing has stopped them from turning up the prairie sod. Land not quite suited for cultivated crops has been turned into tame hay, especially brome grass.

Because of the brome, corn, oats, wheat, and alfalfa, there are no more wild flowers or prairie to greet the eye. The land is a sim-

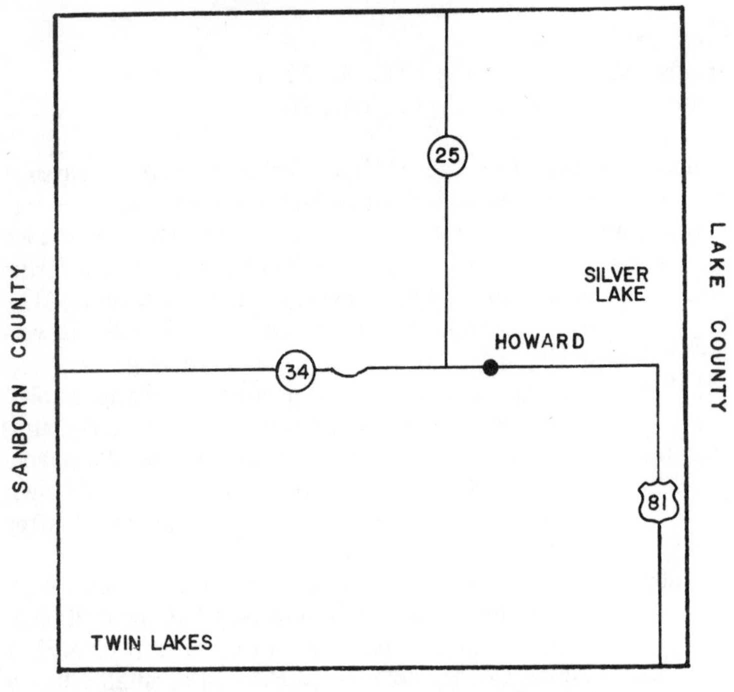

ple ecosystem and a simple food chain of crops, cattle, and man. It is a cycle of man, money, and machinery, played upon the fertile fields of the prairie. By default, or perhaps because no one cared, the prairies, their flowers, and diversity have all disappeared.

The prairie, with the complexity and diversity which led to a stability within its environment, was in a sense forever, since it could change and evolve. It was a balanced system. It was a climax community in Miner County that had some 400 to 500 species of plants, some 800 to 1,000 beneficial insect species which coevolved with the plants, and a host of mammals, reptiles, and birds. To the pioneer, however, it was a threat and a challenge, and from it he carved his fortune. No more did the prairie fire threaten, no more did wildness harbor the unknown, no more did the wolves howl at night; the surroundings offered a satisfied feeling of friendly neighbors. Out of this conquering of the prairie came security and a good level of living. The more energy, power, and new techniques that were developed, the more completely man was able to dominate his landscape.

It has not all been good. The simplified system has been susceptible to new diseases, an increased number of pests, a depletion and erosion of soil, pollution of air and water, and social tension causing increased crime and alcoholism. It has turned, in a sense, into a mundane culture.

The early beginning on the prairie of Miner County was the family farm. Almost everything needed for subsistence was raised on the farm, and what was extra was traded or sold for cash. Patches of untouched land still remained relatively wild. But dreams of economic advancement stirred the farmer's mind and turned the wheels of his tractor until cold or darkness dimmed his ardor. He was no longer a family farmer but an agribusinessman, pitted against the heartless laws of supply and demand. Power and energy were applied to the land as if they were potter's clay. Pastures were renovated, rocks removed, trees planted, potholes drained, land leveled, roads built, and all sorts of things collectively grouped under the heading of improvements were accomplished. Each farmer soon equipped himself with an energy equivalent of 400 to 500 slaves in his gas tank, and with the primitive urge of a slave driver, he flagellated himself into frenzied subjugation of the land. And since a tiger in the tank is not easily turned into a pussycat in the parlor, the trend goes on. Bigger farmers need bigger machines and more energy and hence more mechanical slaves to develop his modern-day feudalism. Soon to arrive is a system requiring more energy to maintain than it can produce and deluding itself that the law of diminishing returns can be avoided by blindness or that increased efficiency is gift-wrapped with free energy.

Not only is man invading the domain of the prairie, but also his introduced plants and animals are continuing to spread. One rapidly spreading plant in Miner County is brome grass — a beneficial grass until it gets out of hand.

Brome grass was introduced from Russia and eastern Europe in 1887. It began to make its impact on the South Dakota farm land after the 1940s. Since then it has penetrated almost every corner of the state. It is a nutritious, fast-growing, drought-resistant, cool-season grass. It spreads by an underground stem system called rhizomes and hence crowds out almost everything that grows with it. It produces abundant seeds and is a plant desired by many. It fits well into a zone that borders the western part of the tall grass prairie and eastern edge of the mixed grass prairie.

Now brome grass reigns ubiquitously. It permeates to all corners of the county, especially road ditches. It forms a grid that frames each section in ribbons of green, and from it comes the seed source that sprinkles the rest of the county with a shower of brome seeds. This, together with the rest of the brome in the county, assures a brome invasion into any area where brome has a chance for survival. Will we develop a new prairie ecosystem? One in which the dominant grass is brome — a brome grass climax community? Already 10 per cent of the cropland is brome, more brome than in any other county.

The county has been brominated, and the people are happy and cheerful in their somewhat mundane surroundings. They have never stopped to ask, "Where have all the flowers gone? Why have many of the beneficial insects decreased in number while a few species like starlings, blackbird, and English sparrows have increased in number? Why are our problems different today from a few years ago?"

With the old system of evolving new species gone and the old species becoming extinct, what will happen? Only those species that can coevolve with man will be filling the biological niches. Imagine, if you wish, feral dogs, cats, and pigs, mini and maxi rats, giant Canada pigeons, red mice with spots to blend in with the kitchen floor, insecticide-dependent grasshoppers, EPA-approved weeds for growing in silted-out reservoirs, crab grass that looks like carrot plants, and giant nut-bearing brome grass. It is hard to imagine what will happen in a man-dependent and directed evolutionary system. Nature's great experiment with natural variation and environmental selection of the fittest will be finished. The land on which nature generates new species will be gone.

What will happen to man himself? How will he evolve in this simplified environment? The diversity and challenges of complex environments resulted in the evolving of the human animal, who could finally understand the world around him. A corollary is that a monotonous environment yields a monotonous individual, which could over a long period evolve into something that you might not even call human. We could be entering into an era in which the big events of the year are the trick knee marathon, a beauty pageant for the nearsighted, and a fortissimo fun fest for the hard-of-hearing.

Who speaks for the flowers of Miner County? Who remembers the flowers? Who even cares? If there is a voice, it is but a whisper borne by the wind. It is a voice that whispers that the forces of life will eventually heal the abuses of man. If you examine the wild wonders of the earth, you may hear this whisper. You will then understand that the creative forces of God are meeting resistance as they evolve new creatures in a wilderness Garden of Eden.

The lowly little pasque flower nods its welcome as the first sign of spring on the prairie. Who will speak for its rights when there is no longer room for things wild and free?

Photo — Ward Miller

Pennington County

Area, 2,792 square miles
Population, 1925 - 14,624; 1945 - 24,729; 1980 - 70,133
County Seat, Rapid City. Population 46,492

It started as a trickle high on the slopes of Mt. Crooks wriggling its way 4,200 feet down and 43 miles out to the foothills. Out past the hay camp where those long bull trains that packed freight from Fort Pierre stopped (1874-82). It grew stronger along the way fed by rivulets, creeks, and springs, springs like Rickgorer, Buck, and Black Fox with their beaver terraced pools extending up the mountains like Chinese Gardens. Black Fox, a National Forest Campground, swells out into a mountain bog full of strange and exotic plants that quake as one steps out on the bouncing bog.

Down and onward, evermore rapidly, it flows past Rochford, Mystic, Silver City, Pactola, Hisega, Cleghorn Fish Hatchery, Dark Canyon, and Canyon Lake. It extends out past its namesake, Rapid City, as it makes its way to the Cheyenne River, 40 miles to the east. Yes, Rapid Creek is one of those many picturesque creeks that flows out of the eastern slopes of the Black Hills to fuel the Cheyenne River. It has attracted a complex of homes, industry, and development.

Then on June 9, 1972, it happened: a 14-inch rain in seven hours fell on the eastern slopes of the hills, and what had been a place for enjoyment and enchantment turned into a rushing torrent of death. Canyon Lake Dam burst, 238 people drowned, millions of dollars of property was destroyed, and it cut a swath of devastation through the northern part of Rapid City. Today a greenbelt along the path of the stream, devoid of the usual clutter, commemorates the power of Rapid Creek.

But Pennington County is much more than a flood scene. It is a county shaped like a hatchet and spread over a million and a half acres. It is the central part of the Hills and stretches out into the badlands. Some have remarked the county and the Hills should have been a National Park, but the discovery of gold in 1875 filled it up with people. Today it is the second most populated county in the state. It, together with Minnehaha, Brookings, and Brown, makes up nearly 40 per cent of the state's population. It continues

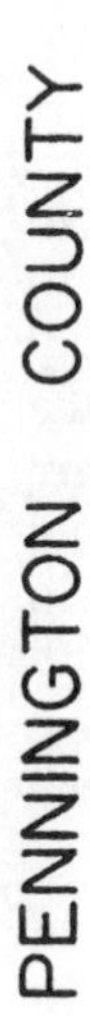

to grow and so a former hay camp, served by bull trains, has turned into a county seat which is the second largest city in the state.

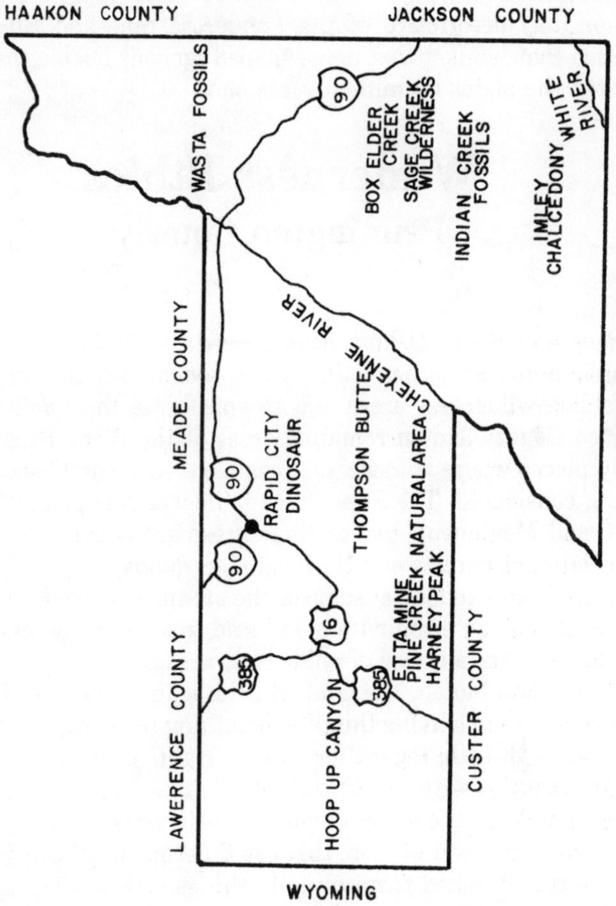

It is a county of contrast with badlands blending into mountains. It is Harney Peak (7,250 feet) rising above cold deep gulches. It is wilderness bordered by a billboard alley. Scattered around the hills are 162 abandoned mines, a host of ghost towns, and scenery that makes the tourist think twice about going on to the Rockies.

Some of the attractions in the Hills are Mt. Rushmore, Museum of Geology, 1880 Train, Dinosaur Park, and Deerfield, Sheridan, and Pactola Lakes, while out in the Badlands there are Wall, Scenic, and the Cedar Pass Visitor Center.

Indians have always called the hills Paha Sapa — a title appropriately descriptive of the Ponderosa pine and Black Hills spruce that blanket that dome-shaped igneous bubble that interrupted the plains 60 million years ago.

Wilderness Ethics

Pennington County

People of South Dakota have a need to develop a wilderness system and a wilderness ethic. There seems to be a reluctance to establish wilderness areas and to appreciate their value. Pennington County and surrounding areas of the Black Hills are the only places where wilderness areas have been established or are being considered. The Sage Creek Wilderness is in the Badland National Monument; two or three areas are being considered in the National Forests and National Grasslands.

It is of value to look at some of the attitudes toward wilderness to see if such an examination will lead to a better understanding of the need for and use of wilderness areas.

To the non-Indian, the land with its wildlife is more a tool or possession than a living thing — something to be managed and exploited, with little regard for its own rights or welfare.

Contrast this with the attitude of the American Indian, who lived as a child of the environment. He believed in a spirit, beyond the ordinary power of men, that could permeate all things. When the spirits attached themselves to things and people, they were said to have Wakan (spirit). Even the commonest sticks and stones could be given spiritual essence. This essence was a manifestation of a pervading, mysterious power that filled the universe. It was as if all the atoms and molecules of the universe were connected with each other and could be manipulated by a divine creator, causing some molecules to fall into place as bears, bugs, barberries, or barefoot boys. Less fortunate molecules would fall into place as sticks and stones. The Great Spirit then gave some of the special creations Wakan (spirit). Some things could receive more Wakan than others.

For example, a little boy walks along the shore, looking at an assortment of stones, which seem of little importance. He picks up one which looks much like the others, but for the moment it becomes more important than the rest, for he has given it his special attention. The stone has Wakan. He now owns the molecules in the rock, as he owns the molecules in his body. But he owns these molecules only for a time. In due time, they will all be released again to the universe, perhaps to be reassembled into another entity. The Indian, feeling this interrelationship of molecules of the boy and the rock, believes that "with all beings and all things we shall be as relatives." Wind, sun, sky, earth, and four directions, and all the things that are on the earth are but extensions of the Great Creator (Wakan Tanka).

Animals were glamorized as being the earth's first inhabitants. Primitive man regarded them as superior in power to man, for they were better adapted to making a living in the wild. Of the trees and plants, he said, "We do not like to harm the trees. If we did not think of their feelings, before cutting them down, all the other trees in the forest would weep, and that would make us sad too."

In order to obtain the spirit (Wakan) and to communicate and understand the spirit of animals, trees, stones and the universe, the Indian searched for a vision. "If you do not obtain a spirit to strengthen you, you will amount to nothing in the estimation of your fellow men." After a period of fasting and stress by the Indian, the Great Earthmaker, feeling compunction that he had made mankind the last and least of all beings on earth, would provide him with a vision that would allow him the power to relate with the world about him.

Once given this power of survival, he would frequently seek to renew it. He would climb the highest hill, and there, at the edge of the sky, facing the rising sun and overlooking the vast land, he would pray to the God of the Universe. This was his earthbound cathedral, where his weakened spirit could be recharged by the powerful spirit of universe. He prayed to be brave like the eagle, strong like the bear, and wise like the owl. Then, having been renewed, he faced a new day with courage.

This is superstition and mysticism, you say, and maybe you are right. But you forget one important point. The Indian's belief engendered respect and care for the earth and its inhabitants. It is lack of respect that will destroy the wilderness, along with mankind and the thin, living blanket of life that clothes the earth. The earth will become lifeless like the moon. But for the few shouted words of alarm across a sea of apathy, the destruction goes unchallenged. Our economic system demands the use of land as a tool. Our religion does not prevent it, for it paints man as a superior being with dominion over all things. Biologically our own greed and avarice feed on the unprotected to create bigger and better egosystems. Man has respect only for himself and his monumental creations. All other things must be destroyed to feed his insatiable appetite.

Many societies and countries in the past have become victims of this creeping blight. As they destroyed the wilderness, they became choked with overproduction; then they suffered from economic constipation; and finally, weakened from inspirational deficiency, they collapsed in chaos, with only history to record their short moment of greatness.

The moral of this story is: learn to respect our wilderness and give rights and privileges to those things wild and free. Thoreau wrote, "Wilderness is the preservation of the world." In Pennington County, and in the rest of the state, we must look forward to emphasizing the importance of wilderness and see that wilderness areas are established, protected, and made available to the people. These areas are needed to feed the intellectual spirit and remedy the inspirational deficiency inherent in the massive, unstable systems created by man.

Potter County

Area, 898 square miles
Population, 1925 - 5,052; 1945 - 4,332; 1980 - 3,623
County Seat, Gettysburg. Population 1,623

Potter County history dates back to 1804 when Lewis and Clark stopped on the banks of the Missouri to visit Medicine Rock, a large rock with mythical implications for the Indians. It had the imprints of very large feet. (Bigfoot, it seems, reappeared at McIntosh, Corson County in 1979.) When the Oahe Reservoir was flooded the rock was moved to Gettysburg. Also at the time of Lewis and Clark's visit, the Arikara had a large village at Steamboat Creek.

Potter County was created in 1873, and like many other counties endured a name change (it was first called Ashmore) and a

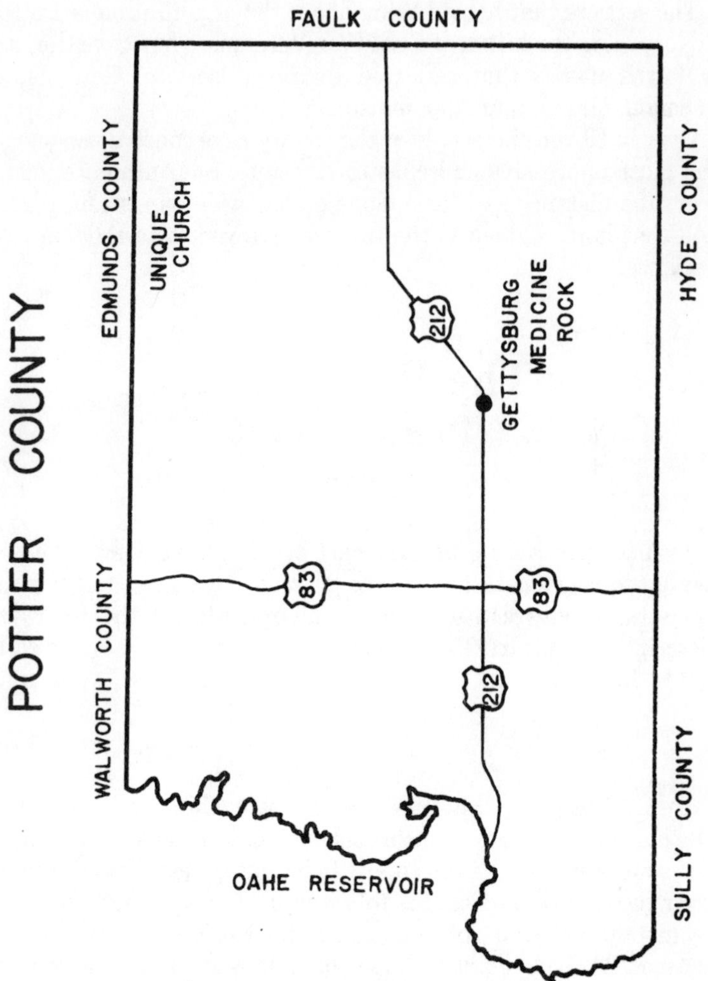

fierce county seat struggle. But unlike several counties its boundaries were never changed.

Ten years after it was created the county was organized. This required approval of the territorial government, an election of a county government, and selection of a county seat. All this was usually accompanied by unorthodox political maneuvering for the honor of being selected as county seat, the spoils being rapid growth for the winner and extinction for the loser. In this case Forest City suffered the latter, and Gettysburg became the city of record.

The settlers that helped bring about the organization of Potter County were the influx of Civil War Veterans. They gave the early towns names that reflected their war service: Gettysburg, Lebanon, Union, and Appomattox.

Over in Hoven the people of the county have constructed one of the most impressive churches in the state. St. Anthony's looms from the distance as if it is alone on the wide windswept plains and that here, suddenly, the prairie gave vent to a religious experience.

The Prairie Fire

Potter County

by Dave Ode

Prairie fires were a natural part of the prairie landscape and served to rejuvenate the prairie grasses as well as limit populations of woody plants, insects, and rodents. In the following description, a prairie fire is portrayed as it may have occurred in South Dakota.

* * * * * *

In a western sky the sun dims to a pale white oval, shaded by the collar of a massive mushroomed thunderhead stalking out of the southwest. As the sun finally fades out, a heavy shadow slides over the prairie bluff and is followed by a silence disturbed only by distant, brief rolls of thunder and the close, dry rustling of tall grasses. The fine golden plumes of Indian grass have long since been scattered by the harsh winter winds. Only the broken stems, uneven and shredded, remain standing, a few limp leaves dangling at their sides.

The prairie bluff overlooks a wide meadow descending toward the east, where a low swale intersects a meandering river enclosed on both sides by tall, widely spaced cottonwoods and scattered colonies of willows. At the lower end of the meadow a female coyote is rigidly poised, a front paw slightly raised, her eyes searching the matted layer of grass and forb litter immediately in front of her. Suddenly she pounces, bringing both paws down together. Her nose follows, plunging beneath the litter surface in search of a pinned rodent. After a few moments of anxious but unsuccessful searching, the coyote raises her head and takes a few steps toward the bluff. She pauses, casting her nose to the west as if she has caught a new scent.

The wind has switched. The thunderhead, no longer looming to the southwest, has moved overhead to the north of the prairie bluff and the hunting coyote. Out of the west the wind increases, raising dust and light plant material. A short barrage of large raindrops sweeps the meadow, followed by a resounding crash of thunder and the female coyote hastens her pace to trot up the bluff toward her den.

Near the river her mate appears, trotting out of the swale toward the meadow. The female reaches the den, a renovated badger hole on the slope of the bluff just a few meters below the rocky crest of the hill. She is greeted by a chorus of high-pitched whines, yips, and yowls emitting from the den opening. The coyote glances back down the meadow toward her mate and then disappears into the entrance of the dark den.

The male coyote finally reaches the den but then continues to the top of the bluff. There he stops and looks to the west, occasionally lifting his nose to sniff the wind. Under the existing dark cloud cover appears another layer of clouds, forming an extensive front along the western horizon. These low white clouds roll and billow in the wind and are being driven eastward with amazing speed. At the ground level along the advancing front, sporadic flashes of red, yellow, and orange contribute to a shrouded red hue permeating the lower level of the swelling white clouds.

The male coyote retreats from the crest of the bluff to the den and pauses. Overhead an increasing number of birds fill the air. Sparrows, meadowlarks, and prairie chickens, carried by the wind, reach the crest and dip down toward the river. From the south side of the swale near the river, the head and forequarters of an elk emerge from a stand of tall reeds as the elk moves downstream along the river bank. Beyond the crest of the bluff a low rumble develops. The male coyote mounts the mound of packed dirt on the downhill side of the den opening. The rumble gets louder and louder until the sound of it drowns out all else. The coyote dives into the den, to reappear with his head and chest protruding from the entrance. He disappears again as hundreds of bison plunge over the crest of the bluff, down the slope, and out onto the meadow. There several small herds of bison merge and ford the river, then thunder away toward the opposing bluff.

The sounds of both the thunderstorm and the buffalo herd are swept away by the wind, leaving only silence. The male coyote again appears at the mouth of the den, only to disappear downward in a flash. Long thin wisps of smoke now sail the wind, and riding upon them are new sounds: sounds of crackling and sounds of snapping; sounds of hissing and popping; sounds of whistling and whooshing and wailing and bursting, amalgamated and intensified into a single ominous roar — the roar of an oncoming prairie fire.

At the crest of the bluff, fine white billows of smoke appear, immediately torn and scattered by the wind. Flaming fragments of grass and buffalo chips shoot up and spiral in the wind, some of them blowing past the bluff top and down the slope and igniting the scattered bunches of little bluestem and muhly.

A wave of fire breaks over the crest of the bluff and floods down the already burning slope. For an instant the dirt mound of the coyote den is a black island in a sea of crimson flame. The front of the fire is not wide, but it stretches for miles both north and south along the river bluff, moving in staggered charges with each burst of wind. Once down the slope, the prairie fire finds increased energy in the denser stand of sod-forming tall grasses in the meadow. The flames of the headfire swell and roar with each driving surge of wind, consuming the dry grass stems, while a lower ground fire marches steadily in pursuit through the accumulated grass litter. As the fire nears the swale, the smoke becomes progressively darker and heavier, until the flames reach the river bank, defended by giant cottonwoods. Here the fire feeds on scattered twigs and branches, which the wind occasionally tosses over the bank and into the river, where the flames are snuffed out after a short hiss.

Meanwhile, the dark heavens finally burst, shrouding the river valley in a curtain of heavy rain and extinguishing the last flames and embers of the prairie fire. The rain continues for several minutes, accompanied by an occasional flash of lightning and roll of thunder. Then, as suddenly as the rain has started, it stops, leaving the river valley and bluffs drenched.

The sun begins to emerge from the scattering clouds, and up on the river bluff the two mature coyotes emerge from their den. After a quick survey of their charred surroundings, the coyotes head out, at a trot, toward the burned swale. There they search diligently among the seared grass remnants and uncover a number of fatally singed rodents, which are gulped down in turn, be they mouse, vole, or shrew. Apparently satisfied, the two coyotes begin their ascent back up the west bluff toward their den, now shadowed from the setting sun.

The east bluff of the river remains illuminated, and several scattered elk and bison now graze along its unburned grassy slopes. A shadow, running the length of the west-facing bluff, slowly stalks up from the flood plain, climbing toward the bluff top until the entire river valley is immersed in twilight. The sun remains, a brilliant orb, shooting its bands of red and orange into feathery wisps of clouds in the dark blue western sky. In moments the orb is gone, and the day of the prairie fire comes to close.

* * * * * *

Man's involvement with prairie fire has a long and varied history. Scientists believe that prehistoric man set fires both accidentally and intentionally, much altering his natural environment.[1] It is well documented that the American Indian set prairie fires. Such fires could be used to flush or drive game, and to stun or kill insects and rodents. In addition, the lush regrowth of prairie plants which follows a prairie fire served to attract and concentrate game animals for hunting.[2]

To the early pioneers of South Dakota, prairie fires were catastrophic. Throughout the state there are historical accounts of early prairie fires which were started by either lightning or human causes. Perhaps one of the most devastating of these fires occurred in McPherson County in 1889. On April 2, rising winds scattered the embers of a smoldering haystack and ignited a prairie fire. Carried by the wind, this fire swept eastward for over eight miles, blackening the prairie, taking one man's life, and

---

[1]E.V. Komarek. 1967. "Fire and the Ecology of Man." Proceedings of the Annual Tall Timbers Fire Ecology Conference. 6: 143-170.

[2]O.C. Stewart. 1951. "Burning and Natural Vegetation in the United States." Geographical Review. 41: 317-320.

destroying 80 buildings in the town of Leola.[3] The widespread destruction resulting from such prairie fires prompted the State legislature in 1893 to enact a law allowing for the establishment of plowed fire guards around each township in the state.[4].

With the plowing of the prairie, both the prairie fires and the prairie flowers disappeared. This is true of the eastern part of the state. The central and western part of South Dakota still support extensive and unplowed grasslands conducive to fires which may burn 20 to 30 miles or more before being brought under control. These modern-day prairie fires, however, have a new name. They are called "wild fires," and when yelled with the proper concern and conviction, this expression will elicit the same alarm and fear as did the cry of "prairie fire" one hundred years ago.

From the flames and ashes of destruction sprout the seedlings of renewal. This statement is genuinely true of all the tall grass prairie. When the prairie was plowed, a few relicts remained on rocky slopes, around wetlands which were not drained, and on many school lands. Some of these relicts have been preserved and represent all that is left of the tall grass prairie in eastern South Dakota. Invaded by Eurasian grasses and weeds like smooth brome and Kentucky bluegrass, these prairie preserves are now being renewed by occasional prairie fires which are more formally called "controlled burns." As a management tool, controlled burns serve to reenact the prairie fires which were once a natural part of the prairie environment. The greatest of care and preparation is required to prevent a controlled burn from turning into a wild fire. It is man who makes this distinction between controlled burns and wild fires. The prairie plants and animals, of course, don't make this distinction and experience both forms as the crackling, whistling, searing flames of the prairie fire.

---

[3]Gertrud L. Becker and B.J. Hilsendeger (eds.). Jubilee Journal — Leola, South Dakota (1884-1959). Sioux Falls: Midwest Beach Co. 1959.

[4]House Bill No. 67, Chapter 91. In Laws Passed at the Third Session of the Legislature of the State of South Dakota. Pierre: Carter Publishing Co. 1893.

A piece of tall grass prairie in eastern South Dakota that has been protected from burning for about 50 years. Note trees, spared because of this protection.

Photo — D. Holden

Part of a tall grass prairie that has had a spring burn. Note the response of the big blue stem and Indian grass in the background. The burn caused the prairie plants to double or triple in height and have a higher protein content. They are sought out by buffalo and grazing animals.

Photo — D. Holden

Turner County

Area, 617 square miles
Population, 1925 - 14,876; 1945 - 12,430; 1980 - 9,255
County Seat, Parker. Population 999

Early settlers in the area embracing Turner County discovered a rich loam soil, excellent for growing corn and beans, and largely for that reason the county has taken its place with the leading agricultural counties in the state.

Swan Lake was the site of the first settlement. It was located on the stage route and had the first post office, which opened in 1869. Located there were also the first school and teacher, the first general store, first town, and first county seat. Now only a marker designates its site.

Today Swan Lake is the recreation center of the county along with Turkey Ridge Creek, which is bordered by scenic gulches.

Turner County, like adjacent McCook County, had its county seat war between Marion, Parker, and Hurley. The legislature finally approved the move to Parker.

Other sites of interest are the Marion Clinic and the Thunder Valley Drag Races. Located on the east edge of the county is Turner Hill, the site of one of the first grist mills and the grave of the namesake of the county.

Education has been a prime consideration of Turner County. It started in 1890 with a 16x14 foot school and a three-month term. In 1939, 93 rural schools served the area. Today eight large districts serve the county with kindergarten to senior high school — all with free bus service.

Gene Conservation

Turner County and All Counties

In the introduction to his Turner County history, W.H. Stoddard quotes John Greenleaf Whittier:

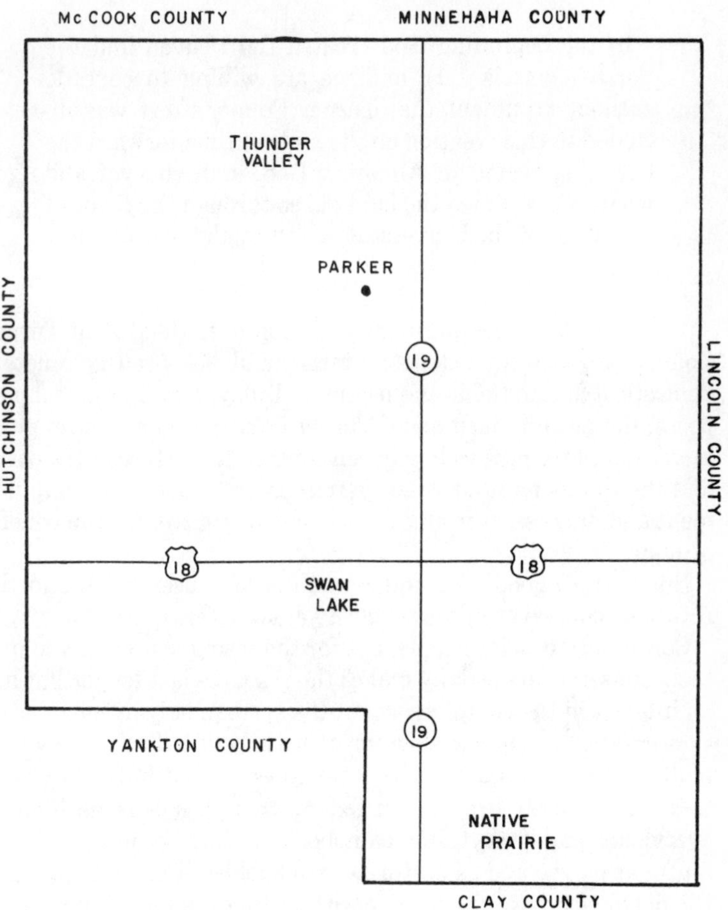

Behind the Indian's birch canoe,
The steamer rocks and raves
And city lots are staked: "For Sale"
Above old Indian graves
I hear the tread of pioneers
O nations yet to be
The first low wash of waves where soon
Shall roll a human sea.

Stoddard continues:

> In the beginning God created the Heaven and the Earth (Genesis 1:1), and we are willing to concede without argument that Turner County's dirt was included in this creation and from that time forward the title was vested in Almighty God, and whoever and whatever occupied the land did so through the favor of the Ruler of the Universe down through the centuries.

Yes, they did come and take dominion over the dirt of Turner County, to such an extent that the land has been completely domesticated into fields and pastures. Today, for all practical purposes, the natural heritage of Turner County is gone. In its place is an example of how well man can control the surface of the earth and the things on it. It is an exercise in the pride of accomplishment and purpose. It is an exercise in gene control for the benefit of man.

But is it all good? An understanding of conservation and the future of conservation may help to answer this question.

Conservation is for people, not for the resource it claims to protect. Conservation usually makes the resource last longer but has no interest in the completeness of the system, only in some parts. Conservation is simply slow (or at least believed to be slow) exploitation of a resource. The term conservation today has been used and abused to such an extent that it means nothing to everybody and everything to nobody. It has become as meaningful as maybe and as useful as soap bubbles. Take, for example, the people who use the term, each twisting the meaning to serve his own special purpose: hunters, fishermen, hikers, naturalists, foresters, ranchers, businessmen, industrialists, dentists, doctors, teachers, teenagers, snowmobilers, senior citizens, and all the rest of the conglomeration that make up our human diversity. They all speak of conservation of energy, water, resources, air quality, and natural resources in the same way they speak of the gross national product and technological fix. They speak of conservation for the benefit of people.

Once eloquently described as "the greatest good for the greatest number for the longest time," conservation has become a euphemism for saving, wise use, ecology, and common sense. Conservation to one group means destruction to another group. Wise use to a forester means exploitation to the Sierra Club. Watershed management to the Soil Conservation Service means habitat destruction to the wildlife manager. Wildlife management means climax destruction to the biologist, and out of it all comes the Corps of Engineers with its own rip-roaring brand of conservation.

On top of this are the established government conservation agencies, each with its own brand of conservation which, they insist, is divinely endorsed. There are the Forest Service, Bureau of Land Management, Fish and Wildlife Service, Department of Agriculture, plus numerous state and local organizations — all practicing conservation with an eye to pleasing a select segment of people. They give lip service to what they are conserving but bend over backward to serve the people. They serve the people more than the system they were given a mandate to protect.

There is a meaning, however, that can be adopted by everybody, one that is unambiguous, necessary, and essential. It is conservation of the gene pools of renewable resources. It is conservation in terms not of what is best for people, but what is best for trees, grass, birds, animals, and natural systems. Instead of meaning something different to everybody, conservation should have limited application to genetic systems, or, in its more total aspect, ecosystems. We must make sure that the genetic systems of the past are made continuous with the genetic systems of the future. It is necessary for survival. There must be a sufficient and representative number of all types of ecosystems, scattered about and preserved in all parts of the country. They must be managed, preserved, and used to maintain the basic integrity of the system. These ecosystems, in essence, will be the seed beds for the biosphere in the event of catastrophe. They will supply the gene banks of tomorrow.

Our present renewable resources, including man himself, are completely dependent upon a high input of energy for existence. Over the years the gene flow in man and these systems has been redirected and is not adapted to natural conditions. Today, if there was a catastrophe, some 90 per cent of these systems, including most of humanity, would disappear because they are no longer adaptable. This includes the gene pool which is our crop, garden, and tree species. It includes the domesticated birds and animals and most of the human race. All these species have been manipulated and selected to the extent that no wild, adaptable genes are left in the population. The gene flow has been directed solely toward production, and these managed organisms are little more than living machines that provide food. All this while we rapidly drain our native gene pools.

In the final analysis, conservation and the proper direction of gene flow in renewable resources are needed for the preservation of the world. By making sure adaptable species are always available, we insure our future. We will, in this way, be able to preserve the stability of the earth's biosphere and, in turn, conserve Turner County with a faith in the future that W.H. Stoddard claims was placed in the hands of man.

What does all this conservation have to do with Turner County? Well, it is motherhood we are talking about. It is the power of the earth to create new life, not just the birth of new individuals, but the birth of new species. We are talking about Mother Earth's capacity of creating, through time, a continuous flow of new species, and by pouring them into a river of life, she floods our planet with the power of growth. To destroy this capacity is to destroy the very birthplace of mankind. Remember, it takes an estimated million years to create a gene; a species comes a bit harder. Should not the people of Turner County, now almost completely agricultural, be awed by these marvelous acts of creation?

Union County

Area, 452 square miles
Population, 1925 - 8,043; 1945 - 7,011; 1980 - 10,938
County Seat, Elk Point. Population 1,661

After the Civil War, Union County gained two things: a name and a batch of veterans who took advantage of the Homestead Act. In fact, five minutes after the Act became official, Mahlon Gore filed for a claim in Union County. He became the first person in the United States on January 1, 1863, to start the floods that filed and helped fill South Dakota with settlers. They came from all walks of life, in all sorts of conveyances, and with all sorts of intentions. They built sod houses, dugouts, log cabins, claim shanties, and put up tents to fulfill the requirements of the Homestead Act. They sat there on the virgin prairie and weathered drought, grasshoppers, floods, hail, and were called

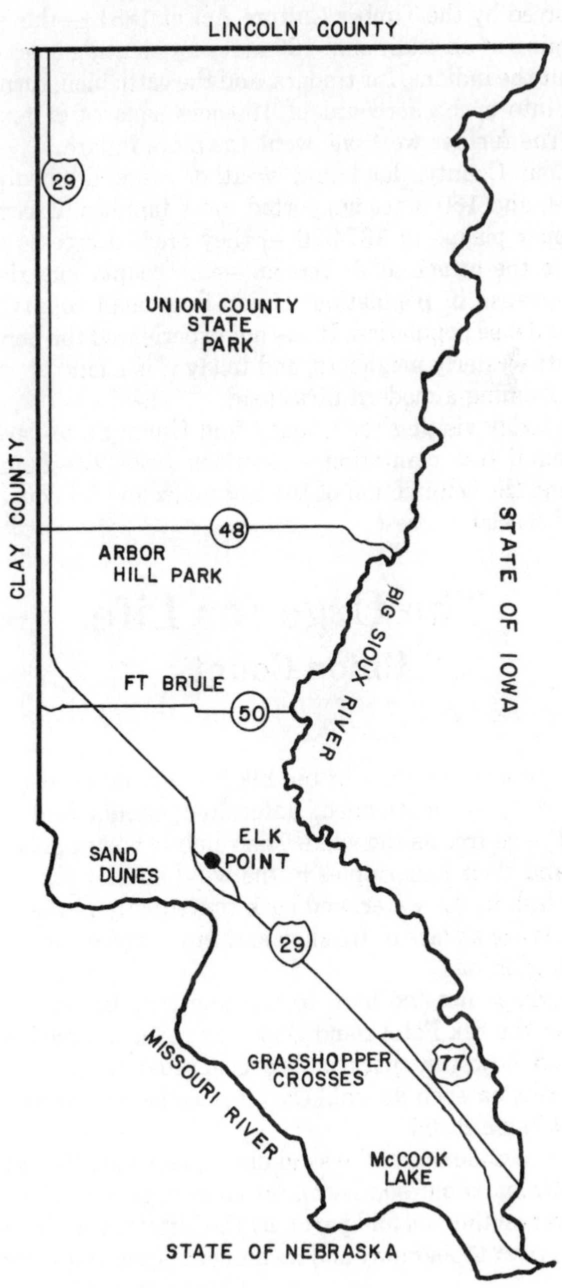
UNION COUNTY
LINCOLN COUNTY
29
UNION COUNTY STATE PARK
CLAY COUNTY
48
ARBOR HILL PARK
STATE OF IOWA
BIG SIOUX RIVER
FT BRULE
50
ELK POINT
SAND DUNES
29
MISSOURI RIVER
GRASSHOPPER CROSSES
77
McCOOK LAKE
STATE OF NEBRASKA

squatters, honyockers, carpet baggers, and ethnic names that were usually more derogatory than descriptive.

Reinforced by the Timber Culture Act of 1881 — this allowed the claiming of an additional 160 acres by planting trees — they forced out the Indians, fur traders, and the cattlemen, turning the country into a checkerboard of 160-acre squares of fence and failure. The further west one went the more failure.

In Union County, land and weather were decidedly more favorable, and 160 acres supported most families. Except for a grasshopper plague in 1874-76 — they erected crosses to commemorate the attack at Jefferson — the county experienced a steady increase in population. Union is a small county with a relatively dense population. It has not experienced the population shift of its westerly neighbors, and today it is a land of corn and soybean framing a modern farmstead.

People today visiting the County find Union State Park — an experimental tree plantation — McCook Lake, Elk Point Sand Dunes, and the conjunction of the Big Sioux and Missouri Rivers points of special interest.

The Urge for Life

Union County

On the pure white sands of the Elk Point Sand Dunes, bathing beauties romp — unattended, unfettered, uninhibited, and unmolested — as free as the wind. Their nubile bodies pulsate with energy, and their hair ripples in the wind as they jog along the beach, splash in the water, and bask contentedly in the sun. The sand dunes are a place of freedom and fun, a place where life can find its beginnings.

It is perhaps not too hard to imagine that life can begin in places like the Elk Point Sand Dunes. It requires imagination to understand how the spark of life generated itself into a full-grown forest on such an unlikely place as barren, white, sterile sand. But begin it did.

In order to understand the sand dunes, let's look first at Union County. Union is our southernmost county. It is flanked by the Sioux River on the east and partly by the Missouri on the west. Its abundant river topography and its numerous soil types, including extensive loess deposits and sand dunes, offer a great diversity of ecological niches. The climate of the southern part, which lies within the fork made by the Missouri and Big Sioux Rivers, is the most mesic in South Dakota. Its rainfall approaches 30 inches, its annual temperature is two degrees higher than that of the surrounding highlands, and its frost-free period is two weeks longer than that of adjacent counties. This combines to make Union County one of the best places in South Dakota to study ecology. Plant succession, from sand dunes to mature basswood-elm communities, can be studied by comparing river terraces of increasing age. On the north-facing slope, abundant woodlands offer a contrast in climate and vegetation to that of the tall grass prairies on the south-facing slope. All this results in an assemblage of plants, animals, and insects that is hard to find anywhere else.

In Union County one can start with pure white sand and see, after a period of 1,000 years, give or take 200, that it has turned into a livable forest community. The whole process is a continuous one. For convenience, it can be divided into stages. Each stage, sometimes called a sere, makes up a pattern of plant succession. Each sere has its own distinct assemblage of organisms — plants, animals, and insects.

In Union County any sun-basking young girl who exercises her mind can trace the exciting progress in the establishment of life from a barren, hostile environment to a stable, livable one. She can understand herself and see and feel the forces of life that mold the raw elements of nature. As this age-old process occurs, extremes are dampened and the environment becomes more livable. Fluctuating temperatures become more average, the wind is reduced, and the humidity remains high but more stable. All of these go into making the dunes a more hospitable and livable place.

The place to start a trip through the system is the sand dunes near the water.

In a large bend in the Missouri River, where it flows southeast for many miles, a vast, wide sand flat is created. The prevailing northwest wind sweeps up this sand and deposits it on the shore. The wind continues to pile the sand into large dunes, which migrate at the rate of 20 to 30 feet a year.

The wind rolls the sand grains up a gradually, sloping, inclined plane, until at the dune's steepest point, the grains suddenly drop on the almost vertical lee side of the dune. The wind, usually traveling faster on the edges of the dune than over the top, causes long tails to stretch out on the edges of the lee side. The sand dune thus appears as a giant sandpile, in which the center of one side has been scooped out as with a shovel. These dunes are called crescent or barchan dunes.

Vegetation must get started on this relatively young surface (less than 10 years old) of what looks like pure white sand. The dry, hot, almost sterile sand shifts and moves. It is a place for sand castles, sunbathing, and sandy picnic sandwiches, not a nursery bed for plants. It is a Sunday afternoon and Fourth of July spot, not a place for plants to grow.

But grow they do, for nature and life are a process programmed to cover the earth. In this case Nature sends out, to battle with the shifting sands, a plant called the sand reed or Calamovilfa longifolia. The reed sends fast-growing, tentacle-like stolons over the sand, binding the sand in a weblike root system. As the system grows, the stolons sprout new shoots and eventually form a dense colony of a grass. The grass colony stops the sand and dust and dies back in the winter. But accumulated nutrients presage a new, and larger, crop in the spring. Soon a shallow zone of soil occurs, and other plants invade it. Helped along by lichens, microorganisms, and insects, organic matter accumulates, and more diverse seedlings find root. The cottonwood was one of the first. After about 10 to 20 years, cottonwood seedlings appear in the sand reed mats. This complex stops more sand and dust. At times the sand is piled up high on the trunks of cottonwood trees, smothering out the original colonizer, the sand reed. The cottonwood adapts to this with a flourish because it has more surface from which to draw nutrients and water. It sends out a network of adventitious roots along a trunk entirely covered by sand.

After a period of 30 to 50 years, the sand has in effect been stabilized by the two veteran sand fighters pitting their talents in a one-two punch against the shifting sand. It would have been hard, or impossible, for either the sand reed or the cottonwood to have accomplished it alone. As partners working in sequence, they stopped the invading sand.

It is now time for nature to send in the second team. Cottonwoods are a high, sunlight-requiring species, and young seedlings cannot tolerate the shade. So in the bottom of the cottonwood forest, which is 50 to 80 years old, under the thick mulch of cottonwood leaves and decaying vegetation, sprouts the more shade-tolerant green ash. In the wetter areas, elm and basswood seedlings appear under the cottonwoods. On a dry south slope, the cottonwood will eventually die out, to be replaced by the tall grass prairie.

So in the 200- to 500-year-old dunes and terraces, or dunes which are a long way from the river, we find three types of climax communities. The type of community depends upon moisture gradient, exposure, slope, and soil. An extremely dry area with a moisture equivalent of less than 20 inches will have short and mixed grasses. Other areas and their moisture equivalents are: 20 to 24 inches, tall grass prairie; 24 to 28 inches, green ash and burr oak; 28 to 32 inches, American elm and basswood. All are climax communities for the area and will remain such unless disturbed.

This process of plant succession is not unique to sand dune areas. It is a process by which plants become established on any virgin area. It is a method by which nature heals those areas which have been injured and abused by man and brings them back to health. It is the universal method by which nature ensures a continuous mantle of green on our planet. It is the reproduction, growth, and development of the supraorganism, the biosphere.

The process is now complete, and the dunes have been made livable for man. But it is now out on the raw sand that the seeds of primeval life are sown. It is a place where the unsuppressible reproductive urge of life conquers all obstacles and clothes the earth with its multitudinous life forms. This dynamic nature of life leads to a diversity and stability into which man must integrate himself. He must form a harmonious balance with nature if he is to be successful.

Even the young bathing beauties sunning themselves on the sugary sand seem to know that the irresistible life force is not lost in the Elk Point Sand Dunes, for deep within them stirs that same primeval urge.

DAKOTA
PIONEERS

Dakota Pioneers

County	Title
Beadle	Beyond the Forest
Jerauld	The First Car
McPherson	The Red Elk Way
Roberts	West of the Sunset
Stanley	Cattle Barons
Sully	Boom Towns
Tripp	Spaced Out in Tripp
Yankton	The Norwegian Connection

The pioneer spirit is like yeast. It grows, spreads, bubbles, and bursts. It is a spirit that turns the hardship, deprivation, and poverty of settlers in a not too hospitable land into optimism. It was a spirit that filled South Dakota with too many people, too fast, and left a situation that was often humorous and pathetic at the same time. In some areas it turned Indian and buffalo grassland almost overnight into settlers who turned the area into a future dust bowl.

It took many years for people to adjust to the environments of the state. This section is about this adjustment. Other parts of the book also reflect on this theme. However, the message is always the same: wise use of the land is the salvation of the people.

> The first man among them to stand on the edge of the Great Plains saw farther over land than he had ever seen before. There is something about the heart of the continent that resides always in the end of vision, some essence of the sun and wind.
>
> —N. Scott Momaday
> House Made of Dawn

> This ocean of earth, undulating in heavy, long-drawn waves, on and on into the blue distance, till the last wave spent itself somewhere beyond the sky-line.
>
> —John Bojer describes the prairie in
> The Emigrant

> Dakota is a mean country. There are no trees and no shade and we get sunburnt. We burn chips for fire. We have lots of thunder and lightning storms. It is a healthy country but it would be nicer if trees would grow. We get lots of wild roses and there are plenty of gophers and plenty of dry weather. We have artesian wells and plenty of winds. Farming is the worst business in Dakota. The animals are horses, cows, oxen and buffaloes.
>
> —A ten-year-old girl reflecting on Dakota in 1890

Beadle County

Area, 1,250 square miles
Population, 1925 - 20,268; 1945 - 18,773; 1980 - 19,195
County Seat, Huron. Population 13,000

Beadle County lies at the boundary, where crop land turns to range land. It is the transition that Hamlin Garland called the "Middle Border." During the wet cycle farmers plow up some of the range land and regret it during the dry cycles. They live in that uneasy zone of pasture or plow. Somehow the tension gets translated into population changes, and maybe this is why Huron is one of the few larger cities in South Dakota that has not grown the last few years; in fact, it is losing a bit. But this is not to say Huron can't grow. It grew 5,000 people in eight years from 1880 to 1888.

What grows in Beadle County are pheasants. It is Beadle, Sanborn, and Spink Counties in the state that are the best known for pheasants, and it is Huron that is considered the Pheasant Capitol.

The chief topographic feature of Beadle County is the James River, which bisects the county into east and west parts. In the western section are the Wessington Hills.

Other historical points are several claim shanties, pioneer trails stamped into virgin sod, legend trees, pioneer cemeteries, and several sites where Indian teepee rings are located.

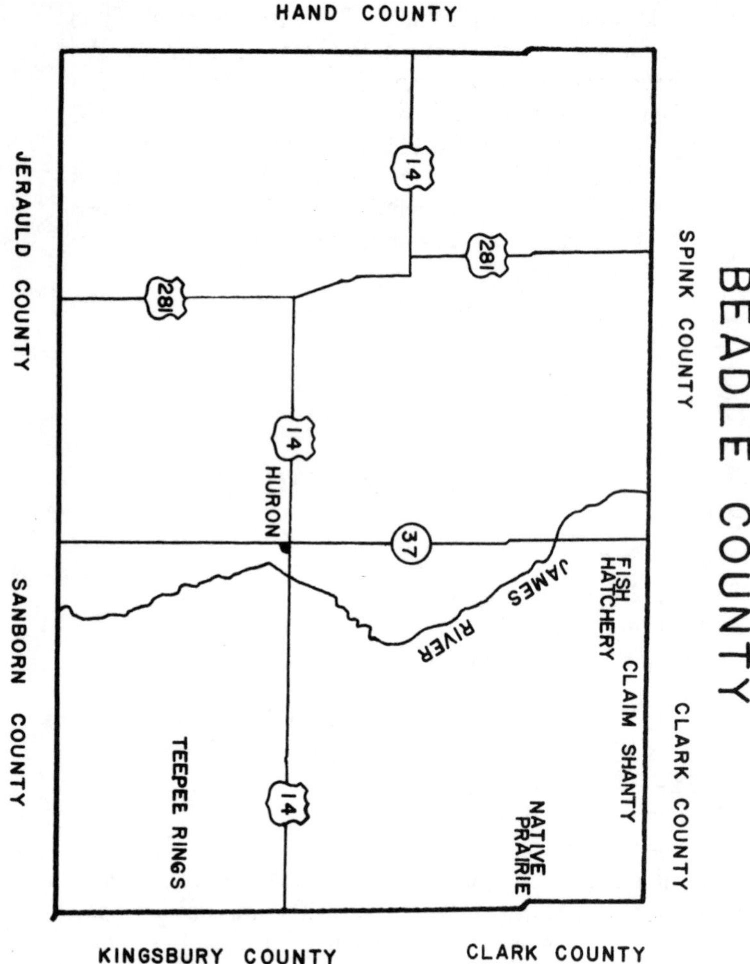

Beyond the Forest

Beadle County

In the settling of our country, waves of settlers came pouring farther and farther west onto less and less habitable land. Out on these western lands, the Government removed one class of people, the Indians, and gave the land to another class, the European immigrants. The railroad, exploding its way into the wilderness, spilled out the pioneers at its terminus. It then continued to serve as the connecting link with the so-called civilized world. It was the nourishing artery that fed the West with goods, services, communication, and transportation.

In 1878-80, as the railroad approached Huron, in Beadle County, it spewed out Germans, Dutch, Norwegians, Swedes, Russians, and a few other immigrants upon the treeless plains. They carried a few worldy possessions and an optimism that climaxed at the Mitchell Land Office. From there, armed with the directions and instructions on claiming land, they set out on rutted, dusty roads to the vast prairie.

Some of the arrivals were speculators and exploiters. All were convinced that land was the necessary prerequisite for success.

With such a mixture of foreign arrivals, a Saturday night in town was a babel of tangled communication. But it soon became apparent to members of the opposite sex that body language was as effective as verbal persuasion. The result was the breaking of the language barrier and a mixing of nationalities.

Most pioneers arrived in the spring, and the flush of the green prairies matched the flush of enthusiasm that glowed in the faces of the settlers. Here was the opportunity for which they had traveled so far. The memories of the old country were dimmed by visions of the future. The promise of the land was like tasting one's dessert before dinner. But the settlers need plans — for a home, livestock, grain crops, and, yes, trees. Trees to make their shelter homelike, to cut the wind, and to break the monotony of the prairie. But where were the trees? The eastern Woodland Indian called Lake Whitewood, a lake to the west, the last lake with trees. Lakes to the west were often muddy and dry. The Indians called the James River, which flowed through the county, Whitewood River because white skeletons of dead trees related a history of drought and prairie fires. The river was, in fact, on the eastern margin of what some early explorers called the Great American Desert.

The pioneer spirit, however, was not bathed in sour waters and dry land. It was buoyed by the Homestead Act, which allowed each settler 160 acres, for living on the land for five years, plus 160 acres by pre-emption at $1.25 per acre. In addition, a settler could claim 160 acres under the Timber Culture Act of 1878 by keeping alive 675 trees per acres, on ten acres, for eight years. So settlers could claim, all told, 480 acres of land for $200, the cost of pre-emption. Needed most were trees, a house, the fortitude to withstand the elements, and a wife with a sacrificing ambition. The first summer, tar-paper claim shanties and sod houses dotted the prairie. That, plus the continuous activity of trying to keep warm, generated enough body heat to survive the winter.

After a home was established, the planting of trees was begun. The 6,750 trees on each 10-acre tree claim had to be cultivated and watered. Water, like trees, was scarce on the plains. It had to be hauled by stone boat from the nearest creek or collected from the roof of the house.

During years of above-average rainfall, the trees flourished. On the upland sites, green ash, American elm, slippery elm, and box elder were planted. In the wetter spots, cottonwood and willow grew. In the dry years, which followed a cycle of wet years, only the most hardy survived. The top branches of the tree were the first to die and, if the whole tree was not killed, it often grew back in distorted form from the lower branches or root sprouts. The dead wood furnished a temporary supply of firewood.

After the dust bowl days, a new cycle of tree planting took place. From 1932 to 1940 government-subsidized shelter belts appeared. This time a greater variety of trees and shrubs was planted. Introduced species were planted alongside the natives. The most common introduced species were the Siberian elm, Russian olive, and Chinese lilac. A few native ponderosa pine and red cedar were included in some plantings.

From these two major tree planting cycles, interacting with cycles of drought and moist years, have come almost all the trees in Beadle County. A total of fourteen species were used. One can look at a group of trees and assign to it one of the two cycles of tree planting activity. The trees planted under the Timber Culture Act are today celebrating a centennial. But only a few of the original 100-year-old trees remain. Most are in towns, where they have been watered. They are noticeably bigger than their country relatives.

The shelterbelt trees, now about 35 to 45 years old, are undergoing considerable stress, and those on the drier soils are dead. One species, the Russian olive, thrives. It has begun to occupy the edges of ponds and creeks and may one day grow more successfully than some of the native trees. It may even become a pest.

Yes, the people in Beadle County now have trees, but the trees are only holding their own with the help of man. Few places exist where conditions are suitable for native trees to establish themselves. The one oasis is the James River Valley, but there most of the trees are young — seldom over 50 to 70 years old. The really old trees are the bur oaks and green ash in the northeast-facing ravines of the Wessington Hills. There, on the very western edge of Beadle County, is one of the last western relicts of what was once a much more extensive forest, which has perhaps been there for five or six thousand years. Some trees approach 400 to 500 years in age.

The mark of success of a forest is its ability to maintain itself by reseeding. The Wessington Hills area and the James River Valley are the only areas in Beadle County where this occurs. They are also the sites of Indian camps and spring-fed rivulets. Pioneers traveled many miles to get to sources of water and wood, and such areas often served as Sunday picnic sites.

The conclusion of this little tale is that it took a tough, special kind of tree to survive the Beadle County climate. It also took a tough, special kind of pioneer to settle the land. Together they made Beadle County a special place to live.

You like a country or you don't
Perhaps it's faith and hope that makes you like it.
Old Johnson died last night.
He believed to his last breath that this was good country.

—A Beadle County Pioneer

Jerauld County

Area, 531 square miles
Population, 1925 - 6,268; 1945 - 4,202; 1980 - 2,929
County Seat, Wessington Springs. Population 1,203

Horse thieving seemed to be the first industry in Jerauld County, but when things got too bad the local Methodist minister took matters into his own hands and drove out the thieves, cleaned up the town, and announced that this was God's Country. So complete was his job that by 1940 Wessington Springs could still boast it never had a saloon or pool hall.

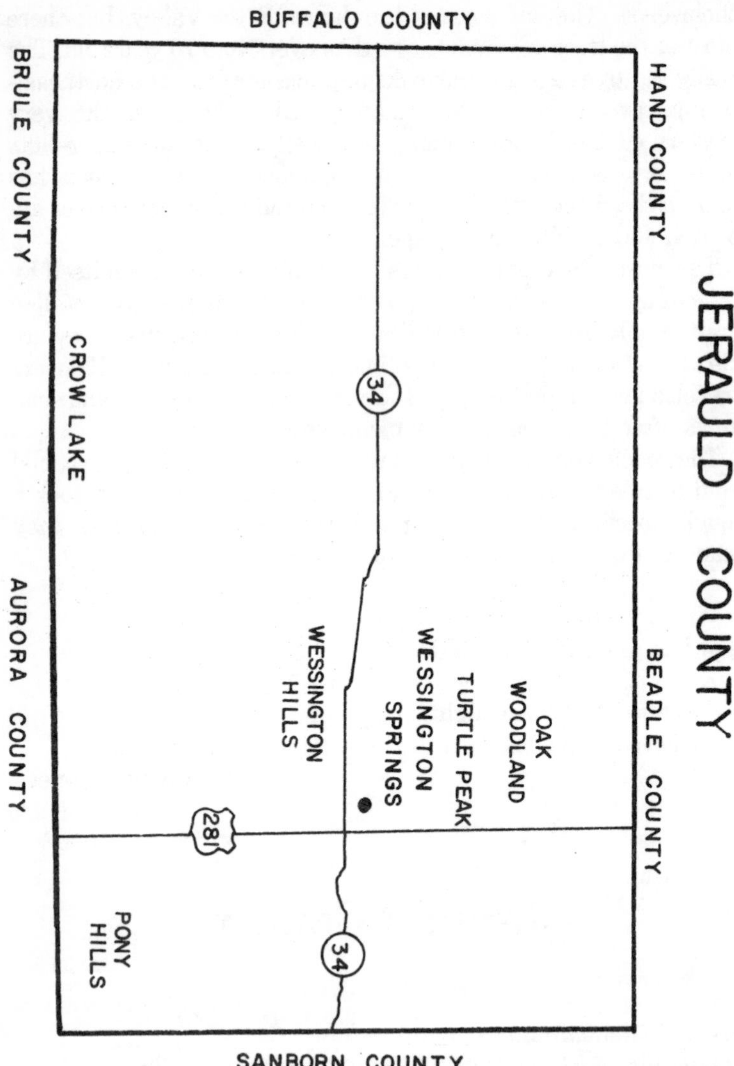

Wessington Springs is an historical city. The Nobles Trail is marked outside the town on top of the hills. It is the first road built in South Dakota (1857) and extended from Fort Ridgley in Minnesota, to Fort Lookout on the Missouri near Chamberlain.

The road brought people into Jerauld County and the county enjoyed a period of prosperity in early 1900s. It reached its zenith in population in 1925. After that it has been a steady decline that has reduced the population 54 per cent. When the people disappeared, the small towns such as Waterburg and most of Lane disappeared. Now only two towns remain in the county, Alpena and Wessington Springs.

The Crow Lake Recreation Area is located in the southwest part of the county and provides a summer recreation spot.

The First Car

Jerauld County

Owning the first car in Jerauld County wasn't easy. Fran and Frank had purchased, a few weeks before, a new 1904 Chalmers with gas lights and pneumatic horn. They had gone all the way to Alpena to pick it up. Now it stood on the main street in Wessington Springs, and everyone stopped by to look.

Frank remembered the first time he had started it on Main Street. He had advanced the gas but had forgotten to retard the spark. It started with one big bang, and horses all along the hitching rail reared back. As he watched scrambling people trying to control their horses, he remembered another incident. He had driven over a hill and there, on the other side, was a farmer mowing prairie grass. The startled farm team took off, hit a rock, and threw the farmer from the mower, dislocating his shoulder and breaking several ribs. Another day his Chalmers had frightened the mailman's team, which stood unhitched and eating while the mailman was having lunch. The mailman hiked for two miles to where his horses stopped.

But the dogs, they were the worst. Every dog in the neighborhood seemed to appear when Frank left the house. Once as he drove out of town, a German shepherd punctured his tire when he stopped at an intersection. When he took the car over to the garage to fix the tire, the rest of the dogs took turns using the right front wheel as a scent station.

Tire on, Frank was challenged to a race by seven dogs. As some dropped out in exhaustion, other barking dogs took up the chase.

The dog episode inspired Frank to hatch a plan. He would have Fran fire blanks in the dogs' faces to scare them off. One bright morning — too early, he thought, for the dogs — Frank and Fran started out for Huron. How wrong he was! One dog aroused the rest. Frank gave the car the gas, while Fran hung out the side, shooting blanks in rapid succession. Over the hill they went, at times hitting 40 miles per hour. Enter the preacher, making an early morning parish call. The preacher's horse, a little bay hitched to a buggy, gave a sudden lurch, flipped the buggy out of its track, and took off across the prairie in a direction never before blazed by weak-wheeled buggies. Frank and Fran missed church the next couple of Sundays.

Roads, in those days, took off at a slant in the shortest distance between two points instead of following straight-angled paths. The low spots were deep ruts that resembled miniature badlands. The ruts were often so deep that the car steered its own course. This presented a problem when two cars in the same rut met. Often it was necessary to stop and lift one car out of the rut so that the other could pass. Going west from Wessington Springs was especially tough after a rain. The only way to make it up the big hill was to back up, since the car had better traction in reverse. Often there was some question about the intended direction when one had to make several runs at the same hill. Once Fran put dinner on the table two hours early because she thought she saw Frank coming, when actually he was going.

It was getting so Fran didn't want to go riding anymore. She had psychosomatic dog fever; she loathed dogs. Her best dresses were mud-spattered, and she hated losing her shoes in mud holes when she had to push.

But times were changing, although some questioned if the change was progress. By 1911, many of their neighbors drove new cars. Runaways and accidents were more frequent. The local doctor, who incidentally was usually the first person in town to get a new car, was kept busy setting broken bones and bandaging bashed heads resulting when spooked horses failed to accept the importance of the new machines.

Later Frank and Fran, accustomed to their new machine, decided on a trip to the Black Hills. Leaving Thursday morning, they arrived Saturday night — 340 miles at 18 miles per hour. They did not, of course, count two flat tires, the three times the engine overheated, or getting stuck five times. They travelled along in ruts, zipped down steep hills at 40 miles an hour, and climbed hills at a turtle's pace. Fran often got out of the car and ran alongside for the exercise on some of the longer hills. Frank was glad it hadn't rained, for then the trip would have taken five days. The local paper reported that the trip was uneventful and made in the remarkably short period of three days.

By 1917 several fatal accidents had occurred in Wessington Springs. Cars tipped over on their occupants, cars banged into each other at intersections, and cars ran down pedestrians.

It was the beginning of the Age of the Automobile.

In the 1920s numerous model-T Fords were being purchased, and by 1922 Jerauld County had built 17 miles of gravel roads. Three years later the first low-priced Chevies were on the market. A new model cost $500, and gas was 15 cents per gallon. Also in 1925, work began on the Chicago-to-Black-Hills road, to be called the Buffalo Trail (now Highway 34).

The decades marked a period of growth for Wessington Springs. It was now the cultural center of the region. Stone steps were built to the top of Legion Hill so that one could view the ridge of hills that cut through central South Dakota. These hills were a preglacial high between two drainage systems and extended in a series from the south; Bijou Hills, Pony Hills, Wessington Hills, and on to Orient Hills in the north. The bedrock in this 400-foot-high ridge is Pierre Shale and Niobrara Chalk, which outcrops where erosion has washed off the thin glacial till. It is all part of what is now the eastern edge of the Missouri Coteau.

At the base of these hills flowed numerous springs that proved a natural setting for a settlement. There were Gravel Pit Springs, Big Springs, Iron Springs, Sulphur Springs, and numerous springs named after people. The most famous is Wessington Springs, named for a guide with W.H. Noble, who laid out the Noble's Trail.

Growing in the larger ravines are small oak woodlands that abound with wild game. On the highest hill are numerous teepee rings and a large stone turtle effigy, believed to be the burial site of Chief Big Turtle. The relics are also proof that the Indians found the Wessington Hills a favorite site for summer hunting camps.

Back now to the thriving little city, showing signs of cultural development. Wessington Springs College and a Free Methodist Seminary with Shakespearian Gardens offered a cultural menu of art, literature, and music. There were a community social club, an opera house, and a symphony orchestra. On the day of a cultural affair, townspeople turned out dressed in garb that stressed the event's importance to the community.

By now Frank and Fran drove a new blue Buick, attended all

the social affairs, and on Sunday afternoon supported the Wessington Springs baseball team. Wessington Springs residents had great social, civic, and church pride and were not reluctant to verbalize it.

Today the college, Methodist seminary, opera house, orchestra, social clubs, and the Wessington Springs baseball team have vanished. Frank and Fran are also gone. But the cars still roll on. Accidents are more frequent, gas has gone up, roads have improved, and the speed is terrific. Most cars speed past the sleepy little town. The cultural vacuum is filled by a drive-in theatre, fast food stops, television, a swimming pool, and teenagers who ramble around in souped-up cars. Old-timers look back to the time when Wessington Springs really had a cultural atmosphere. Some climb the stone steps of Legion Hill to witness the setting sun. As the last gorgeous colors of the sunset paint the sky and darkness spreads across the land, the vastness of the starry universe blends with the sparkling lights of the little city below.

In the dimness of the distance, flickering lights twinkle along the old Buffalo Trail. A parade of the past? The lights are strung in a line, as if history is unrolling. Closer, the watcher on Legion Hills sees a blue Buick, black Olds, Dodge, Moon, Whippet, Essex, Willis, Rambler, Hudson Terroplane, Nash, Studebaker, Franklin, and Reo, mixed in with Model T's, Model A's, and Chevies. Bringing up the rear is a 1904 Chalmers, its pneumatic horn sounding a resonant honk as it tries to make the big hill in one try.

The Antique Auto Club is homeward bound from the annual Fourth of July parade.

McPherson County

Area, 1,157 square miles
Population, 1930 - 8,774; 1945 - 7,679; 1980 - 4,027
County Seat, Leola. Population 645

Eureka, we found it, the largest acclaimed inland wheat shipping center in the world, growing and prospering there in McPherson County together with Hillsview, that town with two banks and a view to the future. Also there is the big sun Wetonka. But all these places dimmed to reality when the people started to disappear. Some 55 per cent of the people were lost in a period of 50 years. They have dribbled away at the rate of about 94 per year since the boom population of the late 20s. Only Eureka and Leola have maintained their population.

Leola, however, did have a couple of good scares when twice it almost got burned out. Once a prairie fire ripped out of the coteau in 1889 and left only 12 buildings standing. But here in the land of kucken and borst, things happen, and Leola rose up again from the ashes and in 1900 was again declared the county seat.

Other things happened in McPherson County, too. Hamlin Garland wrote about the people and his description of blizzards has left an imprint on many a school child's mind.

A look at the sites of interest in McPherson County reveals Ordway Prairie, a sample of the original native grassland that has been preserved by the Nature Conservancy. There is an Indian prayer rock with pictures carved deep into the granite north of Ordway. There are Dead Horse Gulch, teepee rings, buffalo kill sites, and turtle effigies — all marking the past when Indians roamed the area around Ordway.

In the grassland and gulches are sometimes wooded retreats and occasionally, seeping out from the base of the coteau, a prairie fen. They all twist into a pattern and provide a welcome mosaic for the visitor.

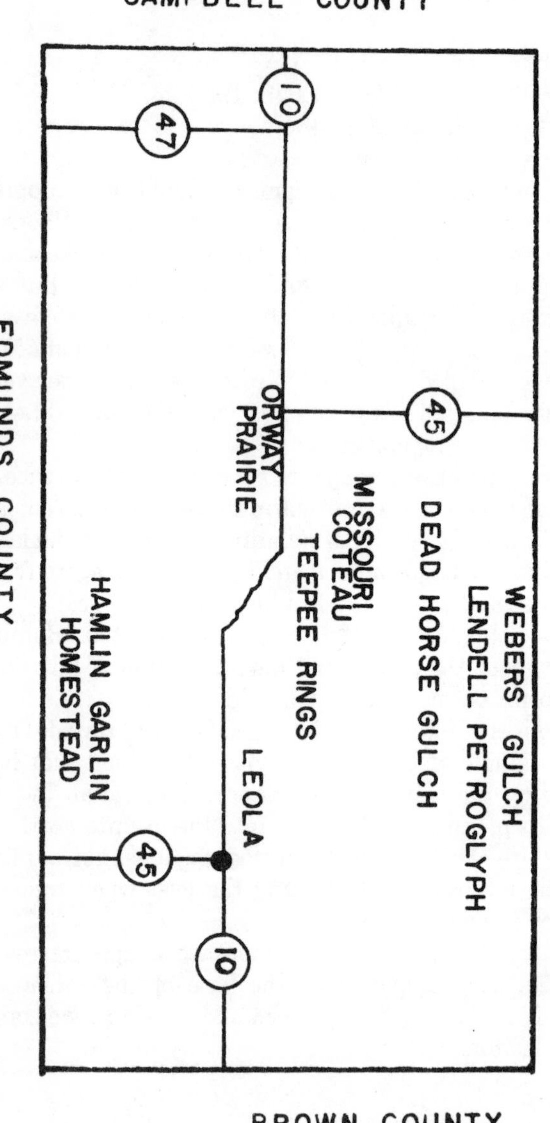
CAMPBELL COUNTY
MCPHERSON COUNTY
STATE OF NORTH DAKOTA
FORBES
WEBERS GULCH
LENDELL PETROGLYPH
DEAD HORSE GULCH
MISSOURI COTEAU
TEEPEE RINGS
ORWAY PRAIRIE
LEOLA
HAMLIN GARLIN HOMESTEAD
EDMUNDS COUNTY
BROWN COUNTY
10
47
45
45
10

The Red Elk Way
McPherson County

> He knew that man's heart away from nature becomes hard; he knew that lack of respect for growing, living things soon led to lack of respect for humans too. So he kept his youth close to its softening influence.
>
> —Luther Standing Bear

> There is yet no ethic dealing with man's relation to land and to the animals and plants which grow upon it . . . The land-relation is strictly economic, entailing privileges but not obligations.
>
> —Aldo Leopold

Red Elk stopped. He turned his ear to the wind. A strange silence hung in the air. Then he heard again a dull trembling roar that seemed to pulse, swell, and fade. He looked to the sky for the ominous thunder clouds that often welled out of the southwest but saw none. He sniffed the air and scanned the skyline for a tattletale whiff of smoke. Still the perceptible roar. Red Elk's eyes strained as he looked down the valley. At the edge of the hills a faint cloud of dust rose and twisted into the sky. With one motion Red Elk was astride his horse and galloping to the highest point on the Missouri Coteau.

There, below him, raced the biggest buffalo herd he had ever seen. They sucked the air into the valley as they went. Dust swirled, to be trampled again and again by the pounding hooves. Behind them, the dry brown grass was beaten into the blackened soil. Red Elk watched until the prairie was again silent. With the tall prairie grass brushing the flanks of his horse, he rode back to the summer camp, where his mate, Bright Water, was preparing food.

Hobbling his horse, he wondered if she would believe him when he told her about the thousands of buffalo he had seen. He thought how he would tell her, as they sat down to a meal of starchy cattail gruel, buffalo beans, Indian turnips, wild onions, and violet leaves flavored with oxalis.

"Ho, you sure are trying to keep us healthy," he stated.

She looked at him rather patronizingly, for she knew that only three weeks ago the whole family felt weak from too few greens in their diet. She though, "Go dig your own turnips," but she said instead, "What did you see today?"

His eyes lit up, and he was about to relate the great excitement he had seen on the plains. Then he remembered that yesterday she had asked that same question. Couldn't she think of something better to say? He went back to quietly munching his turnips, for he remembered last week he had answered the question by bragging about his sighting elk, mule deer, white-tailed deer, bear, beaver, and muskrats, and then the next day had come home with a half-grown rabbit. He was tired of telling her about the ducks, geese, prairie chickens, and grouse out there on the plains and coming home to dried turnips and greens.

Slowly a smile came over his face, and Bright Water, sensing a change, looked at him intently. He adjusted the buffalo hide thrown over his shoulders to keep out the night chill and said, "I'll bet you one papoose carrier filled with cattail fluff that we'll be eating buffalo tongue tomorrow night."

She threw a cottonwood branch on the fire and watched the sparks flash into the darkening night. It was too dark to look at him to see if he was serious, so she said, "Are you going to gather the water rush (the giant reed) necessary for the back support?"

"Yes," he promised, "and I'll get the buffalo sinew necessary to tie it together."

Bright Water now sensed that her mate had really seen the sacred buffalo on the plains, for a great hunter was not easily trapped into women's work. So, turning away from her husband, she reached over and picked up their smallest child, who had been painted with the yellow from the goldenrod, the red ochre from the stream bank, and blue from the woodland berries, and said, "Father is going after buffalo tomorrow, and we will again have meat in abundance."

Red Elk, his family, and tribe lived off the land in a system that provided everything they needed — their food, medicine, shelter, and clothing. The earth created the system that Red Elk depended on, as it had created Red Elk. "The earth was my mother, the sky was my father, and the sun gave power to it all." It was a basic system from which all other systems could be measured. Red Elk lived within it and drew from it what he needed in his winter camp on the Missouri River and his summer hunting camp on the coteau.

Red Elk and tribe had followed this pattern of seasonal camps for many years. As the warm spring came, they loaded their belongings on a travois and headed for a favorite site on the coteau. There the buffalo were abundant, and standing on its high points, Red Elk could look for miles to locate the buffalo grazing range. He looked forward to his first seasonal sighting of the buffalo. It was a time for celebration.

One summer, Red Elk, arriving at camp, rode out to his favorite buffalo lookout point. He felt a strangeness in his bones, for on the way to the summer camp there had been talk of Wasicum (the ones that take the cream, the white men), railroads, fences, and plows.

As he reached the lookout point, he saw in the distant valley what looked like an ant, splitting the verdant carpet with a ribbon of black. For days Red Elk watched from the hill as the ribbon grew wider. More ants and more ribbons appeared, until a patchwork of black festooned the valley. Near each of the black patches stood a structure that resembled a misplaced box. Red Elk's heart was heavy.

One day Red Elk looked over his beloved valley for the last time. To the east he saw a thin wagon trail that wound like a scar across the virgin prairie. He watched a horse-drawn vehicle creep, like an ant, toward a cluster of shacks. Around the shacks the black patches had grown larger.

He closed his eyes, hoping to hear again the thunder of buffalo charging through the valley. In vain he waited for the swirl and swell of dust to fill the sky. Sadness filled his tired body, and he felt lonely. He stood there, almost fixed in space, then slowly turned and drifted off into the past.

Meanwhile, back in the valley, as Red Elk roamed the hills, Ben and Frieda alighted from the immigrant train at Eureka. Frieda had seen a poster back in Germany that proclaimed: "Sued Dakota die reichste Kornkammer die velt." It was enough to make Frieda convince Ben to cut their ties with the European world and start their long journey to America. Their life savings sewed into their clothes, their meager possessions in two large trunks, they stood on the main street in Eureka with many of their compatriots. They wondered what awaited them on the prairie.

Frieda, whose decision it was to leave Germany, looked over at

Ben and, using what little English she could muster, said, "Well." Ben, looking down at the ground, muttered in broken German, "Tomorrow we'll know."

So the next morning Ben and Frieda spent most of their life savings on a rickety wagon, a team of oxen that had seen better days, and supplies to last a couple of weeks. Loading up, they set out for the margin of civilization. The shacks, which showed signs of unskilled construction, became fewer and fewer, until there it was — the land that was free for the taking! Ben felt overwhelmed at the vastness of the land, but Frieda, of more resolute determination, got out of the wagon and capitalized on her command of the English language. "Good," she pronounced. Ben, wondering why he had been talked into coming to this uninviting place, looked around. He looked at Frieda, walked over and located the surveyor mark, then nailed three posts together in triangular fashion. This proclaimed their occupancy of a quarter section of land. He walked back to Frieda, took her by the hand, looked up to the distant coteau where Red Elk had watched their arrival, and said, "Frieda, wir sind heim." Frieda, still with a stubborn determination to master the English language, said, "Home."

Sleeping under a canvas stretched from the side of the wagon was not conducive to the improvement of Frieda's English, and Ben soon learned that mud, cold, mosquitoes, and discomfort were the same in any language. Frieda's natural ability to describe pioneer conditions in vivid German, spiced with expletives, soon prompted Ben to drive back to Eureka to register his claim and buy the lumber to build a tar-paper claim shanty. It was to be their home for the next few years.

With neighbors' help, Frieda and Ben were able to construct their home in a few weeks, and the business of homesteading began. Frieda again went back to learning English. New shanties, some made of sod, popping up at the rate of four per square mile on good level land, thinned out as one approached the coteau.

Ben and Frieda planted wheat, as did all the settlers. Wheat was a way to get rich fast, so they could build a castle on this vast land to replace the shanty. According to European standards, they were rich. But then came the winter. Coal was scarce in Eureka, and money even scarcer. There was no wood within 70 miles of home. So it was out to gather buffalo chips, twist hay, and pile animal manure to dry for later burning. A cold, lonely winter, and the only consolation was that everyone was suffering.

The first few years the wheat fields were small and crops meager, and Ben and Frieda lived partly the way of Red Elk. Herds of antelope, plentiful in the hills, and bogged down in deep snows of the valley, were easily slaughtered for winter food. Ducks, geese, grouse, prairie chicken, rabbit, and deer furnished meat for much of the year, while prairie plants and fish also contributed. But as the fields grew larger, the game grew scarcer. These were the years when towns on the coteau flourished. Railroads hauled in supplies and hauled out wheat. Durum wheat yielded 30 bushels an acre, and the price was up to 90 cents. Frieda and Ben prospered, along with their neighbors.

Ben and Frieda looked to the land and knew it had been good to them. They now had 100 acres plowed out into wheat. The rest was pasture and forage for livestock. They built a sturdy frame house, a barn with a hayloft, and a granary to store their crops. They were no longer dependent on much of the Red Elk system. They looked forward to buying more land and diversifying their operation. They knew that the tall grass prairie, from Texas to Canada, was now almost a continuous field of wheat.

Then came drought, low prices, grasshoppers, hard winters, and rust on the wheat. Rust turned the binders red, settled on the skin like a fine red rouge, and turned the wheat kernel into worthless chaff. What looked like a bumper crop was in reality a waving field of failure. Farmers went broke; bankers and land companies took over the land.

Settlers began their long scientific and technological battle against nature. Wheat had become a massive monoculture, and rust spread like fire through the entire belt. So out of the agricultural colleges came rust-resistant varieties, which were sent into the battle. Koto, Marquis, Ceres, and Thacher all had their day, but the rust fungus was never far behind. The day came when it looked as if rust, drought, and low prices had won. The price of wheat dropped to 32 cents a bushel. But again there was hope — in "Hope," a new variety of wheat with rust resistance that produced Midas, Rival, and Vesta varieties.

Out of the battle with rust and drought emerged a new breed of farmer, for only the hardy persisted. Most of their neighbors had packed and moved away, but Ben and Frieda expanded their farm to 640 acres. Ben, feeling it too risky to plant all wheat, diversified. He began to use fertilizer, for the many crops had taken much from the soil.

By now Frieda's English had improved, and she vented much of her feeling on the government, the weather, and on Ben, when he did not get home in time to milk the cows. She and Ben now had a family, a big family, as did other pioneer farm couples, and at times Frieda was much too busy to worry about English. Her chief words were "get," "help," and adjectives that described food, drink, shelter, and sleep. In between, there was another baby to take care of.

After many years of farming Ben looked at his fields of golden wheat and felt a sense of pride in accomplishment. Their family had grown. One day when Ben came back from the fields, he walked into the kitchen. There he was greeted by the familiar sight of Frieda peeling potatoes. He watched her for a few minutes, then with a resolution that surprised him said, "We're moving to town." The suddenness of the proposal so startled Frieda that she sat and stared. Taking this as an advantage, Ben continued, "I've picked out the place, and we'll move next month."

Frieda knew at last that Ben had beat her to the punch. She picked up the potatoes, put them on the stove, and said, "I suppose William will be taking over the farm? But he isn't even married!"

"Oh, but he will be," Ben said. "He's bringing home the girl he was living with at college." Now Frieda knew it was time to move. She couldn't understand young people and their free and easy ways. Hadn't she told Bill that good girls didn't act that way?

So it was that William and Peggy took over the family farm. Bill's first move was to buy a four-wheel drive tractor, expand the operation by buying more land, and specialize in raising feed for his livestock. He was a farmer who specialized in channeling biological material through biological machines, called cattle, into a salable product called meat. He did this by intensive concentration of capital and energy into one major effort.

As William prospered, his acreage grew, and he relied on hybrid seeds, fertilizer, herbicides, and pesticides. He figured his income and balanced it with his expenses. He was an agri-businessman, a power farmer, whose office was his pickup. He looked at his farm, not as a way to make a living, but as a way to make money. His farm was no longer a way of life but a business that paid off in proportion to his investment. It was an energy-dependent, capital-intensive, production-efficient system.

A comparison of the three systems — Red Elk's, Ben's, and Bill's — is revealing. Red Elk produced enough food for himself and his family; Ben and Frieda produced for themselves and 22 others; Bill and Peggy produced for themselves and 103 others, if the grain produced was fed directly to people, but only 19 when their grain was converted to animal products. Red Elk obtained from 30 to 50 calories from the system for every one he put in; Ben and Frieda, the diversified grain farmers, got three to seven calories for every one put in; and Bill and Peggy, the livestock feeders, got back two-tenths to five-tenths of a calorie for every one calorie put in. On an energy basis Bill was going in the hole. Red Elk used human energy; Ben used wood, coal, and horsepower; and Bill required a huge input of electricity and fossil fuel for operation. If the energy Bill required was calculated on the basis of slave energy, Bill required the equivalent of over 2,000 slaves to run his system.

A comparison of the system on the basis of land conservation shows that during Red Elk's time, soil was being formed on the tall grass prairie at a rate of one inch every 500 years, and lakes and marshes were filled at a rate of one inch every 400 years. During Ben's time, erosion had set in instead of soil deposition on the prairie, and the lakes were filling at a rate of one inch every 100 years. With Bill's massive operation, erosion had speeded up this rate to one inch every 10 years on sloping land and one inch every 100 years on gently rolling land. Deposition in lakes had speeded up to one to two inches in 40 years. In some areas farms were being abandoned and turned back to grass because of erosion.

Bill wondered about these things, but he never once considered making himself part of the system, as Red Elk had. He considered himself the operator of the system, and he operated it as if it were all one big machine that turned out a salable product. He used all the newest techniques that would increase his efficiency and make the system produce more. He used genetic hybrid seed, eliminated competition from foreign species, and controlled the environment as much as possible. This meant large amounts of agricultural chemicals, irrigation, and energy. Bill was completely dependent on fossil fuel for the energy supply to keep him operating.

Bill watched Peggy cooking supper. It was early, because she wanted to drive into town for bowling. She was in a hurry to tell her friends about their new car and the trip they planned to California. "I see the Arabs are going to cut down on their oil production, so we're going to be hard pressed for gas this summer. It probably means we can't make our California trip," Bill said.

"Gosh!" Peggy thought. "What will I tell the girls now?"

Bill continued, "If it gets bad enough, I guess we'll have to let part of the farm go back to grass."

"I'll certainly not let that spoil my bowling party." Peggy said as she took off.

After Peggy left, Bill sat there on the porch a long time, looking up at the distant hills where Red Elk had once stood. A heavy fog covered the tops of the rolling hills, and Bill, who had often heard stories of the Indians in the hills, imagined the shapes and shadows of horsemen. He wondered what the land was like when the Indian roamed it. He wondered about their freedom, and their way of life, and if there was something in their way of living that would help him. There he sat, with the energy equivalent of 2,000 slaves turning a monoculture of a few species into a salable product, and wondered why he had become so dependent on things he could not control. What would happen if his energy supply was cut off? What would happen when the soil eroded away and did not produce? Would the plague of rust come back to ruin his crops? Would he be able to reclaim the land and recover? He dozed off.

The car door slammed, and Peggy called, "What have you been up to?"

Bill looked up and said, as if in a daze, "I wonder, if Red Elk were here today, what he would do."

"Well, I'll bet he wouldn't sit around and sleep all night in a chair!" Peggy jeered. "Let's go to bed."

Asleep again, Bill dreamed about the Red Elk way. Somewhere, deep in his sleep, he thought that he must learn to combine the things that Red Elk knew into his own system. He must try to retain those things of his system that were good and learn from Red Elk's way those things that would help him. He believed he was trapped in a technological web not of his own making, and he felt a need for more freedom. As he turned and tossed, he dreamed of buffalo and Indians thundering through the valley. As the dust settled, a lone Indian rode to the crest of the distant hill, paused for a moment to survey the valley behind him, and disappeared.

When Bill awoke in the morning he had a strange urge to climb to the hill where Red Elk had once stood. As he surveyed the vastness of the valley, a sense of freedom lifted his spirits. He looked for signs of the system that Red Elk had once known. He knew that up there on the coteau, some of the system was still intact, and he felt a sense of satisfaction. He was glad because sometime in the future the system would be needed to develop a new land ethic that would allow him and his family to live in harmony with the land. He recalled the words of Native American N. Scott Momaday:

> In our society as a whole we conceive of the land in terms of ownership and use. It is a lifeless medium of exchange; it has for most of us, I suspect, no more spirituality than has an automobile, say, or a refrigerator. And our laws confirm us in this view, for we can buy and sell the land, we can exclude each other from it, and in the context of ownership we can use it as we will. Ownership implies use, and use implies consumption.

But with the Indian view, Momaday says:

> You say that I use the land, and I reply, yes, it is true; but it is not the first truth. The first truth is that I love the land; I see that it is beautiful; I delight in it; I am alive in it . . . It is this ancient ethic of the Native American that must shape our efforts to preserve the earth and the life upon and within it.

Some of the 42 grain elevators in Eureka in 1902 when wheat was king. Eureka claimed to be the largest primary grain shipping center in the United States. Below is one of the wheat fields that produced the wheat.

Photos — Eureka - 75 Years

Roberts County

Area, 1,111 square miles
Population, 1925 - 7,704; 1945 - 4,972; 1980 - 10,911
County Seat, Sisseton. Population 2,787

Paul War Cloud Grant, Indian artist, had an imagination. He thought about the past and put it on canvas. His habit was to etch into the faces of his people their feeling for their land. He dreamed of the future of Indians and whites using the land together. He put it all on canvas from an Indian scaffold funeral to joyful white and Indian living together on the productiveness of the land. The latter painting now hangs in the Governor's office. He captured the life style of Sisseton Indians and placed it in Pohlen Art Center at Sisseton.

Roberts County remembers the Indian but it also remembers the fur trader and pioneer. In 1819 Hazen Mooers built a trading post on the west shores of Big Stone Lake. Joseph Brown built at Buffalo Lake (1843) and later at Sieche Hollow (1848) a fur trading post. The Renvilles, still a family name in the area, brought religion to the Indians. In 1868 churches were built, and the oldest Christian cemetery in northeastern South Dakota is located in the Big Coulee. It has markers dating from 1860.

Roberts County has 17 ghost towns with the most recent, White Rock, whose last business closed in 1976.

It is here in Roberts County where the Red River of the North begins at the outlet of Lake Traverse. To the south is Big Stone Lake and the beginning of the Minnesota River. Between the two lakes is the continental divide. It has been marked and designated as a National Natural Landmark.

West of the Sunset

Roberts County

Maggie and Willie traveled for 29 days after leaving Old Fort Snelling. It seemed like more to Maggie. Westward, always westward, they traveled. It was now four days since she had seen

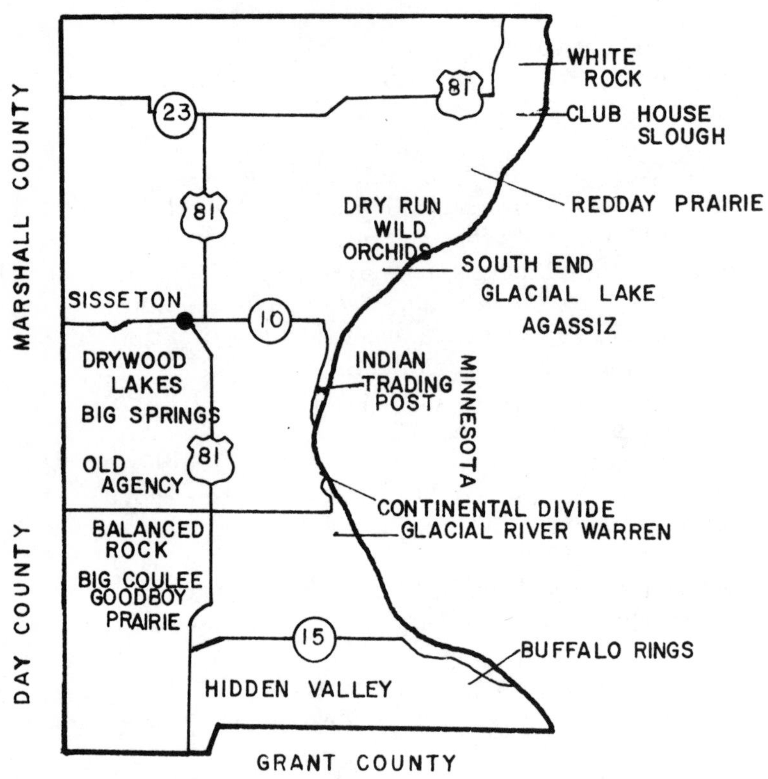

any human beings, except for some Indians on a distant ridge. Every evening Maggie watched the sunset. Every morning, sun to their backs, they moved westward. Maggie imagined they had been traveling west so long and so far that when they finally got to where they were going, it would be west of the sunset.

Two days after their wedding, she had heard Willie ask a trapper the direction to the Red River Valley. The man had told a group of Civil War veterans about free, wonderful land that lay virtually unknown in the northwest. The trapper's flippant reply to a question on location of the valley, had been, "Just two days west of the sunset." Maggie felt that the trapper was serious —

that the land toward which they traveled did indeed lie just west of the sun. What a place for a honeymoon!

She asked Willie if he was tired. One hand clutching the reins of the two stumbling grassburners, Dick and Dan, Willie used his free arm to encircle Maggie's waist.

"Maggie," he said, "it really isn't so bad. What if we had to walk!"

"Great," she said. "I wish we had. We would then have played out when we were still back in civilization. As it is now, we are out here on the edge of nowhere with two worn-out horses and a wagon filled with a plow and other tools. Behind us we're dragging a couple of unsuspecting cows, out into nowhere without a bull."

"Maggie, you haven't seen what's over the hill," replied Willie.

Willie stopped the horses and took Maggie's hand, and they walked to the crest of the hill. As they broke over the edge and looked to the other side, they saw, spreading for miles, the biggest, flattest, longest stretch of land they had ever laid eyes on. There was the fabulous Red River Valley of the north, land of storied legend, where fortune awaited the resourceful. It was the land they sought. Buffalo coming off the hills disappeared into the valley, lost in the tall grasses. It was a place where a fire could rip from one end to the other, leaving the biggest, flattest, longest stretch of utter devastation imaginable.

In the center of the valley Willie spied a shimmer of open water. He pointed the tired animals toward the water, for it was on the western edge of upper Lake Traverse that he wanted to make their home. Water was there in abundance; the soil, heavy and black, would produce a big crop. As they approached the spot, Willie's excitement intensified, but Maggie wanted to turn back. Willie finally managed to coax her off the wagon seat and convince her that in a few days, maybe a few weeks, hundreds of families would arrive to people this fertile land. Maybe even someone with a bull.

Gradually the excitement that Willie felt spread to Maggie. She pushed aside thoughts of Columbus. He was first too but died a pauper and didn't even know what he had discovered. Willie tried to assure her that farther along the lake shore lived a French fur trader named Renville. He didn't mention that Renville's customers, the Indians, also lived nearby.

It was their last night to sleep under the wagon. Maggie slept fitfully. Coyotes howling in the distance seemed to her like children wailing in the wilderness.

An early breakfast of pancakes, salt side pork, and coffee, and Willie was out cutting the dense sod bricks that were to be their home. They built up the walls so that Maggie could barely see over them. They laid two layers of sod lengthwise and one crosswise, using the technique of the bricklayer. They overlapped the joints and dovetailed the corners. In this way the prairie bricks were piled into place, and Willie and Maggie succeeded in bringing shape to the house.

Next they travelled west for miles to the foothills of the coteau for wood for the roof beams. Maggie thought how much nicer a home would be, tucked in the shelter of the trees, but Willie couldn't get away fast enough. He knew that next summer the entire area would be surveyed, and the vast lowlands would be taken first, for it was there that crops could be grown, not in the woods. Reluctantly Maggie consented to go back, unconvinced. If she weren't so busy trying to survive, the vast flat emptiness would drive her mad. While Willie was rhapsodizing over the wonderful country, she secretly stored in the back end of the wagon a little cottonwood tree she had dug up. If she couldn't live in the woods, she'd bring the woods to her home.

Back "home," Willie laid the wooden rafters, added a layer of sod, and thatched the roof off with cord grass to protect the sod and shed the rain. Maggie planted her tree. They agreed the small plant was a sign upon which the eye could focus in the flatness, like an exclamation point announcing the presence of man in a sea of grass. Some day its shadow would provide shelter from the sun.

Maggie suggested they start looking for a bull for their cows. To change the subject (Willie was learning as a new husband), he said, "Maggie, yesterday I saw ducks and geese like you'll never believe on upper Lake Traverse. There were elk, deer, a few buffalo, and even a moose, and who knows what other kinds of game are up there." He omitted mention of the bears and wolves that often came out of the foothills.

"I'll bet they don't give milk" Maggie sniffed.

"Oh, yes," Willie added. "Next year this place will have 10 acres of the nicest wheat you ever saw."

Maggie went in to get supper. And got in the last word. "It sure would be nice to have milk for the pancakes."

Willie's days were filled with plowing, burning a fire break, daydreaming about future wheat crops, and, again and again, hunting and fishing. Maggie hated to stay home alone in the solitude of the prairie. She felt a kinship with the empty cows she had to attend to and stake out every morning. She wondered why she had married a man who wanted only to hunt. She wondered how she could get Willie to stay home, tend to family matters, and not run all over the country exploring. But then, she reasoned, it probably was just as well, since this was certainly no place to bring up a child. When Willie did come home, she wondered how she could convince him to plow up the garden. All that fish to clean and meat to cure!

Summer turned to autumn. Their sod house, turned green by summer rains, was now the red gold of the autumn prairie grasses. Maggie felt like a badger, coming out in the day to live off the land and crawling back into a hole at night. Only the little tree seemed to symbolize the presence of man.

As autumn blended into winter, Maggie grew more lonely. Willie was often away trapping. Sweeping the sodhouse raised a cloud of dust but left the house no cleaner. The tree had lost its leaves, and two unfulfilled cows shared an adjacent room. If she thought about her lot too long, she lost the urge to gather fuel for the winter.

But it was her long trips out into the prairie, with its ceaseless motion of grasses, that eventually soothed her mind. She often wandered for miles, stacking buffalo chips for winter fuel. She found a few pieces of wood along the lake shore. These chips and wood Willie would haul home and stack by the house when he returned.

She was glad she had worked so hard. When winter finally set in, they huddled by the fire during long blizzards. Then she was happy with the sodhouse that seemed part of the prairie, for in the winter it drew heat from the earth and in the summer it cooled from the earth. The winter blizzard shut out the rest of the world. But it kept Willie home long enough to appreciate the benefits of marriage.

With spring, the land awoke. Maggie and Willie looked with new zest toward the future. New neighbors moved in, for the land had recently been surveyed and the word spread. They came from all parts of the country, and Maggie watched with interest for a bull.

This land that attracted a horde of new settlers, this land of Maggie and Willie, started in northeastern South Dakota and spread northward into North Dakota and Canada. One of the biggest valleys in the nation, it measured 300 miles long and extended in places to 100 miles wide. Vermont and New Hampshire would have fitted inside with a bit of valley left over. It was the site of the largest extinct fresh water lake in the country, glacial Lake Agassiz. To the south of this giant lake bed was the Continental Divide and the glacial River Warren (Minnesota River). To the west jutted the tree-sprinkled Coteau des Prairie. There, at the beginning of the valley, was the source of the Red River, Lake Traverse.

It was on upper Lake Traverse, also known as Club House Slough, that Willie and Maggie faced the perils of pioneering. It was there, among the abandoned oxbows and shallow bodies of water where lived abundant wild game, that Willie selected his farm.

Maggie and Willie were squatters or sooners on the land, because they had come before the land was officially opened for settlement. After the valley was surveyed and the settlers came, Maggie and Willie simply readjusted their land boundaries and registered their claim — completely legal.

Settlers poured in at the rate of four per square mile, settling on prime agricultural land. The new neighbors quickly solved Maggie's two problems. She had her choice of bulls. And Willie, hemmed in by neighbors, had to stay home and take care of family matters.

The new settlers planted trees, plowed fields, built fences, put up buildings, and built roads, and in a period of two to three years, the place that had been bypassed in the rush to the west was populated by people who wanted to mine the soil. They found that in the Red River Valley, the 160 acres provided by the Homestead Act could actually support a family.

Today the Red River Valley no longer looks like a sea of grass. It is a mosaic of agricultural productivity, one of the richest agricultural lands in the nation, the producer of food for the world, and the site of industrious farmers and townspeople. It is the place where people, like Maggie and Willie, came, were blessed by the abundance of the earth, and prospered.

Stanley County

Area, 1,521 square miles
Population, 1925 - 2,627; 1945 - 1,688; 1980 - 2,533
County Seat, Ft. Pierre. Population 1,789

Stanley County, along with its neighboring counties of Jones, Jackson, Haakon, and Lyman, shares a western tradition built around the cattle barons, cowboys, Indians, and French fur traders. But even more important, it is a place where the germ of the white man's history was planted. In 1743 the Verendrye party claimed the area for France. In 1817 Fort LaFramboise, later to become Fort Pierre, was started and is the oldest continuous settlement in the state. Here the first church service, by Stephen R. Riggs, was held in 1840, the first white child was born in 1857, and the first school opened in 1870.

When the railroad reached the other side of the river in 1880, a new town was created called Pierre. Ft. Pierre then became the starting point for the freight wagons starting out on the Deadwood Trail to the gold camps in the Black Hills. It was the fur capital and freight center of the upper Missouri for 50 years.

Out on the plains of Stanley County are the Fort Pierre National Grasslands, the Roy Hauck Buffalo Ranch, the home of Scotty Philip (the man who saved the last remnant of the once numerous buffalo), and the two other towns in the county, Hayes, and Wendte.

The county lists at least nine forts, with six being fur trading posts, so that the region was well protected from the Indians. But the final word as to who controls rural areas in that land of cowboy and cattle is that now the Centennial River of Lewis and Clark has been changed to Paul Prairie Chicken Creek.

The Cattle Barons

Stanley County

A lone horseman, momentarily silhouetted against clouds red-streaked by the setting sun, disappears beyond the horizon. On the bleak Pierre Shale badland behind him, little puffs of dust

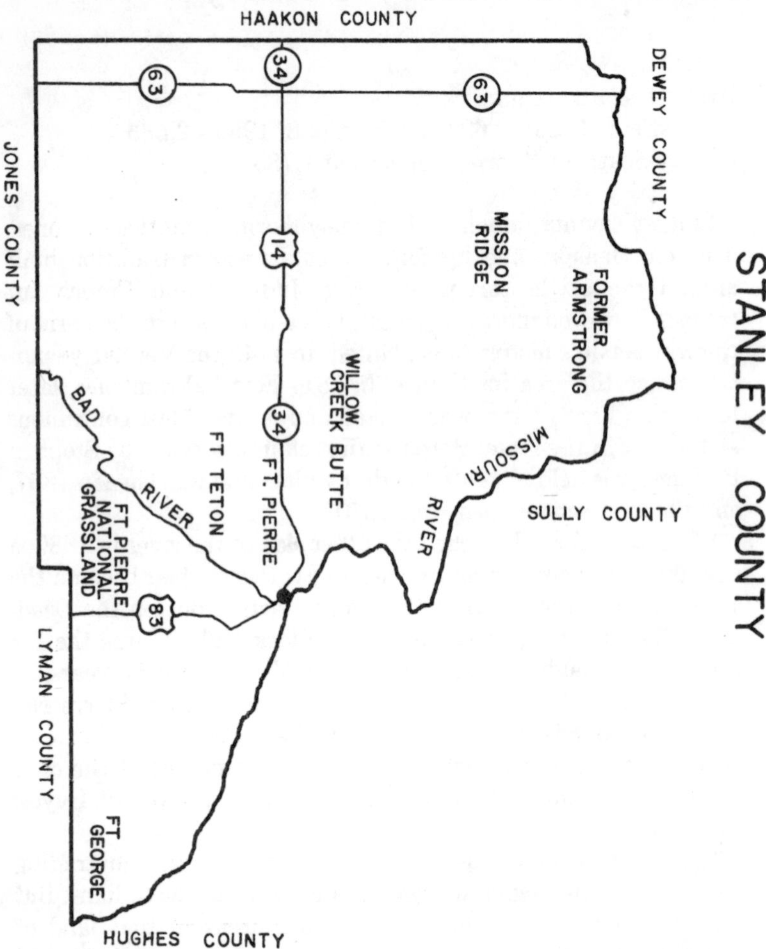

drift upward to vanish into the dusk. Soon all that can be seen as twilight approaches will be the endless rolling hills . . . rolling, rolling into the approaching darkness as if they, like the horseman, will be swallowed by the horizon. What would soon be called Stanley County seemed empty. Empty because by this year 1860, the 3 to 4 million Indians that roamed the plains had been reduced to about a half million. Empty because the 30 million or more buffalo that thundered like black clouds across the plains had been reduced to 200 animals.

What happened to prairies and plains when the Indians and buffalo were exterminated in an almost unbelievable exercise in inhumanity? In those days human rights were not considered a viable means of stabilizing a race relationship. Much easier to kill 'em off. It is hoped that now our moral and ethical principles are directed toward rights and justice for all humanity and other living things. But man still has a long way to go.

The vacuum left by the Indian and buffalo was filled with Texas longhorns. The abundant wheatgrass, blue grama, little blue stem, and buffalo grass were not to be left to decimation by periodic prairie fires. Land was free and the cattlemen knew it. And so they came, from Texas, New Mexico, Colorado and points south. Cattle barons and corporations with strong European connections hired range managers to drive up large herds of Texas longhorns. These barons left a colorful legacy. The area abounds today with their family names.

Three Scotsmen developed the largest ranches in and around Stanley County. They were Murdo McKenzie of the Matador, Cap Mossman of the Diamond A, and Scotty James Philip of the 73 brand. Only Mossman failed to get a town named after him, but he had the distinction of operating the largest ranch in South Dakota. At one time the Diamond A covered over a million acres and ran over 50,000 cattle. It once claimed all of the now defunct Armstrong County and some of the adjoining area for its range. Armstrong County is now part of northern Stanley and southern Dewey counties. The population of Armstrong County in 1939 was 48 Indians and two others. The Diamond A still operates on about 80,000 acres with 5,000 cattle.

Those who travel Interstate 90 may remember Murdo McKenzie as they pass through the town of Murdo. McKenzie operated two large Matador, drag V ranches, one north, the other south of Stanley County.

Those who travel Highway 14 toward the Black Hills will pass through the city of Philip, site of one of Scotty James Philip's ranches. He became known as the Buffalo King for his role in saving the last 200 buffalo on the plains. A second ranch, brand 73, was near Ft. Pierre.

These cattlemen and 50 to 75 others soon filled the void left by the buffalo and Indian. By 1887 the entire area west of the Missouri River was one large unfenced pasture. There, in an area where an estimated 200,000 buffalo had roamed, grazed nearly a million head of cattle.

Why had the cattlemen been able to use, without government intervention, all this free unfenced land? One reason was that the government needed beef to replace buffalo to feed the Indians. At first the Indians were allowed to hunt cattle as if they were buffalo, harvesting the wild longhorns as needed. A second reason was to supply numerous army camps and an increasing number of settlers. As the cattle supply increased and as the railroads developed westward, more and more of the beef was shipped east. One of the shipping points was a town on the Missouri called Evarts. Evarts was literally drowned by the floods of progress; it was inundated by the Oahe.

As time went on the free land became less and less free. At first, all that was needed to hold the land was a gentleman's agreement among neighboring ranchers on land boundaries, a loose contract with the government for supplying beef, or the control of the water supply. But this land on the Great Sioux Reservation was soon to be extracted from the Sioux in a series of treaties. In the meantime, leases became harder and harder to get, and many solved the problem by becoming "squaw men" to gain access to the reservation. Eligible young Indian women that offered this dowry were not, however, all that plentiful.

In some areas along the Missouri, where French trader-trappers had been in business since 1760, a supply of French-Indian women was available. One 102-year-old French-Indian grandmother boasted of nearly 100 grandchildren.

It's easy to see how early settlers left an imprint on the country. Take the cowboys — tired of talking to their horses all week, disgusted with unresponsive cattle, infected with loneliness — and you have men looking for excitement. They meet young French-Indian maids, available, restless with lack of opportunity, and glowing with robust life. Mix them all together on a Saturday night, when youthful energy exceeds common sense, and the result is not a quiet evening at home. Many important names in South Dakota trace their roots to early French-Indian-cowboy adventurers.

The era of the cattle baron was short in South Dakota. It collapsed as rapidly as it developed. Three factors hastened its demise. Southern ranchers were not prepared for the blizzards that occur at periodic intervals in the northland. In the winter of 1887-88 one of the most severe occurred. The cattle on the open range had no hay and no shelter. Up to 90 per cent perished in ravines where snow filled in up to 30 to 40 feet deep. A second factor was the opening by the government of the Great Sioux Reservation to settlers in 1889. Finally, the arrival of railroads brought settlers with barbed wire fences and plows, spelling doom for the free land and big ranches. Some spreads vanished, and others were assimilated by the men with pitchforks and bib overalls.

Stanley County experienced its own growth pains. It started as a small county along the Missouri that boasted the oldest (1817) continuous town in the state, Ft. Pierre. The county's history dates back to 1743, when the Verendrye brothers claimed the territory for France. Its first growth phase was to combine with Jackson and Haakon counties to produce the largest county in the state. In 1910 Stanley County had over 4,000 square miles and a population of nearly 15,000. Its area was over twice the size of Delaware. In 1916 Haakon and Jackson counties were split off, but in 1940 Stanley gained a bit of old Armstrong County to establish its present size.

Today the people of Stanley County are still concerned about their cattle, but barbed wire has replaced the big round up. The farmer-rancher still stands upon the crest of the hill, pushes his hat back, wipes his sweat from his brow, plunges his hands deep into his pocket, and looks off into the red glow of the setting sun. Dust from the pounding hooves of shaggy buffalo and Texas longhorns will never again dim the sun. Behind him the Pierre Shale badland still rolls and rolls into the distance. The farmer on the ridge turns his attention to the future — what he and his neighbors will do now that permits have been issued to irrigate over 50,000 acres.

Sully County

Area, 1,058 square miles
Population, 1925 - 3,611; 1945 - 2,172; 1980 - 1,990
County Seat, Onida. Population 851

Sully County is one of the few counties with a population below 2,000 the others being Buffalo, Harding, and Jones. It, however, remembers the days of greater activity — those days when Fort Sully (1866-1894) was the most important, largest, and longest-lived fort in the Plains. It was an elite fort with all the amenities of a large military post, including a band, baseball, library, roller skating club, and a hunting club equipped with greyhounds.

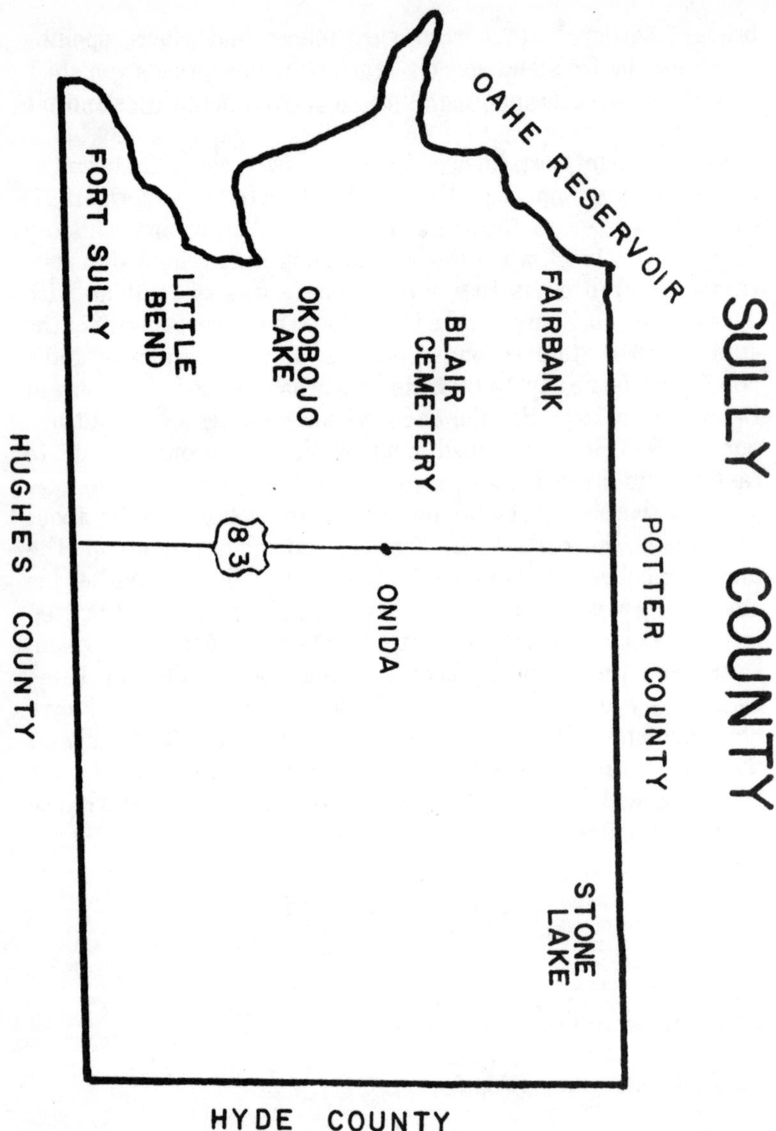

Below the fort and northward, in the little bend area of the Missouri were some of the biggest concentration of Arikara Indians. One village contained over 300 earth lodges. Remains of Indian villages in the area were found every three miles before the filling of the Oahe Reservoir.

It was here, at the Little Bend, in 1823 that General Ashley was ambushed and 13 of his men were killed by the Arikara. This was the first real military action in the state.

As the settlers came, many towns started up on the prairie in Sully County. But the first flush of growth did not last, and now only two remain, Onida and Agar.

The lakes in the county are Cottonwood and Stone Lake. Both are on the east end of the county.

Boom Towns
Sully County

> It is tragic or it is humorous (according to the observer) when a people so hopeful and so vigorous dies out upon a plain as a river loses itself in the sand.
> —Hamlin Garland

An abandoned trail, rutted washboard-fashion, winds over the hills of the Missouri Coteau. Follow it to the other side of the hill. There it disappears into emptiness, an emptiness once filled by a flourishing town with ambitious people. Go backward in time along the trail, to the 1880s and events that were the beginnings of Sully County, where towns boomed and busted even before we became a state.

Along a cottonwood-lined shore, where the Missouri River bends slightly, abandoned mud homes of the Arikara Indian are sighted. They appear like giant ant hills, each with a hole on top to allow smoke out. The early inhabitants of these homes were weakened by (and many died of) small pox, tuberculosis, scarlet fever, venereal disease, the common cold, and a host of other introduced diseases that spread like fire through their close, compact village. Harrassed by the Sioux and exploited by whites, the few that were left in the end disappeared into North Dakota — a whole race of Indians completely wiped out even before a census could be taken.

Corn, tobacco, and three kinds of squash ripened in the fields, and buffalo skin boats remained turned over against the huts. Utensils for cooking stood ready for use. It was as if the Arikaras had all gone on a hunting trip but never returned. In reality, they had died so rapidly, from the last epidemic of smallpox, that they could not even bury their dead. Today no monument commemorates the loss of an entire race of Indians.

On a wide terrace overlooking the abandoned Indian village and the Missouri River once stood a bustling Fort Sully — with some 62 buildings. Nearly 1,000 soldiers and staff stood as a bulwark against dead and dying Indians. After 20 years the fort was abandoned.

From the east in the 1880s came a horde of seekers to claim the land open for settlement. The Missouri River acted as a barrier, and the settlers massed on the east bank awaiting the coming of the railroad and a bridge to get them across to a land stretching into the sun. With visions of growth and riches far exceeding the capacity of the land, the ambitious arrivals plotted new towns. Eighteen post offices were established in the county before 1890, and many towns hoped to become trade centers in the area. Towns at first successful in attracting settlers were Clifton, Carson, Fairbank, Okobojo, and Onida. Only Onida, located in the center of the county, survived, probably because it became the county seat. The rest have been swept clean by the prairie winds.

Fairbank, once selected to be the site for the railroad to cross the Missouri, grew at a rapid rate. By 1885 a Fairbank booster estimated the population between 1,000 to 2,500. The main street was a wagon trail lined with tents, shacks, and dugouts. The trail to Pierre was dotted with ox teams carrying lumber for the new hotels, grocery stores, banks, and other businesses that were in plans for the future.

The only colony of Afro-Americans in South Dakota settled near Fairbank. The group, estimated as high as 400, settled in the area under the leadership of Norvel Blair. For a while it was a thriving settlement of farmers. But alas, the railroad never came. Fairbank became a mudhole and tumbled into Lake Oahe. The Afro-Americans disappeared, leaving behind Blair Cemetery, on a small knoll outside of Fairbank.

Other boomers, outside the county but on or near the Missouri Coteau, are also noteworthy. Evart was a cattle shipping point, noted for once shipping more cattle than any other place in the nation. Its name, on a depot sign, is now in the hands of a collector from Minnesota. La Beau, near Evart, was almost as famous as Evart. Ordway, considered for the capitol of Dakota Territory in 1883, lost by only one vote to Bismarck. McClure boasted a liberated woman, who ran the town and its newspaper. Lamro, in the southern part of the coteau, was another cattle town, marked now by a concrete bank vault, standing in a grove of trees.

The two boom towns that seem to have been the most "successful" in South Dakota are Dallas, in Gregory County, and Blunt, on the Hughes-Sully border. Both claim to have reached populations near 3,000 — at least as estimated by their overly-optimistic, embryonic chambers of commerce. It is interesting to note that some of these boom towns grew, reached their zenith, and popped even before a census could capture their presence. It is also interesting to note the industrial strength of Blunt in 1883: "Hotels 6, stores 21, lumber yards 9, hardwares 6, drugstores 4 and only 5 saloons, and the town is just three months old." Amazing! Today 400 people live in Blunt, and the only institutions that have not declined are the saloons and the churches. The school has combined with Onida's, and the system is now called Sully Buttes.

What about the people that lived in this changing county? The men came mostly packaged in long hair and whiskers, which both protected them from the cold and saved them the inconvenience of shaving. The young women, what few there were, had many men to pick from, but the quality was a bit unpredictable. The visible appearance of most men was meager — a couple of eyes peering out from a face that looked like a horse tail. Often it was not until after the wedding that the prize package was unwrapped. Then, if mistakes were made, it was probably too late to exchange for another model.

Seventeen young ladies from the east coast, who probably felt it a bit much to put up with all the hair, formed a small village called Girlstown. There they were able to hold out until they could examine the hairy merchandise in greater detail.

The causes of the population fluctuation in Sully County were the same as those which affected most rural areas in the state — drought, low prices, and severe winters. One can chart population change with hard times. Note the following shifts: 1885, 3,300 people; 1905, 1,400; 1930, over 3,900; and 1980, 1,990. The present population reflects large farms and ranches, with a high percentage of the grassland being turned into cropland.

So here on the Missouri Coteau, one reflects on the picturesque patterns of the past. There is no longer a Girlstown, nor an Afro-American settlement, nor an elite fort built to give protection from abandoned Indian villages. Only glimpses remain of that period when enthusiasm created failure. Standing on the windswept prairie, viewing the ruts and ridges that were once a road leading to progressive Fairbank, one sees a vision of times past. Ox carts hauling in new lumber are coming. As they draw closer, the creak of the greaseless wagon wheels direct one's attention to a furry faced fellow sitting on the wagon seat, spitting tobacco juice against the wind. His oxen stop, and people rush out to examine the wonderful supplies that have taken five days to haul in.

In the distance and up and down the river, smoke drifts out of the holes in the center of small anthill-like structures. The Arikara are again grinding their corn, and their little bull boats, filled with people, bob up and down on the tree-lined river.

The vision stops, and once again one sees only the vastness of the prairie, sliced by a wide treeless ribbon of water. Now only the thunder booms as it rolls across the silence of the plains.

Tripp County

Area, 1,629 square miles
Population, 1925 - 14,032; 1945 - 8,568; 1980 - 7,268
County Seat, Winner. Population 3,472

Elephant Crossing. Can you imagine a sign like that on the road? Well, would you believe that elephant originated in North America and probably were once almost as numerous as deer? The several species of elephants in the state are now all extinct.

The evidence was provided when Roy Brumbaugh found a mastadon skeleton in the southwestern part of the county. It is now on display at the Museum of Natural History in New York City. This was a short stubby elephant with, for elephants, a short nose.

In Hot Springs they are making a National Landmark out of the site where 19 Columbian elephants were discovered in a sink hole. These elephants are intermediate in size; they have long noses that can curl several times and long ivory tusks.

Near Mina they discovered the Imperial Mammoth. This is the granddaddy of them all in size. Its tusks are so long that they overlap in front. They are apparently worn for decoration rather than protection. Other elephant remains found in the state include the Wooly Mammoth.

Back to Tripp County we find it was settled by a land boom in 1908 when the Congress opened part of the Rosebud Reservation

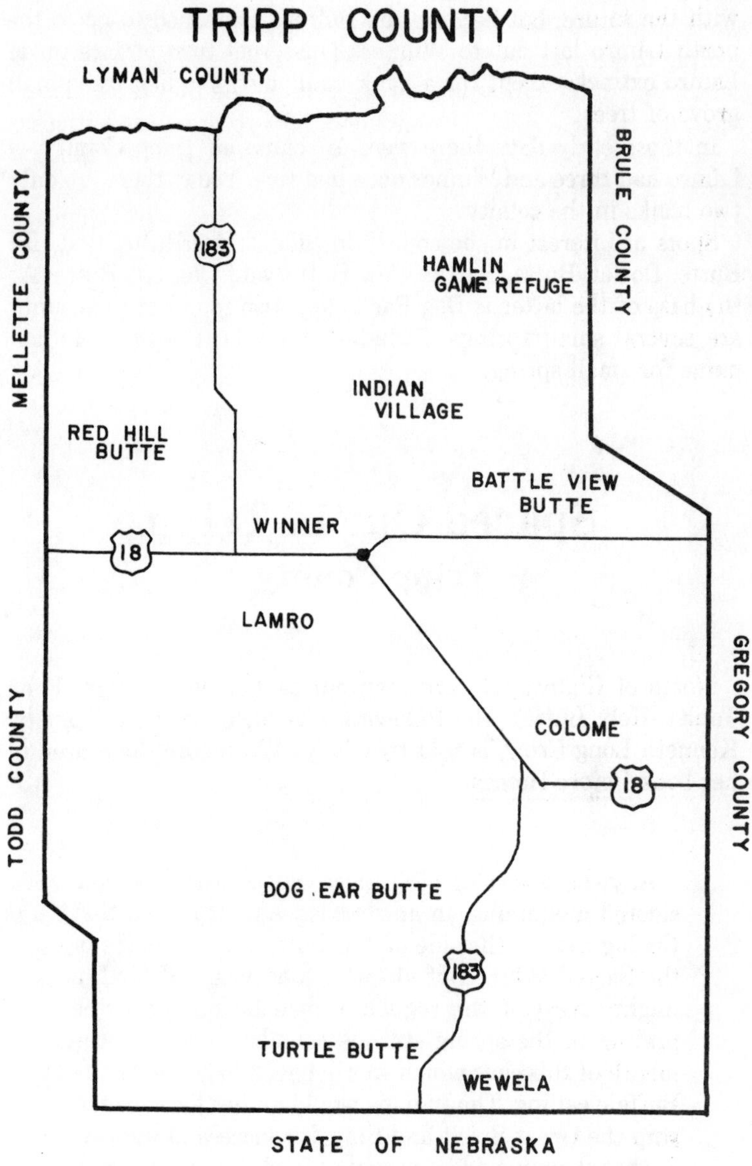

at the same time that the railroad entered the county. Before this only a few people lived in Tripp, but the following year, 1909, the census listed 8,323 people, somewhat over 1,000 more than in 1980.

The first county seat in this booming county was Lamro, the city with the future, but because the railroad happened to go to the north Lamro lost out to Winner. This cruel turn of fate made Lamro extinct, except for a bank vault left standing in a small grove of trees.

In those early days there were 15 banks in Tripp County — Lamro had three and Winner once had five. Today there are only two banks in the county.

Spots of interest in the county include Turtle Butte, Red Hill Butte, Dorian Butte, Battle View Butte, and Dog Ear Butte. At the base of the latter is Dog Ear Lake. Also found in the county are several small springs, including Wewela, the Sioux Indian name for small spring.

Spaced Out in Tripp

Tripp County

North of Highway 44 are twin buttes. One is known as Paha Tanka (Holy Butte). The following legend, based on a story by Kenneth Long Crow, is told by Gladys Whitehorn Jorgensen in her book Before Homesteads.

> Anywhere east of here these buttes would be considered mountains. In ancient legends, it is told that the big cave in the side of this butte was the home of the Sacred White Buffalo who each year led forth a mighty herd of the regular brown buffalo onto the prairie. In the spring strange sounds came from the mouth of this cave which was believed to be the White Buffalo calling. The Indians would gather here to worship the Great Spirit and pray for success in hunting so that there would be plenty of food. No one was permitted to harm the white buffalo and always there was plenty of buffalo until once some foolish young brave shot the white buffalo and wounded it. He led his band back into the cave and they were never seen again. The mouth of the cave collapsed soon after but it is said

> that sometimes in the spring when the wind is right, the sounds can still be heard. Of course the skeptics claim that it is merely the sound made by the wind but the belief still lingers.

A gravel road twists through a pass, which is still known as Buffalo Gap. It is here, in the butte country along Bull Creek, that Indian tradition and legends still live.

The legend of White Buffalo Cave symbolizes the end of the buffalo and the Indian era in South Dakota. In 1889 the great Sioux Reservation west of the Missouri was broken up, and the Sioux were limited to six reservations. The rest of the land west of the Missouri became a vast, unfenced public domain, filled with cattle, cowboys, rustlers, outlaws, and Indians. Out of it came stories of the exploits of Kid Wade, Jack Sully, Doc Middleton, the Lamoureaux Brothers and, perhaps the most colorful of all, Chris Colome. Stories of the hanging tree and the fight at Pete's Ranch are retold today. At a somewhat later date occurred the escapades of the Jackson Brothers, who made a fortune in land deals and engineered the founding of Winner. Their Mulehead Ranch occupied nearly 200,000 acres or about one-fifth of Gregory County.

Then, on April 1, 1909, a great land grab diminished interest in cowboys and Indians. The east half of the Rosebud Reservation was opened for settlement, with 114,000 applicants vying for 6,000 homestead sites. Selection was made by drawing numbers. The lucky homesteaders and their families — some 10,000 people — spread out over the 1,600 square miles of Tripp County, about nine persons, or 3.6 homesteads, per square mile.

"Imagine if you can a whole community set down on the prairie in a day — you might say each one a perfect stranger to all the rest and all coming from different occupations and modes of living. The emigrants consisted of a conglomeration of humanity, ranging all the way from the experienced plainsman to inexperienced eastern merchants, old ladies, school teachers, streetcar conductors, cooks, and almost any other class to be found in the United States at that time, all in high hopes," states Dennis B. Lyons in relating the Tripp County History.

A long period of adjustment followed, as speculation, poverty, and plague took their toll. Rural areas were the first to feel the pinch of too many people. The population shifted into several small towns: Carter, Clearfield, Colome, Hamill, Ideal, Jordan, Lamro, Lakeview, Keyapaha, McNeely, Millboro, Pahapesto, Red Hills, Wewela, Witten, Winoa, and Winner. Most of these towns met the fate of their rural neighbors. Winner remains, sole champion of progress. Colome and Witten are flickering shadows of their former importance. The rest are all but forgotten entries on old highway maps.

After 70 years of settlement and shifting, only 2,000 rural people remain in space once occupied by 10,000. Some 3,000 have left, and nearly 5,000 are located in towns, mostly Winner. The population density, excluding Winner, is now 1.2 people and .8 homes per square mile.

Legends were a large part of the early history of Tripp County. Such legends wove together oral history, from which was derived an understanding of events. Exciting, important events, otherwise unexplainable, became manageable. As man advanced in sophistication, he was able to turn these into measure observations, validated events and repeatable experiments, thus robbing the tales, by logic and science, of their charm, beauty, and mysticism.

Today the people of Tripp County, however, look back on the good old days and remember with pride, nostalgia, and satisfaction the legends that made the country exciting.

The White Buffalo Calf Butte

Photo — D.J. Holden

White Buffalo Calf Cave located in rock outcrop at top of butte (top). One of two cairn of rock erected by the Indians at the top of butte (bottom).

Photos — D.J. Holden

Yankton County

Area, 523 square miles
Population, 1925 - 16,037; 1945 - 15,596; 1980 - 18,952
County Seat, Yankton. Population 12,011

Yankton is a city located along the picturesque Missouri River. It is named from the Sioux, meaning "End Village." It was settled in 1858 and Chief Smutty Bear was there to make trouble in 1859. The Chief was promised a feast at his new home, and he eventually left peacefully for the Reservation.

Yankton is sometimes known as the Mother City of the Dakota since it was the first territorial capitol from 1861 to 1883. The first legislature met in a home and was called the "Pony Congress." It was here at Yankton that Lewis and Clark in 1805 covered Struck by the Ree with an American flag, hence the name Struck by the Ree Valley on the outskirts of town. The present courthouse was once the site of old Fort Yankton.

The natural features of the county include the James River, which bisects the county and empties into the Missouri River east of Yankton. To the west of Yankton are Gavins Point Dam and Lewis and Clark Lake. The most unique stretch of the river is that extending to the east of Yankton on down to Sioux City. It is the wild, not impounded river, of the Lewis and Clark days. Here, along the river Clark made the first sighting of the pronghorn antelope and called them goats.

The Norwegian Connection

Yankton County

Norway has never been known to support a large population, either of people or lemmings. The lemming cured its population problems by periodically committing suicide with a plunge into the sea. Timed by some mysterious biological rhythm, they are programmed for overpopulation by a prolific reproduction urge. Then, as if by a signal, they march to the sea.

The Norwegian people also reproduce at a rate beyond the

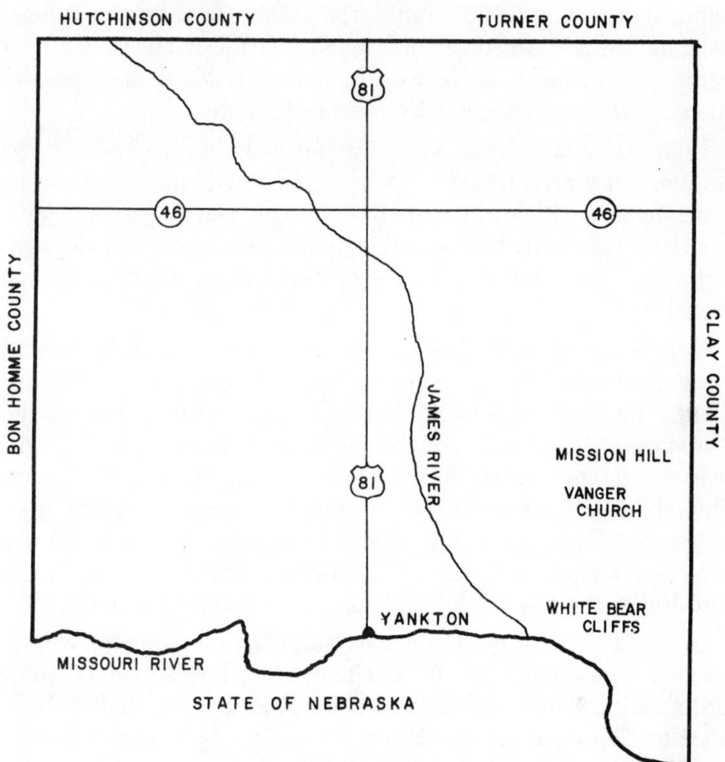

capacity of their beautiful, mountainous country, with its narrow, fertile valleys, to support them. Some 3 million Norwegians find a comfortable home in the scenic grandeur of fjords and mountains. Periodically, however, the population swells over this number. Then, like the lemmings, they depart for the sea. There is no other place to go, especially for the younger people, for the custom is to pass on the land to the oldest son; with the land thus subdivided, each generation gets a smaller and smaller portion.

So they leave, brave Vikings who have always plied the sea. Like the lemmings, they have responded by emigrating. But unlike the lemmings, which swim out into the sea and drown of exhaustion, the Norwegians have reached new lands. They made it to Greenland, Iceland, and other points on the North American continent in one emigration wave a few years after the birth of Christ. Another time they formed colonies in France, Spain, Russia, and Ireland. The last big emigration from the land of fjords and mountains was to the Midwest. More than 700,000 came in the late 1800s and early 1900s to claim land. Most became farmers. In some counties in South Dakota, over 50 per cent of the farmers are Norwegian, and other Midwest states also have a high percentage of Norwegian farmers.

In Norway 2 million acres are farmed. In the Midwest 32 million acres are farmed by Norwegian Americans. This means much food for the world is produced by the men of Norway. Some South Dakota townships are 80 to 90 per cent Norwegian descent. Adjacent townships may be Polish, German, or a mixture of nationalities.

Norwegians were the first people, not trappers or fur traders, to build permanent settlements in South Dakota. They came to farm. The first settlement, in 1857, was on the banks of the Missouri, at the junction of Clay and Yankton counties. This was before the land was given the name Dakota. Norwegian and Indian children grew up using a mixture of Sioux and Norwegian languages. Today, Norway Township in Clay County is 80 per cent Norwegian, with the population spreading northwestward into Volin and Mission Hill Townships in Yankton County.

In the Yankton-Clay County community, the first Norwegian churches were built, the first schools were furnished, and some unflattering words were uttered about Irish and Polish neighbors. Vangen Church at Mission Hill still stands, a memorial to the early settlers. The rest of the early churches were destroyed by disastrous flooding on the Missouri bottoms. Frequently, in the spring, faithful churchgoers would find a floating pulpit to go with a fluid sermon. In 1880, floods were so disastrous that the entire town of Green Island washed away.

Living today in our affluent society, we find it hard to realize hardships the early settlers faced.

They had come mostly in small groups from single areas of Norway and settled in a land completely strange to them. No longer enclosed by mountains, trees, and streams, they encountered a vastness that made them feel small and insignificant. Exposure to the open prairie was like being alone on solid waves of a vast sea. They came in poverty, clutching a few handmade tools and machinery. Often they settled 50 to 75 miles from the nearest town and faced the wilderness with nothing but their own resourcefulness. They existed, those first few years, on sheer determination. They had only two choices — to live or die. Most lived. They became, to succeeding generations, symbols of strength in an environment that frequently exacted death.

It is little wonder that religion had such a strong influence on the Norwegian settlers. Their faith, and a large family, carried them through trying times. The family together combated loneliness and cooperated to survive. The ultimate result of this is that today we have more Norwegians in the United States than in Norway. It is said that nature selects the fittest, and this belief gave the Norwegian pioneers a selective advantage. This, with a trust in God, gave them the strength to carry on and survive, when those of lesser faith gave up.

This religious urge, built into the Norwegian psyche of the period, was amplified by hardship and crisis. They brought with them to South Dakota a fear of God and a mandate to subdue the earth. These helped them to survive on the prairie, to conquer their fear of uncharted seas, and to withstand the desolation of Greenland. In a sense, it was their driving religious influence that allowed them to take almost any lonely place on the prairie and turn it into home. God protected them from blizzard, starvation, prairie fire, drought, and grasshoppers. They worked with an inner-directed zeal throughout the long week. On Sunday they thanked God.

Although a character gap exists between today's descendants and their ancestors, the Norwegians have nonetheless left their mark on all aspects of today's life. Blue-eyed blond Nordics have become a part of the American melting pot. But some descendants, their religion diluted by today's affluence, find it harder to go around the corner to church than did their ancestors to bundle up the whole family and drive several miles in a bobsled for a worship service.

In fact, one can hardly tell second or third generation Norwegians from anyone else since they no longer talk about "good old Norway." Only when one sits down to a dinner of such American dishes as Polish sausage, French bread, and German beer does one note the side dishes — lefse, krumkake, fattigmand, gaffelbiter, lutefisk, and kringler.

The man of the house, waiting to be served, inspects his grease-stained, work-worn hands and states suddenly, "Our daughter wants to marry that damn Kolwalski."

The lady of the house, smiling tolerantly, says, "You'll get over it. Remember when your daughter-in-law named your first grandson Gottlieb?"

The farmer quickly finishes his meal, gets up from the table, shoves another big bite of lefse into his mouth, pulls his cap down hard on his head, mutters that foreigners are taking over the country, and leaves to finish the plowing.

Out in the field the smell of fresh soil seems to fill him with power. He looks at the thick, rich black earth and sees a field of golden grain. His shoulders straighten perceptibly, and he knows that the world is good.

INDIAN HERITAGE

Indian Heritage

County	Title
Buffalo & Brule	The Crow Creek Massacre
Campbell & Walworth	The Old Scaffold
Corson	The Spirit of Sitting Bull
Dewey	Indians in a Land Called Promise
Hand & Hyde	Buffalo Wallow Valley
Mellette & Washabaugh	The Black Pipe Dream
Shannon	A Prairie Yuwipi
Todd	Indian Medicine
Zieback	The Indian Who Looked Both Ways

The Indians were the first people to populate the South Dakota system. They fitted into the ecological gears of the new world like grease and grit: Like grease when they lived in harmony with the land, but grit when peaceful ways spilled over into warfare with other tribes.

In this section, I look at the Indian as he attempts to fit into still another system — a system imposed upon him by the non-Indian. There, mostly in the wilds of western South Dakota, we find him reflecting on the past while looking to the future with feelings of uncertainty. Perhaps the strength of a positive attitude and a faith in himself will again fit him into the ecological gears of the future.

> Our legends tell us that it was hundreds and perhaps thousands of years ago since the first man sprang from the soil in the midst of the great plains. The story says that one morning long ago a lone man awoke, face to the sun, emerging from the soil. Only his head was visible, the rest of his body not yet being fashioned. The man looked about, but saw no mountains, no rivers, no forests. There was nothing but soft and quaking mud, for the earth itself was still young. Up and up the man drew himself until he freed his body from the clinging soil. At last he stood upon the earth, but it was not solid, and his first few steps were slow

and halting. But the sun shone and ever the man kept his face turned toward it. In time the rays of the sun hardened the face of the earth and strengthened the man and he bounded and leaped about, a free and joyous creature. From this man sprang the Lakota nation and, so far as we know, our people have been born and have died upon this plain; and no people have shared it with us until the coming of the European. So this land of the great plains is claimed by the Lakotas as their very own. We are of the soil and the soil is of us.

—The Lakota Genesis Myth, as told by
Chief Luther Standing Bear

Brule County

Area, 837 square miles
Population, 1925 - 8,110; 1945 - 5,605; 1980 - 5,258
County Seat, Chamberlain. Population 2,258

The land of the burnt legs is not exactly what the countless numbers of tourist think about as they whiz over the Missouri on the Interstate bridges. The county, named after Sioux Indians who burnt their thighs in a prairie fire, has always provided a crossing point over the river. First, the crossing was by ferry during the gold rush days; next in 1893 a pontoon bridge was built and it cost 2 cents to walk across and 25 cents to drive a team across. In 1905 the railroad spanned the river, and finally in 1923 the State Legislature provided funds for a highway bridge. Today, a couple bridges later, 6,000 vehicles a day crisscross the river in an endless stream on the two new Interstate bridges. It looks like the race track of life tied to a perpetual motion machine.

Another town east on the Interstate is Pukwana, which was once called "Biggest Little City" in South Dakota. Here J.A. Stransky invented a fuel-saving device for cars. But who, in those countless cars, knows that the fuel injection system in their cars was invented here?

Possibly the most rustic city in the county is Bijou Hills. The

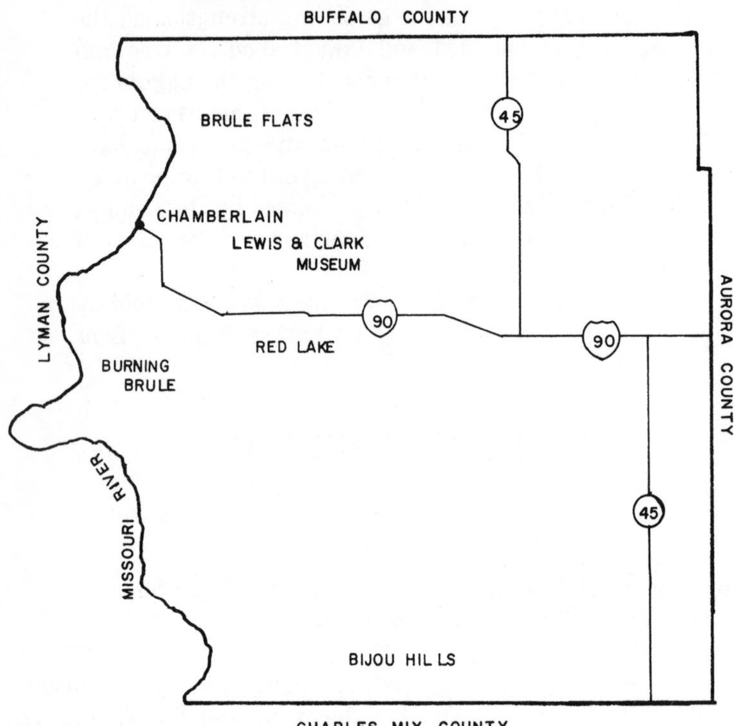

city is mostly gone, but the hills are still there. It was the location of a trading post in 1812. Today we can explore what is left of the city and climb Bijou Peak, where Indians built large ceremonial rock pillars, enjoy Bijou Lake, search for Bijou Springs, and then visit Bijou Quarry. The latter is a site where the Indians obtained green quartzite for his arrows, knives, and scrapers.

Red Lake, near Pukwana, is the county's largest lake. It is filled with grass that gives it a reddish color and is the habitat for marsh dwelling wildlife.

Buffalo County

Area, 479 square miles
Population, 1925 - 2,241; 1945 - 1,831; 1980 - 1,795
County Seat, Gann Valley. Not incorporated.

From the biggest to the smallest, that is the story of Buffalo County. When first organized it included the present Buffalo, Aurora, Jerauld, Sanborn, Davison, Hanson, Brule, Miner, and McCook counties and part of Lake County. It has since been cut down to the third smallest county in both size and population.

What the county lacks in size, however, it makes up for in history. Jean Baptiste Trudeau camped near Fort Thompson on September 30, 1794, and traded with the Indians. In 1804 Lewis and Clark explored the area, and in 1834 Colin Campbell established a trading post near Ft. Thompson.

Ft. Thompson, which was started in 1862, was the first real settlement in the county. It was started by a group of Santee Indians and later became part of Crow Creek Indian Reservation. The Reservation now occupies half of the county.

Another village is Gann Valley, the county seat. Here an Episcopal Church, started in 1886, is still operating using hymnals in both the English and Dakota language.

Villages that no longer exist are Buffalo Center, once the county seat, Duncan, Richards, and Shelby. They were all country stores with post offices. Today there is only one, called Lee's Corner, that still operates. Buffalo County does not have any large towns; in fact, there are no towns in the county. Ft. Thompson is trying hard to be one, and in the last 10 years has gained considerable population. Gann Valley, the county seat, is not incorporated.

Buffalo County is the site of the second largest CCC dam in the United States. It forms the 10-mile long Lake Bedashosha.

Old Indian villages antedating the Arikara are located between Elm and Crow Creek, at Medicine Crow, and Skunk Island.

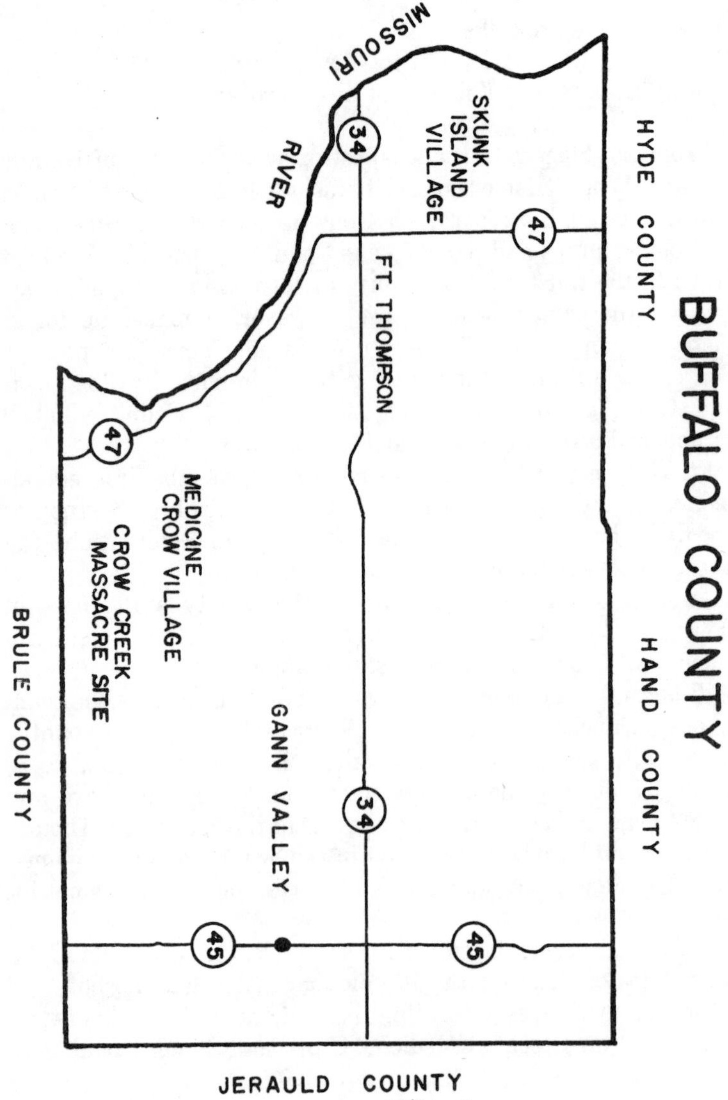
BUFFALO COUNTY
HYDE COUNTY
HAND COUNTY
BRULE COUNTY
JERAULD COUNTY
MISSOURI
RIVER
SKUNK ISLAND VILLAGE
FT. THOMPSON
MEDICINE CROW VILLAGE
CROW CREEK MASSACRE SITE
GANN VALLEY
34
47
47
34
45
45

The Crow Creek Massacre

Brule & Buffalo Counties

Larry J. Zimmerman

It happened here. Here on the brown curving hills overlooking the Missouri. Here where the sun often sinks blood-red into the somber silent night and where the wind plays a never ending game with the soft brown carpet of grass, turning it into a sea of motion. We ask what will the site reveal about man's dark, dim past that will help to illuminate our present condition. It is here that the undercutting wave action of Lake Francis Case has cut into the site of an ancient Indian village, and all along this bluff are the gaping holes left by looters, pot-hunters digging for artifacts and destroying archaeological evidence. But this hole was different. The spoil from the hole was now on the toe of the bluff which was littered with shattered human bones. Back in the hole were the broken ends of many more bones. What had been scheduled as routine maintenance and ultimately stabilization of the wall of the Crow Creek Site opened one of the most mysterious chapters in South Dakota's wealthy prehistory. By the time excavations ended at the site in November 1978, the remains of nearly five hundred individuals, nearly all scalped and mutilated, had been discovered.

The Crow Creek Site, a few miles south of Ft. Thompson, is a National Historic Landmark. Most people recognize that the site is significant from the moment they set foot on the area. Many depressions are visible from the collapsed earthlodges that once provided shelter for the prehistoric inhabitants of the site. Most impressive, however, is the fortification ditch, some 12 feet wide and 1250 feet long, that snakes its way around the landward side of the site. This ditch is interrupted every 125-150 feet by U-shaped protrusions or bastions. The site was first excavated in the mid-1950s by the Nebraska State Historical Society as part of the program to salvage archaeological sites along the reservoirs then being constructed. The site was dated by radiocarbon to the year 1390 A.D. The occupants of the site were culturally part of the Initial Coalescent variant, as the archaeologists label it. They were descended from groups that had come up from the Central Plains during drought and blended with the people already living along the Missouri River. They grew corn, beans, and squash in gardens along the river and hunted bison on the plains nearby. Several similar villages dot the east bank of the Missouri all the way up to the vicinity of Pierre.

Since the site first became known to pot-hunters and since the filling of the reservoir, Crow Creek has been undergoing continual destruction. The Corps of Engineers had been making feasibility studies to see if the erosion could be stopped. Members of the South Dakota Archaeological Society examined this destruction during its late May 1978 annual meeting, when a staff member of the South Dakota Archaeological Research Center spotted what proved to be human bones eroding from the Wolf Creek end of the fortification ditch. The State Archaeologist recommended to the Corps of Engineers that the bones be removed and that the area be immediately stabilized. Necessary "red tape" slowed implementation of his recommendation until July. Over the July 4th holiday, the looter did his work. Many people come to the site to dig illegally for artifacts; this individual probably saw the bones and thought there might be burial goods or salable artifacts.

On July 5, the USD crew arrived at the site with a physical anthropologist to excavate the bones. When they discovered the looter's work, all they could do was document the loss and salvage the many fragmented bones. These were sent to Vermillion to be washed and analyzed. Examination of the fragmented skulls revealed cut marks made during the scalping process in evidence on virtually every piece. The ends of arm bones indicated that hands on many individuals had been cut off. Other pieces of skull showed large fractures. A count of the thigh bones revealed evidence that at least 44 people had been represented in the looter's hole. Since no other remains from the time period had ever been discovered before in such a mutilated condition, the find was of extreme importance in our understanding of Plains village existence. Further, the looter's hole had weakened the bank even more. Immediate intensive excavation had to begin at the site. With funding from the Corps of Engineers, work began to remove what few bones were thought to be left in order that the end of the ditch could be stabilized.

To protect the excavators from bank slumpage and to make stabilization easier, the excavation unit was "stepped" back into the bank. As the level of the bones was reached, the magnitude of the tragedy that occurred at the site became evident; an area nearly 20 feet square was covered with human bones, and the bone bed was nearly three feet thick. The impact of such an incredible site is almost overwhelming. Nearly every skull showed evidence of scalping; many were fractured; the bodies of men, women, and small children were represented. The magnitude of the bone pile was evidence that nearly a whole village had met death in warfare on one terrible day in the 14th century, nearly 300 years before the arrival of Europeans.

The skeletons were carefully excavated and documented. The bones were sent to the archaeology lab in Vermillion to be washed and studied. The discovery made the news around the state and nation, and even the international press carried the story of the Crow Creek Massacre. Thousands of people came to the site to wonder, along with the archaeologists, about who the people were, how they had lived, why they had been massacred, and who had killed them.

Although the excavations ended with some unknown number of victims remaining in the ground, archaeologist and specialists in human bone have attempted to answer some of the questions. We know that at least 489 people were killed; how many more remain in the ground, we don't know. There may also be other bone piles in other sections of the ditch. We know that the victims were ancestral to the Arikara. The pottery styles and decorations at Crow Creek were similar to varieties seen in Arikara villages by the first European explorers. A second radiocarbon date, 1325 A.D., taken from charcoal mixed in with the bone, corroborates the 14th century as the time in which the massacre occurred. This means that the tragedy took place well before the arrival of the white man. While some believe that scalping came with the Whites, such mutilation is actually a trait common to many cultures and many times, including prehistoric North America. We are fairly certain that the people who perpetrated the deed were inhabitants of a nearby village of the same culture, perhaps even distant relatives or friends. The number of people killed and the size of the group needed to attack a well-fortified village indicate that some small unknown nomadic group could not have attacked the village; many more people would be necessary. As well, a conical, socketed bone arrowhead found among the skeletons is known only from Initial Coalescent people. The single most important question, why?, remains; we are not without clues.

Careful analysis of the skulls shows that the people were short of particular nutrients, especially protein and iron. When these elements are in short supply over an extended period, a pitting of the bone on the upper part of the interior of the eye socket, known as Cribira orbitalis, can occur. Many of the Crow Creek skeletons show evidence of this problem. Short supply of food is known as a contributing factor to warfare in many parts of the world and may even cause fighting among close friends and relatives. We know that changes in climate, especially drought, can reduce the yield of crops. Larger and larger amounts of land are needed to grow the necessary amounts of food. Arable land along the Missouri bottoms was in short supply prehistorically, and there may have been competition for this limited resource. Drought also causes changes in animal ranges, perhaps as much as 200 miles in a season. Years of drought may have reduced the number of buffalo in the Crow Creek area, bringing the Crow Creek site occupants into conflict with neighboring groups over hunting territory.

We may never know what the ultimate cause of the massacre was and precisely who committed it. The numerous data gathered on the largest known prehistoric massacre site in North America will be analyzed for years to come. We will undoubtedly know more of the life and death of the Crow Creek inhabitants. We may even be able to substantiate the suspected causes of the warfare. If so, we may have another piece of evidence to demonstrate that competition for scarce resources can lead to disasters unless we control our material appetites. But we can never know the terror that overtook the people of the Crow Creek site on a day when the sunset was blood-red over the Missouri breaks.

On one day in the dim past, a massacre that staggers the imagination occurred in an Indian village overlooking the Missouri. Its magnitude is shown in a grave of skeletons, top and side views.

Photos — L. Zimmerman

Campbell County

Area, 774 square miles
Population, 1925 - 5,532; 1945 - 4,337; 1980 - 2,243
County Seat, Mound City. Population 111

A county that has lost about 60 per cent of its population in the last 55 years must wonder a bit about its past. Will the trend continue and at the end of another 50 years will the inhabitants turn to their neighbors and find them living in the next county? These people, lost at about 42 per year, leave in their wake abandoned farms, deserted cities, and a disillusionment with the land. Why did the land not support them?

Mound City, not spawned by a railroad track, is one of the few county seats to survive the railroad track syndrome. When the railroad was finally established to the north, all Mound City lost was most of its businesses which moved to Herreid. Today Mound City is the second smallest county seat in the state. It is exceeded in dimininutiveness only by Olivet, the county seat of Hutchinson County, whose size and situation parallels that of Mound City.

A historic and natural site in Campbell County is Spring Creek, the campsite of Lewis and Clark which they called Stone Idol Creek. This rock now called Standing Rock is the name of an Indian Reservation. Also along the Missouri are the old Arikara Indian Villages, notably Bramble Village.

Pocasse National Wildlife Refuge is a sandhill crane refuge and is located near Pollock. Notable lakes in the county are Sand, Salt, McClarin, and Campbell.

Other sites in the county include a scenic road along the Missouri past Waneta Bottoms and Bramble, and near Mound City are prehistoric Indian Mounds.

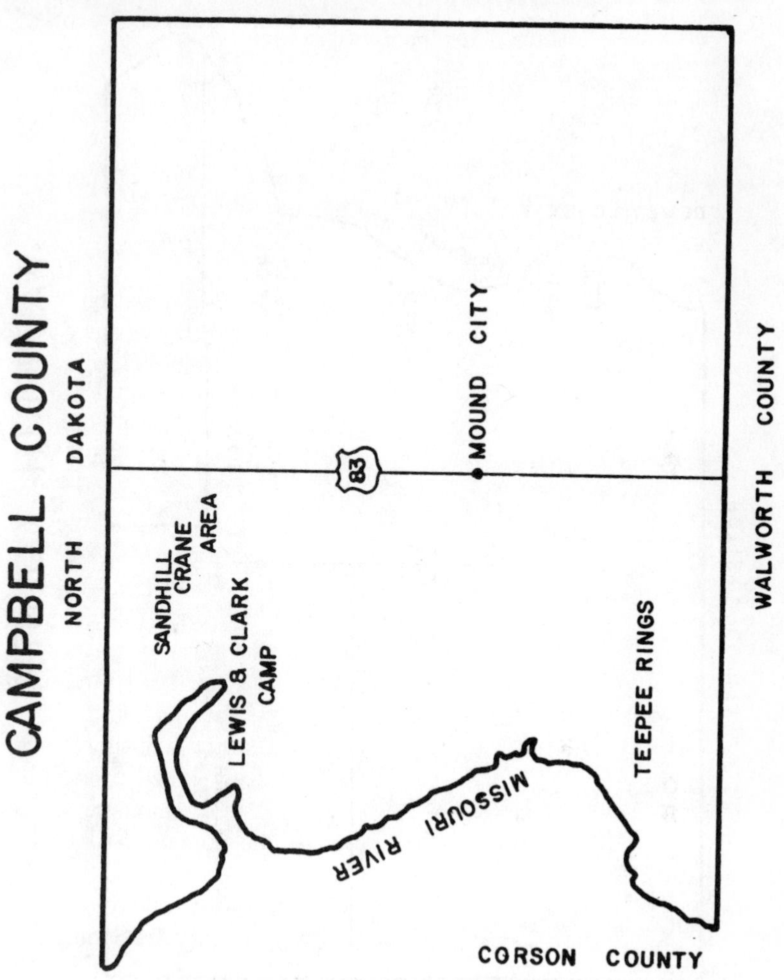

Walworth County

Area, 742 square miles
Population, 1925 - 8,043; 1945 - 7,011; 1980 - 7,011
County Seat, Selby. Population 884

Blue Blanket Valley is a romantic name for a haze-covered cow pasture that once existed along the Missouri River for several miles. Under the haze, seen only from a distance, now are found the industrious farmers of Walworth County.

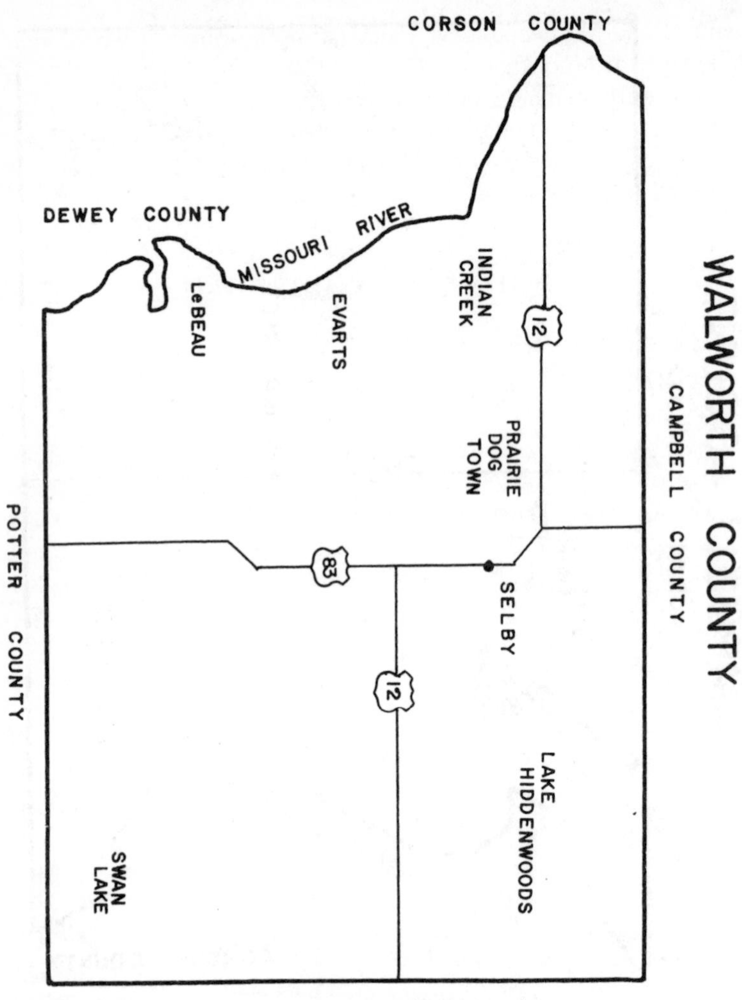

It is a county that traces its history back to the numerous Arikara Villages along the Missouri. To the twin towns of LeBeau and Evarts, from 1900 to 1910, belonged the prestige of being the largest cattle shipping points in the United States. Both now are extinct.

From large areas west of the river, through specially arranged corridors to gain protection from the Indians, came the cattle drives. When they arrived on the west side, the cattle were ferried across the river to the terminus of the railroad on the east side. Evarts was the end of the Milwaukee Road and LeBeau the end of the Minneapolis-St. Paul. Later the railroad would span the river at Mobridge.

Now only memories of those brawling cow towns can be recalled, if one is old enough, can pause for a moment, remember the nine-digit zip code, and concentrate on days when numbers were only on the sides of cattle.

The Old Scaffold

Campbell & Walworth Counties

Overhead fleecy clouds rolled shadows of darkness over the land, setting the distant hills undulating into the horizon. Terry, his school work finished, walked home, wrapped in the joy of a warm spring day. As he approached the old Indian burial ground that he had to cross, he kicked at clumps of dirt. The dust exploded into the air, swirled by the convection currents so common on unevenly heated ground. He flipped a rock at the whistle of a flickertail on a mound near the field. Terry walked with a shifting shuffle, his arms flopping in aimless agreement to the relaxed sway of his youthful body.

As he approached a baseball-size lump of dirt, his right leg tensed and he prepared to spray the particles of soil into the whipping wind. But he paused, for there, on the edge of the clod, glinted an object like one he had seen before. He reached down and extracted a root-beer-colored arrow. He knew what he had found, for he had found other artifacts made from a material known as Knife River Flint on the spot where an old scaffold had stood. He held it to the light and saw streaks of alternating shades of brown that reflected light rays in opalescent patterns. The last time he asked about this curious pattern, he had been told that Knife River Flint was petrified lignite and that the Indians had collected it in North Dakota, hauled it south and made arrows and scrapers from it.

Terry's thoughts played over all the stories he had heard about the old scaffold. He thought he could almost see it standing there in stark relief on top of the knoll, a solitary sentinel of an almost forgotten race. On foggy days, he walked out of his way to avoid the burial site, where he imagined vague, mysterious forms weaving in and out of the dense fog. Once when he detoured, he had found a vertebra on an eroded slope. When he turned it over, he discovered the animal had been killed by an arrow embedded deep in its spinal cord. Did it have a connection with the scaffold? Was it a food sacrifice for the dead? Was it from a horse that was killed to accompany the deceased? Or had a hunting party killed it? All he knew was what the experts had told him, that the animal had lived for some time because calcified bone deposits had grown around the arrow. The mystery of the scaffold deepened.

He stopped off at his house for cookies and milk before doing his chores. As he sat there, he remembered a story told that when the scaffold had blown down, the Indians accused white settlers of pushing it over. After a few crisis-filled days, the Indians re-erected the rickety scaffold and left. The scaffold again stood, forlorn and lonely, the tattered blanket covering the body flapping in the wind.

Each year, for several years, the Indians came in small groups on horse or foot to pay homage to their dead. They stood in silent vigil for a long time, then disappeared to the west. One year when they arrived, the scaffold had completely rotted away and collapsed, and bleached bones were scattered about the prairie. They silently gathered together the bones, wrapped them in a bundle, and buried them in a mound on the highest point of the nearby terminal moraine.

Several years ago, when Terry was just a small boy, he remembered watching the spring migration of ducks and geese as they congregated in the prairie potholes. Overhead the clouds painted shadowy patterns on the swells and swales of the wind-driven grass. As he stood there, he noticed a slow procession of cars cutting a trail over grass that had never been trampled. He watched as they edged up to the fence that now cut off the old Indian graves from the rest of the prairie, for now the flat top of the moraine had been cut by the plow and turned into a large field. The cars stopped at the edge of the field, and Terry felt excitement for the old Indians, who had returned to their burial ground after a long absence — returned for what proved to be the last time. In the past they had always come on horse and dressed in colorful costumes. This time they came in battered cars, with blankets thrown over their stooped shoulders. They walked in single file to the mounds and huddled together silently. They must have felt, on the windswept field, that more than just the prairie had disappeared when their burial ground was plowed. The blackness of the soil matched the bleakness of the moment.

They turned in what looked like a painful gesture and left in single file, the wind flapping their worn blankets. The long and faithful vigil for the dead had ended. They never returned.

Terry had often visited the top of the moraine. He liked to stand on the mounds to view the marsh, prairie and woodlands spread out below. He could visualize a time when Indian camps were strung between the lakes and marshes and off in the distance the buffalo had grazed. He wondered how long the Indians had used this burial ground, for he had found many different types of artifacts around the area. Some said that the oddly unnotched points were really the spear points of the Paleo Indian who occupied the area at the time of the retreating glacier. He had been told that at one time a boreal spruce forest covered parts of the hills, and giant mammoths and horned prehistoric bison roamed the area. Only a few years ago an almost complete mammoth skeleton had been discovered in a gravel pit a few miles east of where he stood. The more he thought about it and the more he heard about it, the more mysterious the old burial ground became.

Terry heard his mother coming, so he quickly grabbed his cap and ran to gather the eggs, fill the woodbox, feed the pigs and chickens, and herd the cows home for milking. He loved doing the latter because the cattle were often grazing up near the Indian mounds, and he could hunt for arrows on the way.

When Terry was finished with chores, it was time for bed. He fingered his new found arrow, admired it awhile, and wondered about the mystery of the scaffold. Had it been a famous chief? Was it some spiritual leader, or was it a loved one of an especially caring family? In a few minutes he was sound asleep.

The next morning a blanket of fog covering the land was lying in long, wispy layers over the ground. As Terry walked to school, he felt strangely uneasy when he neared the Indian scaffold site. The fog and the creeking cottonwood nearby were almost more than he could take. His eyes started to play tricks, so he gripped his lunch box and ran the rest of the way to school. At school he settled in his seat by the window and noticed the sun's rays penetrating the fog on the burial ground. Strange shapes seemed to form in the lifting fog, and for a moment a scaffold appeared and by its side a lone Indian! He rubbed his eyes, then felt a hand on his shoulder. "Getting your school work started, Terry?" Terry, startled, almost blurted at his teacher, "Boy, what a way to destroy a vision!" Instead, he grabbed his book and said, "How many pages do we have to read today?"

Corson County

Area, 2,526 square miles
Population, 1925 - 8,656; 1945 - 6,610; 1980 - 5,196
County Seat, McIntosh. Population 418

You aren't drawn to Clay Butte like some massive impressive monument that you have always wanted to visit. You just sort of wander by imagining hills have names. It seems you are drawn there with the same exuberant enthusiasm you would have in slipping down neighboring Mud Butte on a rainy day. So when you finally arrive at the top of Clay Butte, you wonder why you are there. You let your eyes wander catching the feel of distance, for that is all that there is, distance. What do you write about distance? Emptiness. Loneliness. A place where atoms and molecules have never had a chance to coalesce into beings. Here the molecules of your body, pulled by the vacuum of emptiness, are held only by skin and the energy of life. It seems if you were to remain here you would eventually diffuse out into the nothingness.

But wait, there is something out there. Off in the distance are soft rounded, verdant mounds, like the soft contours of the female form nudging gently into the skyline and vibrating in shimmering haze. Is it Mother Earth? No. The Greek Goddess of Fertility? No. It is just the mind stretching out to greet the vastness of the situation and to bring into focus the things dreams are made of. Yes, the eyes have played into the mind the things Corson County is made up of: space, imagination, and hope.

What else does one think about in Corson County? There is the singing bridge that brings one across the Grand River, past Chief Gall Inn and into the Standing Rock Indian Reservation. It is here where Sitting Bull spent his last day; where Rain-In-The-Face, Gall, John Grass, Running Antelope, together with The Bull, all sought peace after the battle of Little Bighorn. Here is where Sacajawea spent her last days, and there on the banks of the

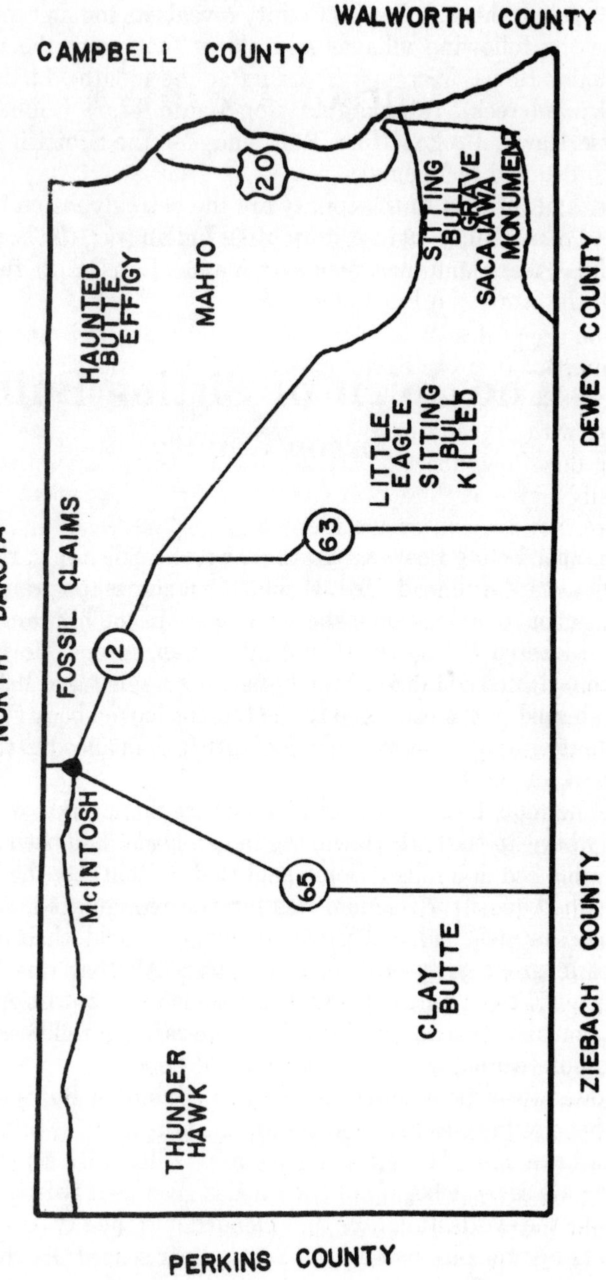
CORSON COUNTY
CAMPBELL COUNTY
WALWORTH COUNTY
NORTH DAKOTA
FOSSIL CLAIMS
HAUNTED BUTTE EFFIGY
MAHTO
SITTING BULL GRAVE
SACAJAWA MONUMENT
DEWEY COUNTY
LITTLE EAGLE
SITTING BULL KILLED
McINTOSH
THUNDER HAWK
CLAY BUTTE
ZIEBACH COUNTY
PERKINS COUNTY
20
12
63
65

Missouri stand two monuments that give tribute to her and The Bull.

Traveling through Corson County reveals its Indian connection. Note the following villages and places that greet the traveler: Thunder Hawk, Watauga (foaming at the mouth), Little Eagle, Wakpala (creek), Tatanka (buffalo), Mahto (bear), Bullhead, Red Horse Hawk, Broken Horn Bull, and, for the Scottish Indians, McIntosh and McLaughlin.

Sites of interest in the county are the petroglyphs on Haunted Butte, Skull Butte and its story of an Indian war, the last village of the Arikara, and the site of Fort Manuel Lisa (1812), fur trader with the American Fur Company.

The Spirit of Sitting Bull

Corson County

Juniper Young Bear skirted the town of Little Eagle, riding his pony toward Bullhead. He had ridden out across the prairie to get the feel of freedom. Somewhere out there in the hills and valleys still flickered the spirit of ancient Indian heroes. He felt that woven within the fabric of the Indian was a spirit that had gotten lost, buried in the past. Today the Indians looked back with painful memories of what they had lost rather than ahead to the spirit needed for the future.

As he rode, he came to the place where Sitting Bull once lived and where, in the early dawn, the Indian leader had been dragged from his bed and killed. Some held that on that day the Indian's cherished quest for freedom was forever extinguished. All seven Indian nations had collapsed; no longer would their councils meet in great gatherings of celebration. All that was left was to ponder, twisting their anguished souls into contortions of indecision and frustration. The Silent Eaters, loyal followers of Sitting Bull, waited in vain for a signal of hope.

Young Bear dismounted his pony at the site of Bull's home on the bend of the Grand River. He watched the river, as Sitting Bull must have done. He felt a timelessness, filled with serenity and peace. He saw the beauty of the wooded river as it twisted its way toward the everlasting hills that blended into the sky. Everything was as Sitting Bull had left it. Young Bear sensed that here was something more than earth, sky, and river; that here beside him and flowing through the entire land was the pulsating strength of a spirit. He continued to look at the distant hills, and the feeling of freedom grew stronger, and the spirit of Sitting Bull swelled around him. His body slowly relaxed. He began to sense the same spirit that Sitting Bull had felt. Now he knew the spirit of the great Indian had not been stilled that eventful day in 1890. It had been released. It had slipped out into the land, a land that was the spawning place of all spirits. Mother Earth was again releasing the spirit and with it a hope for the future. Young Bear's eyes looked to the future as The Bull had looked to the future. The painful events of the past no longer made him bitter. A new spirit gave him confidence.

Young Bear perceived that the spirit of Mother Earth, which gave Sitting Bull strength, had evaded him until today. He remembered other Indian greats and recognized from whence they too had drawn their power. From earth, sun, and the four directions, the spirit of power came to settle in their bodies. This spirit could not be buried, destroyed, bought, sold, or lost.

As Young Bear rode along, he thought about the spirit that had motivated the other great Indians — Red Cloud, Crazy Horse, Gall, and Sacajawea (that wonder woman who had given so unselfishly of herself in her long service with Lewis and Clark). The spirit within him grew stronger. He was thankful for his mother and father, the people of the town of Little Eagle, and the spirit they had given him. He thought of all the people of the world, for he knew the Great Spirit was not the exclusive spirit of the Indian but was possessed by all men of great faith. He knew now that in no way could the Great Spirit disappear. The way to find it was to seek it.

His ride along the Grand River took him to the town of Bullhead. He thought about Lieutenant Bullhead and the other Indians who had been sent out to arrest Sitting Bull. Bullhead had also been killed, as had several others. All lay buried here. It was so wasteful. Indians killed by Indians in a period of misunderstanding and suffering. Their graves merged with those of countless other Indians who had given up the spirit and died a wasted life. Futility replaced the spirit, and despair was the product. Indians had looked toward the coming of an Indian Messiah, had worn ghost shirts that would protect them from bullets, and had drowned their sorrow in alcohol. But events had turned against them.

As Young Bear rode back home, he remembered the Stone Woman (Standing Rock) and it symbolism. He thought of Haunted Butte, Skull Butte, Medicine Rock, and all the other places where the spirit was symbolically strong. He rode past the church where he went on Sunday with his parents. He remembered Jesus, who had also died at the hands of members of His own race and who had released His great spirit upon the world.

He rounded the corner and saw the little house that was his home. On the porch stood his mother, waiting supper for him. With a quick twist he slid off his horse and ran to give her a hug of love and appreciation. He had envisioned much today and grown one step closer to manhood. She patted his head and asked, "Did you have a good ride?"

"Yes," he said, "today I found out that the spirit of Sitting Bull, a man of peace, still lives."

Dewey County

Area, 1,907 square miles
Population, 1925 - 5,682; 1945 - 5,265; 1980 - 5,366
County Seat, Timber Lake. Population 660

Dewey County is in an area of shallow soil and the dry, brittle Pierre Shale often outcrops like huge piles of coal. Here people will walk the farmers' fields looking for nodules, for every nodule will contain fossils. When picked up and tapped with a hammer they will reveal ammonites dating back to the 100-million-year-old Cretaceous Sea. These extinct relatives of the snail and clam provide beautiful examples of extinct life, a pastime for collectors, and a wealth of information for scientists. Specimens from the area are now in museums all over the world.

In addition to fossil sea shells, petrified wood, fossil leaf imprints, and dinosaur bones are found. Near Isabel is a coal mine which reflects the swamps and forests after the passing of the Cretaceous Sea. The fossils here are of an advanced age.

This is the county of the Cheyenne River Indian Reservation, and as one wanders around looking for fossils, he is apt to come across some of the Indian schools in the area such as Bear Creek,

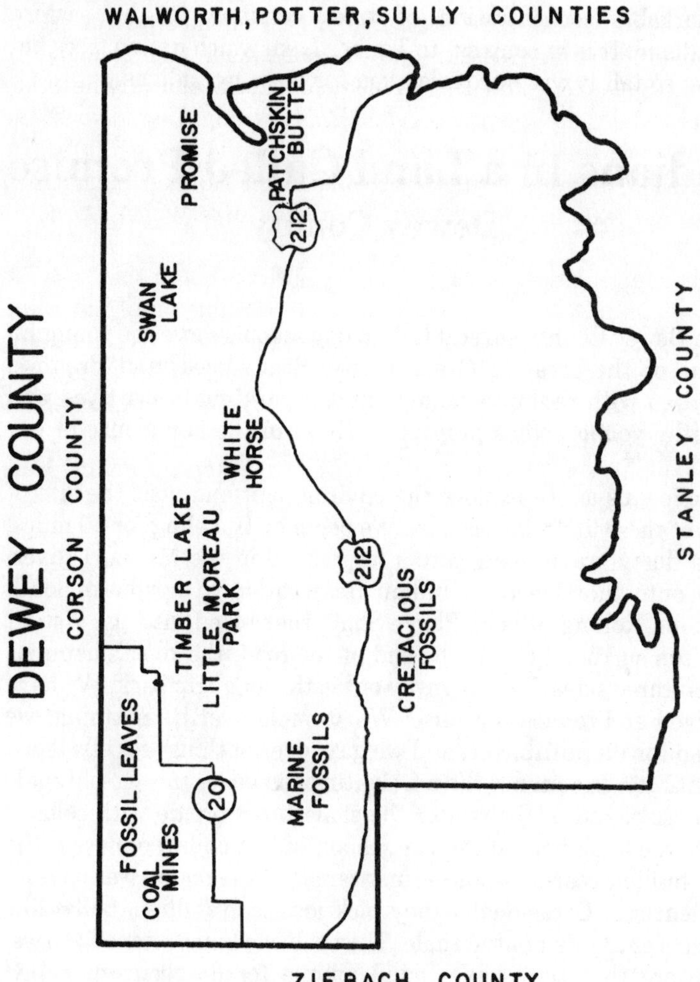

Green Grass, White Horse, Glen Cross, and Promise. The latter named Wahoyapi, meaning "once called," was translated in Washington as Promise. The children here have often their own collection of fossils found in the area.

Other Indian places are Dog Butte, where an Indian dog had puppies, and Eagle Butte, where the Indians were known to capture eagles. The use of eagle feathers was a mark of distinction among the Indians.

An additional site that must be mentioned is the Little Moreau State Park. Here, in a land where trees are hard to grow, is a remarkable concentration of trees common to the eastern woodland. It is in contrast to Timber Lake which has no trees but grass so tall it was once mistaken for trees by Indians.

Indians In a Land Called Promise

Dewey County

In Dewey County several Indian day schools serve the young Indians of the area. In Green Grass, Bear Creek, and Promise, children with receptive young minds, sparkling brown eyes, and healthy young bodies prepare to share in the abundance of our land.

Follow us as we explore the environment and visit the site of one of these little day schools. We begin by traveling for 30 miles, on a dusty gravel road, into a large bend in the Missouri River, and onto the Cheyenne Indian Reservation in northern South Dakota. Rolling hills of Pierre Shale that blend into the distant horizon surround us. At the end of the road, the river surrounds us on three sides. The only way out is the long trip back. We have arrived at Promise. Promise! We stumble over its meaning, we grasp for its fulfillment, and we gaze over nothingness stretched to infinity. In summer the unrelenting sun bakes the age-old shale to a crisp, and in the winter the shale turns brittle with cold.

On the knoll behind the day school, Indian children play on the 150-million-year-old-shale — unaware that the region was once an ancient sea. Occasionally they pick loose, crystalline, bullet-like objects embedded in the shale. They call the bullets pencil agates, unaware that they have found unique fossil specimens called belemnites. The ancient fossils are related to squid or octopi. Their remains are found over much of the Cretaceous formation known as the Pierre Shale. But only at this site has the animal fossilized into a clear, gem-like material.

Across from the children's playground is one of the tallest hills in the area, a place from which to view the vastness that rolls hill over hill and tumbles them into a blue sky seasoned with cumulus clouds. Climbing this hill, we see that someone has been there ahead of us, for scattered around are chips left by an ancient craftsman who used the place as his lookout. We speculate that on this windswept point, he spent many hours making his arrows, for he had found belemnites to be a suitable material to turn into weapons. The 100-million-year-old fossil is transformed into a beautiful, translucent white arrowhead that he has lost in the dry grey shale. Gazing from this vantage point, we see what has attracted the ancient hunter to this site. Curving below us like an emerald necklace, twisting into the somber hills, is a densely wooded river. It is the survival kit of the Indian. It is water, shelter, and food for his people, and for the animals he will hunt with the arrows he is fashioning.

As the shadows lengthen toward evening, the contrast between sky and earth decreases, and the immensity of the place swallows everything in its presence. It is as if our essence has diffused into time and space and become entangled with the spirit of the ancient hunter. No longer living in the present, we tumble along with the ancient squid and all the other organisms that once called this beautiful river valley home. Today little is left of this beautiful river. Gone too is the promise of the past, for most of the life-giving stream has been replaced by mud flats and dying trees. The river is a product of a progressive civilization whose energy needs have displaced a living river with a fluctuating water reservoir. Its level shrinks and swells on the mud flats of death.

Turning and again looking down from the hill, we can see the beginning of a different sort of Promise. Nestled in the hills is a piece of black ground that will provide sustenance for people who no longer may depend on the buffalo, berries, and bounties of the bush. This piece of ground will provide them with some of their future food needs. It is their promise.

As the Indian craftsman on the hilltop prayed for the promise of a good hunt, he also prepared for it by making a supply of sturdy arrows. Perhaps today we, too, can see the promise of an added supply of food from a plot of irrigated land in an area of low rainfall. The fulfillment of a promise means that the past has provided good preparation.

So in Promise, Green Grass, Bear Creek, and scores of other small Indian day schools scattered around the reservation, let there indeed be a promise. A promise that Indians may receive the education and respect that allows them to relate to their culture and their environment, with the understanding that it is the land that gives them nourishment and sustenance. The future of these Indians depends upon it. Like the ancient Indian who prayed on the hilltop, we too should pray that, by working together, we can turn a prayer into a fulfilled promise.

Hand County

Area, 1,426 square miles
Population, 1925 - 9,960; 1945 - 6,643; 1980 - 4,948
County Seat, Miller. Population 1,931

Tommy Fastwalker crossed Hand County, nearly 60 miles, in one day. J.W. Coquillette, champion ladder climber set a world record on the fireman ladder at 5½ seconds. This happened back in the good old days when people were fast afoot. Today people in Hand County get most of their speed from Detroit products that can cover Hand County in less than one hour.

In the flat eastern part of the county, it is easy to speed, but along the western border runs the Wessington and Ree Hills, which slow one down. In the former is Wessington Gulch, a wooded draw with bur oak. The latter is known for its Indian activities and is named for the Rees that were killed by the Sioux for stealing horses. An inspection of the hills reveals a place where thousands of Indians must have gathered. It was here where slumping ground during the wet season would form precipitous drops on clay hills. Over these drops the Indians, B.H. (before horses), would chase the buffalo. Today these buffalo jumps, camps, butchering, and meat-drying sites are an archeologist's bonanza. One of these sites on the Buster Deuter Ranch reveals a period five to six thousand years ago. Up on top of the hill spread out away from the jump area are 200 to 300 teepee rings, rock symbols, ceremonial sites, and signs of Indian congestion.

Down in the valley to the east are buffalo pastures, prairie fires, and big blue stem mixed with Indian grass which once attracted the roaming herds. Now only rubbing rocks, wallows, and, here and there, faint evidence of trails are mute evidence of the thundering herds.

Another site in Hand County that attracts interest is the post glacial fossil fish site. This indicates a fresh water lake once flourished in the area. There is also in the area a convent where nuns homesteaded the land. The lakes in the area are Louise, Jones, Rose Hill, and Johnston's.

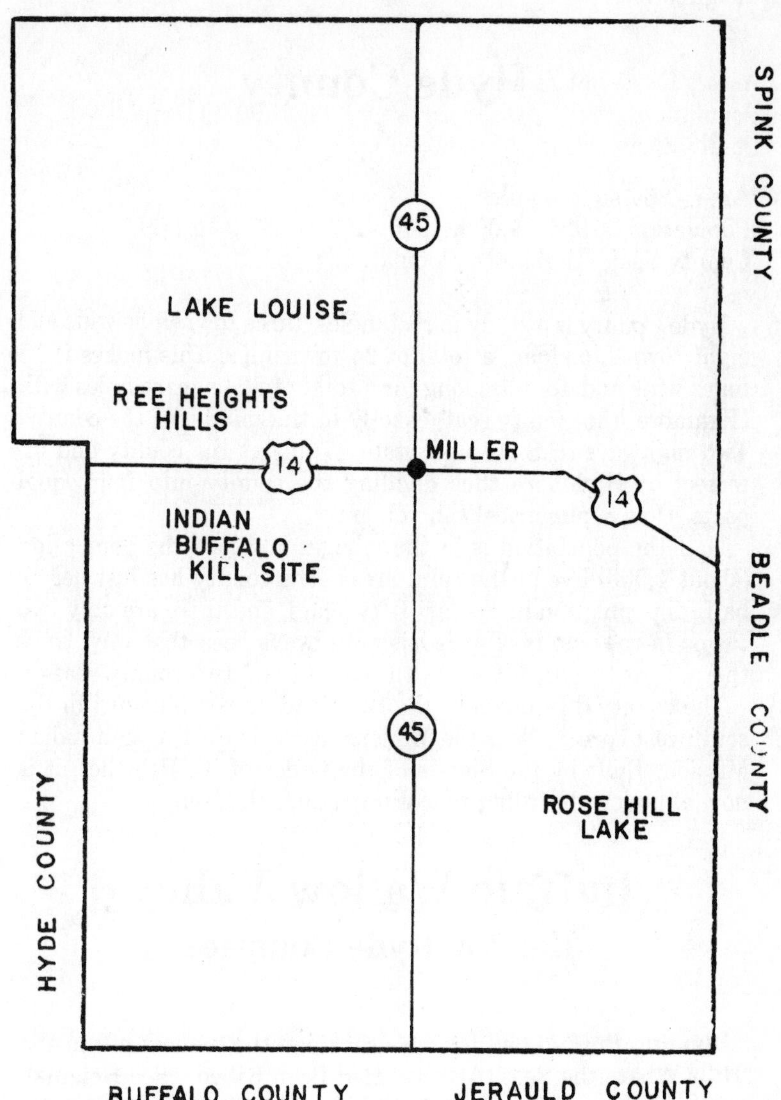
HAND COUNTY
FAULK COUNTY
SPINK COUNTY
45
LAKE LOUISE
REE HEIGHTS
HILLS
14
MILLER
14
INDIAN
BUFFALO
KILL SITE
BEADLE COUNTY
45
ROSE HILL
LAKE
HYDE COUNTY
BUFFALO COUNTY
JERAULD COUNTY

Gone are the rural stores, all extinct except two; gone are the cattle rustlers that found a haven in the Wessington and Ree Hills; gone is half the population of Hand County. Those that remain say it's a good country where you can know and trust your neighbors.

Hyde County

Area, 864 square miles
Population, 1925 - 4,000; 1945 - 2,756; 1980 - 2,069
County Seat, Highmore. Population 1,055

Hyde County is a study in rectangles, three townships wide and eight townships long, a total of 24 townships. This makes it 18 miles wide and 48 miles long for a total of 864 square miles with Highmore, the county seat, exactly in the middle of the county. Two highways (U.S. 14 and State 47) bisect the county and intersect at Highmore thus dividing the county into four equal parts. How symmetrical can you get?

Half the population is in the villages and half the population (about 1,000) live in the rural areas. The county has lost nearly half its population in the last fifty years, and there are only two towns in the county. But it has not always been that way. Once there were 16 post offices in the county and two county seats.

The county dips down to the Big Bend on the Missouri in the southwest corner. Near the Missouri River is the Stephan Indian Mission. Built by the Sisters of the Order of St. Benedict, it is now a modern boarding school for Indian children.

Buffalo Wallow Valley

Hand & Hyde Counties

Running Buffalo had for days sat upon the highest hill in the "Hills Where the Rees (Arikara) Had Been Killed" (Ree Heights), watching the activity of the buffalo herd in the long flat Buffalo Wallow Valley that stretched for 50 miles before him over into what is now Hyde County. In the early spring, members of the

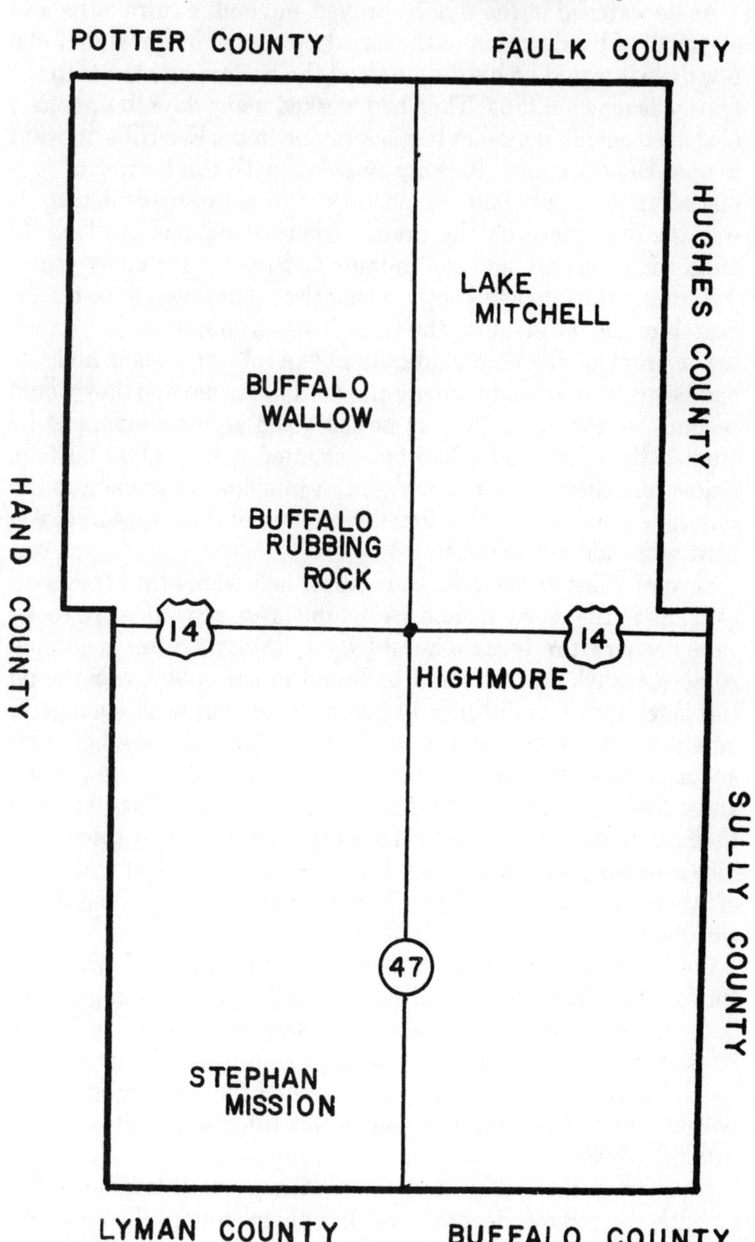
HYDE COUNTY
POTTER COUNTY
FAULK COUNTY
HUGHES COUNTY
LAKE MITCHELL
BUFFALO WALLOW
BUFFALO RUBBING ROCK
HAND COUNTY
14
14
HIGHMORE
SULLY COUNTY
47
STEPHAN MISSION
LYMAN COUNTY
BUFFALO COUNTY

tribe had burned this area, for they knew the buffalo preferred the fresh young grass that grew vigorously on recent burns.

As he watched in the sun, he prayed and built a cairn of rock as a symbol of his devotion to the Great Spirit, for he knew that in a few days it would be his duty to lead the buffalo into the trap the tribe was now building. They had worked many days to prepare a U-shaped corral in a relict bur oak ravine in the Ree Hills, in what is now Hand County. Its narrow sides, with the barrier of logs placed at the upper end, would turn it into an excellent trap. It was the only place on the prairie where wood was available to build such a corral, and the Indians had used it for many years.

Running Buffalo had known a long time that it was to be his duty to lure the buffalo into the trap. It was a dangerous job, crawling in front of the herd clad only in the robe of a giant bull. He had been out practicing among the herd many days so they would become used to him. Now as he marveled at their numbers, he studied their habits. He had once counted nearly 3,000 buffalo. Below him their trails crisscrossed in random fashion across the flat valley bottom. In the distance a cloud of dust appeared as a herd was suddenly spooked.

Several miles to the west was a water hole where they frequently drank in the morning, and stretching off to the left was a rocky valley where the buffalo would later lie down after drinking. Almost always buffalo could be found in the valley, rubbing on the large rocks, wallowing in the dust, engaging in combat to determine dominance in the herd, or resting. Dust clouds puffed above some of the larger wallows, for the buffalo, while pawing and rubbing, would throw dust in all directions. They covered themselves with dust to get rid of the parasites in their thick hair. Lice especially were abundant, but a heavy coat of dust would cut off their oxygen and suffocate them. Another natural insecticide was mud.

Centered in many of the wallows were rubbing rocks. Running Buffalo had frequently watched the buffalo, after taking a dust bath, rub with great intensity on the sharp edges of the rock. The bugs they could not suffocate were ground to death against the rock. The result was a deep groove around the rock and a highly polished rock. In spring the groove was filled with water; in the summer, dust.

Away from the wallow and rest area was a trail leading to the recently burned meadow that lay directly in front of the open end of the trap. Running Buffalo had noticed that the buffalo, after their rest, took this path to the grazing area. He had often sat alone in his buffalo robe along the trail and watched them pass. It was here, he planned, that the hunt would begin. Already he had practiced his buffalo call and watched the beasts' reaction.

Long ago he gave a name to the area — Buffalo Wallow Valley. Once he had sneaked to the edge of the area, clad only in his buffalo robe disguise, and there, hunched over, he had watched as the beasts tossed massive heads back and forth while grazing. One large-sized bull grazed closer and closer but paid no attention to the deformed hulk squatting near a large rock. Suddenly the bull stopped grazing and looked over at the misshapen form. Every muscle in the boy's body tensed. The bull looked him straight in the eye, moved two steps toward him, stopped, pawed the ground, shook his head, sucked in his breath and then, as if in disgust at the lack of response from the curious hulk, continued his grazing.

Just about the time Running Buffalo decided to retreat to safety, a pack of wolves came over the hill, and the buffalo moved into action. With much snorting they rounded themselves into three large circles, with the cows and calves milling in the center. The large bulls, their shaggy heads projecting outward, started circling around the young members of the herd. The wolves began circling in the opposite direction, trying to break in the circle. Running Buffalo had once seen a hunting attack by wolves from a distance. Afterwards he had examined the deep circular ruts cut by the constantly circling buffalo. He had once heard of a wolf attack that had lasted three days, before the wolves were successful in killing a buffalo. Sometimes a wolf ended up impaled on short blunt horns before being trampled to death by sharp hooves. It was predation on the plains, played out in terms of strength, endurance, and survival.

Running Buffalo took one last look at the battle and knew he must leave while the wolves were occupied with the buffalo. Quickly he slipped down in the ravine behind him and retreated to the safety of the hills.

There he rested, for he knew that tomorrow was to be the big day. The tribe had been carrying on preparations for many days. He knew that in the morning tribal members would situate themselves on hills surrounding the buffalo and haze the buffalo in the direction of the trail that led to the trap. He knew that he must station himself near the trap's entrance so the buffalo would not be afraid and would head toward him, not veer off on the trail that branched to the right.

After a night of celebration and prayer, he stood at the selected spot, where he could see the brown mass moving toward him. The large bull leading the herd came to the fork in the trail and hesitated. Then, hearing Running Buffalo's call, he turned and headed in the direction of the trap. The young Indian's heart skipped a beat. He knew the buffalo would not be afraid of the trees, for the animals had often come there to rub on the trunks. His only concern now was to get out of the way when the stampede triggered. Suddenly they came, and he rushed for the protection of the nearest bur oak, reaching it as buffalo brushed past him on both sides. In the protection of the tree, he felt good because he knew the buffalo had been trapped.

Members of the tribe quickly killed the buffalo with arrows and clubs. Sixteen buffalo were dead. The rest escaped. Running Buffalo, looking at the dead buffalo, knew that tonight there would be a big buffalo dance, and he would be given the honor of dancing in the center of the circle. He would at last be considered a great warrior.

After dancing and feasting on buffalo tongue all night, he returned in the morning to the hill where he had for days watched the activity of the buffalo. He gave thanks again to the Great Wakan that had been with him through a dangerous time. He remembered a young friend who had been crippled for life after being crushed against a tree by a charging buffalo. He remembered tales of brave warriors who had died in hunts that had gone wrong. He thought that someday the tribe might get horses that would make the hunt easier. He had heard that Indians to the west were getting horses from the Spaniards.

The sun grew warmer, and he grew sleepy as he basked in the glory of the hunt. He again looked out over Buffalo Wallow Valley and saw the buffalo that he had so come to admire. He felt, as he slipped off to sleep, that things had gone well, and it was the buffalo that had made him happy.

Edging the sky with a ribbon of green loom the distant Ree Heights bluffs. Here the young buffalo caller watched for the gathering of buffalo in the long flat Buffalo Wallow Valley. Down on the valley there are old buffalo wallows and rubbing rocks. The rocks, worn smooth by the rubbing, still stand as mute evidence of the once abundant buffalo. Note the depression around the rock created by the continuous wallowing of the buffalo.

Photos — Top, L. Rezak. Bottom, D.J. Holden

Mellette County

Area, 1,303 square miles
Population, 1925 - 5,177; 1945 - 3,332; 1980 - 2,249
County Seat, White River. Population 561

Although Mellette County has few people, 1.7 per square mile excluding White River, it is rich in history, tradition, and scenery. It boasts Black Pipe Creek, where the famous Black Pipestone is found. The site is known by only a few Indians.

The scenery of the county is created by Cedar Ridge, several buttes, badlands formation, and the White and Little White Rivers.

The town of White River is typically western. Here Indians in modern dress, blanket Indians, ten-gallon hats, gaudy shirts, and a few white collar workers mingle. It was selected as the county seat by "making medicine" and smoking the peace pipe.

The county was opened for settlement in October, 1911, and thousands came to claim land at $2.00 to $6.00 per acre. Of the many that came only a few remained after all the speculation was over. They left in their wake a series of ghost villages and post offices. Some of these are Kary, Red Wing, Ringthunder, Bad Nation, Apex, Chilton, Cody, Farley, Berkley, Runningville, Schamber, Texan, Brave, Gate Way, Neville, and Jorgenson.

Wood and Norris, once active, thriving cities, are but shells of their former past. The drought and dry land have exacted their toll and turned the farming way of life into ranching.

Areas of interest in the county are a sod house in the northwest corner, Horse Creek Day School, Indian burial grounds, and two buttes known as Three Point Butte and Twin Butte.

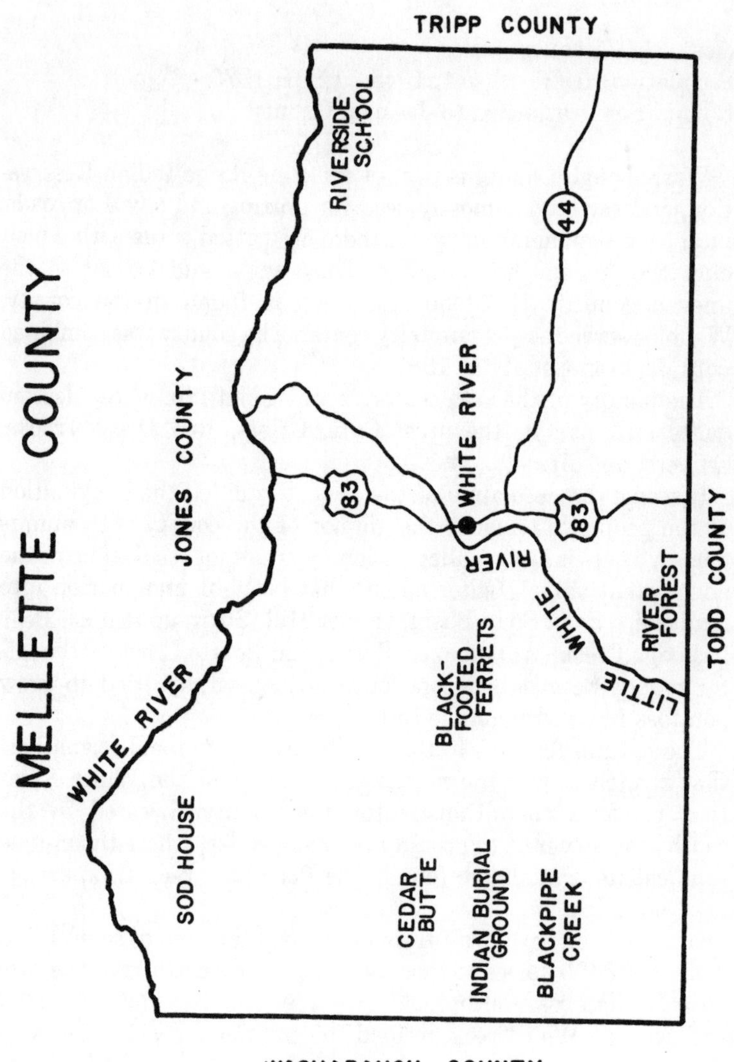
MELLETTE COUNTY
TRIPP COUNTY
JONES COUNTY
TODD COUNTY
WASHABAUGH COUNTY
RIVERSIDE SCHOOL
44
83
83
WHITE RIVER
WHITE RIVER
WHITE RIVER
LITTLE WHITE RIVER
RIVER FOREST
BLACK-FOOTED FERRETS
SOD HOUSE
CEDAR BUTTE
INDIAN BURIAL GROUND
BLACKPIPE CREEK

Washabaugh County

Area, 1,071 square miles
Population, 1925 - 2,474; 1945 - 1,881; 1980 - ?
County Seat, attached to Jackson County.

Washabaugh County is part of the Pine Ridge Indian Reservation, and the land is mostly used for grazing and hay. For roads, except for two main highways, there are rutted trails with which only the Indians are familiar. They angle and crisscross the uneven country. Since no real town is found in the county, Wanblee serves as a community center. The county was combined with Jackson County in 1981.

The history of the area centers about Chief Lip, whose descendants still live in the area: Cuts, Criers, Red Dogs, Tracks, Quivers, and Breasts.

It seems the desolation of the area stimulated the imagination of the people to enhance the glamor of the county with unique names. There is Long Valley, so long you cannot see the end of the nonexistent valley. Other names that brought imagination into reality are Bean Soup Basin, Quiver Hill, Sittin-up School, Bear in Lodge Creek, Wanamaker, Porch, and Potato Creek — the latter named because someone once unsuccessfully tried to grow potatoes in the dry gumbo soil.

The natural features in the county are the badland formations that stretches over the northwest corner and the White River that provides the drainage for the county. Located in the southwest corner of the county is Snake Butte, where the unique sand calcite crystals are found. The Poor Bear recreation area is near Wanblee.

Of note is an early wolf trapper who rid the area of some 1,000 wolves at $400 apiece so that the white man's cattle could be safe on an Indian reservation. Old Two Toes, the last wolf of legend and song on Wolf Creek, evaded the trapper for years. She was shy of baits, poison, trap, and gun. She evaded all methods of capture until one day, old, exhausted, without a mate, she was run down on foot and shot in a cedar grove. With her went a symbol of the prairie, for she was the last wolf in South Dakota.

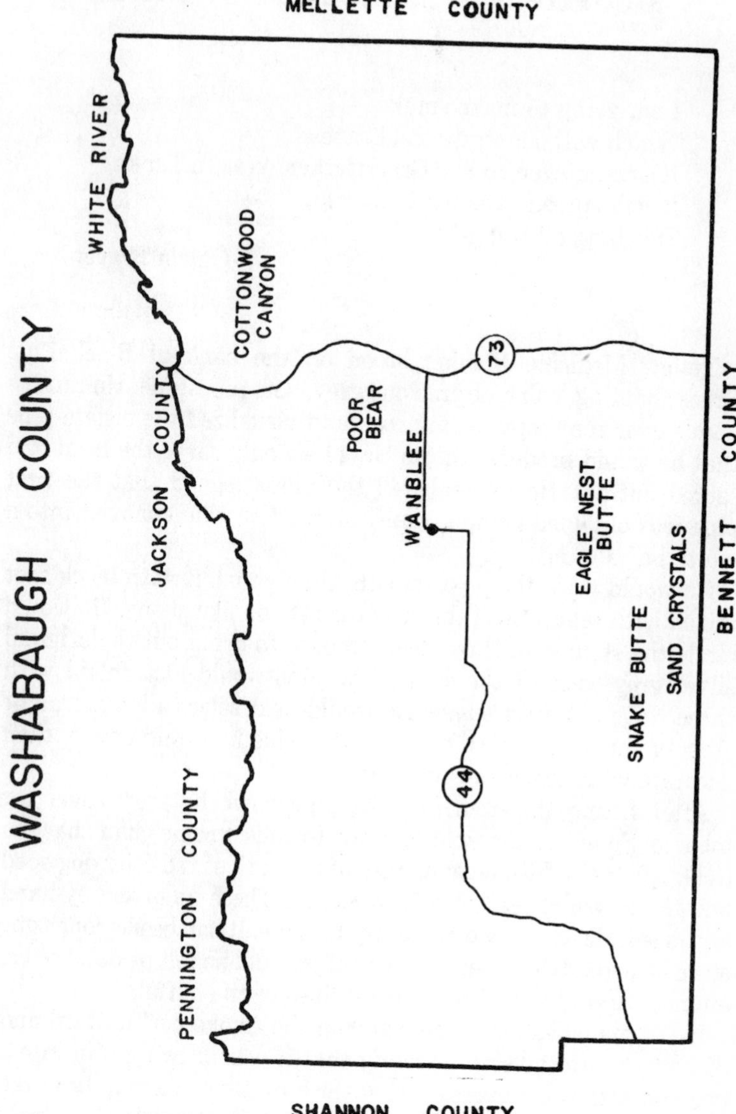
MELLETTE COUNTY
WHITE RIVER
COTTONWOOD CANYON
WASHABAUGH COUNTY
JACKSON COUNTY
POOR BEAR
73
WANBLEE
EAGLE NEST BUTTE
BENNETT COUNTY
SAND CRYSTALS
SNAKE BUTTE
44
PENNINGTON COUNTY
SHANNON COUNTY

The Black Pipe Dream
Mellette & Washabaugh Counties

I am going to make smoke
Which will penetrate the heavens,
Reaching even to our Grandfather, Wakan-Tanka,
It will spread over the Universe,
Touching all things!

—Oglala Prayer

Yellow Medicine Blanket stood on the bank of Black Pipe Creek, holding a slab of precious grey, soft pipestone. He ran his hands over the soapy-feeling rock and visualized the ornate pipe that he would produce. On its bowl he would carve the head of a sacred buffalo. He remembered the Sioux legend that the first pipe was obtained from a beautiful maiden, who changed into a white buffalo calf.

He would work the pipe smooth, then polish it with black soot mixed with tallow until the grey rock shone like ebony. He would circle the stem with three deep grooves to bring out the original silver grey color of the stone. The pipe would look inlaid with three rings of native silver. He would next select a long straight stem of sumac and burn out the pith. This he would polish, then decorate with beads and feathers.

After fitting the stem into the pipe bowl, he grew eager for tobacco. So out in the field he went to collect some chan sha sha (tobacco). He decided on a mixture of the bark of red osier dogwood and the leaves of lead plant and sumac. These he mixed by hand and dried. He was now ready to try his pipe. It had been a long time since he had produced such a work of art, and he felt pride as he examined carefully the finely carved lines of the buffalo.

He lit his pipe, and as he watched the smoke curl upward and disappear into the sky, a feeling that it was drawing him into a oneness with the universe came over him. He had a long time ago felt he had lost the bridge connecting him with the Great Mysterious Creator. Now he felt he was crossing a gap. His pipe smoke had drifted over to diffuse with the spirit of the universe. It drew him close to his maker. With the connection fully made, he was able to pray to the Great Wakan-Tanka and mingle again in the great experiment called Life. There was again a oneness of life, a oneness of spirit, and the Earth, the mother of it all, clasped him in her protective power and made him a part of the whole.

He felt over his entire body the goodness of it all. He must remember to remind other Indians of the power of the pipe, for most of them, too, had drifted from the path that made life complete.

He now knew that Black Pipe Creek must be preserved, for it was a place where Mother Earth yielded the sacred stone from whence came the wholeness of the universe. This 100-million-year-old metamorphic clay embedded in the Pierre Shale was a holy spot, steeped with religion, history, and tradition. The ancient pipes carved from this source predated the more abundant red pipestone. Black Pipe Creek was one place where the Indian came to appreciate his past, look forward to the future, and understand the present. It was the focal point of being and a connection to the oneness of nature.

The non-Indians around Black Pipe Creek have long admired the beautiful figures carved from this responsive stone. They have named a bank, store, school, and saloon after the sought-for stone. People have come from great distances to see the fine products. The Indian must recognize this and respond to the resource in a manner that justifies its use as an economic advantage, for a religious experience, and as a historical heritage. In the future the Indian may look back at Black Pipe Creek and recall with pride that there is an area that combines the earth and his ethereal spirit into one; a place where Yellow Medicine Blanket, his friends, his relatives, and all those with a need may find that the roots of their past are indeed connected with the security of their future. It is a place where the Indian dream, the Indian vision, may again produce a meaningful experience.

An Indian, Ephraim Taylor, and his pipe are like a priest and his Bible. Both signify the ceremonial events that couple man to his God.

Photo — Waltner, Courtesy Pipestone National Monument

Shannon County

Area, 964 square miles
Population, 1925 - 2,211; 1945 - 4,894; 1980 - 11,323
County Seat, Hot Springs in Fall River County. (Main town, Pine Ridge)

Scenic Shannon with its Irish name is filled with Indians. The land of Pajuta Wa Cha Cha (Indian Medicine), Red Cloud, Wounded Knee, and Pine Ridge is steeped with the tradition of the Teton and Oglala Sioux.

It is here, on the second largest reservation in the United States, where the Indians, turned on by their new awareness, are living as closely to their native lifestyles as they are able. There provided with Indian schools (Red Cloud Indian School is the largest in the nation), they weave together a conglomerate of white and Indian tradition. Out of this way of life has come an increase in population, a fivefold increase in the last 55 years. It has proven that we can no longer speak of the Indian as the "Vanishing American."

Shannon is also a picturesque county. It is dotted with buttes and tables: notably Cuny, Stirk, and Red Shirt Tables; Porcupine and Snake Buttes. The latter is the site of the well known sand calcite crystals that are found only two places in the world. Near Wounded Knee is Geiser Geyser and window rock: the former an erosional element that resembles the core of an extinct geyser. And, last, is Sheep Mountain, a point where one can experience the panorama of the National Badlands Park.

A Prairie Yuwipi (U-weep-ee)*

Shannon County

And so the spirits come, from the west and from the south, coming in the shape of bright sparks of light, coming in the soft touch of a feather . . . They come as voices, little voices without bodies or mouths, nonhuman voices which we can understand all the same.

—Lame Deer

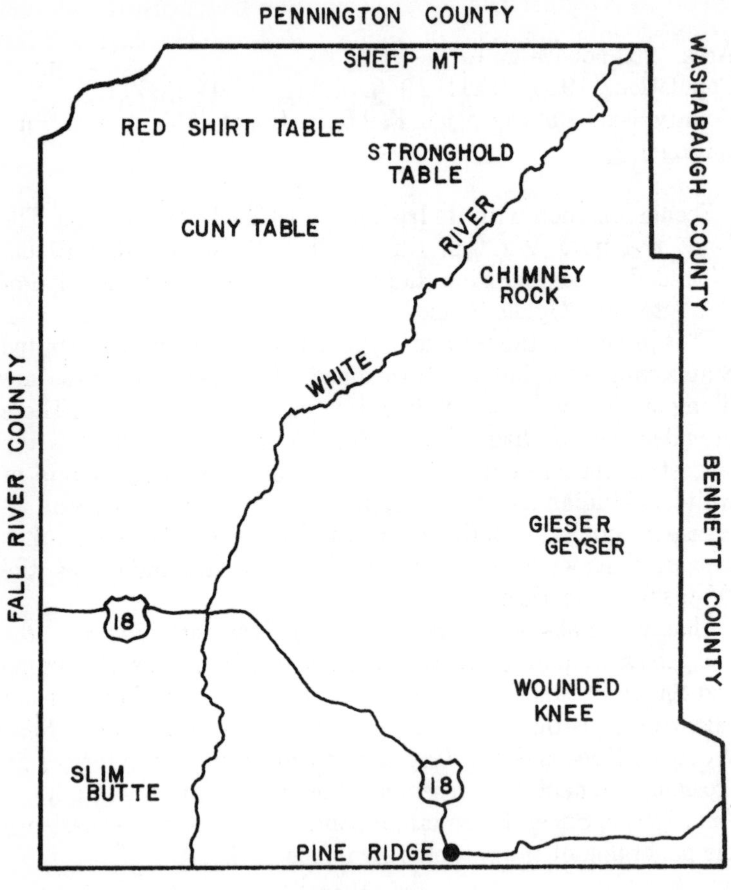

Virginia White Feather drank long, heavy draughts from the cool, clear, crystal springs which trickled from the edge of a moss-covered rock. With one supple motion she straightened up, her long black braid flipped over her shoulder, and her dark brown eyes flashed with an inner light. The two thunderbird symbols on her doeskin vest fluttered with her heavy breathing. As she reached, with her two hands clasped above her head, her supple body twisted into contortions of anguish. Virginia White Feather had just finished with a Yuwipi ceremony, and the twisting, anguished contortions of her body reflected the anguish of her mind.

After many years of attending the schools of the white brethren, Virginia had come home. She had learned well the transcendental philosphy of Kant and Emerson. She had read the Bible and studied the life of Jesus. She had read of the mythical symbolism of Annie Dillard and digested the dogma of science.

She now stood at the outer edge of the circle where a Yuwipi ceremony was going on, drawn there by curiosity. As she pressed closer. It was as if an ancient, unfilled hunger suddenly grasped her and drew her toward fulfillment. Was this what she had sought in all her schooling — fulfillment of an inner need? Was this the intermediary that could connect her life with the mystical force of wholeness?

Quickly she catalogued the things she had learned by which man had transcended the mundane forces of the world and floated sublimely free in the universe of stars. And as she did her mental exercises, she saw the tree of lights that Annie Dillard once saw. She felt that time and space could shrink and grow in mysterious ways. As she floated free, she saw the earthly world shrink to an apple's size. Like Emerson, she ate it. She ate the whole world! She saw the clouds, the water, the place where Jesus walked. At the edge of space she saw the place where Hindu mystics stored their power. She saw the lights of Heaven and glimpsed angels floating by. She felt the heat of Hell and brushed aside a star.

She settled back on earth and flowed into the ground. She felt deeply within her the dragging force of a magnet polarized to pull. Gravity deeply, ever deeply, pulled her into the ancient village of her people. She saw the middle of the earth, with Black Elk as a guide. She saw lights from nowhere, with Lame Deer at her side. They came, the spirits, out of nowhere to flash across her mind. She saw the sacred hoop surround the tree of life. She visited with spiders, owls, and butterflies, as she felt the need to do. Then, as Black Thunder said, a lightning bolt awakened her. Her heart pounded and sweat enclosed her body. She wrenched herself out of the trance and ran exhausted toward the coolness of the spring.

Where, in all this mystic world, did Virginia really live? Would she turn back to her ancestors, or go the white man's way? Or did she have to put it all together and coalesce anew into a completely new Virginia?

As she gazed up at the stars, now twinkling in the sky, she knew the feeling of a new experience, its meaning yet to be understood. She sank to the ground and drifted off to sleep in the warmness of the earth.

When she awoke, all heaviness had left her. The running spring trickled on her hand, and a lightness that she had never felt filled her to the brim; her mind was washed of clutter; her jumbled feelings all had left. She could reach into her mind and grasp the thoughts she wished. When she did this, she found the elusive strength called faith. It was in neither the white man's world nor the Indian's world. What she really wanted lay hidden, unrealized, in the inner depths of her own mind. But now she knew a way to penetrate and release the hidden needs that lay within her psyche. With strength and boldness she could go forth into the world, for deep within her came the will to do it.

She knew that the faith she really needed had always lain deep within her and that searching brought it out. It was a universal faith, awakened by a universal God. It paid no mind to color, race, or creed and spread through all the faiths.

Virginia looked across the land and felt happiness within her heart for being home.

*A Yuwipi ceremony was an attempt to reach the spirits by the use of holy rocks and a Yuwipi medicine man. Rocks were collected from anthills and placed in a rattle. Sometimes sacred medicine rocks were sent out to look for the spirits, and the message they brought back would come in a vision or dream. There were sometimes talking in tongues, strange languages, and strange sensations.

The Yuwipi is one of the many ways the Sioux Indians attempted to communicate with their god, Wakan-Tanka. They also used peyote, the pipe, and various other ceremonies to seek visions.

Todd County

Area, 1,397 square miles
Population, 1925 - 4,758; 1945 - 6,612; 1980 - 7,268
County Seat, Winner in Tripp County. (Main town Mission)

Ghost Hawk Camp Ground and Crazy Horse Canyon, the final resting place of Crazy Horse, are a good place to start your experience with Todd County and the Rosebud Reservation. Here you can camp amid the oak, elm, and ironwood in an area that only receives 12-14 inches of rain a year. Higher on the slopes of the canyon, the deciduous trees blend with the ponderosa pine, and on the top of the canyon blending in with the distances is the short grass prairie. This distinct zonation of vegetation on the canyon wall is made possible by the porosity of the sandstone strata of the canyon wall. The zonation is especially prominent on the north-facing slope. It is as if the canyon floor receives ten inches more of rain a year than the top of the canyon.

Points of interest in the county are St. Francis Mission and its museum. In the county are found Haystack Butte and Hidden Timber.

The Nebraska Sand Hills creep up into the southwestern part of the county and extend into Bennett County, where the Lacreek Wildlife Refuge is located.

Traditional Lakota Uses of Native Plants

Todd County

Dilwyn J. Rogers

Todd County and the Rosebud Sioux Indian Reservation have the same boundaries, although parts of Mellette, Tripp, Gregory, and Lyman counties were included in the Rosebud Reservation until the early 1900s. Todd County/Rosebud Reservation is largely populated by members of the Sicangu (Brule) tribe. The Sicangu and six other tribes comprise the Teton or western Sioux group and speak the Lakota dialect. (Several tribes of eastern

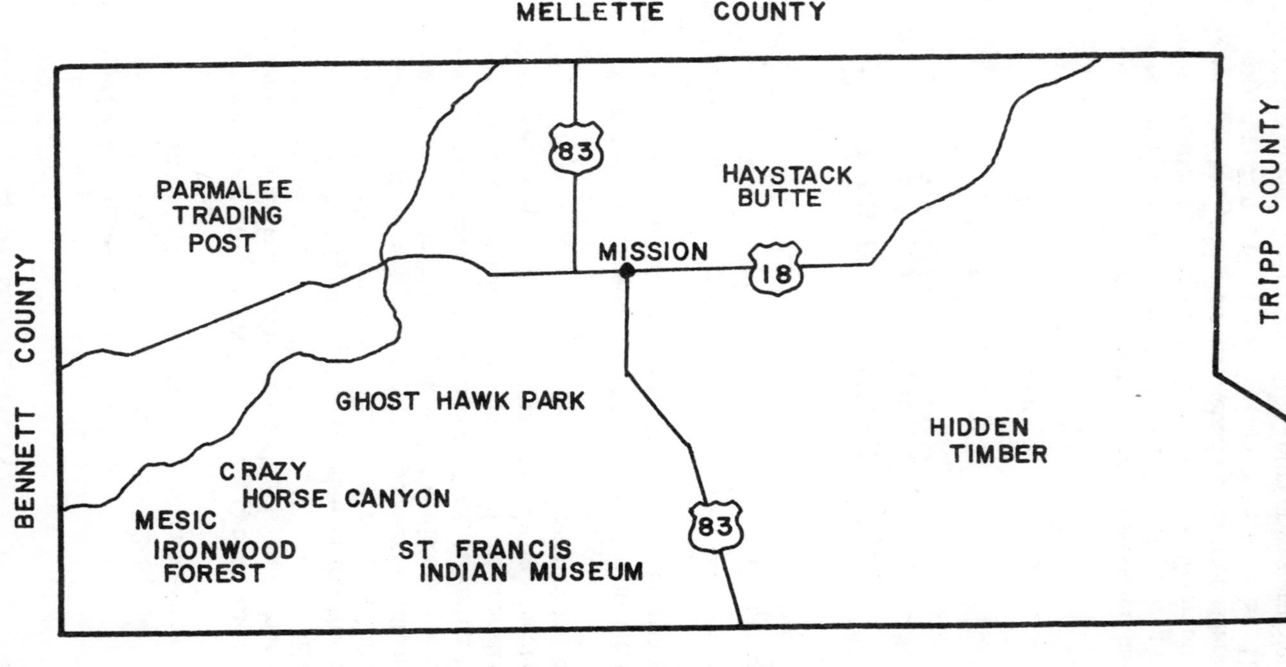
TODD COUNTY
MELLETTE COUNTY
BENNETT COUNTY
TRIPP COUNTY
PARMALEE TRADING POST
83
HAYSTACK BUTTE
MISSION
18
GHOST HAWK PARK
HIDDEN TIMBER
CRAZY HORSE CANYON
MESIC IRONWOOD FOREST
ST FRANCIS INDIAN MUSEUM
83
STATE OF NEBRASKA

Sioux comprise the Santee and Yankton groups and speak the Dakota and Nakota dialects.) Sinte Gleska (Spotted Tail) was the leader of the Sicangu when they were settled at Rosebud Agency in 1878, and he petitioned the President to allow Jesuit Blackrobes to undertake the education of his people. Thus, St. Francis Indian Mission and School were started in 1885 and have helped preserve some aspects of Lakota culture.

Perhaps the person at the Mission who was most involved in cultural studies was Father Eugene Buechel (1874-1954). He was at St. Francis for most of the period from 1902-1954. Father Buechel collected cultural items for many years, and these are preserved in the Buechel Memorial Lakota Museum at St. Francis. Throughout his life on the Reservation, Father Buechel studied the Lakota language, and a Lakota-English Dictionary has been published. He also took many photographs and compiled Lakota stories. A further project of importance is Father Buechel's collection of plants, made between 1917 and 1923 in the Rosebud area. He was able to determine the Lakota names for about 300 species of plants and get information on how the people used many of them. This represents the largest known list of species dealing with Sioux names and uses of plants. Since Buechel's informants had knowledge which dated to pre-reservation life, the list gives information which is little-influenced by white man's ideas. Lakota names and uses of native plants will be described further after a short overview of the physical environment of Todd County.

Most of Todd County is underlain by sandstone and other sedimentary rocks. The topography is primarily rolling hills, but with sharp-edged buttes or level land in a few parts. A northern extension of the Nebraska Sandhills gets into southwestern Todd County. The Little White River passes through the western part of the county, and tributaries and ravines running into it determine the topography. The Keya Paha River and its tributaries dominate eastern Todd County. The climate of this region is continental, characterized by extremes of temperature in both summer and winter. Average annual precipitation for Todd County is about 18 inches but is quite variable. As influence by these geologic, topographic, and climatic conditions, the major plant communities of Todd County are diverse, and include coniferous forest (dominated by ponderosa pine), upland deciduous forest (bur oak, ironwood, green ash), river bottom forest (cottonwood, box elder, elm) sandhills prairie (blue stem, sandreed), mixed-grass upland prairie (wheatgrass, needlegrass), and wetland and aquatic vegetation of marshes, lakes and streams.

Todd County has a large number of plant species, compared to most other South Dakota counties, because of the diverse geological strata, soils, topography, and microclimates. One study showed about 400 species in the western half of Todd County; thus, there could be nearly 500 species in the county, or about one-third of the known species for South Dakota. Father Buechel listed about 250 native species, so at least half the Todd County species have Lakota names. No doubt more species have Lakota names and uses as yet unrecorded. Many Indian people still make use of native plants for medicinal, religious, and other purposes. Some are reluctant to share their knowledge of herbal medicines other than to pass it along to a "disciple." Thus it may not be possible to obtain much additional information on Lakota names and uses. Nevertheless, it may be desirable to attempt to get older people to divulge information from the standpoint of cultural preservation and of potentially useful native plants.

The Lakota technique of naming plants is based primarily on descriptive phrases characterizing the plant's appearance (color, form, etc.) or use. Repeatedly used in names are the Lakota words of leaf, stem, flower, tree or woody plant, grass or herbaceous plant, and medicine. Many names make reference to animals (including insects, snakes, birds, buffalo, dogs, horses, gophers, prairie dogs, black-footed ferrets). Some names allude to a ceremony, game, or story.

There are uses commonly known among other Indian tribes for several of the plants on Rosebud, yet which are not listed by Buechel. No doubt Buechel or his informants neglected to mention some uses. However, it may be that the Lakota people were more oriented to nomadism, the buffalo chase, and an animal economy, so that they did not make as much use of certain plants, other than as medicine, as other tribes. For example, plants with edible fruits or nuts are mentioned, as are some with edible roots or tubers (which store well). However, virtually no plants eaten as greens are listed. Likewise, several plants known for their fiber and cordage uses do not have these uses given. The Lakota may have used sinew, strips of hide, etc., rather than plant materials, for fiber purposes. Many of the plant uses are "medicinal," which in the culture of many Indian tribes, is close to spiritual or religious.

To illustrate the range of Lakota usages of plants as determined by Father Buechel, an incomplete list is given below. The uses listed should not be tried without more detailed information. Only common names, not scientific names, are given. Since common names are not standardized, the wrong plant could be selected. The part of the plant, its stage of development, method of preparation, and other necessary considerations are likewise not listed. It must be noted that several species of plants are poisonous to humans or animals!

NON—MEDICINAL USES

Edible:

Fruits . . . Chokecherry, plum, hawthorn, Juneberry, strawberry, mulberry, grape, currant, gooseberry, buffalo bean, walnut
Underground parts, lower stalk . . . . Arrow-head, sweet flag, rush, onion, orchid, water lily, Jerusalem artichoke, prairie turnip
Sugar (sweet sap) . . . . Box elder
Drink (tea) . . . . Several mints, Coreopsis, red-root
Soup . . . . False pennyroyal, showy milkweed

Other uses:

Smoking . . . . . Sumac, skunk-bush, red osier dogwood, bearberry
Pipe stem . . . . Green ash
Bow . . . . Ironwood, ash, aspen
Arrow . . . . Wolfberry, false indigo, Juneberry, chokecherry, buffalo currant
Crack bones . . . . Juneberry
Use in tanning and bleaching hides . . . . Umbrella plant
Mosquito smudge . . . . Slender-flowered Psoralea
Perfume, hand lotion . . . . Western sagebrush, meadow rue
Soap, vermin killer . . . . Yucca
Paint, dye . . . . Spiderwort, narrow beardtongue (moccasins); ironwood, sand cherry (face), prickly poppy (arrows); lichens (quills)
Mats . . . . Rush
Quilt, diapers . . . . Cattail
Toilet paper . . . . Small ragweed
Musical instruments . . . . Spikenard, water parsnip
Religious uses . . . . Sweet grass, white sage, cocklebur
Magic . . . . Indian hemp, scarlet mallow

Horse taming, catching . . . . Yucca, Canadian milk-vetch, scarlet gaura
Horse stealing . . . . Western sagebrush (pulverized roots on face of sleeping man to prevent his waking up)

MEDICINAL USES

Headache . . . . Yellow coneflower, slender-flowered Psoralea, Clematis
Sore eyes . . . . Wild bergamot
Toothache . . . . Purple coneflower
Sore mouth . . . . Umbrella plant
Swellings . . . . Small ragweed, pussy-toes, purple coneflower, false boneset, false gromwell, snow-on-the-mountain, hog peanut
Swollen glands . . . . Leopard lily, swamp milkweed
Swelling in throat . . . . Prairie-clover
Fainting . . . . Wild bergamot
Flu . . . . Wild licorice
Breathing difficulty . . . . Fetid marigold
Tea for coughs and colds . . . . . Matchbrush, Canadian milk-vetch, wild bergamot, mountain mint
Thirsty or overperspiring . . . . Purple coneflower
Arm or leg cramps . . . . Sweet flag
Chest or back pains . . . . Canadian milk-vetch
Bellyache, stomach cramps . . . . Yucca, purple coneflower, yellow coneflower, bush morning-glory, skunkweed, water dock, cut-leaved nightshade
Improve appetite . . . . Narrow-leaved milkweed, dotted gayfeather, ground-cherry
Diarrhea . . . . Dwarf milkweed, green milkweed, skeleton plant, water dock, alum-root
Constipation . . . . Western sagebrush, prairie-clover
Urination, kidney problems . . . . Western sagebrush, peppergrass, prickly pear cactus, narrow-leaved umbrellawort, umbrella plant
Difficulty giving birth . . . . Yucca and prickly pear cactus; western sagebrush
Induce afterbirth . . . . Winged dock
Enhance mother's milk . . . . Whorled milkweed, green milkweed, snow-on-the-mountain, slender milk-vetch
Stop hemorrhage or blood flow . . . . . . Water dock, wild bergamot

Spitting of blood . . . . Fetid marigold and gumweed; Canadian milk-vetch and wild licorice
Chest wound . . . . Hairy puccoon
Heal sores . . . . Scarlet mallow, alum-root
Snake bite . . . . Slender beardtongue
General medicine . . . . Arrowhead, showy milkweed, giant ragweed, silver-leaved Psoralea, scurf-pea

Horse medicines:
- Lameness . . . . Hymenopappus
- Spine problems . . . . False gromwell
- Urination problems . . . . Yellow coneflower
- Tiredness . . . . Silver-leaved Psoralea, meadow rue
- General . . . . Silvery groundsel, buffalo bean

Indian turnip is one of the Indian's favorite foods. Still harvested today, it is braided into bead-like chains and hung to dry for winter use. The starchy, edible part has been removed from the opened section at the right.

Photo — D.J. Holden

Ziebach County

Area, 1,974 square miles
Population, 1925 - 4,010; 1945 - 2,943; 1980 - 2,308
County Seat, Dupree. Population 562

For miles it looms in the distance. It dominates the landscape. The clouds hanging in a shroud obscure its tip, a searing flash of lightning rips into its sides, then another. For a few moments it is silent; then, crash, a heavy clap of thunder rolls across the plains with only the resistance of the wind to stop it. This is Thunder Butte, that landmark that punctuates the horizon, in a land that never seems to end. It is late afternoon and a July storm has gathered over the crown of the Butte. It is a storm that has formed as the prevailing westernly airstream has been forced up and condensed by the altitude of the butte. It is the local microclimatic conditions that have given the butte its name.

Surrounding the butte are the Cheyenne River Indian Reservation, Mazacaga Draw, Red Elm, Hump Flat, Eagle Chasing Bottom, Bridger Flat, Glad Valley, Snake Butte, and Cherry Creek.

It is a land that seems to attract thunder but not people. A look at the map reveals the only improved roads in the area are those that pass through the county. But to travel one of the unimproved roads is to end up in a unique Indian village that still retains some of those traditional Indian ways of life.

Rattlesnakes abound on the buttes in the county, and to some they are a pastime and profit, but to others they are a peril to be avoided.

Here in Ziebach the nucleus of the once numerous plains buffalo was saved by Fred and Pete Dupree. These buffalo were to eventually form the basis of the herd that Scotty Philips used to bring the buffalo back from the edge of extinction.

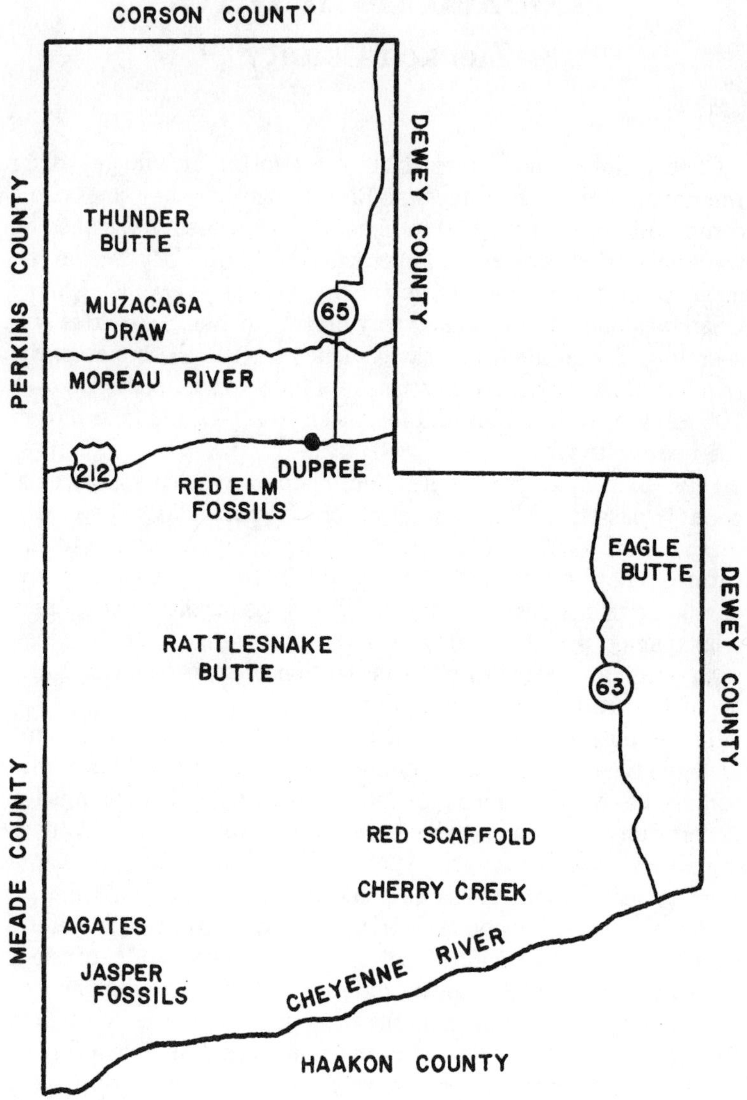
ZIEBACH COUNTY
CORSON COUNTY
PERKINS COUNTY
DEWEY COUNTY
THUNDER BUTTE
MUZACAGA DRAW
65
MOREAU RIVER
212
DUPREE
RED ELM FOSSILS
EAGLE BUTTE
DEWEY COUNTY
RATTLESNAKE BUTTE
63
MEADE COUNTY
RED SCAFFOLD
CHERRY CREEK
AGATES
JASPER FOSSILS
CHEYENNE RIVER
HAAKON COUNTY

The Indian Who Looked Both Ways

Ziebach County

Cherry Creek and Red Scaffold are two Indian villages along the north bank of the Cheyenne River. Together they comprise a community of nearly 1,000 Indians who have been overlooked by the sweep of European man over the continent. They live on the outback of civilization, forgotten by almost everyone. Cherry Creek has made it on the highway maps, but Red Scaffold is still searching for an identity. If one wishes to visit these places, the trip has to be considered in terms of a four- to six-hour drive over 100 miles of rolling hills and forgotten lives — a round trip from the nearest town.

How do people live in these out-of-the-way places that have been bypassed by the surge of civilization? They live with methods embedded in the past and try to turn them into the future. They are torn by the nostalgia for the past and the challenge of the future. They cling to a vision of the old Indian who roamed proud and free over the open range. Yet they look with longing, from within the protection of their own community, at the fruits of the non-Indian world.

These contradictory forces are reflected in the mind and actions of Eagle Bear, as he stands contemplating the future of his grandson. He has gone with his grandson to a hilltop, where Indians for generations have gone, to reflect on the beauty of the surrounding valley. It is his favorite spot, and he would like little Eagle Bear to see and feel the same penetrating power of solitude.

His eyes linger long on the horizon, seeming to search for a dust cloud to tumble out and roll toward him in a swirl of confusion. He waits for the earth to pulse and roar with the pounding hooves of thousands of buffalo. But the only dust he sees is the plume from a distant truck traversing the prairie skyline, like a flag of defiance, as the truck snakes its way across the blue. A dust fleck irritates his eye, and as he rubs it, tears start to flow. They roll along the seamy creases of his wrinkled face, which is a microcosm of the creviced landscape. As the tears wash the dust from the creases in his face, he thinks of all the things that have molded his life and left him standing in the backwash of civilization with his hand on the head of his grandson.

He remembers how he had gotten the name Eagle Bear. It was the day of his vision quest, when an eagle had circled overhead while across the hill a brown bear disappeared into the valley. It was a good omen, and he knew that the Great Mysterious One, Wakan-Tanka, would want him to be brave like an eagle and strong like the bear. But life had given him little chance to be either. He stood there, a saddened man.

He recalled to his grandson how, in the past, the Indians had lived as a product of their environment. It was as if the forces of wind, rain, and sun had molded them as they molded the plants and animals of the plains. Theirs was not an easy life, run by the biological clock of the seasons. In each season there was a task to be performed and a duty to live by. Eagle Bear knew he had to work to prevent hardship. The Moon of the Black Cherries (August) was time to harvest chokecherries and make pemican so there would be food during Moon of Snowblind (March). It was the cold winter months that were terrible, for people starved and froze to death during the long blizzards, even when things were well planned. He knew that during the Moon for the Harvesting of Buffalo (July), he must be successful in providing meat to hang and dry on the buffalo berry tree. It had been so named because, from a distance, when the berries were ripe, the tree was often mistaken for drying buffalo meat. It was a good feeling to see the buffalo berry trees, heavy with buffalo meat instead of berries. This was a sign that it would be a good winter, for the berries were picked and the meat was dry.

After a successful summer, it was time to prepare for the Sun Dance to give thanks to the Mysterious One for the abundant harvest. Eagle Bear would first purify himself in the sweat lodge after he had prepared the lodge with sage and sweet grass. Next he would smoke the pipe. Finally, he would place a rock on the great cairn on the hill as a token of the end of a good celebration. Thus he felt he was living in harmony with the environment.

Eagle Bear told all this to his grandson, for he wanted the boy to know the ways of the Indian. He wanted him to know that there was strength in time-tested tradition and habits. He wanted him to know that Indians were still proud of their heritage.

By this time the truck creating the dust plume that was trailing across the horizon pulled into the village. Getting out of the truck, Little Eagle Bear's father waved his cowboy hat at the two standing on the distant hill. He shouted a greeting and went into his modern-looking home.

Old Eagle Bear looked down at the house and truck and felt he must tell his grandson about the good and evil of the non-Indian world. He must tell him how these new elements must be considered, now that the buffalo were gone. He hoped that young Eagle Bear would be able to weave the good elements of this culture into the traditional values and heritage of the Indian. In this way a new culture could arise that would allow living in harmony with the environment. It would again be a culture that was proud, secure, and self-sufficient.

Eagle Bear told his grandson how the non-Indian worked to straighten the stream, harvest the forest, and manage the wildlife in a manner that conquered nature. He told him of the wonderful fruits of technology but also of the by-products of poison and pollution.

Old Eagle Bear hoped that by looking at both cultures, young Eagle Bear would be able to make the necessary adjustments so that the Indian culture could flourish again. It would be a culture in which nature need not be an adversary to be conquered, for the Indian knew from within that the universe is one and to disturb one strand of life without due regard for the whole is an offense against creation.

Little Eagle Bear looked up at his grandfather, his eyes shining, and said, "I want to grow up like you, Grandfather."

Then the grandfather knew that the name of Eagle Bear would be remembered with pride and dignity. For the first time he felt strong, brave, and wise.

DAKOTA IMAGES

Dakota Images

County	Title
Aurora & Douglas	The Little Red John Deere
Bon Homme & Charles Mix	Sometimes on Sunday River
Brown	Dakota Images
Butte	Tall in the Saddle
Clark	Lonely Eyes
Deuel	Boy Life During the Dust Bowl
Faulk	A Life to Remember
Hanson & Hutchinson	The Confining Community
Mead	North and South of Nothing
Spink	The Land Where the Lake Once Stood

And so the composite of it all, the geology, biology, ecology, climate, and people all run together to reflect our images from the mirrors of the past. They cast upon the viewer an impression of the state that is often superficial by reflecting only the harshness of a blizzard, the destruction of a dust storm, the poverty of depression, and tricks of a variable climate. These events all seem to overpower the more numerous events of happiness, harmony, and satisfaction. But, somehow, maybe propelled by the very forces of adversity that drove the pioneer, the image of the state has blossomed into a heritage of art and literature. It has captured the strength, spirit, and rich traditions of this many-faceted state. It has brought together the vast elements of diversity and coupled them with a living history that makes the state a desirable place.

Here in the final section are bits and pieces of the many images of South Dakota that have molded together a people into a functioning system — a system of unity and diversity into which the seeds of the future can be planted.

The entire book is images that have come to me from the land. So listen to the land, for it speaks a language of survival.

The prairie is no Garden of Eden, even though many writers seem to have pictured it as such. It is moody, consistent only in its inconsistency. The landscape appears to be mostly geometric, especially as divided by section lines, fences, county roads, and the remnants of railroad tracks; but it is full of surprises. Coloring changes with the movement of the sun and clouds, and shadows make abstract patterns on the grasses. Variable winds bend the grass, which sometimes undulates like ocean waves and at other times stands straight up as though peering for rain. The weather is predictable only in terms of change.

—John R. Milton
South Dakota

Wherever I go, and talk turns to home states, someone invariably says, "I've never met anyone from South Dakota before," and then asks a series of condescending questions suggesting that part of the prairie remains frozen in the nineteenth century, a primitive frontier where the buffalo and Indians still prevail and the weather is a never-ending cycle of dust storms and blizzards. "Well," I used to explain, "certainly it isn't a place of bright lights, crowded streets, chic dinner parties where the rich and famous gather to be witty and wise, but South Dakotans stopped living in sod houses and gathering buffalo chips some time ago." My explanations, no matter how clever, failed to generate little more than small smiles of little tolerance or fixed stars of boredom. So I have relaxed about my South Dakota birthright and the burden of explanation it carries with it. Instead, I've started thinking about what the state means to me and not what I might be able to make it seem to others.

—Tom Brokaw
Letter to John R. Milton

For a time, some people in later years nicknamed South Dakota "The Blizzard State." But others called it "The Sunshine State" . . . Eventually the paradox was resolved when South Dakota was dubbed "The Land of Infinite Variety."

—John R. Milton
South Dakota

Aurora County

Area, 719 square miles
Population, 1925 - 7,534; 1945 - 4,301; 1980 - 3,628
County Seat, Plankinton. Population 644

Aurora named in honor of the Goddess of Dawn awaits a new gleam from the east. So far it has lost over half of its population but has to its credit 17 artificial lakes and nine natural ones, the largest White Lake.

The town White Lake, which is not on the lake White Lake but

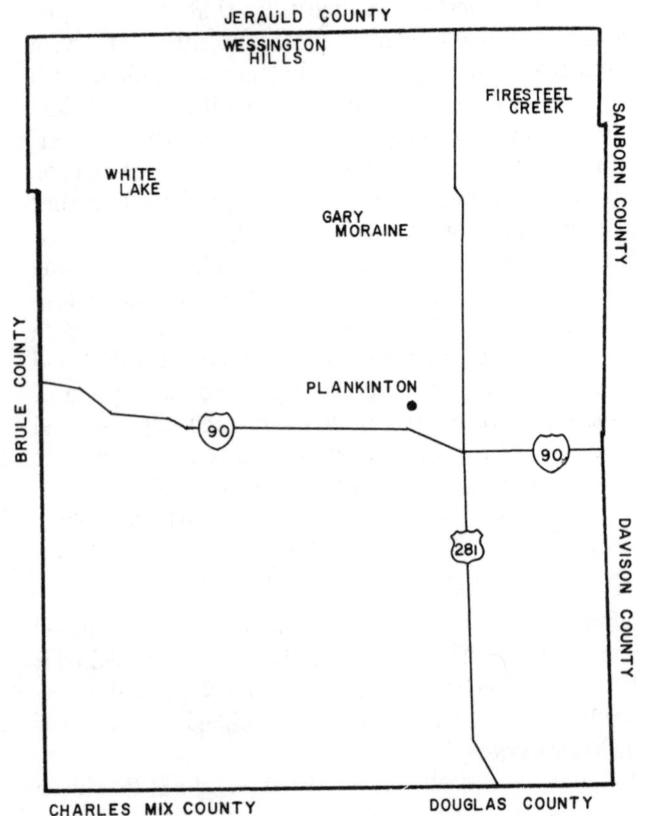

five miles south, had a bit of time deciding on a name. First it was known as Siding 36, later Windsor, then Yorktown, but finally, the influence of the nearby lake dominated and it became White Lake.

Farther south is Gondola Lake, named after the stratophere balloon Explorer II that set an altitude record of 79,395 feet on November 11, 1935. It was launched in the Strata Bowl near Rapid City and landed near the lake.

Other natural features of the county are the Wessington Hills, on the north edge; Gary Moraine Hills, in the northcentral; Arrowhead Lake, the site of a large Indian Camp, and Downey Grove in the southwestern corner.

Plankinton, the first city to try out the corn palace concept, proclaimed "Dakota Feeds the World." Today the concept is the sole property of Mitchell, which announces "The World's Only Corn Palace."

Douglas County

Area, 445 square miles
Population, 1925 - 7,156; 1945 - 5,293; 1980 - 4,181
County Seat, Armour. Population 819

Douglas County got off to a fraudulent start when a Mr. Brown set up a corrupt county government in 1880. When he was about to be apprehended, he left town on a fast horse with $200,000 he had collected for operating the county. With his departure the mythical county seat of Brownsdale ceased to exist.

In 1882 Douglas County made another attempt to organize, and this time succeeded in setting up Huston as the county seat, but later that year it moved to Grandview.

By 1885 all the land had been filed upon in Douglas County, and Grandview and Huston were growing towns. But in 1894 the center of county government was moved to the new town of Armour, and Grandview and Huston soon achieved the status of historical markers along the highway.

Areas of interest in the county are Oak Hollow, a Hutterite colony, and the Hieb sandpit. The latter is the site of many fossil finds.

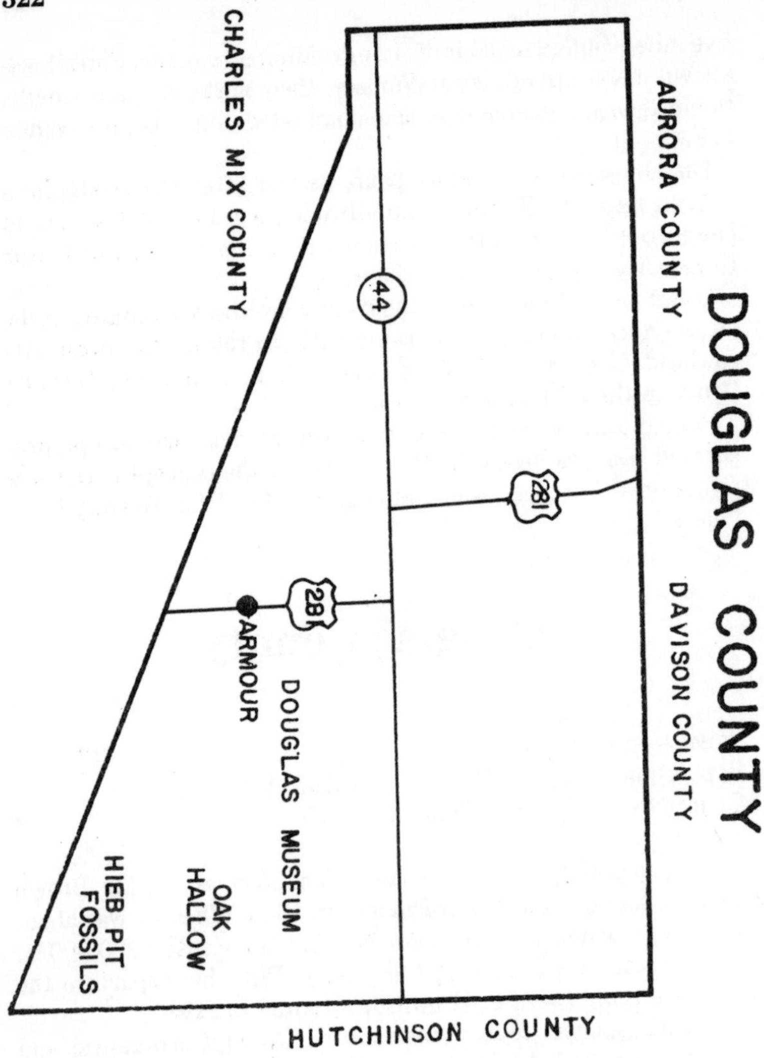

DOUGLAS COUNTY
AURORA COUNTY
CHARLES MIX COUNTY
DAVISON COUNTY
HUTCHINSON COUNTY
44
281
281
ARMOUR
DOUGLAS MUSEUM
OAK HALLOW
HIEB PIT FOSSILS

The Little Red John Deere

Aurora & Douglas Counties

Small rural towns are bits of euphoric contentment placed beyond the usually hectic mainstream of future shock. Suffering a bit from cultural lag, aloof from the needs of class three sewage processing plants while at the same time opposing sanitary landfill, they await the shock of an energy crunch. The biggest news is that last year's double winner in the rhubarb pie baking contest has done it again.

The annual events this week are the church circle meetings, a Cub Scout jamboree, and an open house at the local John Deere implement dealer's. The latter gives out free donuts and coffee and has become the place for a social encounter of the third kind; i.e., one does not have to talk about the weather, girl topics are reserved for the pool room, and all that is left are motors and power.

As one enters the showroom, he finds several segments of rural America present. At the front of the tractor are the real power buffs. They eye the world with motor mentality. Terms like piston displacement, horsepower, drawbar, and fuel consumption are mixed with bank loans and wheat prices.

Others are there, not so much to look at the new models as to see who is in town. One retired farmer, Old Bill, sits with a cup in his hand watching the crowd. He has just related, for the third time, how the old Rumley Challenger went 36 days without a breakdown in the 30s. He has already made it to three open houses and completed two visits to the pool hall so far this week. Now Old Bill wonders about either returning the empty cake pan to the widow Williams, who is getting awfully sweet, or going home.

As he gets up to leave, Big John, an old McCormick Deering man (and former John Deere man), comes in. Instantly the shop is quiet. Tenseness settles over the shop, for everyone remembers the last time Big John came in. Old Bill recalled the day as if it were yesterday.

As Big John, whose farm lies just south of Old Bill's, walked in, his eyes were riveted on the walls of the shop. He was careful not to look at the green monster in the center of the room. Could arthritis have twisted his neck, forcing his head at right angles with his body? But no. As if to make sure no one was watching, he whipped a quick glance at the new model. His broad shoulders shuddered as his head snapped back into normal position. It was again that awful day in 1961 when he had come to the annual opening with $4,000 in his pocket. He wanted to be the first in his neighborhood to buy the new John Deere. He could see himself as he drove down the straight and narrow corn rows with Young John following on the old John Deere putt-putt. What a picture it would paint for the neighbors. And what a feeling of pride would fill his body!

He approached the new model, slapped the radiator cap with a loud bang to assure attention, and announced loudly, "How much will you take for this?" His left hand fingered the bills in his pocket as he looked around for the impact of his statement. The owner of the shop quickly sensed a deal and jumped to the seat of the tractor to demonstrate its raw, tough pulling power. With a clear, crisp whir it started, the engine pulsing and roaring with a crescendo of power that pulled at the very guts of the customers' primitive urge to plow.

Big John's chin dropped to his chest, as if the chug-chug of the past had been forever submerged in a sea of power. He stared in disbelief as it slowly dawned on him that what he was looking at seemed like a green McCormick Deering. John Deere had changed to a four-cylinder tractor, and the old two-cylinder putt-putt that he had so loyally defended from the onslaughts of the McCormick people had been swallowed on its terrible trail toward progress.

A distinct sound would be gone from the landscape. No longer would people say, "Here comes Big John." On still, clear fall nights, when sound carries for miles, who would listen for the putt-putt of Big John, echoing as if it were the very pulse of the earth? The land would no longer throb to its steady beat.

Big John withdrew his hand from the hood of the Deere, his shoulders slumped and, trying not to create any attention, he shuffled toward the door. With a feeble excuse that didn't make sense, he headed for the pool hall. Not even the beer tasted good, but it did deaden his senses. He stared with disbelief into the mirror over the bar. Then, with the suddenness of a rabbit startled from its hiding place, he wheeled and, like a robot, stalked out the door and down the street to the empty show room of the International Harvester dealer. Within minutes he had purchased a red McCormick Deering tractor.

He jumped on the seat, looking neither to right nor left, drove past the John Deere yard, and headed home. As he drove into the yard, his wife stared in amazement as she turned the donuts in the fryer. Little John jumped up and down with glee, for now he would get the old John Deere.

Big John parked the new tractor by the old, green putt-putt. Something was wrong. He went into the barn for red paint, and in one hour two shiny red tractors stood side by side in his yard.

Then he went into the house, and for two days he didn't say a word.

For years people stopped to stare at the putt-putting red John Deere following the red McCormick through long, straight rows of corn.

Now, after all these years, Big John had come back into the John Deere showroom. Old Bill settled back into his chair as all eyes turned on Big John. The dealer stopped in the middle of an explanation of the power take off to a young farmer's wife whose obvious interest was the cost of the tractor.

A hush fell over the building as Big John sat on a folding chair. The sudden slam of a door startled the group, which turned to see Little John, now grown big, enter the room. He looked at the various models with the manner of one who had already studied them for a long time and said, "I'll take that one, Pop."

Little John, who had spent all those years driving the little red John Deere, now was celebrating his 21st birthday and taking over the family farm. Big John decided to give his son the tractor of his choice. Little John's devotion to the John Deere was complete. He didn't care if they were two-cylinder or four-cylinder. So Big John made out a check for $20,000, and Little John said, "Will you take it home, Pop?" Big John got on and, without a word, drove out the door, the silent stares of the neighbors following him down the street.

Old Bill got up and hobbled over to the pool hall. The old Rumley stories seemed unimportant in the face of real news.

In the meantime Little John got in his revved up car with the oversize springs, monstrous tires, mag wheels, and maxi power. He felt good, and as he revved the motor, the power vibrated through his body. He looked around for his friends, already beginning to gather at the various corners for the weekly Saturday night looping. Dragging Main and cruising for girls would be a special treat tonight. He gave all his friends rides. Even some of the other loopers would stop their rigs and get in with him so that he could tell about his new tractor. The boys would tingle with the roar of the revved up engine and discuss the drag races at Thunder Valley.

After an evening of ripping, roaring, and racing, his twin chrome plated tailpipes spewing smoke into the face of a defiant world, Little John made one last loop. The sheriff, who earlier was conveniently located in another part of town and could tolerate only so much looping, now stood on the corner. Little

John took one look and went home. Anyway, he thought, he was getting a bit old for this stuff, now that he had his own tractor.

On Monday morning, as the sun burst clear and crisp from the eastern sky, a big, new, shiny green John Deere purred down the long, straight rows of corn. Behind it followed a small red John Deere. Big John heard only the putt-putt as he rode the fading red machine. His mind was occupied with the days when his putt-putt had been the symbol of power in the country. Little John, feeling the surge of the new tractor under him, wondered if Case, Massey Ferguson, Allis Chalmer, or the new White were really any good. Would he soon be getting one of them? Or would he settle for a four-wheel drive Steiger as his next tractor?

Back at the house the appetizing aroma of freshly fried donuts drifted out to mix with the cool country air. And over the land, if one stopped to listen, the putt-putt of the little red machine could be heard, a muffled heartbeat echoing from the distant hills for the last time.

Bon Homme County

Area, 573 square miles
Population, 1925 - 11,885; 1945 - 9,051; 1980 - 8,059
County Seat, Tyndall. Population 1,253

There, located along the north edge of the Missouri River, is a county that relates back to Lewis and Clark, who visited Bon Homme Island in 1804. There they reported puzzling earthworks, now known to have been made by the river. In 1828 a French trader, Zephyr Renconter, operated a fur trading post on the island. The first actual mainland settlement, across from the island, came in 1858. That same year Smutty Bear came to give them trouble before leaving for the reservation. In 1860 the first schoolhouse in the Dakota territory was built here in Bon Homme village.

Into this new county with its French name (meaning the man) came the Czechs in 1871 and started the town of Tabor. Today the Tabor-Tyndall area has the largest Czech population in the state and celebrates Czech Days in June, which feature Czech kolaces and polka music.

In 1879 Scots founded the town of Scotland. Later the Russo-

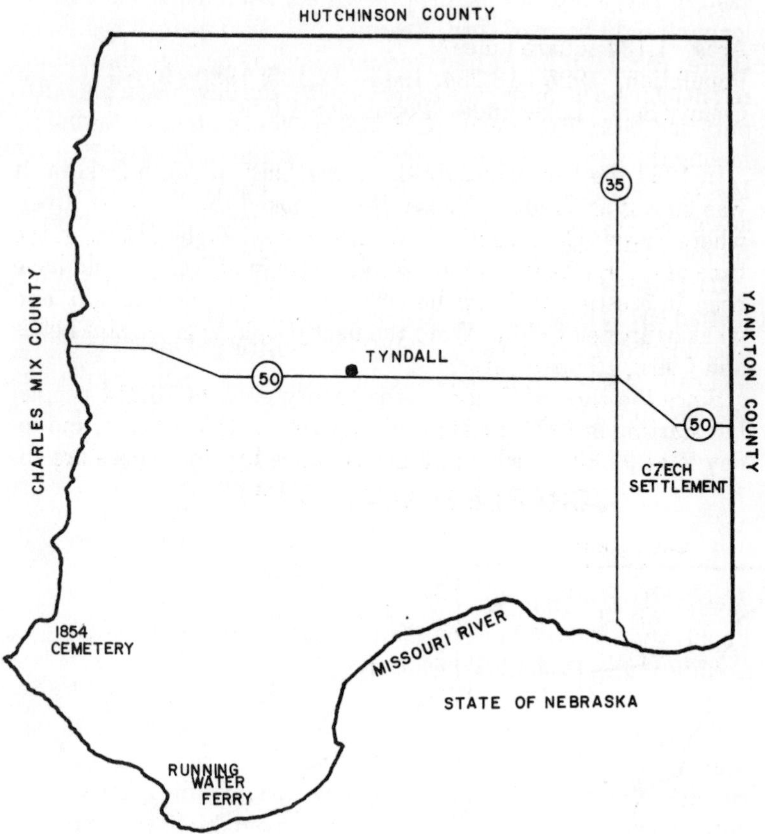

Germans settled along the James River. Now include the Dutch and Scandinavians, and Bon Homme becomes a melting pot.

Heritage sites in the county include: St. Marys, a school for Indian girls; Running Water, oldest operating ferry over the Missouri; the birthplace of George McGovern; and one of the first cemeteries in Dakota. Here four-year-old Sophia Brown was buried in 1859. But the most attractive place is the Missouri itself. Its cliffs, islands, and wooded banks speak of the wilderness that once surrounded Lewis and Clark when they first met the Sioux.

Charles Mix County

Area, 1,134 square miles
Population, 1925 - 18,254; 1945 - 12,185; 1980 - 9,680
County Seat, Lake Andes. Population 1,029

In 1794 the first white dwelling was built in South Dakota. It was known as Trudeau House. It overlooked the Missouri River, where basswood, oak and elm formed a wooded glen. Here, at the time of George Washington's second term in office, it would have been interesting to know how Trudeau lived, what he did, and what happened to him. Were the next people to greet him Lewis and Clark, 10 years later?

Since the time of Trudeau, the county grew to 18,254 people, but starting in 1925 it lost people at a rate of 155 per year, and today is at 9,680, of which 33 per cent are Indians. These are In-

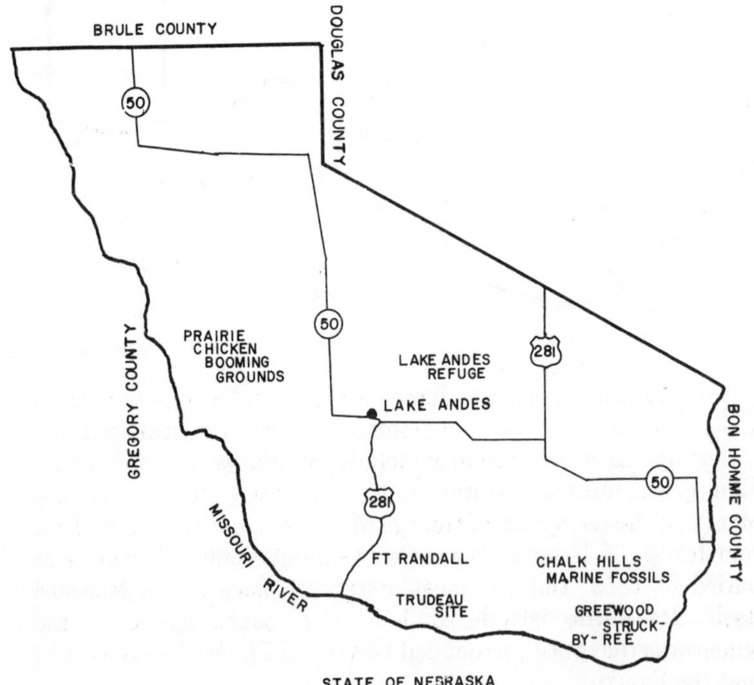

dians located on the Yankton Reservation, where Struck-By-the-Ree Monument stands and Greenwood village with its churches, and the side street schools create the impression people are living here on only faith and education.

Papineau Trading Post, now a museum at Geddes, is also an old part of the pioneer tradition. Below Papineau's old post is Fort Randall, one of a chain of army forts that was constructed from Kansas to Canada. The ruins of the old army chapel and the cemetery still mark the spot.

It is here at the Fort that one can stand on Fort Randall Dam and look to the west to see Lake Sharp, the newly formed lake, then look to the east and see the Missouri as Lewis and Clark saw it. It is as if the new and the old are split by a ribbon of concrete.

Lake Andes National Wildlife Refuge is a lake with a flowing artesian well. It is known for its large concentrations of waterfowl that overwinter. Many of these birds are dying of lead poisoning, wounds, starvation, winter cold, etc. The result is a build-up of predators: bald and golden eagles, hawks, owls — the snowy owl is often abundant here — and mammal predators.

Sometimes on Sunday River

Bon Homme & Charles Mix Counties

Marlene and Marty had been going together for two years, but Marty couldn't settle down. He talked about getting a job in Minneapolis. Marlene, ever since she had finished college, wondered why she had even bothered to come back. If her mother hadn't gotten sick, she probably would have taken a job in Sioux Falls. Now, as she sat in the old '64 Chevy on a beautiful Saturday evening, she wondered if it was to be bowling, car races, movies, or driving around the streets aimlessly. She looked out the window, looked at her watch, stared at the dashboard, looked over at Marty fidgeting with his keys, and wondered if he would notice her new dress. She had made it from a pattern in a Paris magazine. Her girlfriends said it looked great, but Marty's only comment was "I hope it's not going to rain." Marlene was about to tell him that she was going next week to look for a job in the Cities. She had her fill of lifeless dates. She turned toward him so he could see how smartly the new dress fitted and how hard she had worked to make herself enticing, but he kept looking at a new Ford Mustang across the street.

She opened her mouth to inform him that her mother was now completely recovered and that she was not needed at home any more, when Marty jammed the keys in the switch. He jerked the car to a start and took off with a roar. "Gee," he thought, "here she is all dolled up like something out of the Ladies' Home Journal, and I'm about to take her on a canoeing trip. Gosh, I guess I should have called her. She usually never gets dressed up for these weekend flings." The only time he had really seen her in a dress was the one time she had talked him into going to church. Now, when he had this great idea, there she was looking like a Paradise Island Resort model.

He jammed the car into second, spun around the corner and, as centrifugal force whipped her over against him, whispered into her ear, "How about a canoe trip down the old Missouri?" Then, gripping the wheel firmly in both hands, he pointed the car out on a dusty road that bumped along toward the river.

Marlene forgot about her mother, her plans for a job, her new dress, and her hairdo and thought, "Wow! This isn't going to be a dull, monotonous weekend after all. A canoe trip down the Missouri! Why haven't I thought about that? Maybe there's some romance in the world after all." Then, with a hesitating glance and an effort not to seem too eager, she replied, "Well, all right."

He breathed a sigh of relief, drove a few more miles, and stopped the car by the river. He took one look at the supplies he had purchased and the equipment he had rented from the camping center in Sioux Falls. He wondered what he would have done if she had said no.

In short order they were in the center of the river, drifting downstream. Marlene felt the charm and romance of soft yellow moonlight. Reflected in the rippling water, it made them appear to be drifting over a bed of jewels. They paddled through a tunnel of trees, where the leaves whispered "The Song of Hiawatha" — "By the shores of Gichi Gumee, By the shining Big-Sea-Waters." Marlene leaned back and closed her eyes to imagine the wonders of it all.

Marty did not know much about paddling, and occasionally he sent a spray of water over her. Once he tried to turn around and almost tipped the canoe over. Brought back to reality, Marlene grabbed the other paddle and guided the canoe back on its course.

Now that everything was going smoothly, Marty got out a map, and they began to enjoy the many sights and sounds of river life. As they drifted, they counted the birds and animals. By being especially quiet, they could often drift by without disturbing them. The geology advanced from Pierre Shales to Niobrara Chalk, which stood in massive cliffs on both sides. The river spread out on a wide river plain, and the braided stream made selection of the right channel difficult. The trees thinned to grassland on the exposed South Dakota side, and a forest covered the north-facing slopes on the Nebraska side.

In order to complete the trip, Marty had planned to catch a few hours of sleep in a hastily built camp, then at the first break of dawn continue the trip by retracing the path of Lewis and Clark.

Here was the original river, no dams, just the wild Missouri. Here was the tower where the Lewis and Clark crew tried to drown out the petite chien or prairie dog. It was their first recorded sight for science. Further on, Clark made the first sighting of antelope and later described them for science. He called them goats. A bit farther on is the site where Lewis and Clark first met the Sioux. The antelope and prairie dog are gone today, but at Greenwood the Yankton Sioux still live amid memories of their famous chiefs, Struck by the Ree and White Crane. As they passed Running Water, the canoers saw, still operating, one of the oldest ferries in the United States.

All along the way they found little streams entering the Missouri. Where they entered, sand bars and deltas formed. The rapid Niobrara, which flared at its mouth into a picturesque wooded valley, entered with such a load of sand that it almost clogged the upper end of Lewis and Clark Lake.

The modern explorers found, all along the river, islands and sand bars, some so extensive that Lewis and Clark described them as ancient fortifications. On the islands are morels and muskrats mixed with wood duck and woodbine and here and there nesting colonies of cormorants, pelicans, and herons.

They also found a panorama of history, starting with Fort Randall, one of the old (1856) chain of forts on the Indian frontier. Continuing down river, they found the site of Trudeau's cabin. The first white man to enter South Dakota, he built his cabin when George Washington was President. Just below the cabin, in a beautiful wooded ravine, is a relict eastern woodland where numerous basswood flourish.

The Missouri was really the pipeline of civilization and served as the main artery of transportation long before South Dakota was a state. The first steamboat, the Yellowstone, reached Ft. Pierre in 1831. One of the islands it passed was Bon Homme Island. Near there is the oldest cemetery still used in South Dakota. Seven of Custer's men are buried there. Farther on is the first school in South Dakota (1860).

All this, and more of the natural heritage of South Dakota, Marlene and Marty absorbed and explored as they traveled downstream on the Missouri River.

On a limb overhanging the river, a scarlet tanager landed. Its bright red body and black wings flickered like a small flame on the swaying branch. Marlene and Marty twisted around in the canoe at the same time to see, for the first time, this strikingly beautiful bird. As they did so, the canoe tipped, and there in the middle of the river two completely soaked explorers gasped for air. For a moment they were stunned, then both quickly scrambled for shore. To Marty it felt refreshingly cool after all that paddling. Then he looked at Marlene. There she stood, her new hairdo streaming down her face, her new dress clinging to every curve of her body, and in her hand a cattail she had grabbed as she fell out of the canoe. Marty thought she had never looked so beautiful and, overcome by guilt for not telling her earlier, said, "I really like that dress on you."

Marlene looked down at herself, squished the water in her new shoes, kicked them off, brushed hair out of her face, and ran her hands down the length of her body. She glanced up to see if Marty was watching. She saw a gleam of fascination in his eyes that she had never seen before. She felt a warm glow in her body; she felt good. Her eyes had a new sparkle, her smile lit up her face, and it was as if a rose hue had settled on the land. He had finally noticed her as she liked to be noticed. She walked over, handed him the cattail, gave him a hug, and kissed him softly. "Marty," she said, "you ought to take me canoeing more often, but please try to be a bit more careful."

From that time on Marlene and Marty enjoyed the river frequently, especially on Sundays when they looked forward to extended trips planned with much anticipation. They were no longer just company for each other on a boring weekend. They were lovers, and there on the river, whenever they saw a scarlet tanager, they recognized it as a symbol of their love.

"Cruising down the river on a Sunday afternoon" is a joyous refrain for canoeing through the woody sections of the wild Missouri. Here trees, water, and people blend into an experience of happiness. Top shows the river flowing by a sizable island. Bottom shows the river broadening out at the upper end of Lewis and Clark Lake.

Photos — Jeanne Kilen

Brown County

Area, 1,750 square miles
Population, 1925 - 30,533; 1945 - 29,345; 1980 - 36,962
County Seat, Aberdeen

Back in the 40s they found the giant 29-foot lizard skeleton (Mosasaurs) when they dug the Elm Creek Dam. It was near Mina, where they uncovered the Imperial Mammoth skeleton, largest mammal ever known. What kind of land is it anyway around Aberdeen? Hamlin Garland never wrote about this; he just described blizzards.

Well, Brown County is a county of both the urban and the rural. It is the big city of Aberdeen and farmland spread across old glacial Lake Dakota. The county was organized when river transportation was going up and down the James. There were two large boats, the Fanny Peck and the Nettle Baldwin; the latter fell apart in a cow pasture. Brown County is also a place of quadruplets (Schense), quintuplets (Fischer), and ordinary people.

Colin Campbell started a Hudson Bay trading post in 1922 near the site of the birthplace of Waneta, famous Cuthead Indian chief. To the south of Aberdeen is the Oakwood Indian rendezvous and Rondell trading post.

Brown County is also the site of ghost towns: Gage, Winship, Detroit, New Dehli, Rudolph, and Ordway. The latter once was one of the most promising towns in Dakota but lost out to Grand Crossing, now known as Aberdeen.

Other sites of interest in Brown County are Sand Lake Wildlife Refuge, Dakota Prairie Museum, Putney Slough, and the birthplace of Hamlin Garland.

Dakota Images

Brown County

The flat expanse was depressing. The town was ugly and the little park along the muddy "Jim" pathetic, with its tiny unkempt grove of water elms and box elders filled with flimsy cabins and huts.

—Hamlin Garland

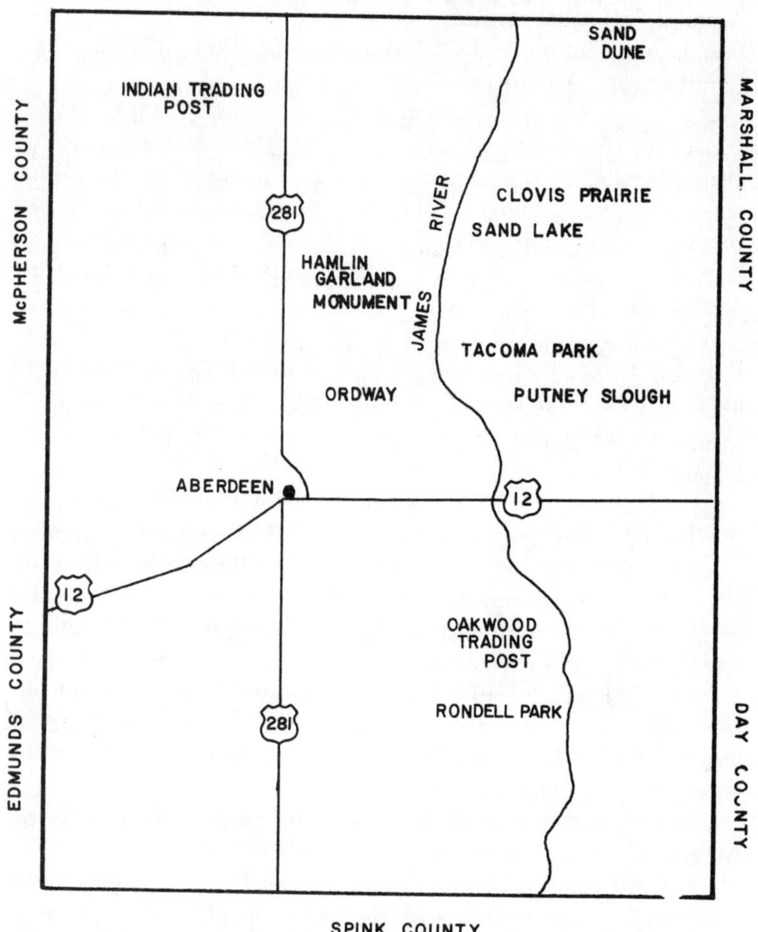

Sometimes at a party or in visits with friends outside the state, I get brave and inject casually into the conversation, "I'm from South Dakota." As if suddenly confronted by a bit of news on par with the birth of guinea pigs, they look at me in amazement. The more polite volunteer that they saw Mount Rushmore once, before lights were strung to illuminate the faces. Once, just before the conversation was about to die, a young fellow said, "I once met a swell gal from Sioux City at an Interstate rest stop who had just lost her contact lens, and I had fun helping her find them." Braver ones simply shrug and mutter, "Where the hell is South Dakota?" Mostly, however, a look of indifference settles over the crowd, and a sigh of relief ripples through the room when the subject is changed.

To serious students living outside the state's boundaries, who are required to learn geography, South Dakota is not a land of infinite variety, as the sign proclaims, but a frontier of Indians, cowboys, and an endless, treeless plain — a curious collection of disjointed images intermingling into a vague blur. We have dust storms, blizzards, hailstorms, heat, cold, wind, grasshoppers, and poverty. And striding out of it comes the farmer in his bib overalls. Against a red, round, roofed barn, pitchfork in hand, he stands as the image of South Dakota, looking out across a field of golden grain — an image held by our urban friends.

Where do our images come from? In part from a collection of literature that has flowed into the main channels of learning. It forms the classical milk upon which the youth of the nation are nourished.

One of the first set of images of the Great Plains to pour out of the jug of learning originated with the experiences of Hamlin Garland in Brown and McPherson Counties. The author's description of blizzards, poverty, and people rendered broken and helpless by endless toil and drudgery leaves one with a feeling of having just made a rest stop on the way to hell. Garland claimed his writing was accurate. "I resumed by writing in a mood of bitter resentment, with full intention of telling the truth about western farm life, irrespective of the land-boomer or the politicians." Then he described the pain, suffering, and heartrending poverty that the land exacted from its people, especially the women.

His description of a blizzard, which he blew through almost every book he wrote, is typical. He turned the blizzard in his claim shanty into a poem:

My cabin cowers in the pathless sweep
Of the terrible northern blast;
Above its roof the wild clouds leap
And shriek as they hurtle past.
The swift clouds drive across the light
And all the plain is lost to sight,
The cabin rocks, and on my palm
The sifted snow falls, cold and calm.

Garland's stories of the "Middle Border" (the Great Plains), land of the straddle bug (a tripod of posts used to claim occupancy of land), have become classics of pioneer poverty and misery.

Amplifying this image was one of morbidity, bordering on death and insanity, as Ole E. Rolvaag explained the plight of pioneers. By blizzard and loneliness, he drove his characters to madness. Ambition hung frozen in the grip of fear. "Bleak, grey, God-forsaken, the empty desolation stretched on every hand . . . Many took their own lives; asylum after asylum was filled with disordered beings who had once been human. It is hard for the eye to wander from sky line to sky line, year in and year out, without finding a resting place! . . ."

Blizzards did not single-handedly account for the pioneer's plight. Summer produced dust storms, prairie fires, and grasshoppers. These Three Horsemen of Disaster combined to stamp out what little spirit remained after the long winter.

Marilyn Coffey related effects of dust storms: "If hot sun and high wind didn't drive folks mad in summer, then winter blizzards would. Or hail. Or grasshopper plagues. Or prairie fire . . . After the dust blizzards . . . dirt covered fence lines until only scattered post tops remained visible. It drifted as high as the eaves of houses, blocked roads and railroad tracks so badly that snowplows had to clear them."

Historical records of Brown and its sister county McPherson also reflect the pioneer hardship. The county seat, Leola, was twice almost destroyed by prairie fires. "Flame points flashed out as far as two rods or more ahead. Farmsteads in the path of the flames were burned, and the little city of Leola suffered almost complete annihilation . . . One person lost his life . . . He was terribly burned about the body, and nothing remained of his clothing except a part of his lace boots."

Brown County reports a mail carrier frozen to death by a blizzard. A settler, driven by the loneliness of the winter, started back to his folks in Iowa in the middle of February. His body was found in sitting position, a la Rolvaag, in the spring, a few miles south of his claim.

These hardships and many more form grist for the writer's pen. Added together they equal an image of grim unhappiness, embedded in our past.

South Dakota is just a young state. Author John R. Milton observes that as a state of just 75 years, we have one foot on the frontier and the other poised on the moon.

In Brown County, pioneering was not all suffering and sorrow. A spirit of optimism and achievement bubbled like a spring in the desert. Pioneering was a place of being — being in the right place at the right time. A case of being is Ordway, the Hamlin Garland boom town that would but couldn't. It couldn't become the biggest town in the northern plains, it couldn't become the capital of Dakota Territory, it couldn't become a big railroad center, it couldn't become the site for a large Methodist University, and it couldn't, in a final effort, even get on the highway maps. On the other hand, Aberdeen, by being in a place where two railroad tracks finally crossed, became in a few short years a thriving metropolis. It was soon the third largest city in the state.

The image of South Dakota is slowly changing. It is developing into an image of place, with roots in art, literature, and music to describe its own unique heritage. Now the image of South Dakota is not always projected in dreary, dismal moods. Tempering it will be the memories of pleasant experiences and beautiful places.

Why, just last winter when I mentioned I was from South Dakota, someone popped up with, "Is it true that the really big blizzards correlate with a population increase?" Then, while I was groping for an answer, a storm warning was broadcast.

"Oh, boy, we sure hated to miss that last big one," he said, with a sidelong glance at the young lady across the table.

Then it dawned on me. Hamlin Garland's blizzard had at last blown itself out.

Butte County

Area, 2,289 square miles
Population, 1925 - 6,438; 1945 - 7,167; 1980 - 8,372
County Seat, Belle Fourche. Population 4,682

Butte County is in the northwest part of South Dakota. Belle Fourche, the county seat, is in the southwestern part of the county and accounts for over half of the population. In fact, if one removes Belle Fourche and the irrigated section around it, one comes up with the most thinly populated area in the state. Other towns and villages are Fruitdale, Newell, Nisland, and Vale. All are connected with the irrigation section. Post offices and rural stores are at Arpan, Castle Rock, and Hoover.

Water in the county is provided for by dams on streams and includes two-thirds of the county which is drained by the Belle Fourche River. There are 10,560 acres of water area in the county, and 8,000 acres of this form the Belle Fourche Reservoir.

About 90 per cent of the county is used for grazing, 5 per cent for dry land farming, and 4 per cent for irrigation. Winter wheat is the main dry land crop, with corn, alfalfa, sugar beets, and edible beans the main crop on irrigated land.

The interesting natural areas in Butte County are the rough hogbacks that abut the Black Hills, and scattered through the county are other steeply sloping ridges and buttes. Some of the larger buttes are Owl, Castle Rock, Antelope, Deers Ears, Two Top, North Haystack and, to the south, a series of Haystack buttes. Located some 20 miles north of Belle Fourche is a butte with a visitor's viewpoint. This is the Geographic Center of the Nation Butte. Sundance Hill, an Indian ceremonial site, is located just outside of Belle Fourche.

Butte is a Western county wrapped in the tradition of the West. The annual Black Hills Roundup is one of the largest rodeos in the nation. Throughout the year Western tradition and activities abound in Butte County.

Tall in the Saddle

Butte County

You don't have to be an easterner to realize when you're in the presence of a real westerner. He rides tall in the saddle. Riding tall in northern Butte County helps the real westerner see where distance has merged with time. In a land of buttes and bumps, a man sitting tall in the saddle casts a manly shadow on that portion of earth that is Butte County. He becomes a romantic figure, symbolized by stories of the West that thrilled the days of our childhood.

Where and what is Butte County? It is in the northwest part of South Dakota and contains a butte which is the center of the Nation. The southwestern part of the county is irrigated and farmed intensively. The remaining part is rolling hills, punctuated by buttes. In one area of this thinly populated part, there are 36 square miles without a dwelling place — only prairie and buttes.

Many of the buttes have names although some are mere bumps.

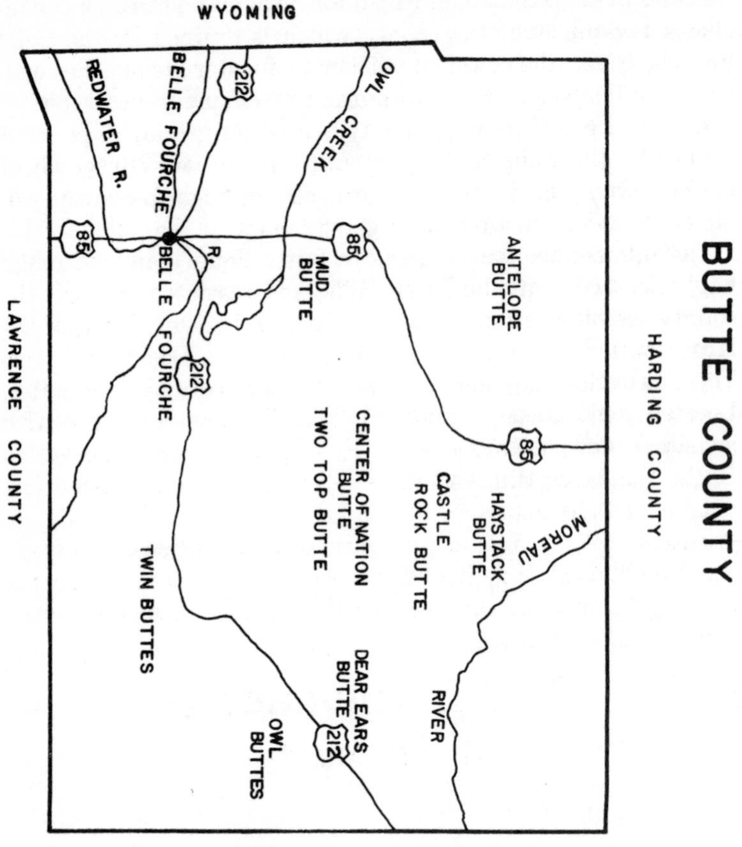

These buttes are described as a landform somewhere between a mesa and a pinnacle. They represent the erosional remnants of an ancient landscape (peneplain), where only the most resistant elements remain. The layers in the buttes are a series of strata that reflect the geological history of the ancient surface. Many of the strata contain distinctive fossils. The buttes were often ceremonial sites for the Indians in their vision quests. They are landmarks for the traveler, sites of Indian battles, campgrounds, and Indian eagle-catching sites. They have picturesque names: Castle Rock, Two Top, Haystack, Deer's Ears, Twin Buttes, Middle Creek, Susie Peak, Mud Butte, Owl, Crow, Antelope, and Eagle Butte. They often have names of animals — Eagle Butte was known to have had an eagle nest for many years. The butte area today is a land of cattle and cowboys.

In butte land the cowboy is as American as apple pie, baseball, and the Fourth of July. He is a tradition upon which the Old West was built. He still roams the range as a cowboy should.

The first thing one notices about him is his hat. It is a symbol of his character and is removed primarily for funerals and weddings. Permeated with dirt and dust, it is cemented together with sweat into a shape that reflects the character of the owner. Stiff with age, it can withstand the tearing of the prairie wind. It is as if it were slowly becoming ossified to the head. But it is not dirty. It is petrified.

The cowboy's blue denim jeans bend at the knees, as if they were hinged. As with the cattle he tends, the purifying power of the wind and rain have made them both fresh and clean.

You can always tell a westerner from an easterner out in butte country, even if they are dressed identically. The man in the saddle has trained his eye to look at distance, and he appears to be looking over your shoulder. Involuntarily you also turn to look at the distance. When two westerners meet on the plains, they stand side by side, looking out at the distance and viewing the surroundings with an appraising eye. When two easterners meet on the plains, they look at each other, oblivious to their surroundings.

The western plains have also produced a distinct language, passed on from generation to generation. It consists of two words, Yup and Nope. Westerners don't need much more, because activities in life have become so routine that they can almost always anticipate the question. If one heads for the range, chow, bathroom, or town, in a scheduled manner, the answer is always Yup. Everyone seems to know where everyone else is going, so who needs to ask? On those rare occasions when one has to make a sudden run to the bathroom instead of to town or to some other unscheduled activity, the response is Nope. Isn't it wonderful when people act in such a predictable manner that two words can serve as the entire English language? Language that anticipates the question with an answer leaves a great deal to the imagination. It has little appeal for English teachers.

The ruggedness in Butte County symbolizes true western traditions. The tall, rugged buttes silhouetted against the sky stand as a vast two-storied structure, the top story eroded away except for the supporting pillars. These pillars stand in grotesque relief on the bottom story. The people of Butte County can operate on two levels; mostly they operate on the bottom. But they can climb to the second level and wave to each other across the distance. And standing on top of the buttes is probably the only way they can see that there are other people living in the country.

The horseman, like the Buttes, also stands out against the vast sky. Tall in the saddle, he appears even taller than he is. The buttes and the cowboy personify the West. He makes one feel the spirit of the Old West all over again in his characteristic manners that blend in so well with the butte-accentuated landscape. One can really be captured by the nostalgia of the Old West. Almost, but not quite, you put the question: "Do you always ride so tall in the saddle?"

The cowboy turns and answers the unspoken question, "Yup." Which, translated, means: "You get a pain in the back when you ride slumped over."

A cowboy is never far from his horse. Together, they reflect traditions when the range was wide and wild.

Photo — D.J. Holden

Clark County

Area, 974 square miles
Population, 1925 - 11,364; 1945 - 8,126; 1980 - 4,894
County Seat, Clark. Population 1,351

Clark County illustrates the dramatic shift from the rural north central counties to the more populated southeast counties. It shows a loss of 6,470 people since its peak population of 11,364 people. Over the last 55 years it lost people at the rate of 117 per year or 57 per cent of its population. If Clark County continues to lose population at this rate it will have a negative population in 42 years or by 2023.

Of the 4,894 people now living in Clark County, one half live in the city of Clark and the small villages. This means the rural population occupies the land at a level of 2.5 persons per square mile as contrasted to 1925 when it was 8.1 per square mile. This illustrates the dramatic shift in population and where the loss of people has occurred.

Clark County also has its share of ghost towns such as Elrod. This once prosperous little business place has now only the shell of an abandoned school and memory of S.H. Elrod, Governor 1905-07, who gave the town a name.

The natural areas in Clark County are the many lakes and marshes in the area. These include Willow, Bailey's, and Cherry Lakes. In the northwest corner of the county is Oak Gulch.

Clark is often called the potato county in the state and has a large industry devoted to processing potatoes.

Lonely Eyes

Clark County

Loneliness is not confined to the rolling plains and prairies. But the vastness and apparent emptiness of the surroundings seem to magnify the effect. To many pioneers, especially women, the vastness acted as a prison with no walls. Imprisoned in nothingness, they were worn out by the endless drudgery

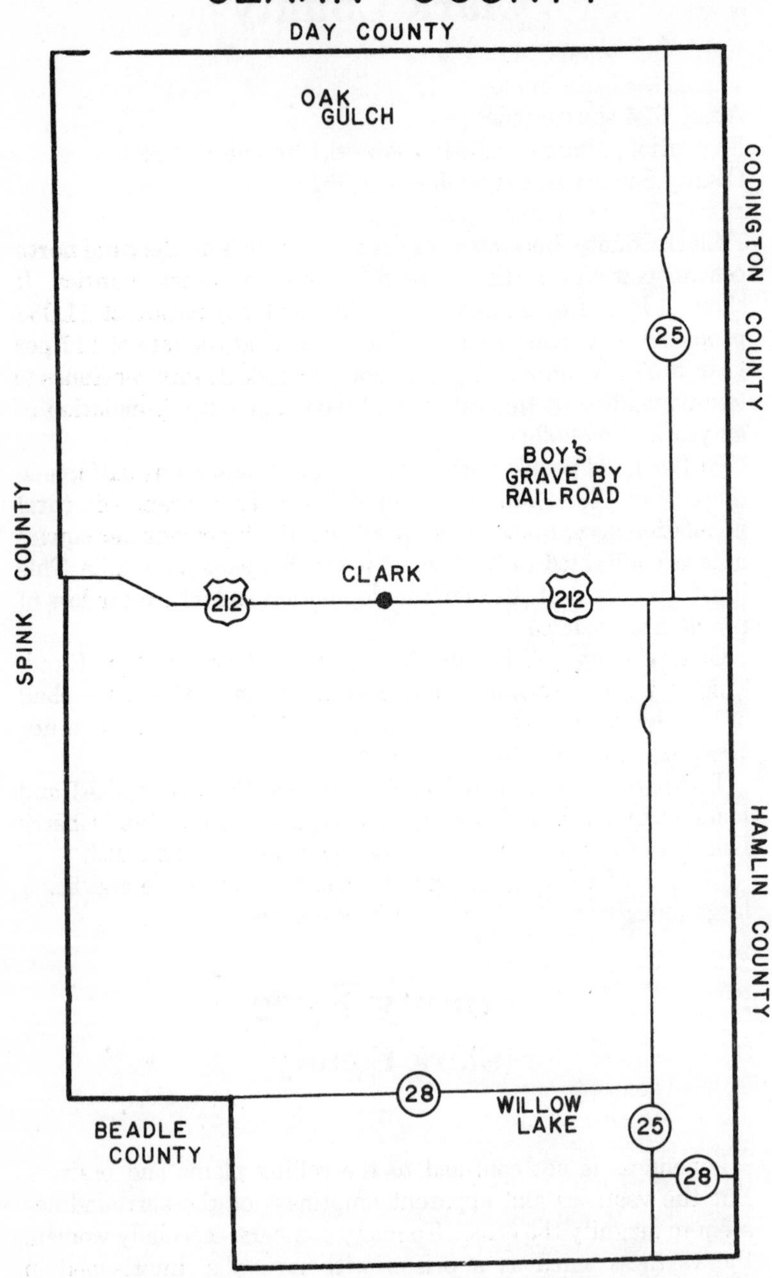
CLARK COUNTY
DAY COUNTY
OAK GULCH
CODINGTON COUNTY
25
BOY'S GRAVE BY RAILROAD
SPINK COUNTY
CLARK
212
212
HAMLIN COUNTY
28
WILLOW LAKE
25
BEADLE COUNTY
28
KINGSBURY COUNTY

associated with life. Their very essence seemed to evaporate and diffuse into the vastness of the prairie. First went their spirit, next their minds, and finally their bodies — all diffused out to mingle with the molecules from which they were created. The forces of disintegration were greater than the forces of creation. The more fortunate ran away to more hospitable regions. Only the strong stayed, to turn the prairie into the breadbasket of the world. These fortunate few, through luck, ingenuity, or maybe even craftiness, were able to produce more than enough energy to offset the forces of destruction.

From them came the ideas associated with the term *pioneer spirit*— energy, power, opportunity; growing, taking, conquering. These were converted into a pioneer's dream, a dream that often crashed headlong into tragedy when individual rights were carried beyond the limits of environmental and ethical constraints. This theme of empire-building and tragedy influenced many authors of pioneer life. Herbert Krause's *The Thresher* and Ole Rolvaag's *Giants in the Earth* are morbid examples of pioneers who were killed by the grasp of their own selfish ambitions. Johnny Black (*The Thresher*), with ever bigger and better machines, and Per Hansa (*Giants*), with more and more land, effectively destroyed their families before being themselves destroyed by their pioneer brand of aggressive greed. The loneliness of the prairie played no part in their lives because their pioneer spirit was obsessed with subduing the land. In the end, the tragedy is completed when Johnny dies in the flames of his biggest threshing machine and Per, lost in a winter blizzard, is found dead in a haystack the following spring. The victims and futility of their struggle are clearly tied to the endlessness of the prairie. Willa Cather's *My Antonia* and Frederick Manfred's *Lord Grizzly*, together with the Harvey Dunn pictures, look at the prairie as a friend, not an enemy.

The loneliness of the prairie is exemplified by a story of the little boy who loved trains. Near the center of Clark County, in an isolated strip of prairie where the little blue stem still waves, is an almost forgotten grave. The grave is a memory link to the past and to the friendship developed between Big Bill, a trainman, and the child with no playmates.

Imagine, if you will, some hundred years ago in a lonely sod house a little boy who lived with his parents. Every day he stood on a side hill outside the house and watched for the Chicago and

Northwestern's No. 106. His eyes lit up at the sight of the approaching train; he waved a greeting to his friends as the train rumbled by. The train fascinated the boy. Every day, rain or shine, snow or blow, he was there to greet the trainmen. And the trainmen grew to look forward to their daily meeting on the vast lonely prairie.

One day, no boy greeted the train, and a small grave appeared on the site where he once waited. Stricken by a strange disease, he was buried on the spot he loved so well. The parents, disillusioned by the harshness of pioneer life, left with a promise one day to return. But only the trainman, Big Bill, who promised to tend the grave, remained to carry on the memory of the boy. The parents did not return.

Today this memory of a trainman's love for a nameless boy of the prairie is still carried by trainmen, relatives of Big Bill, and the people of Clark County, who on Memorial Day visit the grave.

Through the remaining 364 days of the year, the trillions of molecules that made up the body of the little boy are playfully resonating with the molecules of the vast prairie. They diffuse and resonate with the molecules of the universe in a continuous network. Some molecules have become part of the spiders that weave the prairie grasses surrounding the grave into basketlike cavities. Countless spider generations have sat on web edges and watched for eons of time. Their webs vibrate with the wind, and their body molecules resonate with the molecules of the universe.

There are, according to Indian legend, spiders everywhere. Wherever God is, there must also be spiders. Through communication with spiders, whose molecular network connects with the molecular web of the universe, the Indians believe they are in direct communication with God. But how do we communicate with spiders? Again, according to Indian legend, we must first be receptive. We must be attuned by virtue of the emanating wave lengths of good energy. Bad energy (bad intention) turns off the receptivity. When all systems are "go," a direct communication with God is achieved by communicating with spiders. The lines are always open. God is always there, and the spiders, together with the molecules of the universe, form the connecting network. All we have to do is tune in. There are, however, people who do not seem to have receptive molecules. Some lose them or fail to tune in; others receive a weak or intermittent signal. Then there are those who radiate only the good energy and seem to be on a direct line.

If this is true of spiders, it could extend to other living systems. We are all islands of molecular organization, held together by energy bonds in a sea of molecular disorganization. If we can adjust to receiving a message from God, we can channel our molecular vibration into radiating good energy and creating good things. On the other hand, if we are a special kind of pig (Wilbur in Charlotte's Web), we should have no trouble communicating with spiders.

Surely the little boy on the prairie appreciated the goodness of life, and his molecular organization radiated love of life as he learned to communicate with the men on the passing train.

This molecular sociability seems still to grasp us as we stand on the windswept prairie by the grave and watch for the train. We can feel the spirit of the young lad and sense the presence of spiders as the molecular vibrations bring us all together. Then, suddenly, a shift in the breeze brings awareness as a train whistle wails in the distance. Our lonely eyes light up, and we feel the message brought by the molecules of the boy, the spiders, the prairie, and the universe.

We have joined the dance of the celestial molecules.

On the lonely prairie by an abandoned railroad track is the equally lonely grave of the little boy who loved trains. Here spiders and little blue stem connect him with the eternal cycle of life.

Photo — D.J. Holden

Deuel County

Area, 632 square miles
Population, 1925 - 9,004; 1945 - 7,617; 1980 - 5,289
County Seat, Clear Lake. Population 1,310

There situated on the east slope of the Coteau des Prairie is Deuel County. It is covered by prairie and ponds. The west and south part of the county has felt the bite of the plow and most of the land has been turned into productive farms. Along the east edge of the Coteau are the lakes: Cochrane, Fish, Oliver, Rush, Alice, Goddard, School, Bullhead, Round, Sutton, and ones still waiting for a name are called Coteau lakes. In the center of the county is Clear Lake and appended to the shore is Clear Lake City. Fortunately the city did not take its name from the other adjacent lake, Slippery Dick.

Salt Lake, the lake with the highest concentration of Epsom salts in the county, is shared with Minnesota. It is a Nature Conservancy Preserve. Here shore birds are known to concentrate in the spring. Anther Nature Conservancy project is the Altamont Prairie, where native forbs, legumes, and prairie grasses can be observed. On this prairie is a high point overlooking the Minnesota River Valley. The Indians have marked it with a cairn of rocks. It was noted as a place where the Indian could sight water.

Lakes in the northwest corner of the county also reflect early Indian use. Round Lake, in this group, also reflects a past history of dryness. A rock found on the lake bears the inscription, "Trapper Jim Dry Lake, 1854." The lake was also dry in 1894, 1934, and nearly dry in the 50s.

Boy Life During the Dust Bowl

Deuel County

Much has been written about the Dust Bowl years, when dust and despondency were the major features of the era. Accounts tell of people who lived in poverty and hardship while they struggled to make a living.

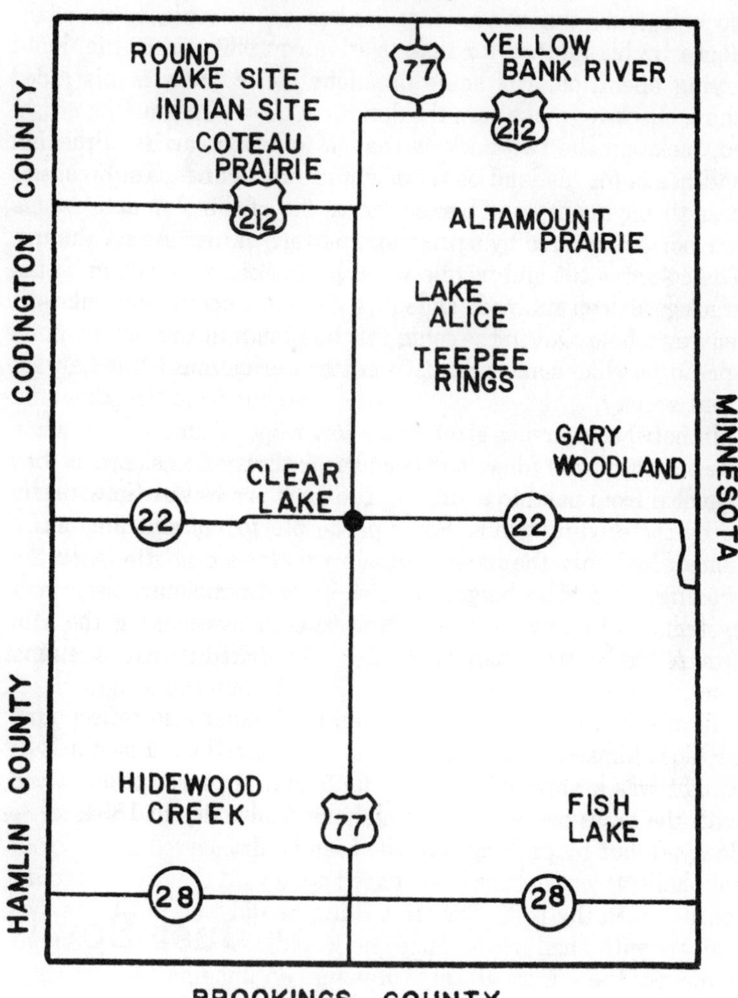

What did the youngsters do who were too young to help with the continuous toil needed to provide food and fuel for the family? Well, they were usually free to wander about and explore the country on their own . . . anything that kept them from getting in the way of the more serious business of making a living.

It is interesting to follow the adventures of a young boy as he wanders about, exploring the family farm and neighborhood in Deuel County during the Dust Bowl years. We find him, standing outside his home, dressed in patched overalls, hands in his pockets, and a smile on his face. He has just been kicked out of the house by his mother for his negative contribution to the donut frying operation. His smile broadens as he tucks in his faded shirt, checks to make sure the donuts in his pockets are not crushed, picks up the two buckets that he so often carries with him, and heads for his land of fantasy and fun. As he goes, he has to pass through a dry and barren marsh (he calls it a slough), its entire bottom covered by a prismatic pattern of hexagonal columns. The columns tilt and wiggle when he walks on them and, if the cracks are deep and wide enough, a column sometimes breaks off, leaving a hole. Out in the center of the slough, the repeating units spread out like some primitive pattern of paving left by an ancient society.

In between marshes stretched a low ridge of land which, when the marshes were filled, had been the pathway ducks used as they traveled from pond to pond. But the duck passes were now cut into by the eroding winds. Some parts, plowed up and then abandoned, had only the hated Russian thistle to do battle with the eroding wind. The bigger thistles grew on mounds, their root systems and bulky tops providing some protection for the soil. Other thistles were half covered by the drifting dust, dirt, and sand.

It was on these eroded fields and duck passes that the young boy lost himself in thinking about the past. The first place he sought was a narrow stretch of land that appeared to be paved with the brass bases of shotgun shells. The paper had long since decayed, but by probing into the base he discovered the color of the shells. It was on this brass paved boulevard that he started his journey into the past. The first thing he did was to fill the two buckets with shell bases. These he would save for a rainy day at home, for there were all sorts of games an imaginative boy could play with the various sized metal discs. One game he was weary of playing, however, was a shell hide and seek, which Mother usually won. So it was back to the pass for a couple more bucketloads.

The two buckets of shell bases collected, it was time for the more leisurely searching for other artifacts of the hunting trade. Many items were purposely discarded, some were lost in the excitement of the hunt, and some were simply forgotten. Bottles and bottle openers were scattered among almost completely rusted tin cans. There were coins, especially Indianhead pennies, occasionally a knife. And always there was the dream of finding a silver engraved shotgun, reportedly lost in the marsh.

When the search got a bit slow, he sat down under a tree, reached into his pocket for one of the prize donuts. There is nothing better than a fresh donut that has remained intact in the pocket after a trip over the prairie. As he sat daydreaming and munching on his slightly sandy donuts, the past seemed to drift slowly over the land. The sloughs were again filled with water. The teal, shovelers, and some of the dabbling ducks had departed for the South. Only the big canvasbacks, redheads, and green-headed mallards, mixed with a few other species, collected in the distant sloughs. Some disturbance caused them suddenly to fly up, darkening the sky. Hundreds of thousands of them started winging away, cutting low over the pass as they fought a stiff northwest wind. The shooting started and rippled from one end of the pass to the other like the muffled roar of a giant popcorn popper. When it was over, the ground was littered with dead and dying ducks. No need to remember who shot what since there were enough for everybody and some left over. The ducks were divided and stacked into piles. The desirable ones were loaded into Model T's and wagons. The less desirable were left to rot. Conservation was not an ideal of some of the old-time hunters.

After the hunt, silence crept over the slough until the quacking of distant ducks again surged over the land. Scattered over the ground was the litter of the hunt — cigarettes, beer cans, whisky bottles, and matchbooks. Matchbooks from Chicago, D.C., Minneapolis, Baton Rouge, Houston, Aberdeen, and other places.

The most conspicuous items of the litter were the spent shells. Scattered around the area were 20-, 16-, 12-, 10- and a few 8-gauge shells in vivid reds, greens, and blues. A question never answered entered the boy's mind. What will a double-barrel 8-gauge do to a compact flock of ducks? There were the usual Remingtons, Winchesters, and Peters shells, but also some with foreign names, French-sounding names. Prize finds were the yellow ones, but the best finds were the shiny black ones called Ajaxes. They were manufactured by the U.S. Cartridge Co., and some are known to have been loaded with old-fashioned black, smoky powder.

The sting of flying dust particles upon his face reminded the boy where he was, and the daydream was over. He got to his feet and headed back to the ridge between the sloughs. This time his search led him to an even more distant past. His first finds were flint chips and a hide scraper or two. Then, on a mushroom-like pedestal, was a beautiful arrowhead made of Knife River Flint. The arrow had protected the soil underneath, while the wind had eroded away the material around it. The week before it had been a pipestone peace pipe, two clubs, and several broken arrows that were found.

This time the youngster had visions of an Indian party occupying the site, and he saw wave after wave of ducks flying over. The Indians had lost many of the artifacts from the hunt which the boy picked up, inspected, and wondered about. He knew the Indians had been in the area, for only a few hundred yards to the north was a hill with an Indian burial ground and nearby teepee rings. Near the base of the hill with the teepee rings was a salt lick and a spring, where once were scattered the skeletons of hundreds of buffalo. They had been killed by the Indians as they came to drink. Today only a few scattered bones are found in the area of the Indian graves.

A quick check of his pockets revealed that he was out of donuts, so he circled up to one of his favorite sites, where he could look over the entire Minnesota River Valley. There, on the highest point, was a cairn of rocks, which the Indian had made as a lookout. To the Indian it served as a Holy Site, where young braves went on a vision quest. It was a site where water could be seen, buffalo sighted, and a vast area surveyed. As the boy circled back to the duck pass, he followed a rutted prairie trail that indecisively searched for direction as it wiggled down the hill.

A few rods off to the side of the road was a jumble of rocks that was once a claim shanty or sod house. Now all that remained was a pit circled by odd shaped rocks. He had visited the site many times before, and he looked around for something new that recent erosion might have uncovered. He picked up a large piece of blue and white china, probably once a plate. He pulled on the door of the wood-burning stove that was embedded in the sod and remembered the time he had found an entire cup, minus the handle. Did a little boy once share this home?

Nobody seemed to remember who lived here and where they went. No one cared. He thought about several similar sites he had found on his afternoon walks, all equally mysterious and most dug into sidehills around marshes.

Backtracking to the duck pass, he crossed a fence beaded with

Russian thistle. It looked like a spiny necklace as it threaded its way around the neck of the valley leading to the pass. He looked at the rip in his shirt he got crossing the last time. This time he crawled under. On the other side he released three Russian thistles and watched the wind tumble them across the marsh in a race that only the mind of a little boy could transform into a Russian Thistle Thoroughbred Derby.

On his return to the duck pass, he heard a faint cry that sounded like "Supper." Then the boy with patched overalls quickly grasped his two buckets filled with shotgun shell bases and trotted home. This time he'd hide them so Mother would have it a bit harder finding them. Then, sliding into his place at the table, he heard his concerned mother say, "Where you've been, Son?" With a quick look at Sister, whose duty it was to keep an eye on his whereabouts, he mumbled, mouth full of potatoes, "Outside, Mom"

Silence again fills the dining room, for there is nothing good to talk about. Everyone is hoping that the rains will come, break the drought, and bring the promise of renewed activity in the country.

A farmstead in Dust Bowl days, showing windblown soil piling up on the buildings, and the ubiquitous Russian thistle.
Photo — SCS

The same view a few years later, when the rains came and the area was planted to grasses.

Photo — SCS

Faulk County

Area, 1,018 square miles
Population, 1925 - 6,969; 1945 - 4,747; 1980 - 3,327
County Seat, Faulkton. Population 981

The people who settled Faulk County had dreams — dreams that the plains of waving grass could be turned into a populous center of industry and learning. But even before the depression of the thirties hit, the disillusioned were already leaving. The population continued to decrease so that today over 50 per cent have left. The farms are turning into larger and larger units operated by fewer and fewer people. The small towns, milked of their farmer support, have grown smaller and smaller until only a wistful memory remains.

Gone are the railroads that once controlled where the townsite was to be located. Gone are the schools and local post offices. Now only the cars and the roads that are paved to the large market place remain.

For the people seeking recreation, they can find it at the Scatterwood Lakes, one of the few places in South Dakota where the cattle egret nest. At Lakes Cresbard, Gerkin, and Faulkton are also areas of recreation and waterfowl production.

A Life To Remember

Faulk County

A little boy growing up on the prairie in the old days had several options for occupying his time. He was too little to be much help around the house and yard, yet too big to be watched over all the time. He was free to roam and amuse himself in a manner that only little boys can dream up. So there he is, out on the prairie bashing gophers to death with a stick. Equipped with traps, snares, and a water bucket for drowning, he is there to rid the pasture of the plague and at the same time make some money by collecting gopher tails at a bounty of one penny.

Still not strong enough to set the trap, he would have it set at home and carry it out to the pasture. He had not far to go before he could place it gently in front of a burrow. Then it was not long before excitement reigned and a quick trip home with "Mom! Boy, I got something big in my trap!" Big Sister, hearing about it from the next room, took off in disgust for fear of having to help. Mother, too busy to help, sent him back to deal with his own problem. So with a bit of apprehension, he took a stick and went out and beat the gopher to death. Its eyes popped out and blood ran out its nose, but that didn't matter. By now he had five other traps to look after. Besides, he had just gotten his first gopher (flickertail) and earned his first penny without the help of grownups. He had taken his first step toward independence.

After an afternoon of collecting gopher tails, it was off to find a Copenhagen snuff box to keep them in. So over he went to the snuff-chewing neighbors, who scattered the boxes all over the place. There he found his friends also had snuff boxes full of gopher tails. Going home he foresaw it was going to be tough trying to keep up with his friends in the gopher-catching business, for while there were many more gophers in their pasture, he

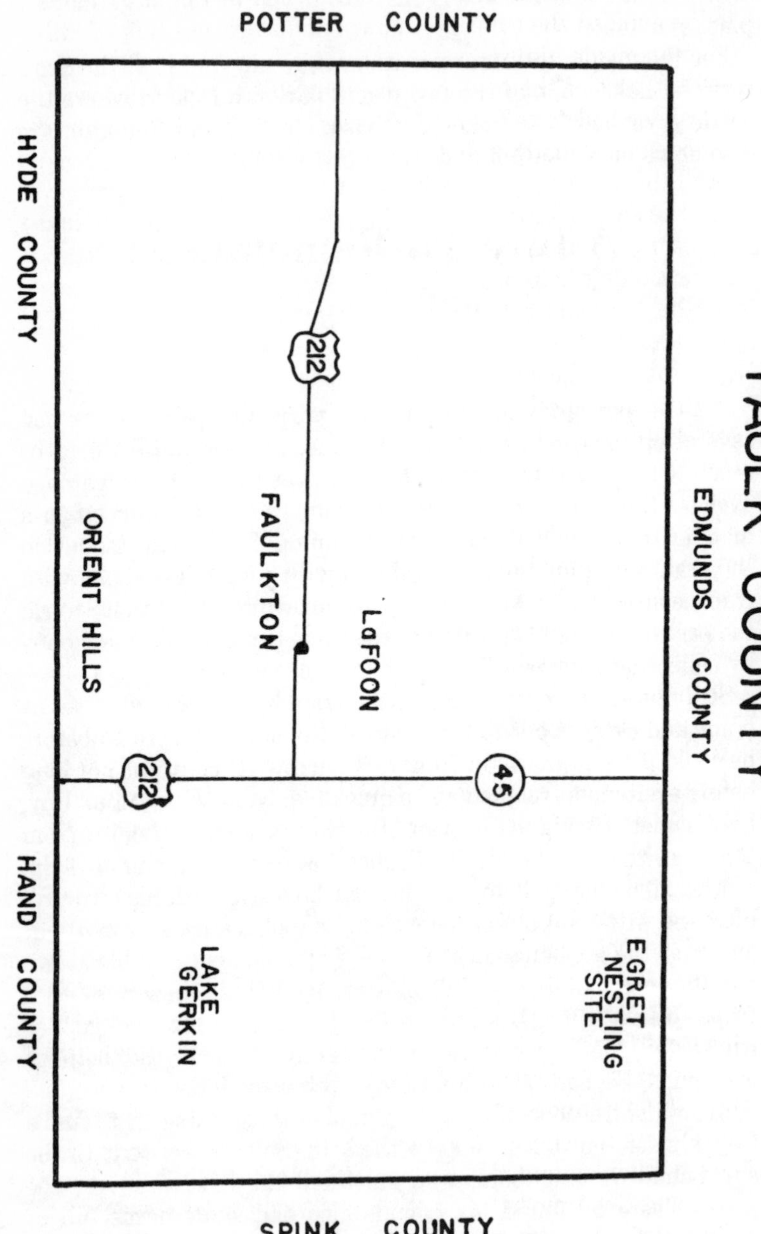
POTTER COUNTY
HYDE COUNTY
212
ORIENT HILLS
FAULKTON
LaFOON
FAULK COUNTY
EDMUNDS COUNTY
45
212
HAND COUNTY
LAKE GERKIN
EGRET NESTING SITE
SPINK COUNTY

noticed that most of them had no tails. When he saw his friends again, he avoided the subject of gopher tails because talk of killing gophers made him sick.

The best part of the business was the selling, especially when his big sister had to take smelly two-week-old gopher tails in to the independent young girls at the county court house. He loved to see all the stuck-up girls turn their heads in disgust when they opened the smelly snuff boxes to count the tails. At last he had gotten back a bit at those helpless girls who made fun of his trapping. He couldn't help but smile at the thought of their spending part of the day counting smelly gopher tails. It made him feel better when he went out to the pasture to work.

About this time he grew into the slingshot age. With one weapon in his hand and another in his pocket, he would select a pocket full of small rounded rocks for target practice. Bottles arranged in a line were an excellent enemy because they popped with a loud crack when hit. The ground soon became littered with broken glass, and everybody in the family showed much concern over where the new firing range was to be located. There wasn't much chance of getting this kind of information beforehand, because a little boy never knows from what direction the imaginary enemy will attack. The best solution was to set most of the farm off limits to war games.

After sufficient practice on bottles, it was time to plan a trip for some real wild game. English sparrows and barn pigeons were likely targets, but he could never get close enough to hit any. Then one day a lousy eastern kingbird started bothering him. It apparently had a nest nearby and kept buzzing over his head and alighting on a nearby branch. So he let him have it. The dead bird lay on the ground at his feet. He picked up its limp body and watched the blood running out of its beak. As he slowly turned its black and white body over with his hand, he noticed for the first time that under the black outer feathers on top of the head were brilliant red feathers. It was truly a beautiful bird. He looked up to the top of the tree where its mate was fluttering in a frantic manner. A tear slipped out of the corner of his eye, and he cried for having done such a foolish thing. Never again did his mother have to tell him to quit shooting at song birds.

Just about this time he began itching for bigger things. He had for the last couple of years eyed the guns in the house with anticipation. He had handled them many times when nobody was looking, and he knew exactly how they worked. The ammunition was always hidden, so he had problems there. But the gopher tail business was going great, and he was beginning to accumulate money to buy shells of his own. So one day when he got home from town with his own shells, the family decided to give him the necessary lessons in care and handling of a gun. Now the gopher tail business would accelerate with a bang and boom into a really big operation.

His first experience with a rifle was to hunt, but there really wasn't much game that was legal to take with a rifle. There was, however, a plentiful supply of barn pigeons (rock doves), and he had heard doves were good to eat. He set out to supply the family with doves. This was done after several older family members filed an impact statement on behalf of the barn roof. After the hunt, mealtime was a proud moment, with two good-sized, oven-baked doves in the center of the table. During the meal only one small member of the family ate rock dove. The rest watched and made unsolicited remarks about a leaky barn roof and little boys with big ideas. The experiment was not a success. The family never had doves again.

The family was always reluctant and anxious when the boy went hunting alone with a gun, especially after he demonstrated his expertise by shooting a hole in the living room door. There was a feeling of relief when he got home. Nevertheless, he finally graduated to the shotgun. This required more gopher tails to buy shells, and the government suddenly decided to discontinue the bounty payments. The ducks and pheasants he hunted provided no income, so it was time to look for a better way to earn money.

This led to long nights of reading Fur, Fish and Game and related magazines about the latest methods for capturing muskrat, mink, fox, weasel, and skunk with common sense and smelly scents. Combining sense and scents proved successful when used in the right places. It resulted in numerous pelts drying in the granary. Skinning skunk, however, proved to be a problem if older brother wouldn't do it, especially if he had to go to school the next day. Just how successful his trapping was can be attested to by looking back over his best month, when 499 muskrats and various other game were captured. By now he had become adept at killing. He no longer clubbed the muskrat in the head because that would injure the pelt and make a messy skin. He simply grabbed it in the back of the head and the middle of the back and with a quick jerk separated the head from the spinal column. The animal died instantly.

By now he had a sizable bank account (muskrat sold for $2 apiece) and was making more than almost everybody in the neighborhood. But it was not to last long, for the U.S. army's desire for 18-year-olds was in no way diminished by dead muskrats and smelly skunks.

It was in the U.S. Infantry that life turned to reality. No longer did he deal with clubbing gophers, shooting pigeons, and extirpating muskrats. Real people were involved — dead, dying, mutilated people. He was on that borderline of life where his automatic rifle told him he was a man, but the unused razor in his pack said he was still a boy. A boy who was beginning to realize that death was not just the end of life but that it carried a meaning and a purpose. The killing that started with a dead kingbird ended with people.

He could now look back at that little boy growing up in Faulk County, and he would always remember the moment of truth when a dead kingbird turned on his reverence for life. It was the kingbird's gift to him. It was a gift that gave purpose to the kingbird's death by strengthening his own moral convictions. He now knew that all life was given to be experienced, fulfilled, cherished, and respected. Even with the denizens of the wild, a purpose and meaning of life existed. To those wild and free, as well as people, "Life is real! Life is earnest! And the grave is not its goal." — Longfellow.

Hanson County

Area, 432 square miles
Population, 1925 - 6,354; 1945 - 4,620; 1980 - 3,415
County Seat, Alexandria. Population 588

Hanson County is one of the smallest in the state and 97.2 per cent of the land is farmland. The farms, many of them established in that eventful two-year period (1880-82) when every bit of the vacant land was claimed, is today still occupied by offspring of the original settlers. This despite the winter of 1880, the blizzard of 1888, and the drought of the thirties.

Along the James River that cuts across the southwest corner of the county is the site of old Fort James. It operated for two years from 1864-66 with a contingent of 80 men. It was established to

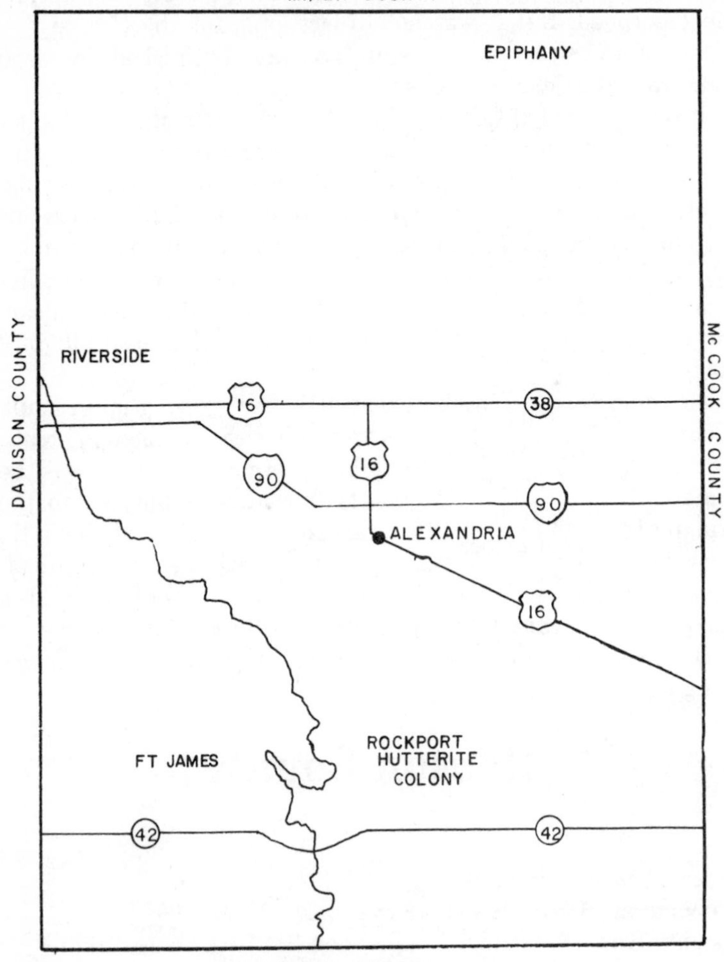

protect the Whites from the Indians. Its major battle was a firing of the cannon which resulted in one dead Indian and a dead horse. Today only broken pottery, rusty horseshoe nails, mules shoes, and a few foundation stones mark the place where it once stood.

Also along the James are the Hutterite colonies of Rosedale and Rockport. These industrious Russo-German people pride themselves in never asking the government for aid. Their prosperous farms and accomplishment in rural living mark them as successful farmers.

Bard and old Rockport were once successful towns in the county but today are just memories of those early days when the horse and buggy were the common mode of transportation.

Hutchinson County

Area, 817 square miles
Population, 1925 - 13,769; 1945 - 10,900; 1980 - 9,350
County Seat, Olivet. Population 96

James River Maxwell was the first white boy born in Hutchinson County, and since that time the Maxwells have multiplied in Hutchinson County. There has become a Maxwell Hutterite Colony along with five other colonies. The whole county, in fact, is steeped in the German tradition of industrious farmers. The Mennonites coming from the Black Sea, Hutterites from the Swiss Alps, and mixed in between a few other Germans consitute the bulk of the population. In October they all eat their way through a

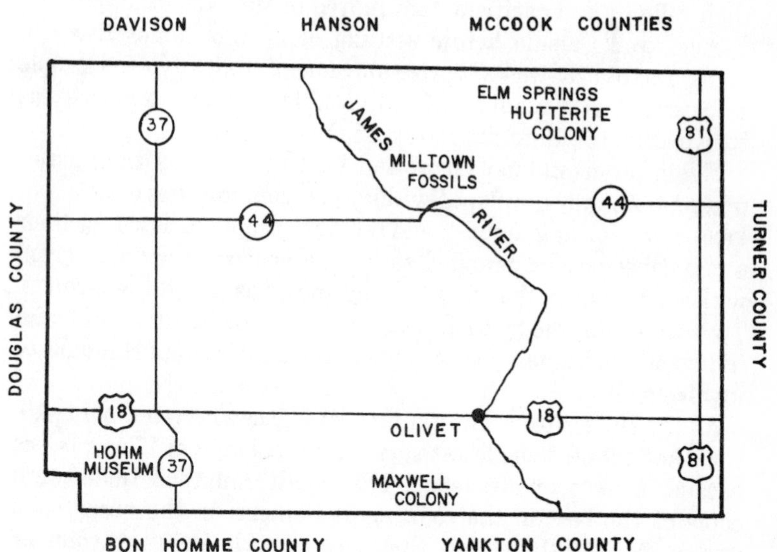

two-day Schmeckfest at Freeman. The order of the day is beer and German food all served by gaily dressed German maids in such a manner that even the Norwegian, Swede, and Irish cannot resist.

Freeman, whose name was supposed to be Menno, got its name switched with Menno when a railroad official accidentally nailed the wrong signboards on the depots — probably after some sort of a Schmeckfest of his own. So, if it makes any sense, Freeman got its name from Menno and Menno got its name from Freeman.

Olivet, the oldest city in the county, built a two-cell jail (1879) before its courthouse (1881) because of the more pressing need for the former. The courthouse is the oldest in use in the state, and the jail was just recently replaced. Olivet, population 96, is the smallest county seat in the state.

The Confining Community

Hanson & Hutchinson Counties

From out of the Tyrols of Switzerland they came, hardworking communal farmers called the Hutterites. Persecuted because of their religion and pacifism, they moved to Moravia, other parts of Europe, and Canada before settling along the James River in South Dakota. It was a "Swiss movement" that involved people who carried with them many of the skills, manners, and customs spawned by the Reformation in 1525.

Living on communal farms and held together by the glue of persecution, they developed within their communities a society of loyal, hardworking, honest, and religious people. Known for their social cohesion and branded as human isolates, they multiplied with such rapidity that they became known as the fertile farmers. They were admired by their neighbors for their industry, peaceful living, and politeness, but resented because of lack of community involvement.

As the Hutterites grew and prospered, they retained old traditions but adopted the latest agricultural technology. Their farms became models of efficiency. Their corn and bean fields were some of the best in the country. It is there, in the bean fields under the hot July sun, that one sometimes finds younger members of the community working.

Lisel and Ludwig had been hoeing corn out of the beans on the communal farm for three days. The hot, oppressive weather and the dullness of the job played tricks on Ludwig's mind. He watched with fascination as Lisel swung her hoe with a golfer's grace. He wondered how she could go on so steadily without stopping. He noticed the roundness of her body, even under the long loose dress. After two hours, her clothes clung to her body, and sweat streamed down her face. Ludwig, watching, could no longer concentrate on hoeing.

Everyone expected that she would soon be his bride, for she was about the only girl left in his colony not spoken for. To everyone in the colony they were always spoken of as one — Ludwig and Lisel. It was all so smug that he felt trapped. Not that she wasn't pretty and desirable. He had noticed how some of the older men in church had watched her as she entered church last Sunday dressed in a new spring dress and polka dot scarf. For him, the courtship, if you could call it that, seemed unexciting. All he needed to do was walk across the six bean rows where she was working and say, "Will you marry me next week?" What was romance and love all about anyway?

As he continued to hoe, his mind jumped off to last month when he was in Freeman with his father. He had been shopping for some garden seeds, and he could not help noticing the Freeman girls his own age in their tightfitting jeans. Once one had impishly looked him in the eye and said, "Hi, Butch." He had smiled, and suddenly her white teeth flashed, she tossed her head and then, grinning at him, said, "You sure got a nice mess of curly hair." His face flushed, his smile grew broader, and he glanced at her blond tresses rippling in the wind. With an impulsiveness that surprised him, he said, "I'll comb yours if you'll comb mine." Suddenly her eyes grew darker, and she said in a teasing way, "Why don't you come to the dance Saturday night? I'll let you try." Then knowing full well he wouldn't, she turned with a wave and walked off down the street. As he felt watched, the blood rushed to his face and he clenched his fist and wondered if he had sinned. All the way home he could think of nothing but the curly blond-haired girl with the red lips and flashing blue eyes. How nice she looked in her faded blue jeans and white T-shirt.

A drop of sweat ran down his brow, the salt stung his eyes, the sun grew hotter and the hoe heavier, and he grew more restless. Suddenly he could stand it no longer. He threw down the hoe, walked across the six rows of beans and grabbed Lisel by the hand. She, startled by his appearance, dropped her hoe, looked at him shyly at first and then, noticing a sense of determination in his face, she turned to him and asked, "Is something wrong?" With the reservation of a steamroller, he blurted, "Will you marry me?" Taken back by the explosive proposal in the bean field, she looked down, for she had nothing to say, although she had been expecting him to ask for almost a year now. Only last week when they had been walking down by the edge of the lake, and as the red full moon had pushed its way up through the pine, he had taken her hand and she felt he might have asked. She had hinted that her father was wondering what his plans were, but he had shrugged his shoulders and said, "It's getting a bit chilly." Her girlfriends had asked when Ludwig would be getting around to ask her, and she would change the subject. Recently she had been having second thoughts about her dull romance with Ludwig. She too felt that love and romance should be exciting, and she would have liked to know other boys to consider. She knew Ludwig would be a successful member of the community, for he was already respected for having some of the best corn and beans in the colony, but it was unexciting to be connected only with good beans and corn.

She looked up again, and the reality of the situation grasped her. As suddenly as she had lost her composure, she regained it. She reached down in the bean row, scooped up a handful of dirt, ground it to fineness in her hand, and with a broad sweep of her arm threw it on his sweaty head and ran off across the field. He gasped, spit out the dust from his mouth, and took off after her. It wasn't until she had reached the lake that he caught up with her. She had slipped out on a large flat rock and was cooling her bare feet in the water. He made as if to sit down beside her, but with a sudden shift he slid her neatly into the inviting water below the rock. She gasped with its sudden coldness, but then, relieved from heat of the burning sun, she slid out into the deeper water. Her long dress became water soaked and heavy, and with a twist of her shoulders, she slipped out of her clothes and swam toward the center of the lake. He watched for a moment the graceful figure, and then, almost with one movement, he shed his shoes and blue denim overall. He, too, now was swimming toward the center of the lake. What had started as a dragging, dull, drudging day had turned into the most exciting day of his life.

It was over an hour before their impromptu swim was finished, but it seemed as if a whole new world had opened up. Wading back to shore, Lisel stopped to gather up her wet clothes. As he turned to watch her, she ran her fingers through her tangled, wet hair, and tiny drops of water, like jewels reflecting in the sun, rolled smoothly off her body and dropped onto the ground. He visualized her standing there in faded blue jeans with a slightly too small T-shirt, and the haunting vision of the girl in town no longer inflamed him.

No longer were beans and corn on their minds as they walked, hand in hand, to the colony's dining hall, their wet hair and clothes drying as they walked. It was now all settled, and a new seriousness settled over the couple. They both had felt trapped in their ultimate fate and strangely rebellious toward it. They had both wished the freedom of the people on the outside but valued the sense of security the colony provided. They both remembered their discussion with a distant relative who had left the colony but had returned for a short time. They had learned that of some 10,000 Hutterites, there were only 15 family names. They learned that inbreeding can be dangerous and that an inflexible genetic base can bring out bad, weak, recessive characteristics. They talked about the high fertility rate of their people. At 4.9 per cent, it was the highest in the nation and resulted in an uneven sex ratio. It also caused stress on the colonies, for new land was hard to find. Some people lately had been leaving the colonies, but they found life hard in the outside world with only an eighth grade education.

They turned, looked into each other's eyes, and knew it was too late for them to do differently, for they knew they were in love. But as they gazed at each other and fondly thought of the future, they vowed that their children would not be caught within the confines of an invisible trap but would be given the opportunity and freedom to investigate all options that the world had to offer.

The clock in the colony's dining room struck 2:00 p.m., and Ludwig's beans became his concern. As he walked back to the field, he felt at last he could concentrate on hoeing.

Lisel went home to put up her wet hair.

Meade County

Area, 3,491 square miles
Population, 1925 - 9,486; 1945 - 8,080; 1980 - 20,717
County Seat, Sturgis. Population 5,180

Meade, that gigantic county, exceeds all other counties in size. Even the recently combined counties of Jackson and Washabaugh do not reach the size of Meade. Eight and one half Clay Counties, our smallest county, would not completely cover Meade. Meade,

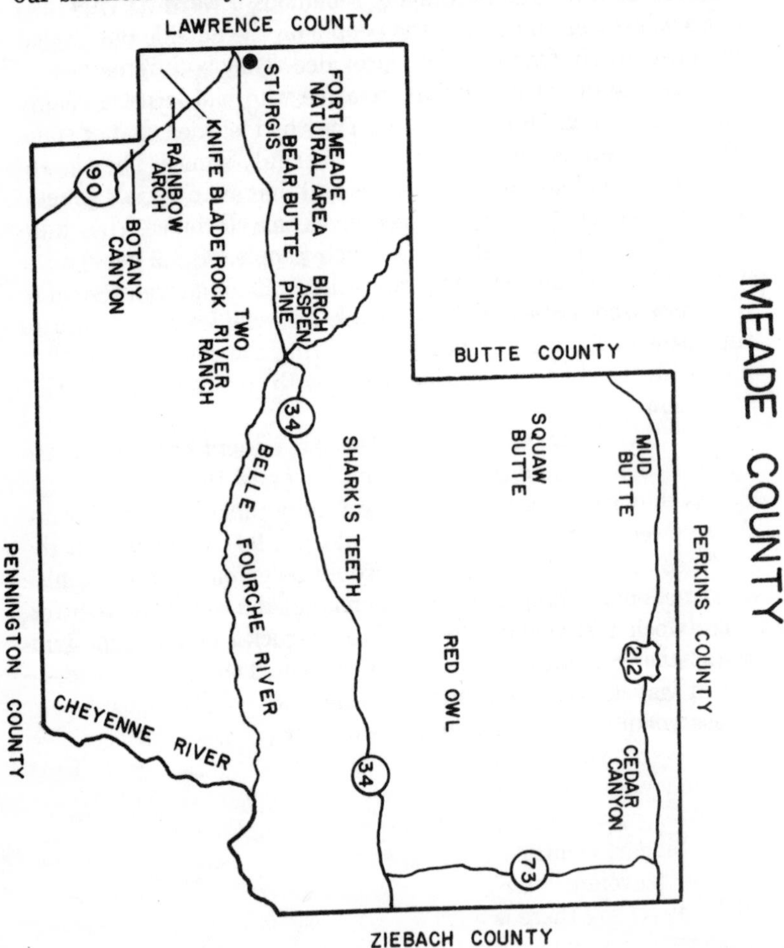

larger than the combined size of Delaware and Rhode Island, is 140 miles from one corner to the other.

The county starts in the northeastern edge of the Black Hills and stretches out across the expansive plains. It is a county endowed with many natural resources, and notable are its many caves. Three of the larger are Bethlehem, Wonderland, and Stagebarn. The latter was the site of a stage station and barns. Below this cave is the delightful Botany Canyon with its wild orchids, moss-covered rocks, and in the summer its almost arctic-like climate. Near Crystal Cave is Knife Blade Rock.

Ghost towns also are numerous in Meade with Calcite probably the best known. Others are Caton and Elk Creek. At one time there were some 50 post offices in the county, but these have dwindled to 15. One post office that operated until a few years ago was said to be the only sod house mail dispensary in the country. At one time 160 rural schools dotted the county, but they, too, have been consolidated. Some small villages that still serve the area are White Owl, Red Owl, Enning, Plainview, and Howes.

Indian legends and activities are common at Bear Butte State Park. This is an old volcanic plug but is more youthful than Devils Tower. Another butte, Squaw Butte, has a legend of an abandoned squaw who recovered from her illness and lived out her life on the butte.

North & South of Nothing

Meade County

There is something unsettling about rolling along on Highway 34 between Pierre and Sturgis. You look out the window of the car at the undulating hills, rolling to left and right like giant brown waves. You get the feeling they are rolling toward you; that if you stopped, you would be submerged by a swelling wave. A sign warns you it is 48 miles to the next gas station. If you have a tendency toward motion sickness, hold on, because you're about to cross a grassy prairie sea. You are entering Meade County, one of the biggest counties in the nation.

Some travelers who have crossed this prairie sea on lonely Highway 34 say there is nothing out there. Not so. A look out the window assures you it is a pleasant country, with wide blue skies and running room for jackrabbits. Up ahead looms a cluster of buildings at the side of the road. They seem out of place in a land shaped for curves. Low, rounded hills, like upended rocking chairs, press against the sky, and the few silhouetted block buildings tear holes in the sky.

Coming to a stop at the local combination gas station, post office, grocery store, and supplier of local news, travelers can pause for a bit of refreshment. The air is fresh, the view is excellent. You're told that out on a distant hill, you can look so far that it takes three seconds for the image to return! It is a place where, when you ask what is going on, the standard reply is "Nothing." What did you do last week? "Not much." What are you going to do next week? "Same thing."

This can be interpreted to mean that Nothing is the normal course of events, events repeated so often they seem like Nothing. People get excited only when Nothing stops happening. And then, as if by some magic diffusion process, everyone knows who got married, had a baby, died, or got drunk last night. Nothing always means good news, that everything is normal, as expected. Nothing is a drag to the teenager; to older people, it is a blessing.

So out here in Nothing, USA, next to Red Owl, a little way on the other side of White Owl, and surrounded by great horned owls, one gets the feeling that, yes, it really looks like Nothing, for it's hard to see something. It's like being in a giant covered dish. The bottom is brown (green in spring), and the top is blue, splashed with dabs of whipped cream. It is not a place for ordinary people, who want to get to their destination. It is a place for special people, who wish to pop out of the big covered dish and explore to find out if there is really something to Nothing.

The first place to go is south of Nothing. After about five or six miles, you come to the edge of a range of hills that overlooks the confluence of the Cheyenne and the Belle Fourche Rivers. It suddenly looks like the foothills of the Black Hills. On the northeast-facing slope are ridges of ponderosa pine. Here and there are aspen groves. On the drier sites, western red cedar form ribbons of green on the ridges. At the bottom, two silver streams wind in snakelike fashion to coalesce into one. The Cheyenne washes sediments into the area from the southern Black Hills; the Belle, from the northern Hills. Down on the sand flats, you can pick up rocks, minerals, and gems that originated in far places. Also, as the streams cut through the numerous layers of the Pierre shales and chalks, fossils are eroded out and scattered through the area.

Here and there petrified wood has washed in from the Hell Creek Formation.

Wildlife, birds, and fish funnel in by following the river valleys into the area. Experience builds to a high when you step out onto the prairie and find all the plants the Indian used for survival. Here the horned lizard flashes across the little sand blowouts that surround the mushroom-like rocks that eroded out of the sandstone. Down around the base of these multicolored mushroom rocks, numerous shark teeth are scattered on the sand. As you wander around, exploring the crevices of the past, looking across the valley into visions of the future, you enjoy the splendor of the present. It is an experience that few know about and still fewer enjoy.

Back to Nothingsville, and then off you go to the north. There, on the border shared by Meade and Perkins Counties, the Cedar River meanders into the Moreau River. It has cut deeply into horizontal layers of sandstone and shale, creating 30 miles of badland formations. It is a place where you can wander for days without seeing anyone. Cattle lost in the canyon take days to find and sometimes die, lost in the depths. Turkey vultures and golden eagles watch from favorite perches overlooking the canyon, and one plateau has a colony of partially albino prairie dogs. The red cedar roots washing out of the slopes are collected and polished for driftwood decorations and furniture. At every turn in Cedar Canyon is a scenic view.

People who live in the area relate to the area in a manner that does not bring about much change. They blend into the area, rather than disrupt it. Their friendly nature is a product of their isolation, and their openness blends with the openness of the country, creating a sense of trust. They are people who depend little on the outside world, and young and old find a place of usefulness in the family circle. Their quaint schools and comfortable ranches are tucked away in hills. All this adds up to an experience at Nothingsville that is hard to forget.

A quick look at the gas gauge reveals it's nearly empty. You have traveled nearly 300 miles. Pulling into the first gas station, you are greeted by a product of the women's lib movement, only she had done this work for a long time, since there are only girls in the family. You ask her what's going on. "Nothin' " is her reply. Then quietly you spring on her the announcement that you have just driven over the great divide between the Moreau and Cheyenne Rivers and that bisecting it is the rapidly flowing Belle

Fourche River. "Aw, shucks," she replies. "That's nothin'. My boyfriend does it most every day." Then, suddenly, you realize out in Meade County, which is bigger than the combined states of Rhode Island and Delaware, Nothing is really a state of mind waiting for something to happen. And happen it does when boys and girls get together and when one looks around and explores the country. By doing so, Nothing turns into something very special in Meade County. Really! Where else can you get something for Nothing these days?

In a valley where two rivers meet is the land on the edge of Nothing. Nearby are the relict pine, birch, aspen. It is a whole new land that seems to explode out of the endless prairie. The Belle Fourche River is to the left, the Cheyenne at the bottom. United, they flow on to the Missouri as the Cheyenne.

Photo — SDSU - Remote Sensing

On the north edge of Nothing stands the turkey vulture tree, overlooking picturesque Cedar Canyon.

Photo — D.J. Holden

Spink County

Area, 1,511 square miles
Population, 1925 - 16,054; 1945 - 11,216; 1980 - 9,201
County Seat, Redfield. Population 3,027

Spink definitely is flat. One fellow, thinking he was going down hill, started out at an altitude of 1304 feet and after six miles bottomed out at 1302 feet. The entire elevation of the county varies less than 15 feet except where streams have incised their shallow valleys. It is this level land on the dry bed of glacial Lake Dakota that makes Spink County one of the greatest wheat producing counties in the world.

The history of Spink County is rich in the Indian tradition. Prehistoric Indians date back to the mound builders. The Rees lived there in 1762. It was only in 1880 that the last Indians left the county when Chief Drifting Goose pulled up stakes for the Crow Creek Reservation, but only after several confrontations with white settlers forced the closing of the Spink County Indian Reservation.

Here in the county is Council Rock, where the Indian God Wakan lived. It has been the site much reverenced by the Indian, and many Indian ceremonial activities were known to have taken place here. A replica of the site has been constructed at the site. The original stones, skeletons, and artifacts were lost at the Chicago's World Fair in 1895.

Near here at Armadale Island in the 1800s, Indian rendezvous were a yearly event. Here at these trade fairs as many as 2,000 lodges from many tribes were camped. It is at this site in 1827 that a fur trading center was established.

No history of Spink County is complete without a mention of the county seat war. This war complete with armed groups led by preachers and bankers, the militia from Fargo, and fraudulent elections, made for much excitement in the early 1880s.

Redfield, winner of the war, is now known as the Pheasant City. It got its name because in 1908 Spink County sportsmen introduced the ring-necked pheasant along the James River. Today the pheasant population is a matter of considerable concern in most parts of the state.

The Land Where the Lake Once Stood

Spink County

Spread out across glacial Lake Dakota in northeast South Dakota is one of the greatest wheat producing counties in the nation. The large dry, flat, rockless glacial lake bed is a study in geometrical angularity.

Standing there on all this flatness, it seems as if the end is the beginning with the straight geometric lines of roads, railroads, and fields all seeming to vanish into the distance. The horizon appears like a meeting place, where atoms, molecules, and compounds create it all and where the primeval soup is poured into square molds to create the earth. There is no more. It is all the same. In one great sweep of the eye, through a 360-degree arc, the four cardinal directions seem to wrap around themselves. The

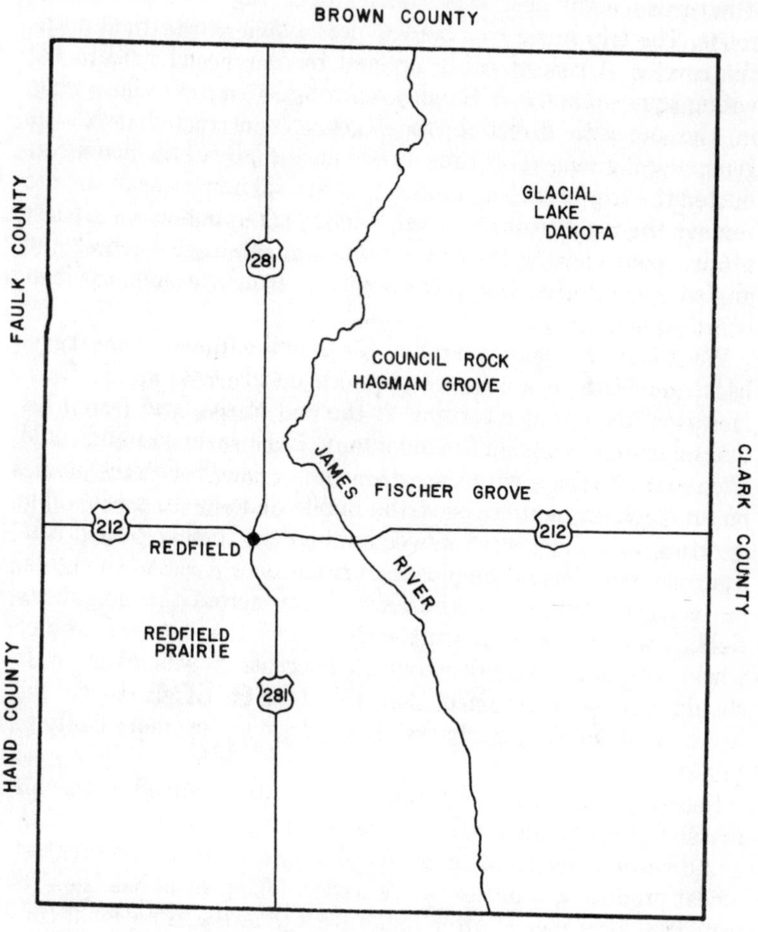

land establishes the habits and patterns of the people. It must have been a place like this where man first suggested that the world was flat.

Working with this immense flatness, man found it easy to permit his reductive impulses to tumble square onto square: square county, square township, square section, square farm, square field, square farmstead, and square buildings. And, could it not be said, square people? Square to the extent that their minds run in square patterns dictated by topographic flatness. It is like living life in two dimensions. Angular roads follow section lines. Only a nut would venture across the country at a slant. Going to town for a Saturday night beer was a series of zigzags on right angled roads. The trip home was maneuvered like a geometrical maze, the reveler at risk of being greeted by the wrong wife in the wrong square when lost. Sunday morning led to more zigzagging, in the opposite direction to a geometrical church with its geometrical graves. This time, however, the lady of the house conducted the trip in such a manner that arrival home was in time to remove the roast from the oven. Sunday afternoon was a modest affair, spent viewing the countryside through angled fences and angled shelterbelts, but occasionally passing through checkerboard square towns.

Weekdays brought some relief, for then the farmer could travel back and forth in a ceaseless pattern on his flat, square field. However, the circular turning at the end of the field jarred his mental state loose from the monotony. His awakened mind could then soar into space with the astronauts, crash through the jungles on an elephant, and envision the nubile dancing girls of Arabia gyrating with suggestive movements on the freshly seeded soil. Since no rocks jarred the plowman from these pleasant thoughts, he could suddenly find himself halfway across the neighbor's field. It was probably in some such manner that a mixed crop of wheat, oat, and barley (locally called succotash) was invented. It should also be mentioned that this is more likely to be the behavior of the younger bucks. The older ones are more likely to fall asleep.

Recently the Oahe Irrigation Project was coupled with this massive mess of angularity. A series of angular dams, ditches, and dikes will zigzag Missouri River water to one of the greatest wheat producing counties in the nation. The project has been rejected by local people after much local, state, and national controversy. Could it be that state and federal planners forgot that compounding squareness does not lead to inspiration?

Dakota images? Yes, we are all part of them. We are stamped out like Xerox copies, only to be diluted by an avalanche of time. We live and grow in a mold, controlled inwardly by our selfish genes and outwardly by an overpowering environment. Tricked, though we are, into believing we are masters of our destiny by an overwhelming ego, we have two revealing virtues — reflection and self adjustment. It is as it should be today and ever will be. God be with us.

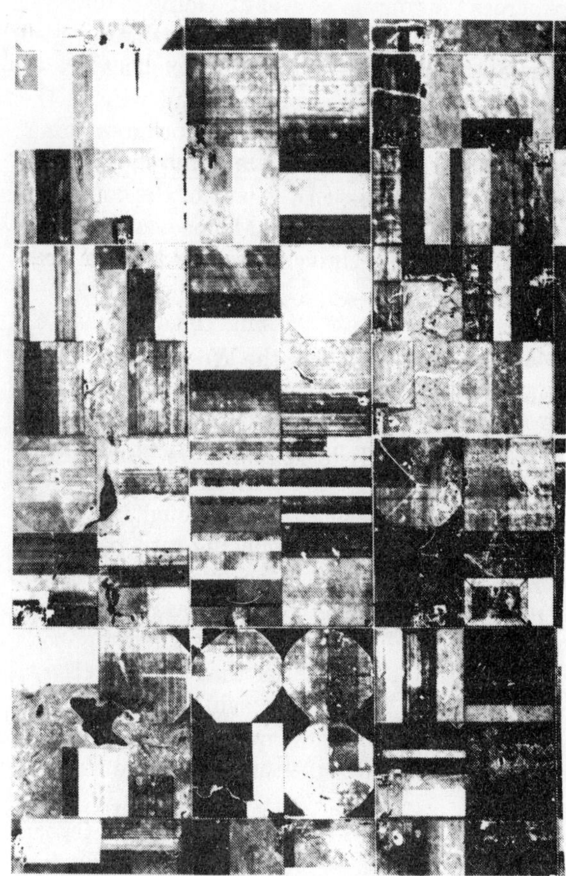

On the broad plain of glacial Lake Dakota, a geometric pattern was imposed upon the once vast sea of grass. Today the angular patterns of straight-line farming have given way to the bent of people who like to go in circles, and a new pattern is emerging.
Photo — SDSU, Remote Sensing

Selected Literature

Blegen, H.M. 1978. The Norwegians in America. Center for Western Studies, Sioux Falls, SD.

Coffeey, M. 1978. "Dust Storms." Natural History 87:72

Dick, E. 1954. Sod House Frontier. Johnson Publishing Co., Lincoln, Neb.

Ellis, C.H. 1909. The History of Faulk County. North Plains Press, Aberdeen, SD. (Also many other county histories are available.)

Froiland, S.G. 1978. Natural History of the Black Hills. Center for Western Studies, Sioux Falls, SD.

Hassrick, R.B. 1964. The Sioux. University of Oklahoma Press, Press, Norman, Okla.

Huseboe, A.R. & W. Geyer 1978. Where the West Begins. Center for Western Studies, Sioux Falls, SD.

Hunt, J.N. 1974. South Dakota Historical Markers. Brevet Press, Sioux Falls, SD.

Janovy, J. 1978. Keith County Journal. St. Martin Press, NY.

Jennewein, J.L. & L. Boorman. 1973. Dakota Panorama. Brevet Press, Sioux Falls, SD.

Lewis, F.C. 1971. Nothing to Make a Shadow. Iowa State Uni versity Press, Iowa City, Iowa.

Milton, J.R. 1977. South Dakota. W.W. Norton Publishing Co., NY

Rogers, D.J. 1980. Edible, Medicinal, Useful and Poisonous Wild Plants of the Northern Great Plains. St. Francis Press, St. Francis, SD.

South Dakota Ornithologists' Union. 1978. The Birds of South Dakota. W.H. Over Museum, Vermillion, SD.

Underhill, R.M. 1972. Red Man's Religion. University of Chicago Press, Chicago.

Van Bruggen, T. 1976. The Vascular Plants of South Dakota. University of Iowa Press. Iowa City, Iowa.

Vogel, V.J. 1970. American Indian Medicine. University of Oklahoma Press, Norman, Okla.

Wedel, W.R. 1961. Prehistoric Man on the Great Plains. University of Oklahoma Press, Norman Okla.

Natural Heritage Site List

A list of Natural Heritage sites is never complete. Following is a list of responses to nearly 1,000 letters sent out to knowledgeable people in the state in 1971. These responses, plus conversations with many people from many parts of the state, have generated the list. It is a preliminary list, and much works needs to be done on each county to approach adequacy. The number of areas reported is somewhat proportional to the population. The more heavily populated areas turned in more responses and more sites, whereas some of the less populated areas, which really have many sites, failed to report them.

Ideally, each county should be surveyed and each area catalogued, investigated, evaluated, written up, and accurately mapped. When this survey is completed, we can begin to develop programs to protect unique and important sites for future use.

It is important that this work be started in South Dakota. It has already started on the national level and in several states.

The first step is passage of a state law proclaiming the need, giving the protection, and providing the machinery to implement the program. With such a law, future generations will be indebted to our foresight in preserving a part of our natural heritage.

Alphabetical List of Sites

Site	County	Site reported by
Altamont Prairie	Deuel	Max Myers, Brookings
Ancient Bog	Bennett	Dilwyn Rogers, Sioux Falls

Site	County	Site reported by
Ardmore Agate Beds, Ogalala National Grasslands	Fall River	D.J. Holden
Armstrong County, Historical	Stanley	Sigurd Anderson, Webster
Aspen Grove, Lemmon	Perkins	Lloyd Dale, Lemmon
Aurora Prairie	Brookings	D.J. Holden
Bad River	Jones	Ext. Homemakers
Balanced Glacial Erratic	Roberts	R. Ben Swanberg, Sisseton
Beaver Creek	Minnehaha	D.J. Holden
Beecher's Rock	Custer	Richard Edie, Bruce
Big Moreau & Little Moreau	Dewey	D.J. Holden
Big Spring (The)	Robert	Bruce Harris, Clear Lake
Big Spring Canyon	Bennett	Morton Green, Rapid City
Big Tom Formation	Grant	Lowry Elliott, Milbank
Bijou Hills	Brule	Francis H. Ugolini, Landmarks Denver, Colorado
Bitter Lake	Day	George M. Jonkel, Laurel, MD
Black Pipe Creek	Todd	June Zietner, Mission
Blair Cemetery	Sully	Charles Rogge, Sioux Falls
Blue Cloud Abby	Grant	Ext. Homemakers
Botany Canyon	Meade	Nat Whitney, Rapid City
Box Elder Creek	Pennington	Francis Ugolini, Landmarks, Denver, Colo.
Boyd Prairie	Lake	Ruth Habeger, Madison
Boy's Grave by Railroad	Clark	D.J. Holden
Buffalo Gap & Hogbacks	Custer	D.J. Holden
Buffalo Gap National Grassland	Custer	D.J. Holden
Buffalo Jump	Custer	Dick Rebbeck, Rapid City

Site	County	Site reported by
Buffalo Jump, Short Pine Hills (east)	Harding	Les Baylor, Rapid City
Buffalo Kill Area (Shadehill)	Perkins	Dave Hanson, Waubay
Buffalo Lake	Roberts	Richard Durland, Sisseton
Buffalo Rings	Roberts	Don Allen, Pierre
Buffalo Rubbing Rocks	Hyde	D.J. Holden
Buffalo Slough	Lake	M.E. Anderson, Pierre
Buffalo Trading Post Prairie	Lake	Robert Buckman, Madison
Buffalo Wallow at Highmore	Hyde	D.J. Holden
Buffalo Wallow at Manchester	Beadle	George Jonkel, Laurel, MD
Bull Creek Indian Village	Gregory	Max Myers, Brookings
Burning Bluff	Gregory	D.J. Holden
Cactus Hills	Minnehaha	Ronald R. Nelson, Sioux Falls
Calico Canyon & Elm Creek Canyon	Custer	D.J. Holden
Camp Crook	Harding	D.J. Holden
Cannon Balls	Harding	Charles Foster, Meadow
Capitol Rock (Just over the border in Montana)		John Sherrod, Camp Crook
Cascade Spring	Fall River	D.J. Holden
Castle Rock	Butte	Don Adolphson, Mpls.
Cedar Butte	Jackson	Ext. Homemakers
Cedar Canyon	Perkins & Meade	Paul Bishop, Bison
Cement Ridge	Lawrence	Marion Hilpert, Spearfish
Cemetery Site on Missouri, 1859	Bon Homme	Ext. Homemakers
Chalk Hills - Marine fossils	Charles Mix	D.J. Holden
Cherry Creek	Zieback	D.J. Holden

Site	County	Site reported by
Cheyenne River near White Owl - Birch, Aspen, Ponderosa Pine on the Glenn Spears Ranch	Meade	Glenn Spears, White Owl
Cheyenne River Bridge on Highway 34 - agates, jasper, and fossils	Ziebach & Haakon	D.J. Holden
Clovis Prairie	Brown	D.J. Holden
Club House Slough, White Rock Slough, Mud Lake and Upper Lake Traverse	Roberts	Francis Ugolini, Landmarks, Denver, Colorado
Coal Creek Indian Village	Fall River	Ext. Homemakers
Columnar Juniper - near the border in North Dakota		D.J. Holden
Cormorant Island	Day	Clem Kehrwald, Webster
Coteau Prairie	Deuel	Jim Sieh, Pierre
Craven Canyon Pictographs	Fall River	Jim Larson, Rapid City
Cretaceous Fossils	Dewey	June Zietner, Mission
Crow Butte Teepee Rings	Butte	Ralph Cole, Rapid City
Cuny Table	Shannon	Ext. Homemakers
Dallas - Once one of larger towns in S.D.	Gregory	Ext. Homemakers
Dantes Inferno	Jackson	Ext. Homemakers
Dead Horse Gulch	McPherson	Dave Ode, Sioux Falls
Deadwood Trail	Haakon	Ext. Homemakers
Deer Draw	Harding	Ext. Homemakers
Deers Ears Butte - Indian ceremonial site	Butte	Mrs. Alfred Hinds, Prairie City
Dells of the Big Sioux	Minnehaha	James O. Berdahl, Sioux Falls
Devil's Gulch	Minnehaha	James O. Berdahl, Sioux Falls

Site	County	Site reported by
Deciduous Forest near Bonesteel	Gregory	Terry Spitzenberger, Brookings
Dinosaur Park	Pennington	Francis Ugolini, Landmarks, Denver, Colo.
Dinosaur Tracks	Harding	Paul Bishop, Perkins Co.
Drumlen and Glacial Features	Roberts	R. Ben Swanberg, Sisseton
Dry Run or Cottonwood Slough	Roberts	Rolf Wallenstrom, Pierre
Dry Wood Lake	Roberts	Ken Husmann, Brookings
Eagle Butte Marine Fossils	Dewey	D.J. Holden
Eagle Nest Butte	Washabaugh	Ext. Homemakers
East Central South Dakota Forest	Jerauld	Dilwyn Rogers, Sioux Falls
Eisher Spring and South Slim Buttes	Harding	John Sherrod, Camp Crook
Elk Point Sand Dunes	Union	Charles Rogge, Sioux Falls
Elm Springs Hutterite Colony	Hutchinson	D.J. Holden
Eros Data Center	Minnehaha	D.J. Holden
Etta Mine	Pennington	J.P. Gries, Rapid City
Evarts	Walworth	Ext. Homemakers
Fairburn Agate	Custer	D.J. Holden
Fairview	Sully	Charles Rogge, Sioux Falls
Farm Island	Hughes	D.J. Holden
Firesteel Creek - Shark Teeth - Pierre Shale	Davison	Ext. Homemakers
Firesteel Coal Mine - Isabel	Dewey	Sigurd Anderson, Webster
Flint Hill	Fall River	Jim Larson, Rapid City
Fort James	Hanson	Ext. Homemakers
Fort Meade Natural Area	Meade	Ralph Cole, Rapid City
Fort Pierre National Grasslands	Stanley	James Hughes, Pierre

Site	County	Site reported by
Fort Sisseton	Marshall	Sigurd Anderson, Webster
Fort Sully	Sully	Charles Rogge, Sioux Falls
Fossil Clams - McIntosh	Corson	D.J. Holden
Fossil Site - Ed Hess Ranch	Harding	Ed Hess, Redig
Fossil Leaf Imprints at Timber Lake	Dewey	D.J. Holden
Gary Moraine Hills	Aurora	Ext. Homemakers
Gary Woodland and Stream	Deuel	D.J. Holden
Giants in the Earth	Minnehaha	Ext. Homemakers
Gieser Geyser & Window Rock	Bennett	Don Adolphson, Mpls.
Gilley's Grove	Brookings	Dwayne J. Breyer, Mpls.
Glacial Lake Dakota	Spink	D.J. Holden
Greenwood - Part of Original Missouri River	Charles Mix	Ext. Homemakers
Grindstone Buttes	Haakon	Will Robinson, Pierre
Harney Peak Area	Custer	Edna Grieb, Spearfish
Hartford Glacial Example	Minnehaha	Bruno Petesch, Vermillion
Harvey Dunn Birthplace	Kingsbury	Ext. Homemakers
Haunted Butte Effigy	Corson	Ext. Homemakers
Haystack Butte	Perkins	Mrs. Alfred Hinds, Prairie City
Hedtke Pass	Day	Mrs. Chester Duerre, Webster
Hell's Half Acre & Crow Peak	Lawrence	Marion Hilpert, Spearfish
Hidden Valley Ranch	Roberts	D.J. Holden
Hidewood Creek	Deuel	Ext. Homemakers
Hidewoods	Brookings	D.J. Holden
Hieb Sand Pit - Fossils	Douglas	Ext. Homemakers
Homestake Open Cut	Lawrence	J.P. Gries, Rapid City
Honeycombs (Jump Off Country)	Harding	Dick Rebbeck, Rapid City

Site	County	Site reported by
Hoop Up Canyon - S.D. border near Pennington County		June Zietner, Mission
Horseshoe Lake	Codington	Kent N. Olson, Huron
Hot Springs and Battle Mountain	Fall River	D.J. Holden
Hushers Grove, Winter habitat for birds	Brookings	Nelda Holden, Brookings
Igloo	Fall River	Ext. Homemakers
Imley Chalcedony	Pennington	June Zietner, Mission
Indian Camp Site - Roland Miller Ranch	Perkins	Roland Miller, Lodgepole
Indian Cemetery - Big Coulee	Roberts	Reed Sanderson, Waubay
Indian Church	Grant	Ext. Homemakers
Indian Creek Fossil Site	Pennington	Jim Larson, Rapid City
Indian Mounds	Kingsbury	Ext. Homemakers
Indian Mounds in Sherman Park	Minnehaha	James Berdahl, Sioux Falls
Indian Rock	Harding	Doug R. West, Lemmon
Indian Rock Shelters - Bounty, Steven's & Lord's Ranches	Fall River	Ext. Homemakers
Indian Trading Post	Brown	William Oliver
Indian village	Minnehaha	Dwight Marrow, Sioux Falls
Island in Red Iron Lake	Marshall	Richard Durland, Sisseton
Joel Bishop Ranch - Beautiful Leaf Imprints	Perkins	D.J. Holden
John Brown's Mound	Sanborn	George Jonkel, Laurel, MD
Jumpoff Country	Harding	Dick Rebbeck, Rapid City
Karl Mundt Wildlife Refuge - Eagle Refuge	Gregory	D.J. Holden

Site	County	Site reported by
Lacreek Wildlife Refuge - Trumpeter Swans	Bennett	Gary Nies, Martin
Lake Andes Wildlife Refuge	Charles Mix	Ext. Homemakers
Lake Dumarce	Roberts	Richard Durland, Sisseton
Lake Hiddenwood	Walworth	Ext. Homemakers
Lake Thompson	Kingsbury	George Jonkel, Laurel, MD
Lambro	Tripp	D.J. Holden
Laura Ingalls Wilder Birthplace	Kingsbury	Ext. Homemakers
Le Beau	Walworth	Ext. Homemakers
Lendell Petroglyph	McPherson	John Lokemoen, Jamestown, ND
Letcher Conifer Grove	Sanborn	Bruce Harris, Clear Lake
Lewis Clark Pillars	Bon Homme	D.J. Holden
Limber Pine Relict & Cathedral Spires	Custer	J.P. Gries, Rapid City
Little Badlands at Oelrichs	Fall River	D.J. Holden
Little Bend Area	Sully	Charles Rogge, Sioux Falls
Little White River - Ironwood Grove	Mellette	Dilwyn Rogers, Sioux Falls
Lodgepole Pine Relict	Lawrence	Dilwyn Rogers, Sioux Falls
Lone Rock	Moody	V.A. Fenner, Flandreau
Ludlow Cave	Harding	Sigurd Anderson, Webster
Lynn Lake and Mydland Pass	Day	Rolf Wallenstrom, Pierre
Makoce Washte	Minnehaha	D.J. Holden
Marsh Lake	Hamlin	D.J. Holden
Medicine Butte	Shannon	Ralph Cole, Rapid City
Medicine Knoll	Hughes	Ext. Homemakers
Medicine Lake	Codington	Ext. Homemakers
Medicine Rock	Potter	Ext. Homemakers

Site	County	Site reported by
Meng-Hudson Buffalo Jump, south of Ardmore in Nebraska		D.J. Holden
Mesic Ironwood Forest	Todd	Dilwyn Rogers, Sioux Falls
Milbank Quarries	Grant	D.J. Holden
Milk Camp	Gregory	Max Myers, Brookings
Mina-Pierre Shale - Glacial Till Unconformity	Edmunds	D.J. Holden
Mission Vertebrate Fossil Quarry	Mellette	Mort Green, Rapid City
Missouri Coteau	McPherson	D.J. Holden
Missouri River - Yankton to Sioux City	Clay & Union	Webster Sill, Vermillion
Missouri River Terminal Moraine & Prairie Dog Town (Black-footed ferret)	Hughes	James P. Hughes, Pierre
Moreau River Fossils-North of Faith	Perkins	Paul Bishop, Bison
Mud Butte	Butte	D.J. Holden
Native Prairie near Watertown	Codington	Mrs. Lou Woostencroft, Watertown
Needles in Black Hills	Pennington	D.J. Holden
Newton Hills State Park	Lincoln	Robert D. Richter, Sioux Falls
No Moccasin Dam	Tripp	Regina Conrath, Rapid City
Northern Hills Spruce Forest	Lawrence	Les Sugart, Spearfish
Oak Hallow	Douglas	Ext. Homemakers
Oak Lake Girl Scout Camp - Native Prairie	Brookings	D.J. Holden
Oakwood Lakes	Brookings	D.J. Holden
Old Indian Trading Post	Roberts	Russell Smith, Milbank

Site	County	Site reported by
Ordway - Near the claim of Hamlin Garland	Brown	Ext. Homemakers
Orient Hills or Bald Mountain	Faulk	Ext. Homemakers
Oyster Butte	Dewey	Bruno Petesch, Vermillion
Packskin Buttes	Dewey	Leslie Labahm, Timber Lake
Palisades	Minnehaha	Sigurd Anderson, Webster
Paradise Hill or Fletcher Prairie	Union	Ted Van Bruggen, Vermillion
Parkers Peak, Hot Springs, Fossils	Fall River	June Zietner, Mission
Pelican Lake	Codington	Ext. Homemakers
Petrified Grass and Rocks near Prairie City	Perkins	Paul M. Bishop, Bison
Petrified Grass and Rock and Tipi Rings	Perkins	Paul M. Bishop, Bison
Petrified Wood Area - Lemmon	Perkins	D.J. Holden
Picnic Springs	Harding	Ext. Homemakers
Pine-Aspen Community	Meade	Ralph Cole, Rapid City
Pine Creek Natural Area	Pennington	Clinton L. Currey, Forest Service
Pine Ridge Reservation Natural Area	Shannon	Ralph Cole, Rapid City
Pipestone Quarries	Minnehaha	Jim Gleich, Sioux Falls
Pony Hills	Jerauld	Ext. Homemakers
Prairie Chicken Booming Grounds	Charles Mix	D.J. Holden
Prairie Dog Town and Black-footed Ferret	Walworth	Johnny Skogberg, Selby
Prairie Homestead	Jackson	Ext. Homemakers
Prairieland near Emery	McCook	William Uphoff, Emery
Prairie Village	Lake	D.J. Holden
Promise Day School	Dewey	D.J. Holden

Site	County	Site reported by
Punished Woman's Lake	Codington	Carl Beskow, South Shore
Putney Slough	Brown	Ext. Homemakers
Quarries area - Dell Rapids	Minnehaha	Sigurd Anderson, Webster
Rainbow Arch	Meade	J.P. Gries, Rapid City
Ralph Sandstone Formation	Perkins	D.J. Holden
Rattlesnake Butte	Washabaugh	Robert W. Wilson, Rapid City
Red Canyon	Fall River	Jim Larson, Rapid City
Redday Prairie	Roberts	Verlyn Marth, Herman, MN
Redfield Prairie	Spink	Larry Fine, Brookings
Red Lake	Brule	Francis Ugolini, Landmarks, Denver, Colo.
Red Rock	Gregory	D.J. Holden
Red Scaffold	Ziebach	Charles Rogge, Sioux Falls
Red Shirt Table	Shannon	Ext. Homemakers
Redwood Fossil	Gregory	Ed Kleen, Big Stone City
Reed Cave - Pringle	Custer	Bill Roberts, Rapid City
Ree Heights Hills Buffalo Jump	Hand	Buster Deuter, Ree Heights
Reva Gap	Harding	Douglas West, Lemmon
Ripley Pass	Harding	John Sherrod, Camp Crook
Rockport Hutterite Colony	Hanson	D.J. Holden
Rondell	Brown	Wayne Phillip, Aberdeen
Roughlock Falls & Spearfish Canyon	Lawrence	D.J. Holden
Round Lake Area	Deuel	Ext. Homemakers
Roy Lake	Marshall	Dick Durland, Sisseton
Sacajawea Monument	Corson	Ext. Homemakers
Sage Creek Wilderness Area	Pennington	D.J. Holden

Site	County	Site reported by
Sand Dunes - East of Hecla	Brown	Max Myers, Brookings
Sandhill Cranes Area	Campbell	Bruce Harris, Clear Lake
Sandhills	Bennett	D.J. Holden
Sandpit North of Milltown	Hutchinson	Dale Carey
Sand Lake Wildlife Refuge	Brown	D.J. Holden
Sarah Goodboy Prairie - Alto Township	Roberts	D.J. Holden
Scalp Mountain	Gregory	Leroy K. Lamp
Scatterwood Lakes - Nesting Egret Colonies	Faulk	Harold Wagar, Mitchell
Sharks Teeth - White Owl - Glenn Spears Ranch	Meade	Glenn Spears, White Owl
Sheep Mountain	Shannon	Ralph Cole, Rapid City
Silent Guide Monument	Haakon	Ext. Homemakers
Sioux Prairie	Moody	D.J. Holden
Site of First Gold Discovery	Custer	U.S. Forest Service, Custer
Sitting Bull Grave	Corson	Ext. Homemakers
Sitting Bull Killed	Corson	Ext. Homemakers
Slim Butte	Harding	Sigurd Anderson, Webster
Smithwick - Claude Barr Ranch - Native Plant Gardens	Fall River	D.J. Holden
Snake Butte (effigy)	Shannon	Dave Fischer, Pierre
Snake Butte Effigy - Blunt	Hughes	Charles McMullen, Brookings
Sod House	Harding	Rapid City Journal
Sod House	Mellette	Ext. Homemakers
South Slim Buttes - J.B. Rock, Kelly Canyon, Original Ranger Station	Harding	Buck Thybo, Buffalo
Spirit Mound	Clay	Dave Ode, Sioux Falls

Site	County	Site reported by
Spring Creek	Todd	Max Myers, Brookings
Squaw Creek	Lawrence	Marion Hilpert, Spearfish
St. Francis Indian Museum	Todd	Dilwyn Rogers, Sioux Falls
Stronghold Table	Shannon	Ralph Cole, Rapid City
Swan Lake	Walworth	M.E. Anderson, Pierre
Tacoma Park	Brown	D.J. Holden
Teepee Canyon & Aspen abandoned teepee - John Helms Ranch	Harding	Ralph Waugh, Reva
Teepee Rings	Beadle	Ext. Homemakers
Teepee Rings	McPherson	D.J. Holden
Teepee Rings & Buffalo Jump	Custer	Carl Sanson, Custer
Teepee Rings - Hermosa	Custer	D.J. Holden
Teepee Ruins and Eagle Catching Site - Slim Buttes	Harding	Ralph Waugh & Carl Cornell, Buffalo
Thompson Ranch (Denis) - Badland Formation and Teepee Rings	Harding	D.J. Holden
Thompson's Butte	Pennington	C.D. Wisehart, Caputa
Thunder Butte	Ziebach	Sigurd Anderson Webster
Thunder Valley Drag Races	Turner	D.J. Holden
Trudeau Site (1794) Basswood on River Eastern Type Dicid-uous Forest	Charles Mix	Dilwyn Rogers, Sioux Falls
Turtle Buttes	Tripp	June Zietner, Mission
Turtle Peak	Jerauld	D.J. Holden
Twin Buttes	Border Tripp-Gregory	Max Myers, Brookings
Twin Buttes - near center of nation	Butte	D.J. Holden
Twin Lake	Miner	D.J. Holden

Site	County	Site reported by
Two River Ranch	Meade	D.J. Holden
Union County State Park	Union	Paul Nordstrom, Brookings
Upper Belle Fourche River	Butte	Dick Rebbeck, Rapid City
Vangen Church - Mission Hill	Yankton	Ext. Homemakers
Vermillion Prairie	Clay	Ted Van Bruggen, Vermillion
Wall Lake	Hand	George Jonkel, Laurel, MD
Wasta Fossils & Prairie Agates - Gravel Pits	Pennington	D.J. Holden
Waubay Wildlife Refuge	Day	D.J. Holden
Webers Gulch	McPherson	Dave Ode, Sioux Falls
Wessington Hills	Jerauld	Marion Solberg, Wessington Springs
White Bear Cliffs	Yankton	Herbert R. Davis, Yankton
White Butte - Petrified Wood Site	Perkins	Guy Henshew, White Butte
White Horse Area - Grand River Prairie	Dewey	Tom Pozarnsky, Pierre
Wieda Agate Beds - 10 W. & 6 S. Kadoka	Jackson	Franklin Shaw, Brookings
Willow Creek Butte	Stanley	Francis Ugolini, Landmarks, Denver, Colo.
Windy Mound - Tip of Coteau des Prairie	Marshall	D.J. Holden
Wounded Knee Area	Shannon	Sigurd Anderson, Webster
Yellowbank River	Deuel	Bruce Harris, Clear Lake